THERAPISTS ON THERAPY

THERAPISTS
ON THERAPY

Bob Mullan

FREE ASSOCIATION BOOKS / LONDON / NEW YORK

Published in 1996 by
Free Association Books
39–41 North Road, London N7 9DP
and 70 Washington Square South
New York NY 10012–1091

© Bob Mullan, 1996

The right of Bob Mullan to be identified as the author
of this work has been asserted by him in accordance with
the Copyright, Designs and Patents Act 1988.

ISBN 1 85343 329 2 hbk

A CIP record for this book is available from the British Library

Printing history: 99 98 97 96   5 4 3 2 1

Produced for Free Association Books by
Chase Production Services, Chipping Norton, OX7 5QR
Printed in the EC by J W Arrowsmith Ltd, Bristol

Contents

Preface   vii

1   DEREK GALE   Humanistic Psychology   1
2   SUSIE ORBACH   Psychoanalysis   19
3   BRIAN THORNE   Person-centred Therapy   37
4   CHARLOTTE SILLS   Transactional Analysis   56
5   PETER LOMAS   Psychoanalysis   76
6   DOROTHY ROWE   Personal Construct Psychology   89
7   PAUL TAYLOR   Humanistic/Transpersonal Psychology   105
8   BRIAN SHELDON   Cognitive-Behavioural Therapy   127
9   ERNESTO SPINELLI   Existential Therapy   146
10 PEGGY SHERNO   Gestalt Therapy   171
11 ANNIE KELLER   Neuro-Linguistic Programming (NLP)   189
12 LENNOX THOMAS   Psychotherapy and Race/Ethnicity   202
13 ADAM PHILLIPS   Psychoanalysis   223
14 NAONA
    BEECHER-MOORE   Psychosynthesis   241
15 JOHN ANDREW
    MILLER   Bioenergetics   259
16 ANNE GERAGHTY   Groupwork   276
17 FAY FRANSELLA   Personal Construct Psychology   294
18 IAN
    GORDON-BROWN   Transpersonal Psychology   307
19 MARGOT
    MESSENGER   Rebirthing   322
20 SALLY BERRY   Psychotherapy for Women   340
21 NOEL COBB   Archetypal Psychology   359

'I've never been in therapy', I murmured.

'Not even *group*?'

I shook my head.

'God, you must be really neurotic', she said respectfully.

Sue Grafton, *A is for Alibi*

Preface

The irreducible elements of psychotherapy are a therapist, a patient, and a regular and reliable time and place. But given these, it is not so easy for two people to meet. We all live on the hope that authentic meeting between human beings can still occur.

R.D. Laing, *The Politics of Experience*

My first personal experience with therapy was in the late '70s when I endured a number of less than fruitful consultations with an analyst. With the benefit of hindsight I see all too clearly that my disappointment was due mainly to my complete lack of understanding as to the nature of such encounters. At the time I was in distress, desperately sought a 'quick fix' and was simply unaware of the precise purpose, procedures and language of the analytical enterprise. Handing over a considerable sum of money after listening to my *own* voice for well over 45 minutes each week merely added to my displeasure.

Shortly afterwards I joined a sensitivity training group – an *encounter* as it was called by others – not, on this occasion, for the purpose of problem-solving, but rather for experiential education. By the end of the second meeting at least half of us were close allies, rolling on the floor, hugging each other, and with tears streaming down our pained but relieved faces. The manner in which I was encouraged to face *myself* came as a great shock. There was nowhere to run, or to hide. Sitting uneasily on a chair, in the middle of a group of interested and attentive onlookers, it took a mere five minutes for my facade to crumble and for my somewhat less-confident and confused self to emerge.

A decade later, following an intense period of emotional turmoil and personal dislocation, I spent almost a year with an NHS counsellor-cum-psychotherapist. I would eagerly look forward to this weekly meeting and invariably left with my heart lifted. These were often painful and sad occasions but nonetheless by the end of the hour a degree of clarification and understanding had invariably been achieved. More importantly, I felt I was with someone who professionally *cared* for me, and was a person who understood.

It is through such experiences, together with a fleeting acquaintance with various psychiatric institutions and professions, that I am compelled to agree with Joel Kovel's simple observation that therapy 'can touch the human heart and promote freedom' but that 'it can just as likely mechanize, enslave and drive a person crazy'.[1] The term therapy has its origins in the Greek word meaning to *attend* (medically). More recently R.D. Laing has expanded this meaning to argue that the therapist should be a specialist in attentiveness and awareness.[2]

Despite the numerous and varied forms of psychotherapy that abound,[3] it appears to be almost self-evident that it is the *relationship between therapist and client* that is *the* most important element involved, especially as the techniques employed vary to *such* a degree. Indeed it has been suggested that actually there is no 'clear evidence that the form of psychotherapy makes a material difference to the outcome'.[4]

The *types* of therapy on offer grow annually. Some are new versions of old techniques, others extremely new, some seemingly bizarre. Estimates as to the number of different models of therapy in existence range from 250 to well over 400. And of course each practitioner *within* a particular tradition will express their own personalities and emphases within such traditions. Thus a consumer may find themselves face to face with a conventional analyst, engaged in a cathartic rebirthing or Gestalt session, being gently encouraged in a Rogerian counselling environment, or may be enjoined to chant joyfully their anxieties or fears away.

Petrūska Clarkson helpfully divides the myriad of therapies into 'three major traditions', the psychoanalytic, behavioural and humanistic, although sensibly she adds that 'individual psychotherapists rarely fit into categories, particularly the more experienced they become'. Indeed she further argues that there is a 'discernible trend toward integrative' approaches which 'draw upon many traditions and do not adhere to only one "truth"'.[5]

For the potential consumer of therapy the major issues are whether the therapy on offer may increase their awareness/understanding, remove neurotic (or even psychotic) symptoms, and be available or affordable. Sadly it is fair to say that the extensive research on the efficacy (or outcome) of therapy is utterly inconclusive, although it seems somewhat churlish not to accept the fact that talking regularly to *any* therapist is *likely* to be more helpful than harmful.[6]

But of course abuse occurs. And ever since Sir John Foster, in his Report, *An Enquiry into the Practice and Effects of Scientology* (HMSO, 1971), recommended the registration of psychotherapists, the protective (and defensive) professionalisation process has gathered apace. The contemporary therapeutic industry is determined to register and attempt to monitor therapeutic practice. Accordingly ethical guidelines have been developed in a decent and laudable attempt to stem the abuse of power by therapists. Though this, of course, can never be completely eradicated.

Over the past decade the cultural milieu in which therapy in the UK operates has slightly warmed to the enterprise. Therapy is no longer seen as suitable for only the sick and needy or merely a manifestation of what Christopher Lasch famously termed the 'culture of narcissism'.[7] Undoubtedly there are individuals whose intense self-awareness borders on self-absorption. However, the majority of those who enter the psychotherapist's doors are in some form of mental

distress, social dislocation or pain, and require understanding, advice
and help.

But what should we expect from a therapist, whether it is in the
consulting rooms of a well-known analyst or the less clinical setting of a
cathartic group? What will actually happen? Will I get *better*? Is it value
for money? What are the dangers involved? With such questions in mind
I talked with a range of therapists whose good nature and patience
towards me was uniform. I thank them all for their generosity and
co-operation. Also I would like to thank Diane Owen who painstakingly
transcribed the tapes, and Andrea Brown who also helped with the
project.

Notes

1. Joel Kovel (1978) *A Complete Guide To Therapy*, Harmondsworth:
   Penguin, p. 19.
2. See Helen Graham (1986) *The Human Face of Psychology*, Milton
   Keynes and Philadelphia: Open University Press, p.45.
3. On the various definitions of psychotherapy see Petruska Clarkson,
   'The nature and range of psychotherapy', in Petruska Clarkson and
   Michael Pokorny, eds (1994) *The Handbook of Psychotherapy*, London: Routledge, pp. 3–27.
4. Ibid., p. 5.
5. Ibid., p. 22.
6. Jenifer Elton Wilson and Michael Barkham, 'A practitioner-scientist
   approach to psychotherapy process and outcome research', pp.49–74
   in Clarkson and Pokorny, eds, *The Handbook of Psychotherapy*,
   argue that studies suggest that the 'average client receiving psychotherapy is better off than 80 per cent of a control population', and
   suggest that only a possible '8 per cent of clients' are '"harmed" by
   psychotherapy' (p. 63).
7. Christopher Lasch (1978) *The Culture of Narcissism*, New York:
   W.W. Norton.

CHAPTER 1

Humanistic Psychology

Derek Gale

Derek Gale is a humanistic psychotherapist who has also written widely on both counselling and psychotherapy. Based in Essex, he runs groups and workshops as well as one-to-one work.

Tell me a bit about how you came to do these men's groups

Well I suppose my main qualification for doing a men's group is that I'm a man. I did once do a group for women, I'm not sure if that was a good thing or a bad thing. I think perhaps they weren't as relaxed as they would have been with a woman leader, or as forthcoming. Interestingly enough the women denied that when we talked about it.

A very interesting question for me is why I do any of it. Normally when I'm thinking about a workshop, my story is that I'm trying to increase my income. I suspect that that isn't really true. I think normally I think about a group that I feel particularly drawn to, an idea that I feel particularly drawn to, or an idea that I think is creative, and then if other people say 'Yes, we think that is a good idea too', then I'll probably get it off the ground. But it's an interesting dichotomy that one deals with as a therapist, because obviously you are doing it for a living. Even if you work in a university and you're employed to run 20 groups a year, you're still doing it for a living because if people don't come, then they don't produce income for the university.

However I don't tend to run groups called 'Introduction to Basic Counselling Skills' or 'How to be a Psychotherapist' or whatever. So I think what I do is that I say I do it to earn a living, but I actually do it to entertain myself. I'm quite interested in what people focus on. For example, there are quite extensive therapy centres that focus specifically on abuse and on relationships, and issues centring very much around relationships. What interests me is whether the people who set something like that up have actually sat and thought 'What is a good economic idea? What will get the punters in?' Or have they actually thought 'Well these are the issues that we're most interested in', and started to develop, and then discovered that people want to come towards them.

In my own case, any attempt I've made to do something that I've thought would be commercial has been a dreadful flop. I'm going back 20 years when I say that. Anything I've done which I really wanted to do has had a much better chance of being a financial success. And some things that I really wanted to do which weren't a financial success, I've stuck at. So how did I get to be doing a men's group? Well basically, men that I was working with asked me if I would do something for them. They started to talk about things like 'What does it mean to be a real man? Am I a man if I can't mend my car? Surely that's what men are supposed to be able to do? How am I supposed to be able to engage in sexual intercourse, or how attractive am I supposed to be to women?'

So I spoke to a group of men that I was working with individually, and some that I wasn't working with individually, and said 'How would you feel about doing a workshop?' The problem then was 'Well what are we going to do in this workshop?' I didn't have a long association with Robert Bly, Shepherd Bliss, or *Achilles Heel* or John Rowan, or any of these people. I suspect a lot of people in the men's movement would say I was fairly unreconstructed. There was a certain amount of tears in the workshop, which I was quite happy about. There was no hugging trees, no wild racing round the woods and being hunter–gatherers. We focused much more on issues that were appropriate to the people at that time. Quite what would have happened if they'd said 'We want to go out and hug trees, have male bonding in the forest, which is all around us', I don't know. I suppose we would have done that.

Myself, I'm not terribly enthusiastic on some of the things that are promulgated in the forefront of the men's movement. I prefer sleeping in my own bed at night, nice and warm with a hot shower in the morning. I'm quite athletic, I'm quite sporty, I'm fitter than I've ever been in my life, but I don't necessarily think that's anything to do with being a man. I think some of the things that came up in the workshop were more about feminine sides of being a man. About flirting, about feelings towards women. Practical issues like – how do you get women to talk to you? Having said all that there was an enormous sense of men together, and men bonding together. And because I work in the grounds of my house it was very significant to me that my wife went away for the weekend. So it was very powerfully a 'men together' workshop.

It's quite clear to anybody who's got their eyes open that, whether the women's lib movement is a good or a bad thing, it certainly alerted women to the idea that they could relate among themselves, that they could be a resource for themselves. They didn't need men or teachers, or dictionaries or whatever to tell them what to do: they could get together and say 'What we want to do on a Saturday night is ...' – whatever it is they decided they wanted to do. Men are quite a long way behind in that area. We got a group of men together and I said 'What are we going to do for the weekend?' and they looked at me a bit sort of 'That's your job'. So in fact we spent most of the first day of the weekend just looking at how we would answer that question; looking at what it was that made us feel that we were men.

I suppose to some extent therefore one is learning from the women's movement, because they went out and got their act together. One is always very reluctant to make any generalisation, but it always seems to me that the person in the apparently down position is actually the person with the real strength. So I always say to my clients 'You are the ones with all the power in this relationship, because you can choose not to come, you can choose not to pay. If you don't come, you don't pay, I can't come round and drag you off for therapy.' And it seemed to me interesting that women who perceive themselves or are perceived by men as being in a down position actually had an enormous amount of power. And I think what we were trying to do in some sense was to re-empower men, because my own experience of men today is that although they won't admit it, although they speak in a different sort of idiom, they feel very vulnerable. One only has to see how excited a lot of men get when they're in the presence of strong women, who are saying 'Well we don't want this, or we don't want that, or we do want this, we do want the other', to see how vulnerable a lot of men feel. That was basically where we were at.

Could you tell me a bit about your therapeutic past? Any interests?

Have you got a couple of weeks?

I just want to know where you trained ...

I suppose actually, compared to the majority of people that I consider as colleagues, I've been at it longer than most. I'm 46 this month, and I started in my 16th year. When I started, basically what was available was not much. You could go for analysis, or you could go for some offshoot of analysis. If I remember rightly the first Quaesitor [sensitivity training] groups were in about 1968, and I started in '66. And I met someone who trained in a method that no-one's ever heard of, which doesn't have a name – at school – where I was very rapidly going mad. And it was quite clear to me at the age of 16 that I was either going to end up in a mental hospital, or in prison, I wasn't quite sure which. And I don't really think I want to rescind that view.

I met this guy called Manny Klein, who had worked with two people – one was called Alfred Wolfsohn and another was called Roy Hart. Wolfsohn's idea was that the voice and the personality, the soul of the person, are very intimately connected. Wolfsohn had been in the First World War and when he left for the War he was already training to be a singer. In the War he heard the most extraordinary sounds made by people who were injured, dying. He also had some fairly hair's breadth escapes, not least of which was being buried under a pile of dead bodies. And I think this had two effects on him. One was that he came out of the War thinking that if he'd survived, there must have been a reason that he'd survived. And the other was, that he was fascinated by why people made these sounds when they were in agony, that apparently they couldn't make when they were in normal life.

Anyway he then failed to develop as a singer, at least as a conventional singer. And he started working with his voice, trying to recreate these sounds that he'd heard in the battlefield. He discovered that this had quite a remarkable effect on the voice of his pupil, Roy Hart, who I think you will still find in the *Guinness Book of Records* as having a voice which covers eight octaves – or having had a voice: he's dead now. And Wolfsohn really researched into the voice. What could you do? He had a reputation, he lived in Berlin, as a voice doctor. And what he discovered was that working with people's voices – getting them to scream, getting them to shout, getting them to whisper, to whine, to make every single sort of sound that he could think of – had quite an emotional effect on people. And I think, combined with these experiences that he'd had in the War, because he was – I never met him – but he was apparently someone who had an enormous love for humanity, he felt that he had in some way to train himself as a therapist. And judging by what his followers have done, he obviously read very extensively in Jung, was very impressed with Jung. Took an enormous interest in dreams.

He was Jewish, and in '38 he came to Britain where he was taken up by someone who – at least the legend has it – in the First World War, he'd been fighting against in the same village. He lived through the War, and in '48 Roy Hart came from South Africa, gave up the very promising career at RADA where he was a contemporary of Laurence Harvey, and dedicated himself to studying with Wolfsohn. As a result, he developed this thing which he called the Roy Hart Theatre. By the time I came on the scene Wolfsohn was dead, Roy Hart was moving to France, my teacher had split off from Roy, and – he was a teacher in my school – taught in his spare time. I say taught in his spare time because I think Wolfsohn's ideas and working with people was much more important. And I told him a bit of my story, and he said 'Well would you like to work with me?' And as I was in such a desperate state – if he'd said to me 'Well I can help you by swinging from the chandeliers' – I would probably have accepted. But Manny was a very warm man. He had a tremendous capacity to look after others and to intuit what other people needed. Whether he had a tremendous ability to look after himself, I'm not so sure.

I found two things. One, someone who was willing to listen to me, and someone whose company, whose advice, whose questioning, whose analysis, whose interpretation seemed to change my life. He once told me that someone at school had said to him 'Why do you spend so much time with that dreadful Derek Gale?' And he said, 'That's why.' And I *was* dreadful, I was a complete mess. I couldn't have a relationship with anyone – I couldn't have a relationship with myself. So it must be some credit to the work that we did together – admittedly over 13 years – that I reached the stage where, being in a marriage for nearly 20 years,

I've got two kids who seem to be reasonably all right, people want to be my friend, and, amazing as it may seem, someone who started off as mad as me not only can work as a therapist but can be successful as a therapist. And I suppose my view of therapy would be that the really successful therapists are the people who've gone through the mill. I tend to be rather sceptical of people who say to me 'Well you know I had my three years of training therapy, I don't need it any more.'

I seem to find that I need therapy more than I need supervision, and I find the willingness to go on working on myself after 25 years or whatever it is – it's 30 years – something that I'm quite proud of. I don't feel that I should have reached some end point or that I'm willing to accept that that's the way I am. I think that is to some extent related to the work with voice, because once you say that the voice is an instrument with limitless range, not just confined to a couple of octaves, or that it's an instrument with limitless colour, you're not just a male voice or a female voice, you're not just a tenor, or a baritone or a soprano. You get into this feeling of thinking 'Well I could do anything.' I suppose rather than accepting my normal neuroses, and thinking 'Well I could live with them', I think 'Well, if that's troubling me, maybe I can find something I can do about it.' And that's what I tend to do.

While I was working with Manny I trained as a teacher, and I thought I had an interest in working with disturbed kids, kids who were like me. I think I'd probably still be doing that now, if it hadn't become obvious to me, mainly through getting married to someone who was much better at it than I was, that I wasn't as good at it as I could possibly be. That's not to say that the kids I worked with didn't get a lot of benefit from working with me, but I didn't enjoy it 101 per cent. And we used to have these open evenings which I would force my wife to come to, or maybe she came because she wanted to – I don't know. I used to feel 'Well if I've got to work in the evening, I may as well take my wife along and enjoy it.' I used to see her sometimes relating to the kids, or teaching – she is a teacher – teaching the kids things. She had a capacity with them which I knew I didn't have, and, combined with the fact that I never totally enjoyed it, I eventually bowed out of working with disturbed kids. At the time that I bowed out, I was training as a drama therapist, and people would occasionally say to me 'You seem to be much more at home running the therapy groups than doing the teaching, which is a bit irritating because you're employed to teach.' It was also irritating because I was employed to teach six hours a day, and most of the kids we worked with had an educational attention span of about six minutes. But I was quite creative as a teacher, I would not say 'You've done your maths, there's nothing else to do today.'

But it was true I was more interested in the therapy side, and when I left I had this drama therapy qualification, and basically I had this building in my garden that was rented out to someone else, and I started to think 'Well maybe I could run workshops, maybe I could be a therapist.' It was at about that time that I split with Manny, or he split with me, more accurately. The reasons that we split are quite interesting in that I'm Jewish, he had by then become a Rabbi, and I had decided to marry someone who wasn't Jewish, and finally this was a situation that he couldn't cope with any longer. So the split was not about therapy or approaches to people, it was actually a religious split. And we've never spoken or communicated since.

The interesting question is what I would have become if we hadn't split, because I always felt myself very much in the shadow of the Master, and by splitting with him I had not only to learn to stand on my own two feet, but to learn what to do. I think to begin with I was quite arrogant. But over a period of time I came to understand, I think, something quite fundamental about the nature of therapy. I read a lot, I used to talk to people a lot. One of the things I learnt from Manny was that you can learn a lot more about another human being by asking questions and listening, than by reading a textbook. And quite innocent statements like 'I think that person's got an extrovert personality' would get you in a lot of trouble. Manny was more likely to say 'I observe that that person in this situation, did so and so, or does so and so.' We were very against jargon, but very in favour of people. And if my therapeutic method has an underlying approach, it's that I'm more interested in people than in methodology, ideology, or any other 'ology'.

I have enough clients – *just* – most of the time to pay my bills at Sainsbury's and British Gas. Therefore I don't tend to worry too much if telling the truth, as I see it, upsets people.

Are these clients one-to-one?

I do both one-to-one, and groupwork. The drama therapy gives you quite an insight into groupwork. I also do a fair bit of psychodrama. I do voice groups and – although I don't really subscribe to it – I'm a member of the Association of Humanistic Psychology Practitioners, and when the whole UKCP [UK Council for Psychotherapy – the organisation of organisations which registers psychotehrapists] thing came up, I felt it was important to have a driving licence, as it were, even though I may never want to drive the car. And one of the objections was that I didn't have a qualification as a therapist. In the Association of Humanistic Psychology Practitioners we were at that point where, I don't know if you still can, you could get in under a 'grandparenting clause', but you had to satisfy the Board that you were competent. They had two objections. One was about my supervision, and the other was about my client load.

I suppose one of the mistakes I made was to be clear, honest, and frank about what I did. Rather than to couch it in a way that they could handle in terms of the formulae they tried to create. But it had some good effects for me because they said to me 'You don't have enough individual clients, and we don't think you've had enough supervision.' And rather than trying to convince them otherwise, which I suppose I might have been able to do, I thought 'Well, there's not really a great hurry', but I made a note in my diary, and I went off and changed my client load, and engaged in the sort of supervision they wanted, and at the end of two years I merely wrote and said that 'I've now fulfilled the requirements of your letter dated so-and-so and so-and-so.' They made some enquiries to me about how I fulfilled those requirements, and one day the rubber stamp just appeared.

What kind of people come to see you? What are their 'presenting problems', and what happens when someone comes to see you?

Okay, well first of all what sorts of people come. Virtually all the people I see have a head, two arms and two legs, although I think a head is probably a prerequisite. What do I do? Well obviously the first contact's on the phone, nine times out of ten. I normally ask them if they'd like to sit down, and ask them if they'd like to tell me why they've come. I try often to give them some flavour of what talking to me might be like. And I explain to them my terms and conditions of working.

Because I don't live in Hampstead a lot of the people who come to me may know nothing about therapy at all. They may think they're going to a doctor. So I probably explain quite a bit about how I work to them. I don't push people to tell me what their problems are in the first session – if they want to they can. I try and behave, as far as I can, in a way which will make them feel safe and comfortable. Some people come in and they just want to talk non-stop; some people come in and they're very embarrassed or frightened. I will often say to somebody with a bit of smile 'You find this rather a nerve-wracking experience', and if they nod I say 'Well, it's nerve-wracking for me too.' And I try and be as amenable as possible really.

I wouldn't say that that doesn't stop me being quite confronting if necessary, or honest: I don't try and get them to think that coming and having therapy with me is going to be like a warm bath once a week. I might say to them in the first session, 'I think you need to be aware that the sort of work that you do with me might be very tough for you.' Whatever I say to somebody, if they don't come back there's always a part of you that's saying 'Well should I have said something different?' I often say to people 'Do you want to book four sessions, and review it after four?' The question that they often ask me is 'How will I know if it's doing me any good?' To which my answer is 'You'll know.'

So what do you do with people?

What I do is I share a fixed length of time with a client, which is, for reasons which I can't even explain, 55 minutes. It must have some historical significance. Maybe that was how long it took me to make a cup of tea or go to the toilet, I don't know. Originally I used to see people for an hour. In that 55 minutes I try and be as much myself as I can. If a client's engrossing me then I might say 'I'm finding what you're saying is making me feel interested.' If they're boring the pants off me, then I might say 'I wonder if it's significant that you seem to be talking about something which is very significant for you, but I'm yawning', or I'm feeling tired.

I find my own feelings wonderfully useful in therapy. I used to feel rather guilty when I was with someone and I felt like dropping off. But I've come to realise that's a very good indicator of the fact that they're not really working on what they need to be working on. And I have once or twice dropped off in a session, with very positive results. Once I dropped off in a session and I dreamt the answer to the issue that was being discussed. I was working with a woman, and she was droning on and on and on and on, and I dropped off and I dreamt about a medieval army on horses with knights racing across the plain, and I came to with a start and she rather angrily said 'Were you asleep?', and I said 'Yes, but I've got the answer to your problem. You're furiously angry aren't you?' And she said 'What do you mean? I'm not angry at all.' And I said 'You are.' And she said 'How would you know anyway?' – well I told her my dream, and it was quite a turning point in her therapy. From being a rather wimpy doormat, she's quite a powerful woman today.

The other was a man who was very, very depressed and he came and I said 'Hello, how are you Billy?' in a cheerful voice, and he said 'Oh Derek, I'm so depressed.' And he whinged on like this for quite a while, and I know I was asleep for ten minutes, because I remember looking at the clock, thinking 'How much longer do I have to put up with this?' And I was woken by this very depressed man's raucous, screeching laughter, because what he'd realised was that he'd put me to sleep and then he'd just gone on talking without even noticing I was asleep. And I think that might have been a turning point for him. Certainly he went away a lot happier than he came.

I listen to people's dreams, I try and interpret them in conjunction with their own thoughts and feelings about the dream. I don't say 'This is what your dream means', but I try to get them to look at what their dreams might mean to them. I might challenge someone's behaviour in the session. I might say 'It seems to me that you don't treat me with a great deal of respect, or you treat me with far too much respect.' I'm quite happy to talk about material they bring in from outside. I think anything the client brings to the session is grist to the mill. Whether it's dealt with in the way that they hope it will be dealt with is another matter. And often I'll suggest to them that they put members of their family on a cushion. I'm a great user of broomsticks, and often they'll get a broomstick out and have a good whack, a good scream, a good shout. I don't view the catharsis as an end in itself, but there's quite a lot of criticism of cathartic work in terms of it giving you a high followed by an even bigger low. To which all I can say is either I'm very lucky, or I must be better at it than most, because that isn't the experience of my clients.

I've learnt a lot about that from a woman called Zerka Moreno, who's very good at reintegrating whatever has come out in the catharsis. So if somebody has had a good scream, and a shout, and a cry, and all the rest of it, I tend to think of that as the beginning of the work, and I'll look for ways of establishing what's come out in new behaviour. So, for example, if they shout and scream at their mother and say 'You never looked after me, you never loved me ...', and they have obviously a wonderful sense of relief from that, then perhaps we'll talk about 'Well how are you going to get the love, the attention that you actually need?' I might suggest to them that they have a conversation with their ideal mother, in which she gives them what they need, and they ask for what they need. And I think it's a shame that cathartic work really has such a bad press, because I think it's as much to do with the turn of mind as anything else. I mean, if I was taking a bus to visit a very beautiful woman, I wouldn't blame the bus if she wasn't there when I got there, or if we had an argument when I got there. And I think to blame the catharsis for getting you somewhere because you haven't then been able, or your therapist hasn't helped you to make something out of where you've got, is a bit of a cop out. So I guess if you wanted a box to put round me, you'd have to say I was a Humanistic Psychodynamic Action Therapist. In fact I'll probably use that in my next biography, myself.

Are there people that you feel you can't work with? Are there people you turn down?

Yes. I suppose you want me to say who they are, do you? [Laughs] One of my clients gave me a birthday card of a therapist sitting next to an ubliat with a handle, and the patient's obviously going down the ubliat, and the caption is 'You're too fucked up, next customer please'. Or 'You're too fucked up for therapy, next patient please', something like that. I think she gave it to me because she thought I was someone who was willing to work with people who were too fucked up. Some of the people who I work with, I've been working with for seven or eight years. Obviously if I were cleverer, betterer, whateverer, I'd have helped them a lot more a lot more quickly.

However, I'm not cheap, and they keep coming, despite my asking them if they don't think they've had enough. So presumably I am willing to take on people who some people would consider too 'fucked up'. I'm thinking of one client in particular, who when she came to me was actually in a group counselling situation. And the counsellor kept saying to her 'Well I think you've really got it together now, you could leave.' She could hardly get it together to stand up, let alone leave. And I see this woman after some six or seven years, just beginning to look like she's about ready to start making a life for herself. I can't say in a moral or a therapeutic sense whether that's good or bad. All I can say is that she comes and she pays her money, and that I work with her to the very best of my ability.

I sometimes get the screaming abdabs when people come and they don't say anything, or they're not going to say very much. But if they come back and they pay their money, then, well, if the worst comes to the worst I can always do the money mantra, or think about what I'm going to have for dinner. So I don't think it's right as a human being to say to somebody who wants to work with you 'I'm not willing to', unless I think they're going to be physically violent and going to do me damage. But there are people who come and I just think 'Oh, I don't think I can cope with this person', or I don't want to have to. It's more likely to be a personality thing. And normally they don't come back, so I don't have to handle it. I have worked in mental hospitals, unlike an awful lot of psychotherapists, so I have got some experience of working with people who are pretty disturbed, and pretty damaged. I'm working with someone at the moment with whom I have enormous arguments about whether she's mad or not at the moment. Well I don't know what mad means, but it's certainly very difficult to have a conversation with her about herself which seems to follow some normally neurotic thought pattern, or normally neurotic emotional pattern. So I guess I'm willing to work with anybody who's willing to work with me, really.

What about the issue of dependency?

Some of the people I work with, when I say 'Well you have the choice', say 'Well we don't have the choice, because we're dependent on you.' I think that's a bit of a cop-out. This normally comes up when I put my fees up. And I suppose if I thought that someone I was working with was in the middle of a very difficult transference where in fact they didn't have the choice, I probably wouldn't mention to them that I was putting my fees up, and I'd wait however long it took – in one case 18 months. So I managed to put them up twice in one go. [Laughs] I think you've got to become dependent on your therapist if you're going to have any change. I think you've got to let go of stuff, you've got to live in the flow and you've got to learn something new. And I think at that moment you've got to have someone who's holding you up, and it's probably your therapist. But I don't encourage dependency.

So in some sense they've got to become dependent, in another sense they've got to live their own lives. I don't want them to be *me*, I have enough trouble living my life without them living it for me as well. I think the humanistic psychologists who ignore or don't find transference significant ... well put it this way: I speak English and French, which seems to me that I've got two possibilities – if I only speak English, I've only got one possibility. I was rather pleased that my son is studying German at school, because that means that we've got three possibilities. If you ignore transference, it seems to me that you're saying 'Well, if anybody wants to speak to me they can speak to me in English', which means that there's a limit to what you can do. I think I'm an enormous transference object. People have the most wonderful fantasies about me, and I find it a very useful part of what we do. And as I said, however many hours ago we started, that the counter transference that I experience, I bring into the session all the time.

I've been very influenced by a Swiss Jungian called Jacoby, who wrote a book called *The Analytic Encounter*, which is about countertransference, and I also like Guggenbuhl-Craig who talks a lot about the analytic situation and the analytic relationship. Somebody once told me, I don't think I read it in a book, that even Freud said 'Well, transference has to have some hook in reality.' I've been so critical of analysis that eventually I decided to have a go at it for three years. Quite what insanity led me into that I don't know, but it seemed to me that my transference on to the analyst was handled extremely badly. When I discussed this with analysts, they said 'Well, that's how we do it.' So if somebody comes in and says to me 'Well I know you hate me' – assuming that I don't hate them – I'm likely to say 'Well I think this might be more to do with how you feel about yourself, or how you think people feel about you, than it is about how I actually feel.' And then I might ask them who they think is standing behind me, or sitting behind me and try and have a look at the issues, rather than what I understand the analyst to do which is to leave the patient floundering in the transference. I won't be the first person to have made the observation – this may be good for the analyst's bank balance. When I stopped being in analytic therapy it was quite clear that the woman I worked with thought I'd only just got started after three years, and was quite shocked at my feeling that I could make up my own mind about when I started and when I ended.

So at least if I'm critical of analysis it's from some experience. Of course you could then say 'Well, of course you didn't go to a good enough analyst', and this story can go on for ever. And of course, that's what I say when people are critical of me: if they'd stayed longer they'd have done better, or if they'd understood better what I was trying to tell them, or if they were less proud, or less mad or whatever it is. John Heron once said that he thought therapy was much closer to education than it was to medicine. And I rather agree with that. I think it's an education about how to live. I was very shocked once when I was doing some supply teaching, and I was asked to go and teach something about sex education. And I said to whoever asked me, 'What shall I do?', and they said, 'Well they only want to know whether they should sleep with their boyfriends/girlfriends and we don't know the answer, so we don't discuss it.' And I thought, 'Well I don't know the answer either, but I do know the issues', and I suppose that's what I do, I try to say 'Well, what are the issues? What are we talking about? What are you feeling? What's going on? What's happening in the here and now? And if what's happening in the here and now is that you hate my guts, well then we'd better have that out in the open.'

Do I sense that you prefer groupwork?

When I'm doing a lot of groupwork I think I enjoy one-to-one, when I'm doing a lot of one-to-one, I like doing groupwork. I'm not one of these people who says 'Oh it's a wonderfully exciting privilege to be observing people's development and their story unfolding.' If I have an hour with someone, and it feels good, and the time passes relatively quickly, I think that's great. And if the time goes slowly because they're struggling – with enormous difficulty – over the issue, I think 'Well that's the way it's got to be', but I find it a bit boring. If I'm working with a group where there's lots of action and lots of outspoken people, and plenty of transference, and people complaining, or having wonderful catharsis, especially if their catharsis leaves them beaten and thinking I'm wonderful, then I like groupwork. If it's a group in which nobody wants to say anything, and you sit there wishing the time was over – I don't do that. I'd probably introduce things and raise issues. But you can only take a group to water, you can't make it drink. Then I think 'Well maybe I was better off in one-to-one.' You're probably right. I think the real answer is that I do a lot of one-to-one work because that's what comes to me, and when I feel a bit stale or jaded I'm glad to get into a group and meet some new people. One of the advantages of workshops as opposed to an ongoing group is that you meet new people, and you have new challenges.

And do you tend to think that rather than being a group worker who (say) is associated with Gestalt, you're a group worker who thematises workshops?

Both. I run two psychodrama workshops a year, two residential psychodrama workshops, which don't have a theme. I run one or two long voice workshops a year, week-long, which don't have a theme. But I've also done the men's group. Sometimes I'll do a voice workshop maybe with someone else where they brought in a specific theme. Perhaps I'll do something on group dynamics, so it's a bit of a mixture of both. I'm always fascinated by the wonderful groups you can think up. A number of my clients were fiddle-faddling about their careers recently, and I put it to them, I said: 'Well how would you like to do a six-week careers workshop?' 'Yes' they said, and off we went. I didn't know anything about how you do a careers workshop, but I – we – sat down and we thought, 'Well what do you need to develop a career?' And I brought my very extensive knowledge of active groupwork techniques to bear, then we worked out a syllabus and off we went.

I noticed that a lot of my clients had trouble understanding what was being said, as opposed to hearing what they wanted to hear, and then communicating back what they wanted to say. And we did a couple of one-day workshops, which seemed to have quite a profound effect on people.

It seems to me that in therapy, therapists want to align themselves to 'ologies' and to parties. They want to be a member of the British

Association of Psychologically Psychodynamic Counselling Actors. And they probably want to be a member of the sub-sect of that group which is politically aware of the needs of women and the disabled or someone. And then they want people to operate very specifically in the modality that the Association has. I'm not sure that I won't get letters from people in the Association of Humanistic Psychology saying 'How dare you have analytic therapy?' Hopefully I won't because we're supposed to be a bit more liberal. Maybe my therapist will get a letter saying 'Why did you take on that ridiculous humanistic guy?'

Quite frankly I think it's a load of rubbish. I've had people come to me and say 'I want analytic therapy. I want to lie down, and I want you to be an analyst.' Well I've *had* a person say that to me. And actually I found it absolutely fascinating. I don't know if she got anything out of it. Eventually, because she wanted to do a training course in the Tavi [Tavistock Institute], she had to go off and have therapy with someone at the Tavi. I'm not averse to sometimes meeting my clients outside of the consulting room. I'm not averse to my clients knowing that I'm a real person, that I have a life. I'm not averse to switching my methods. What I do have an allegiance to, is the people I work with; most of whom know that I'm often criticised for not having any boundaries, and they always have a good laugh when I say 'No' to something, because their general response is that 'You're not supposed to have any boundaries, Derek.' I think I have very secure and very firm boundaries. I think that I've done an enormous amount of work on myself, and that has made my ability to feel secure in much wider boundaries manifest.

I've never slept with a patient that I've worked with. I've never stolen money from a patient that I've worked with or a client. I've never felt uncomfortable that I've taken money from someone when I haven't given them a good service. I've often lost sleep over whether what I was doing was the right thing, and I've tried as far as I possibly can to focus on the individual needs of each person that I've worked with. And if that might include, at the end of the session, inviting them into my kitchen and having a cup of coffee, then I'm not worried about that, I don't feel I've suddenly broken some dreadful therapeutic boundary. One of my clients turned up, and I was actually in my house when she arrived, and I can't exactly remember the context – anyway she ended up with me in my kitchen, and I said, 'You look a bit peaky', and she said, 'Well I haven't eaten since yesterday morning', or something. I said, 'I think we'd better sit down and have a sandwich or something.' In actual fact I cooked her an omelette, and she told me some time later that this was one of the most significant things that had ever happened to her in her life. Well I'm sure that a lot of people would find this an extraordinary way for a therapist to carry on.

I've been interested – I've read Patrick Casement's *On Learning from the Patient* twice, and frankly I think he's wrong. I think his obsession with being separate from the patient is unnecessary. I don't find that the way I behave prevents transference, I don't find it prevents projection. And as far as I'm concerned, the more the merrier, because it gives the person something to work on.

Do you have a notion or a model of what a person's optimum mental health is? Is it about autonomy, becoming in control of their own destiny, is it that kind of thing?

I think people are born whole. I don't believe in the Freudian view that you're born a mess. I often say to my clients 'You were born a perfect baby, with all that you needed for your life.' If bad things happen to people, and they develop psychic, psychological injury, obviously you can't see it you can't touch it, but you can see its manifestations. And I think therapy can heal those scars, I've seen it done. I've experienced it myself. I think the brain is a very multi-faceted model, because I can see how, in myself for example, getting into some extraordinarily complex cathartic experience has healed something. On the other hand, there is the different issue of being healed just by talking. I wouldn't say that the analytic work I did was useless – far from it. I've been hypnotised; actually I found that totally useless, but I – you know sometimes I might take a behavioural or a cognitive approach. So all I know is that there's a person here and that all sorts of things have happened to them, and that all sorts of things could help to put that right. I've forgotten what the question is now.

What is optimum mental health?

I think it's pretty good if people could see their parents as human beings, as opposed to their parents. I think if they can see them as people who've got good and bad sides, as opposed to a package of all their projections, what their parents ought to be, I think that's a very healthy thing. I think being able to do what you call autonomy, being able to do what you want to do when you want to do it, without feeling that you've emotionally got one leg tied behind you. I think being able to voice what you believe in in life without being inhibited by other people's responses. So people will sometimes say to me 'Well I can say that in therapy, because I know you understand.' I can sometimes be critical of that and say 'Well why can't you say that in the bar?' And they say 'Well, they'll make fun of me.' To which my response is, 'Only insofar as you choose to let them.'

I sometimes find myself in quite macho male environments and somebody says 'Look at the tits on that one', or something. And I say 'You know I don't really find that terribly pleasant when you talk in that way', to which their reply might be something like, 'What are you, one of these left-wing poofters, or something?' To which my answer is 'Well I don't particularly vote one way or the other, so I don't know what wing I'm on. I don't think I'm a poofter, whatever that means. I just don't think you talking about that woman as though she's a lump of meat makes me feel particularly happy. I don't want to make a big thing about it, I'd just rather you didn't do it.' To which my clients then reply, 'Oh yes, but you're very strong, you've got a lot of confidence', and all the rest of it, to which my answer must be, 'Then to have some strength and confidence is mental health.'

I also think it's very important if somebody wants to claim to be mentally healthy, to have had a good outcome of therapy, that they treat other human beings well. I'm not very happy with one or two people that I've worked with who seem to treat their fellow human beings in a rather cavalier manner, and say 'Well I can cope with that, I feel happy with that.' I don't think that's a very good outcome for therapy.

I like the way you talked about how it helped you enormously in your work the fact that you were in distress. Is that the crucial thing you think you have in terms of your skills as a therapist? Do you think that's a necessary condition?

Like you mean that if you haven't had a bad life, you should have one before you become a therapist? [Pause] No I think the essential skills are common to all traditions, I just think some people ignore them more than others. I very much doubt that anybody that hasn't had a reasonably difficult childhood, a reasonably difficult life, would even want to be a therapist. All the therapists I know strike me as being pretty screwed up now, so I assume they were a lot more screwed up before they got involved. I tend to be more drawn to the people who seem to have been able to use therapy to work on themselves and to make themselves less screwed up. I was extremely critical of someone who's very prominent in the psychodrama world, who went to a psychiatrist in Harley Street to try and deal with some problems of her own.

I don't really see how you can be a psychotherapist as opposed to perhaps a cognitive or a behavioural therapist unless you've had therapy yourself, and unless you've been willing to go down into your own personal sewer and give it a good cleaning out. What I know is that the more of that I do, even after 30 years of doing it, the better I am as a therapist. I do refer people, and therefore I obviously don't believe that you've got to be me in order to do therapy. But I think the best therapists are people who've worked quite fundamentally on themselves. The problem is you can work quite fundamentally on yourself and still know nothing about therapy. Which is, I suppose, the situation I was in when I started. And I think today, I'm much less involved in my foundations, and much more kind of working from my penthouse flat, than perhaps I was when I started. So I don't have to keep going back to thinking 'What was it like for me, and what have I worked on?' I kind of know how it's done.

Occasionally I'll be working with someone and I find myself very in touch with some very old primitive stuff of my own. And I think the fact that I've done so much work on myself enables me to treat that with equanimity and not get panicky about it. But you've got to learn to listen, you've got to learn to know which parts of your client's behaviour to pick up on, which of their comments to pick up on. You've got to know how to interpret, and in my view, you've got to take – and this is something I've never seen anybody else say, but I'm sure lots of other people have – in my view you've got to take a lively and active interest in all facets of human life. I do that often by listening to a lot of Radio 4.

In fact, sometimes, especially in the voice group, I'll start off by saying, 'Oh I heard something on the radio this morning which is relevant', and you can see people sort of glazing over – Derek's on his hobby horse. But I understand a reasonable amount about computers, I understand some-thing about the internal combustion engine, I understand something about building, I understand something about art, I know something about glass-making, I've learned some stuff about dressmaking, I know a lot about the theatre, and about film-making, I think I can talk about air-conditioning. Well I am a teacher, so I ought to be able to talk about teaching. I think those issues will give you some idea of who I'm currently working with, and what their jobs are. And I think to be able to have some understand-ing of the focus and the interests of your clients is very important. I find a lot of therapists are very, very narrow in their outlook, and I find that a bit off-putting.

I was going to ask you how you view the ethics of psychotherapy. The issues of power, responsibility. You've answered it obliquely.

I suppose if I was going to be really open I would say that we havn't even scratched the surface of the ethics of psychotherapy. A lot of crap is talked about it. I used to have a column, in the counselling journal – British Association of Counselling Journal – called 'Gale Force 10', which I was asked to cease writing, and in this column I used to call the odds. People found this rather uncomfortable-making, and eventually asked me not to come back. There is a rule, for example, in the BAC that you're not allowed to have sexual relations with a client within 12 weeks of ceasing therapy. I think my response to this started off as something like: 'I don't need a code of ethics to tell me whether or not to have sex with my clients.' Actually I had a couple of quite complimentary letters about that.

I think ethics or an ethical view comes from being an ethical person. You have a code, and that will probably help some people who are on the borderline. But I think the people who aren't ethical people will try and get round the code. I'd rather have a code of ethics than not have one. But so long as we cannot accept and deal with criticism in a more grown-up manner, we're always going to have trouble, and what worries me is the idea that a code of ethics somehow protects us from having to look at ourselves. I viewed 'Gale Force 10' as something that was very sincerely written. As I understand it people viewed it as the raving outpourings of a rather odd character, and I found that very disturbing and very worrying, because what I was doing was taking difficult issues that confronted us as counsellors, and trying to get people to look at them.

So for example, I wrote a piece that I don't think was ever published about an obituary that appeared in *Counselling*, in which the author of the obit spoke of the wonderful emotional atmosphere that surrounded the dead person, the wonderful work that she'd done, and slipped in that she'd committed suicide. I wrote a piece saying that I didn't think you could hold someone up as a paragon of virtue if they killed themselves, and that probably the family and friends of this person were not helped by this rather one-sided obit. I also said, and I quote: '... suicide whatever else it is, is a very aggressive act ...' And the editor wrote back to me saying that he didn't feel that this was publishable in *Counselling*, and he said – one part that I remember quite clearly was – 'that it was only my view that suicide was an aggressive act'. Well maybe there are thousands of other views which personally I would love to hear. Because I never think really that I know the answer to anything. I know my wife sometimes says to me 'Oh, for God's sake Derek, just put it down, forget about it, leave it.' I'm like a dog with a bone, I'm always worrying it, I really want to know: what does somebody think, what do they mean? So the problem that I have with ethical issues is that really when we're challenged, I don't think we want to discuss them. I've often been challenged. I've never been brought before an ethical committee, although I think that in itself might be an interesting experience, though I hope it's one I'll never have to take on. When I'm challenged I give my responses. 'This is what I was aiming for, this is what I was trying to do.' If I'm wrong, I admit it, and if I'm not wrong, or if there's a disagreement, then I stick to my guns.

What are your views, Derek, concerning money – if a client is paying for the service will he really have more incentive to want to get better?

That's my experience. That is my experience. [Pause] It's not true actually, I must rephrase that. When I worked in the National Health Service – I worked at a day hospital at one time, so the people who came to the day hospital were at least unemployed if not unemployable. And instead of saying 'I'm wasting my money', they used to say 'I'm wasting my time.' Which was a very interesting eye-opener for me. But I do think people in the main value it more if they pay for it. The people that seem to get the most out of what they get from me are the ones who pay my full fee. I often reduce my fee because I think either my client won't pay any more or they can't pay any more. Now that's okay. I have on occasions reduced it very, very substantially, or waived it altogether, and it doesn't seem to have been a good idea. I don't think the client likes it. The client feels demeaned by it.

The humanistic tradition is often seen as quasi-transpersonal, and then there's the interface between psychotherapy and spirituality. Have you thought about that issue?

Don't know what it means. How can psychotherapy not be spiritual? And how can a spiritual experience not be a therapeutic one?

Lots of therapists wouldn't agree ...

Well I don't understand it. I don't understand it. The minute you say to somebody, 'What do you remember? What are your fantasies? What are your beliefs? How do you relate?' I think therapy is a moral issue, much more, as I've said, much more than a medical issue. How can it be anything other than spiritual? I don't go to church, I don't go to synagogue, I don't pray. I don't have experiences at the tops of mountains. But I would describe myself as someone who hasn't any problem with spirituality. I sometimes think that probably I've got quite an interesting awakening ahead of me, but when I look out of the window I look at the trees, I see the seasons change, I hurt, I laugh, I enjoy – I sometimes talk to my parents who are both dead, talk to them a lot more lively than I did when they were alive. There's a lot of fools in therapy, and a lot of foolish attitudes. On the other hand if it works for a client, go ahead, but I don't see how you can separate the two.

Do you know when you need a break?

By the hour, by the week, by the holiday?

Well I was thinking of the notion of therapeutic burn-out.

Yes, I take quite good care of myself. I have a limited number of sessions that I'm willing to do in a day, except in very extreme circumstances, and they'll probably be extreme that I need the money. Or that it just so happens that I've got somebody who needs to see me urgently, and that for some reason I can't cancel someone else on that day. I swim, I ride a bike and I do go-kart racing. I think the swimming and the cycling might be seen as psychotherapists' activities, the go-kart racing, I think I partly do it because it's so unusual. I don't know any other people involved in therapy who do it, although Diana Spaghetti's husband, Sir John Whitmore, was actually quite a well-known racing driver in his day, and has written a book on the psychology of motor-racing. I generally don't work at weekends, unless I'm doing a workshop, and I more or less take school holidays.

CHAPTER 2

Psychoanalysis

Susie Orbach

Susie Orbach is a London-based psychoanalyst. She co-founded
and currently co-directs the Women's Therapy Centres in London
and New York. She is the author of a number of books including
the international best-seller *Fat is a Feminist Issue* and, more
recently, *What's Really Going On Here?*

*Can you tell me a bit about your background, how it pertains to why you
do therapy?*

Well the problem with that question is that I would give a different
account on a daily basis. One always creates a new narrative about *why*.
I mean now why it pertains is because I've been doing it for so long.
[Pause]

Put another way, what did you do before you did therapy?

Well, I studied Russian history, then I worked as a city planner, then I
studied Law. And all those things had a bearing. Given the sort of psychoanalytic edge you could say that I've studied Russian history because I was
interested in contemporary politics; that I studied city planning because I
lived in very bad housing and I was really interested in that; that I studied
Law because I got caught up in the political struggles of the late '60s and
needed to understand the legal issues. And then that I got into therapy
because I had my own personal difficulties.
   Therapy interested me from three different areas really. There was
the intellectual area, which was coming out of feminism, which is if we
understood certain kinds of things about inequality and subordination,
why were women still second-class citizens? What was it internally that
made it impossible for women to shift? So I was interested in what
another language or another discourse, or another kind of conversation
had to say about that. So that led me into therapy and the interest in
the unconscious. So that's one strain.
   The other strain was that I was in my own form of difficulty and our
women's group – which was the political form in those days – unbeknown
to itself, used therapeutic methods of trying to understand ourselves,
although there we focused on the meanings for us as a group rather than

the meanings for us as individuals. And I was interested in how does an individual get made?

And the third reason is that I developed all this work on understanding women's eating problems, and I needed to learn more about therapy. But I suppose I've always been a critic of therapy, even though I'm very much inside the field, and my particular background has made me a critic. Because I didn't go to the Institute [of Psychoanalysis], and then swallowed that and then critiqued it. Because I was interested in how people come to be who they are, in particular cultures, and because I had an interest in wider anthropological, and social and political questions, I was interested in what psychoanalysis – any kind of psychotherapy – might be able to tell us about how people are and who they are. And my political background – I was a child of the '60s, and I am one of those people that actually came of age at the point where youth suddenly was on the agenda, and I think we thought we were going to take over the world, and change things and create new agendas. I was I suppose the generation that felt I was interested in something wider than Labour Party politics and canvassing. I was interested in a politics of meaning. And I'm just part of that generation. So that political thing intersects with a kind of interest in the therapeutic, in a particular way.

How do you describe the tradition you come from?

But I'm not a tradition. I think we're in the making. Now I can fit myself in with and say, 'Look I really like the work of the interpersonalists in the United States. I think that they're doing the most interesting work.' Luise and I created a lot of new theory on women, and on beginning to think about men and gender consciousness – Fairbairnian object-relations therapy. I can do that but actually our base was different. So it's not so easy to fit in. I can talk all those languages, but I don't necessarily fit into any of those places.

Put another way then, how do you describe what you do? What kind of people come to you, and when they come to you what do you do with them?

All sorts of people come to me. Obviously very, very few people come to me, because you don't see very many people, but across the class, across the age, and across the ethnic spectrum. Some people come because they think, 'Ah, Susie Orbach is a feminist'; other people come because, 'Ah, Susie Orbach is technically very good in psychoanalysis.' Some people come because – I don't know, they've never even heard of me, they don't know I'm a writer or anything like that. They don't know that I have a whole set of ideas. But what do I do with them – I guess I listen. My first point is to make a relationship, and to try and enter into how they experience the world, and what's troubling them, and what makes it so difficult for them. And so I will engage, I'm somebody who is interested in engagement.

This might sound terribly stupid but do you normally have two chairs?

Yes.

You're traditional in that sense?

I have two chairs and a couch in my room. I also see couples; I should say that. My chair is exactly the same as the chair the person sits in. I see people at different frequencies. It could be once, twice, three times a week. I see people on an open-ended basis. Although once in a while I'll see somebody for a short term. But I'll greet people, I'm not silent or withholding. I don't believe that the way you create therapeutic safety is by being uptight. I think I'm aware enough of my own boundaries to engage but still be a human being, which I think is a crucial feature of therapy.

When you're not listening, how often are you talking? And relatedly do you interpret?

I don't like the word *interpretation*, because interpretation has now come to mean utterances by the analyst about the unconscious processes of the patient, and I don't actually think that that's what therapy is about. I think therapy is about making a relationship in which it's possible to understand the person, for them to understand themselves – and that that process itself is transformative. Am I noisy? Of course I'm not noisy in the therapy. That's not my job. But my job is to, perhaps – having entered into the world of the person, to try and show them that I've understood it by perhaps putting it into another set of words so that it expands their experience or speaks to them. I don't know, you'd have to listen to a session – each therapy relationship is completely unique. There are some people that I would laugh with, and some people would never know that I have a sense of humour, and some people who experience me as very tall. The whole point about the therapeutic encounter is that it is an intimate and quite special encounter in which two people's psyches get mixed up in particular ways, only one person's meant to be terribly responsible for what's going on. But I wouldn't say that the driving force for me is interpretation. The driving force for me is relating and reflecting all the time on my response to what's happening. Reflecting so much that it's automatic really. And some of that I will share and some of it I won't.

Which concepts underpin your understanding of how you see what is going on between the two of you? You mention the unconscious. How important is that? How important is childhood? How important is the here and now?

Here's the problem. You have to have a theory, because otherwise you can't assess what the hell you're doing. But if you pre-formulate as the analyst your responses to the person, you're no good to them whatsoever, so the question is how to have theoretical understanding that's wide enough, is multiple – has multiple understandings – but yet has precision within it for the person. Right? So – I think that you're raising important questions. How important is the unconscious? *What do we mean by the unconscious?* It's not a physically located place, it's a way of talking about things that we think affect us at another level ... [Pause] ... it's a way of describing and I do think it's a useful way – it's a metaphor for describing problematic states or states that we don't understand, emotional tableaux that we've internalised, that impact on our conscious lives. So, of course I have a concept of the unconscious, I also have a concept of an inner life, where the person will impose a set of ideas on an external situation that reflects their understanding of how relationships have gone before, and their capacity to modify that is obviously a sign of our mental health, isn't it? In terms of concepts, I suppose I do think Fairbairn's schema is useful for me, which to put it in really simple terms is that good relationships provide the food to create in you a human being and they make it possible for you to enter the environment and see it as reasonably benevolent, but when you have rotten experiences and nobody helps you with them, you can't digest them or assimilate them and they repeat on you. If I can put it in this very simple way. And the mind then does a very complicated thing with those, it takes them inside of itself and it refashions the experience – which is usually experience with another person – but instead of the person being the victim of that experience, in order to gain power over it, they become the perpetrator in some way. So there is a very complicated schema that Fairbairn has about what he calls 'internal object relations' which is completely different than the Kleinian schema or other schemas – although everybody uses the same words. And that I find very, very useful, because I think it accords both with my experience clinically in the room and with what I think people are saying. So that's one concept. Another concept is what happens in the therapy relationship. In the transference and the countertransference. I think in the therapy relationship we unbeknown to ourself enact our fantasy or our experience of relationships in particular ways. And we both seek confirmation of that enactment as well as wish to transform it. So the therapy relationship for me – what happens between me and the person in therapy – is important in terms of being able to provide a different kind of relationship, to be able to comment on what's happening between the two of us, and also provide a space in which something different can be tried. The anxiety about doing something differently can be lived through.

Do you turn anyone away?

I turn people away, I'd say, on a weekly basis. Because I don't have time, not ...

Would you turn someone away because you feel you can't in any way help ...

Of course.

And what kind of things would you turn them away for? What are the criteria you use to decide whether a person is ...

... therapeutically amenable? Well it wouldn't be therapeutically amenable, it would be to me. Recently I wrote about this so I don't think it's actually private, do you see what I mean, it's published. I referred somebody on with whom I felt no physical exchange. This was a woman who sought help for vaginismus actually. And although I felt that a lot of her problems related to her relationship with her mother, I felt that it would have been unproductive therapy in the short term, because since she came with the symptom that she wanted help with, she might actually get more help if she had an empathic man rather than me. This very unusual decision on my part is formulated posthoc. I referred her to a man, with whom she had a very successful therapy. At the time it was somehow that I felt there wasn't something there, there wasn't some empathy that I could find.

Now I suppose I'm more interested in older women and older men than I am in absolute youngsters. I'm for ever being sent people's 25-year-old daughters, and I'm more interested I suppose in the 35-year-olds, the 60-year-olds.

Although each therapeutic relationship is different, do you anticipate (at a conceptual level) that people will go through definite types of experiences and stages?

Yes, I think there are definite things that people go through. I think there is a tremendous relief that people feel when they first embark upon therapy. Then there's a certain amount of shame about the indulgence level and everything's all sorted out, and then there's a certain amount – particularly with women – of them saying 'Well I've got enough now, thank you very much, I don't need any more.' Then there are phases in which there is a loss of the whole construction that's built up. And you may be sitting there weathering an enormous depression, by which I mean loss of the kind of the conception of self, and you may be with the person sitting in a tunnel, with the therapist's confidence that they're going to get out and reconstruct something that feels much more substantial, but for them it feels very shaky and very scary. I think the shift in our relationship is significant in terms of being perceived as being an enabler, and then being perceived as being quite – not a torturer, that's far too strong – but being perceived as somebody who's being unhelpful. Or not magical enough or whatever.

How strong a concept for you, a reality for you, is transference?

I don't call it transference – of course I call it transference when I'm teaching – but actually I'm much more interested in the way in which the present is both a re-enactment, i.e., it's a transference, but it's also a new possibility. I use the word countertransference all the time, i.e., my response to the total therapeutic situation not simply the patient's transference, and I'm well aware that there's something called transference because people can see me as their 60-year-old mother. I know I don't look 60 – I have got that! Or their dad, or their brother or whatever. And really the feelings in the room seem to have nothing to do with what just happened. So of course for me transference is a completely central concept. But it's another one of these things that I don't really like. Transference developed – was a word that Freud used – to explain something, and now it explains *everything*. I'm very unhappy with the language that we use to describe practice, so I'm rather wanting to talk about the kinds of things that occur within the therapy relationship, and I would include both the transference aspects and the stuff extra-transferential, the stuff that isn't all about projection.

Is it an important issue for you, the idea of dependence on the therapist?

Well, I think it's absolutely crucial but not in maybe the way you understand that I understand it. For me I think – and this is where there is a gender divide – for women their defences against dependency are so profound that they will spend a tremendous amount of time looking after everybody else, and in that way somehow find a way to look after themselves, by imagining they're in the other person's shoes. And so in therapy there is a real reticence to believe the therapist can be there for them, and be walking alongside them. There may not be a concept of attachment that isn't humiliating. So for me dependency is absolutely crucial and it is one of the major things that I find that I have to struggle around to allow those desires for dependency to be within the room. And when I say there is a gender divide, I think that women have this set of defences against it that have to do with feeling it's very unsafe. Men also have a set of defences against it but manage to depend without being so conscious of it. So in a way, men, once you tell them it's okay to attach, they relax and do it, whereas women fight it much longer within the therapy.

How do you end these relationships?

Hopefully by mutual consent.

That's more tricky than it sounds, though, isn't it ...

Well therapy's very interesting for a period of time, then it's very painful, and then there can be very exhilarating bits. To me the therapy is successful when the person is able to leave having felt supported in their change, not at the point of change, but where they've consolidated some of that change. Where they've risked doing things in a different way, and they've had all that stuff fold inside of them rather than just be these external ... I have sat – I've been doing it now for 25 years, so it's not like I haven't had some experience with ending – and my experience is that I feel it a little bit before it comes up in the therapy. Now you could say, 'Does that mean that I want to get out and I'm transmitting that?' Obviously I have to ask myself that question. But there is some way in which the person tentatively raises it, and then we talk about it, then – sometimes I think it will màke sense, and sometimes I don't think it will make sense – so I'll be absolutely up-front about what's on the agenda, why. And I'd want to have the kind of ending that was the one where we were both – celebrating is too glorious a word – but we were both able to enjoy the struggles that the person has achieved and the fact that they exist within their own lives and bodies. But having had a significant relationship with me that's now on the wane.

When you first meet do you jointly set goals?

No. I might with a couple, and I might with somebody on a short-term basis. No I don't. We'd enunciate a set of things – somebody comes in and says, 'I don't know who I am, 17 different bits of me can come out wherever. I always have to get myself so stressed at work that I only do the thing at the last moment', or 'I just don't know why, I really feel like I just want to beat my kid up.' They might say those kind of things. I might think about all those things and say, 'So these are the things that you are really worried about, and you're concerned about, that you want to work on', or 'these are the things that are bringing you here.' And I will hold them in mind, but no, I don't have a set of goals or a programme. However if somebody came to me with a phobia, or with anorexia or something that they want specific help with, I would always keep that very much in the forefront of our discussions. How *this* relates to *that*, because otherwise I think it's a real disservice, somebody comes with a symptom and you think 'Oh no, I want to have a really interesting, productive analysis, and let's ...', no, so I wouldn't do that.

But someone who comes to you, they know your name, perhaps they've read your books, whatever.

That's unusual. People will come to me, and after they've been here a while they say, 'Do you write, because I mentioned it to my friend and they say you write in the *Guardian*.'

Say they know very little about the therapeutic encounter, do you always tell them what you do, and what they can expect from you?

I try to demonstrate what I am doing in the course of our first meeting. I don't give them a speech about what therapy is, because I don't know where it's going to go, but also because certain things don't make any sense unless you're in the process. It's not that I would *not* explain – I will explain anything, at any point in the therapy – but for me to say 'Actually I think you're going to need a seven-year therapy ... and what I will do is this.' I'll say, 'Well I think the things that we've been discussing, how I understand that we might be able to be helpful to you is ... and I think also, the kinds of feeling that you are talking about with your boyfriend or your mother may actually come up with me, and what will be different is that we will be able to observe them and talk about them while they're happening, and in a way I'll be not caught up in the same way.' So I will explain, but I hope I won't over-explain, because I don't think it's meaningful.

Using clinical terms, what is the range of issues and problems and descriptions of self that arrive on your doorstep? Are your patients people who really aren't that distressed?

No. I mean are they high-functioning, yes. They could be very high-functioning, but are they not distressed ... no, they're very distressed. I don't think Britain is a therapeutic culture. I don't think people come unless they're really in incredible difficulty. It's not a recreation. It's not a piece of cultural development.

Using the language of clinical psychiatry, do you get the whole range of ...

Well I don't get people I would say who are actively psychotic, but I certainly get people that are schizoid, I certainly get people who are dissociated, I certainly get people who are – I don't think I've seen in my whole practice, I've probably seen two neurotics in the course of 25 years – that's as healthy as you get, as far as I can tell.

What other kind of theoretical perspectives do you find useful or interesting?

Well I like Stephen Mitchell's work. He runs a journal in New York called *Psychoanalytic Dialogues*, and I like it a lot, and it involves the interpersonal, the relational theorists, I really like that. I think they're doing work that's very much like some of the contemporary Freudians here, and also some of the independents.

[Pause] ... Put another way. Presumably there must be some techniques which are better than others?

Obviously I do what I do because I think it's very, very useful. I'm sure there's stuff in Bioenergetics that's useful, and I'm sure there's stuff in all sorts of theories that's useful, but I'm not someone who's studying what's useful in those theories. And yes, I would have a hierarchy of things that I think work for particular people, there's no doubt about that. Within psychoanalysis, within my own field, I think the splits and the divisions are really, really absolutely profound, between relationally oriented therapists and the Kleinians. I just think the divisions are massive. Some psychotherapy I think is iatrogenic, I think it is damaging.

Which?

I think the tendency to attack people's defence structures is really damaging, and the conduct of a lot of therapists is appalling. And I'm forever receiving letters about 'this happened', and I don't always take the analyst's side, I will often see it from the patient's point of view. I think relational theories are much better than instinctual/drive theory and I think theories of engagement and reflection are much better, and I'm sure the body therapies have a lot to tell us, but I don't know enough about them to say.

Within your own therapeutic endeavour, what qualities do you feel it necessary for you to have, for you to possess? Say you were training other therapists. What kind of people would you want them to be?

I have a lot of trainees, a lot of supervisees. And these are people who will never write. They have no interest in that. I think a fantastic capacity for compassion and empathy is absolutely crucial, without the need to empty their own distress into that other person. So obviously quite a highly-developed sense of their own issues and struggles. The capacity to describe – I feel I can tell whether somebody's a good therapist in the picture they draw me of their patients: whether I get a picture of who this person is or I don't. So the capacity to not simply absorb their patient's experience, but to articulate it and share it with their supervisor, let's say. A capacity for technical skills and reflection. I absolutely hate sloppiness, I really cannot stand – I suppose the capacity to think really, under fire, but also to think reflectively afterwards. To understand the difference between – when you're aroused in the therapy because you're caught in an enactment with the person – to understand whose bit of what is going on, and whose defence structures are in – that capacity to create inside of yourself an internal reflector at the same moment as your – so you need to have quite a high level of analytic and you need to be able to both be detached and attached at the same moment. I know some good therapists who are not very theoretically inclined which I find fascinating, because I would say you actually have to have a good theory to work, but in fact I do know a couple of clinicians who are far more eclectic than I am. You have to have confidence. It's a good question – I do think the capacity to read and assimilate material is important, I don't actually just think how you are in the room matters.

That's interesting, because it's not a widely held view is it?

No, but somebody comes in with a case – their patient suddenly stops speaking – I'm going to talk to them a lot about that, but I'm also going to give them a paper that I think is important that bears on this, and I want them to read it and I want them to be able to reflect on whether it's right, because the paper may speak to me but I need to speak to them, and then I want them to be able to judge whether it does or it doesn't. I suppose in my supervisees or trainees, I go for quite a high level of intellectual competence. I wouldn't say that means people have to be university graduates, it's not that, but they have to be able to know what's important when you read a paper.

You mentioned earlier about Britain not being a, particularly England maybe, a therapeutic culture. Are there any societies which are ...

Well metropolitan New York, California, Chicago, Philadelphia.

Sure. But I'm thinking more of European cultures.

Therapy was for the intellectual elite in Britain, in the inter-war period, and then it was one option for the distressed. But it never entered the culture in the same way that it did in the United States. You didn't get therapy entering the school system, social work in the same kind of way. Much, much lower. I'm sure it had something to do with class society and how we value the capacity to cope in ways that are very unproductive actually. I think it's a very, very complicated and long answer; I'm not a historian of feelings, and I'm not a historian either of the shift from agrarian to the industrial world, but I'm sure it's right in there. And now, of course, I think there's a real battle on, because on the one hand Britain – the fire services, the police – know they cannot actually function unless they have in-house counselling. But we're getting an attack on the therapising of this culture and the enervating of it, that somehow there are counsellors in every GP's office, and then there's all the attacks on the false memory people, and then there's intellectual attack from Frederick Crews, and then there's the attack from Grunbaum. I think therapy is really under fire at the same moment as everybody's realising that there's something about the therapeutic that's valuable.

How do you view the arguments of Jeffrey Masson and others, sceptics who have practised themselves, and then recanted?

I think lots of what Jeffrey has to say is completely valid, but I mean it's not my position. I think you can make a critique of conventional psychiatry, and conventional psychoanalysis, but I think the problem with Masson is that he – you get it in his autobiographical thing about his father, and his father being caught up with the guru – hated psychoanalytic fundamentalism, lots of us hate that. Contemporary psychoanalysis contains within it fundamentalists, but it contains within it people who I think have a capacity to manage complexity and to think through and who would develop practices that are completely authentically useful to people. So yes he's fine as a critic, but he's so out-of-date, he doesn't really know what's going on.

Do people always have to fundamentally help themselves?

In partnership. If they could help themselves they wouldn't be at the front door would they?

But in the end, isn't it having to help themselves that makes them better?

Yes and no, because it's a therapy relationship, and if you have a relational theory that says that people develop and grow in a decent medium, and it's in a decent medium that people understand their defences and problems around intimacy, or around growth, then you have to see it as something that's implicit – of course it's about them, but it's not about them stranded or alone, it's about them in concert with you. I'm in concert with them, definitely. But on the other hand I don't think five years from now they'll be thinking 'Oh God, wasn't she great', they'll be thinking, 'It's over, and it was fine, and it did its job.'

How do you take on board in your encounters, the fact that people live lives outside your rooms. That could be incredibly stressful ...

I support that those are things that are stressful. The inner world is made up of people's experience of the external world, and then what they make of it. I don't know anybody who doesn't have a life that's stressful. It is true that half of my clients don't have to worry about where the next penny comes from, and so that isn't a major therapeutic issue. But it is for other ones. It isn't something I can make better, but it isn't something I would deny, or interpret as their desire to be deprived. If somebody's economically deprived I think we have to take that as a reality.

How do you feel about the economics of therapy?

I hate it. I think that the therapists made a big mistake in not fighting to be within the National Health Service in 1945/46. As a result they've got a whole bunch of crazy theories about how you have to charge for therapy and it matters. I've worked in places where I've been the recipient of a salary and people haven't paid for therapy, it's made absolutely no therapeutic difference. People value or are unable to value their sessions, having absolutely bugger all to do with money. In fact, if they don't pay directly, but it's coming, let's say, out of the state purse, it highlights the issues about the difficulties people have with receiving an entitlement and deserving which are very profound issues. And money

actually covers that up. Most therapists will say 'Oh well.' I want to be
paid for my labour, don't get me wrong, but I would love to do away
with direct payment. I find it of no significant value. However, having
said that, once it's in the therapy relationship, because people mostly do
pay me directly – not everybody because some people are paid by the
insurance companies – then we have to deal with it all the time. We
have to adjust fees, the meaning of the money – and it carries a whole
lot of meanings. But if it wasn't there we would be doing all those
meanings around something else, not around the money.

*You mentioned earlier about some therapists not behaving in the way that
you would like them to behave. You mentioned that you hear about these
things. What would be the rational way of dealing with this, other than
some back-handed register?*

You're asking a very fundamental question. I think training has to be
transformed. All the trainings look the same now, the psychoanalytic
ones. All the originality about why people set up these different trainings is disappearing. I think the fact that they're private trainings, that
they don't operate in university settings, that they're not proper postgraduate trainings like most academic disciplines or the fact that people
have to pay for them in a particular way, the fact that people pay for
therapy and that's separate, and then they pay for supervision. It's not
that that is a corrupt set of practices, but it does something to the way
in which we train therapists. The fact that most trainings are a bit like
column A and column B: you go down a bit of Freud and then you get
a bit of Klein, and then if you're lucky you get a bit of object relations,
and maybe you get the independents, or Jung; I don't see how that
equips people very well. I think you need to learn a set of ideas; either
look at Freud from a relational perspective, and look at all the other
people who followed, or you need to look at attachment theory, so
people actually understand. And I think you need to have close relationships between tutors and trainees. You're talking about a reform of
training completely.

Do we know much of what happens to the spouses of clients?

They get disturbed, unless ...

No-one talks about it to me. It just seems to me – obviously if you're in ...

It can be very, very threatening. I can think of somebody I see now who
came into therapy. Her husband was rather brutal, cruel – physically
cruel, but as well emotionally very cruel – she conceptualised her life as
surviving through being very, very proud of what she could survive. But
she'd had it – this is not atypical – so of course the husband then is very
uptight about when she goes into therapy, a real fear of the loss of the

relationship on his part, a real trying to pull her back to old conceptions that she had. A real wish on her part that he would go into therapy so that they could do all of this stuff and still be in a partnership together. Sometimes we've talked about the kinds of sentences she could generate, so that she could still hang into that relationship and have the reassurance – she may not get the support – but she could give him some reassurance, and she wouldn't be battered by her endeavours. But I do think it is difficult. Some spouses benefit by default, don't they, because if the person has been dumping a lot of stuff out into the relationship that they are now able to hold within their own physical membrane, then actually something shifts in the relationship, it forces a shift.

If the client brings this up in a session ...

... often does, yes ...

... do you wait for them to say 'Could you see my husband as well?' or do you sometimes initiate ...

Well I might initiate it, but I wouldn't say that. I would say 'I think you might have a hope that I could see your husband and that somehow we could all be in a dialogue together, and that he could have a chance to understand you better and understand himself better. And I think if that's something that you want, it's not something I can offer, but I would be happy to – if he felt at all that he wanted to do that – it is something that we could think about in terms of a referral.' I wouldn't take him into therapy. I either commit myself to an individual therapy, or to a couple therapy.

How do you answer those people who just have no conception of the efficacy of what they would call a talking cure?

But everybody knows that a conversation with a friend can sometimes have an 'aha' quality, where you begin to enter a conversation and something is different at the end of it. So there is something very powerful about human interaction. And I suppose I would say – I'm not into convincing people – I'm much more into saying that what happens in a conversation of this kind is that you have two people reflecting and daring to look from different perspectives at things. And that in itself makes one think and possibly feel very differently ... There is something very transformative. I'd say 'Look, it seems to me X is rather upset. He presents himself in the world as rather angry, and actually behind that there's a lot of extra dimensions that we don't know, which I think are difficult for X', and when they know them they're richer, and they can manage things more. I write about emotional literacy in the *Guardian*, but I don't know that I would be a propagandist for therapy per se. I feel more complicated about it, but that's because I'm a critic of so much therapy that goes on.

Would society be a much healthier place if – whether the NHS took it or it became a culture where we accepted that it's a legitimate thing to do?

I don't think there's any doubt that that would be better, but I'm not really interested in that. I'm not interested in everybody being in therapy. What I am interested in is how what we've understood about emotional life and about damage, and cruelty and hurt, how we might incorporate that understanding into the national curriculum, day care centres, child rearing practices, schools. All of that, how that might be imbued with a completely different sensibility. It's not that I want everybody to go to their therapist; I'm interested in seeing emotional literacy in all of our institutions.

And school being particularly critical and pertinent?

I think it is, because I think it is a very difficult institution that children spend most of their time in.

What are your thoughts on false memory syndrome? I hear very different views.

Well I've got a lot of views on it. For me the critical issue is still sexual abuse. Why we as a culture cannot take on board sexual abuse. In other words we find it easier to take on board that people are being falsely accused than we take on board the fact of the kind of level of transgression that occurs. So to me the really interesting question is why. I myself find it indigestible to take on board the level of sexual abuse that I believe exists. I don't want to think about it, it's too painful, it's too horrible. As to false memory, I'm sure there is some false memory. I don't think we can contest that. Why does it come to prominence? ... [Pause] ... we've only really been able to take on board the idea of sexual abuse since women have been able to articulate their own experiences and that's somehow allowed them to be subjects, and then we have children who are now finally allowed to be heard. It's to do with the whole social process in which children actually, and women, have reshaped some of the agenda. So false memory could be the backlash against that, and given that we know the kind of paedophiliac practices of the American False Memory Society, some of their membership, and given the BPS's report on the British False Memory Society, I think we have a right to be very careful about what the false memory societies are about. I'm sure there are some genuinely falsely accused parents in there but there are others who are either amnesiac ... it's quite possible that they were not aware that they were involved in sexual relations with their children, that they were dissociated at the time. Because for me the question is why do children make, or adults make, this an account? Why do they fashion their distress into an account of sexual abuse if that isn't on the agenda? That's a pretty heavy thing to do, what the hell is going on there? Why are they being – quote un-quote – 'duped' into that, if the distress is of a minor level? Something must have gone very seriously wrong.

Do you think therapists monitor their own performance enough? Are there times when you know that you're not attending as much as you like to?

New theory allows you to regard the phenomenon of 'floating off': let's say you realise during a session that you're actually in the supermarket, as opposed to sitting in the room with the person. I think most contemporary psychoanalytic theory has a way of helping you understand why you're doing that.

Which is what?

What is it in the interaction that's allowed you to drift off. Not what's that patient done to you, but where have you gone and why? Why the supermarket – is there an unconscious meaning to this? On another level I think most therapists are overworked. They're rushing in a million different directions, and a lot of them don't have enough study time and reflective time. And I don't know how good a record most of them keep. There aren't those requirements in this profession.

Do you keep written records?

I do actually, I keep written records, but not always. But I don't want to say that, that's the problem. Because I once went to court on a case in which I didn't. So from time to time – I keep *notes*.

But although you keep notes ...

I don't do it verbatim, which is what I did when I trained, but I have a way of noticing the process.

Is this necessarily a developmental record? Do you have the notes for the next session; you bear in mind what was said in the last session? Or is each session different and new from the beginning?

Both. It's both. You're both in a constant dialogue, but you're also meeting anew with whatever's on this agenda. But I might bring it in, and I might bring in something from two years ago.

Might you also give people practical advice?

Me? I think I'm very much like the Anna Freud Centre, which has worked out that 70 per cent of their – I don't know if it's 70 per cent, you'd have to check this figure – an enormous amount of their interventions were

extra-psychoanalytic, so they called them socio-educational or something.
Which I thought was very funny. There's no therapist I know who doesn't
make suggestions, it's impossible not to. How you phrase it might be very
different. You might say 'Well I wonder why ...?' – 'it's interesting that it
didn't occur to you to do x, y, and z, given that you ...' You may do it
indirectly rather than directly. But I don't actually want to exclude those
from the psychoanalytic dialogue, because I want to include – everything
that goes on in there is psychoanalytic – I don't want to divide up the
interventions and say 'Well this was psychoanalytic, and this was counselling, and this was practical', because if it is a relationship you are going to
find different things that are appropriate to say at different moments.

Do you think therapists should retire? Should there be an age of retirement?

I definitely don't think they should take on people over a certain age,
for clinical treatment. I think they can take them on for supervision.
Because who wants to have a therapist die on you? I think it depends –
some people are very alert, and get wiser, and some people don't get
wiser as they get older. I don't actually believe in mandatory retirement.

*Correct me if I'm wrong, but you were involved in the foundation of the
Women's Therapy Centre, weren't you?*

I started it with Luise Eichenbaum.

Do you see yourself as fundamentally moving away from that perspective?

Well I think the Women's Therapy Centre is very different from when
Luise and I started it, and I feel very connected and attached to it, and
great-grannyish, if you like, and I look forward to celebrating the twen-
tieth anniversary. But there are lots of things that are very different
than I would do.

*The lay person's point of view. The idea of the Women's Therapy Centre
equals feminist ideas ...*

I am a feminist. I don't think there's anything about me that isn't
feminist really.

I think most people find this hard to square. Psychoanalysis ...

Yes, because they're looking at it, I think it's a good question, they're
looking at it from the point of view of – you have to swallow psychoanalysis, and then you tack your feminism on. Well that's impossible.
But if you start from a basis of trying to understand how human beings
develop with their genders, with their class, with everything about them,
then you can take from psychoanalysis what you find useful, in personal

development and individual development. It's interesting, I haven't heard that I'm a sell-out, I'm intrigued by that but I'm sure people must think that.

Just a couple of people have mentioned it.

When Luise and I started the Women's Therapy Centre, the other women who we brought in immediately did have practices, you can't survive on what we did there. We couldn't survive on the £30 a week that we managed to pull out of the centre, so we all did other things.

Presumably it was an idea that women were far more 'deserving of help' than men ...

No. It was rather trying to understand and focus on women's experiences. I still see many more women. But I think feminism has advanced to a point now where it is in a position to talk about the crisis of masculinity. I don't think it needs to exclude that from its conversation. Luise and I started the Women's Therapy Centre in a very different political climate. We still had the GLC, we hadn't had 16 years, 17 years of a kind of Thatcherite government. It was possible to think in terms of changing a lot of practice and of getting funded and all those kinds of things. Now, it's very convenient for me to work on my own because I have to juggle so many things.

Could you describe a patient and the movement they've made over time with you?

Well I don't know how compelling an account this is because it's going to sound like a small change, and yet I think it's a big change. This was a woman who wasn't from Britain, who came to me. She was professional, she'd come here at a certain point in her life. So she was torn away from her background, although she came with her family, and they didn't know how to act in England. She really tried to integrate into British culture, but it wasn't that easy because her parents didn't know how to do it and she was very unsupported, and she got into all sorts of trouble, had a child very young. Somehow got herself together enough to get a professional training, but felt that nothing that she did was meaningful. That everything good about her was fraudulent, that she only did it to create a very temporary sense of self-esteem, that there was no continuity running through her. That she existed in a lot of different compartments. She was a very angry woman, and she sought a kind of confirmation of self in confrontation. But she was very, very deeply lonely, but couldn't know that she was lonely. And so she had a series of unfortunate relationships, and difficult times at work. I think that what happened to her was learning to understand that the strength that she had developed, like all these tasks she set herself to succeed in, were actually things that belonged to her, although she just saw them as these very superficial things that she knew how to do. And in the course of the therapy, she came to mourn a lot about living in two cultures and she came to accept not only being a displaced person but having a different experience, and she came to understand her anger as expressing lots of fear and vulnerability and helplessness, and she learnt how to tolerate feelings of helplessness, so that she could transform those into knowing when she *was* helpless, and knowing when she wasn't. And initiating not from the point of view of seeking external confirmation every second, which then when she got it she didn't believe, but by feeling a certain internal satisfaction. And being able to be much less rigid with herself, and much less rigid with her ideas.

Are there times when you find human misery and human difficulty just too much to bear?

Well, I'm sure I do. I'm sure being a writer is a way, not just being a writer, I think that I have ways that I try to transform my own experience of absorbing and sharing in a lot of misery. So obviously I have a conceptual political framework, and I think that's what keeps me as sane as I can be.

Even when there is something going on between you and a client, are there times when it's just too tedious to bear?

It can be very, very hard to bear, but that's what being a therapist is. It's learning how to bear that. That's my bread and butter. I think that if I didn't have a set of relationships myself, that mattered to me and sustained me, I couldn't do the work.

CHAPTER 3

Person-centred Therapy

Brian Thorne

Brian Thorne is Director of Student Counselling, University of
East Anglia, Norwich. He has written widely on counselling,
including the books *Carl Rogers* and *Person-centred Counselling*.

*Can we talk a little about your background? As it pertains to your chosen
profession?*

Yes, sure. It's quite a long story, that's the difficulty of course. I think it
probably started when I was a boy in the War. I was an only child, my
own father did not serve in the War because he was in a reserved trade,
but most of the other families around us, the fathers had gone to the
War. Therefore there were a lot of children without fathers, and there
were a lot of women without husbands. And looking back on it now,
that actually created a kind of environment of relating which I think
was very unusual. A lot of community development in a way, a lot of
going in and out of others' houses. A lot of children coming through our
house, principally I think because they wanted contact with a man, and
my father was one of the few available. As an only child, of course, it
was a very rich time for me, because there were on tap all these
potential brothers and sisters.

So looking back on it I think I grew up in a very unusual situation
where people were actually at times quite literally talking about their
feelings, particularly the women. I remember the mothers of so many of
my friends would sometimes pour their hearts out to me, a little boy, or
to my mother or father, whatever it was. So I think that's where my
real, as it were, fascination with human nature, and also human anxiety
to an extent, began.

In terms of more clear cut influences. When I was in the Army,
when I did my National Service, I was actually serving in Cyprus during
the Eoka time – which again was a very crisis-ridden existence, because
serving on so-called internal security duties, you were never quite sure if
somebody wasn't up on the roof just about to put a bullet through you.
Living as it were with risk all the time. Being with a lot of other young
men obviously my age. But being in a position as a young officer of
some responsibility, again through being sort of cheek by jowl with
people, who were in a very difficult situation, experiencing all sorts of

feelings, and anxieties, and emotions. And actually having to really try
and respond to them.

So I think that was a second baptism really. It was strange how in a
way aggression and hostility and warfare contributed to creating environments in which I think I learned to become very, very fascinated with
human nature, and with my own, of course, too.

The Church was your first profession?

The Church as my chosen profession?

I thought you were a man of the cloth ...

Well you're absolutely wrong. But it's very interesting that you should
have made that mistake. As it's quite interesting for me that I often get
letters here addressed to the Reverend Brian Thorne. But I've never
been a priest.

It's a common misunderstanding then ...

Yes, yes, so I'd better say something about that. I've actually written
about this. I wrote a book a little while ago called *Behold The Man*,
which is a therapist's meditations on the passion of Christ. In that book
I referred to a childhood experience which was just after the War,
strangely enough, and which happened to me on a Good Friday, when I
was playing cricket in a still war-devastated park.

I won't go into all the details of it, but suffice it to say that I did
have, I think, a very profound experience as a young boy, and that that
was really for me the turning point of my life, and has remained the
cornerstone, I think, of my whole existence ever since.

Basically what I experienced on that Good Friday afternoon was that
in the last analysis all that really matters is that we should attempt to
love. And also to attempt to receive love when it's there on offer. I'm
sure I didn't conceptualise it in those terms at the time. Although I
think in a fairly marked way I knew something about what the priorities
were, and I don't think they've ever really left me.

Can you elaborate?

I was there, playing cricket, it was the year 1946. Is that right? Yes, I
was nine. Just after four o'clock. It was Good Friday, not that that was
a matter of great significance to me at the time, although I knew a bit
about some of the essential Christian understandings, and therefore I
knew that Good Friday was actually a rather special day – when the
crucifixion of Christ was central in some people's understandings. That
bit I knew.

As we were playing cricket in this park, suddenly a great procession appeared, going along the street at the top of the park. It was what they call a procession of witness, with the crucifer and a couple of acolytes, and the clergy and the robed choir, and the congregation as it were, going through the streets, actually saying 'This is a rather important day.' And for whatever reason, at that particular moment, I was totally overwhelmed by a sense of the magnitude of all of that.

I actually ran home – I left the cricket match – and what I remember now is simply going up to my bedroom. I don't remember my parents at all, whether they were in the house, I've no idea. But going up to my bedroom and just simply sobbing, and sobbing, and sobbing for a very long time. With a deep conviction that what I had somehow experienced was the essential meaning of reality. That here was a kind of personal, if you like, manifestation to me. What actually mattered more than anything else was that I could prove capable of loving my fellow human beings, and that that's what God had himself done, and that that was a rather expensive thing in terms of human pain and suffering, but that whether I liked it, wanted it, or whatever, that was going to be where my life was going.

And then ... later ...

I became a school teacher. After the army, I went to Cambridge to study Modern Languages, which still remains one of my great delights. I graduated as a specialist principally in German, and there also hangs another interesting tale, which again coloured my later adolescence. When I first went to Germany, which was again in the early 1950s, when Germany was still showing all the signs of the ravages of War, and becoming very close to a family in Hamburg, where the father had actually died on the Russian Front, and experiencing really enormous feelings and emotions about living in this culture of the enemy.

Again, looking back on it, I think it was a very important experience of somehow living in depth with tremendous pain, really, all round me, of which in a sense I was myself part of the history.

I decided to be a school teacher because I liked people, I loved my subject, and I thought teaching German and French wouldn't be a bad thing to do. It felt to me at the time as if that was very much in keeping with my own sense of vocation. I'd wrestled with the notion of 'was I actually called to be a priest?' and had very firmly decided that was not what God was wanting me to do, and that school teaching would be an admirable milieu. The direct, I suppose, answer to your question, in a sense – how on earth did I find myself in counselling and psychotherapy? – was my experiences as a school master.

I went to teach in an independent school, which was principally a boarding school, and you probably don't need to hear much more because that school, like, I suppose, most independent boarding schools then and now, was full of young people in pretty awful states of misery. I soon discovered that, although I was being paid to teach sixth formers

German and French, I seemed to be spending an awful lot of time
doing something else, which I suppose now I would call a kind of
informal, amateurish counselling. As time went on I had really to make
a fairly dramatic decision. Because it was, I think, fairly obvious to me
and to others, that I was really rather a good school teacher, and
therefore there were all sorts of possibilities ahead for me. The Head of
Department, the Headship and all that, looked a very real possibility.

But increasingly, I found that I was being drawn to this other activity,
and a crucial time was when – I think I'd been teaching about four years,
three or four years – when I was trying to be of use to a lad of about 17,
who was clearly highly disturbed, and I think looking back on it now, was
drifting in and out of almost a psychotic state at times. I'd seen this lad on
one particular evening, and felt hopelessly out of my depth, and really very
perturbed and anxious, and although I'd discussed it with colleagues in
school, and also with a consultant physician in the school, I didn't feel at
all comforted or reassured really about him evidently.

So I decided on the spur of the moment to get in touch with a man
called George Lyward, whom I'd heard about, who ran a residential therapeutic community, although he never called it that. He simply said that he
offered hospitality, particularly to young men who had really gone through
all the other possible forms of help, and had fallen through the bottom. I
knew about his work, particularly with the 16–20-year-old age group. And
on the spur of the moment I rang him up, and got him on the line at a
place called Finchden Manor which was the name of the place he offered
hospitality, and told him a bit about the predicament I was in, and to cut a
long story short, he said 'Why don't you come over and see me this
weekend?' So I went over to see him.

We talked about this particular situation and this particular young
man, and he simply said to me at the end, 'Well you must come back
any time you want here, you'll be very welcome, but you do clearly
already know don't you, that you're a therapist?'

How would you describe what you do?

I think the best way I can describe it is that I hope to offer a particular
kind of relationship. And that if I'm successful in offering that particular
kind of relationship then there is at least a very good chance that the
person who is seeking my help will begin to find a way forward for
themselves. But if I had to respond simply to the question – what am I
trying to do? How would I label it? – I would say that I am trying to
offer a particular kind of relationship.

*For the uninitiated could you talk of the importance of Carl Rogers' work
... what he stood for ...*

Yes I think so, and it might be easier in a way to look just a moment or
two at what we might call the potential clients. Because from that I

think the philosophical underpinning, if you like, of Rogers' work becomes more evident. It seems to me that a lot of people who seek help from counsellors and therapists are people who have a pretty poor opinion of themselves, that may not be necessarily totally evident in the lives that they're leading, and other people meeting them or perceiving them and so on, may not actually cotton on to that fact. But almost invariably my experience is that the person coming for help is actually thinking pretty badly of themselves. Or to use the jargon has fairly low self-esteem.

Now one of the primary reasons for that, it seems to me, is that person has experienced in their lives a very considerable degree of adverse judgement. Some of that may be quite clearly attributable to parental upbringing or other significant people in the life of that individual. Sometimes it's actually reinforced very much by the societal norms. And particularly nowadays, when we live in such a very competitive culture, the opportunities for being failed at this, that and the other, are growing apace. So here we have a person, therefore, who is not feeling very good about themselves.

Secondly, I think a lot of people who come for therapy feel that they have never really been paid much attention. A sense of – people say it – never having been properly listened to. That they've been, in a way, regarded rather more as objects or people who have to go through some kind of process, rather than being attended to as individuals who are worth listening to, worth understanding.

I think, too, the third thing which characterises a lot of the people who see me is that they have found it almost impossible to be authentic. They've spent a lot of their time really leading concealed lives, pretending actually to be people that they aren't; sometimes, as a result of that, achieving positions of very high eminence, so a very deep, basic inauthenticity. And allied to that, too, the experience of being surrounded by other people who seem basically to be lacking really in any kind of real honesty.

Now if those sorts of things characterise the clients, then I think it's fairly easy to see in a way where the approach that Carl Rogers developed came from. Because he was very concerned – it's very interesting reading about his experiences in his life in the 1930s for example – he was very concerned to discover what worked. Very pragmatic in a sense, and gradually tumbled to the fact that, as he put it, 'the client knows best', that the person coming for help knows what he or she needs: may not initially be able to articulate that very well, but essentially the therapist's task is to really follow the lead of the client.

Many clients, as they begin to get in touch with what they need, realise that they actually need, more than anything else, a relationship which is characterised by the very things which they have up to that point lacked. Instead of having adverse judgement thrown at them, or feeling all the time that they're up for criticism, or big brother's watching them, they would like a relationship where they feel a pretty good modicum of acceptance. That they're not perpetually having to be on their guard; they can relax. That the person they're with is not going to be passing negative judgements on them, but is in fact going to be acceptant of them. They also discover that it's really incredibly liberating to be with somebody who appears to be genuinely interested in them and wanting to listen to them, and wanting to understand them – if they've had a lifetime really of feeling unlistened to and ignored.

Then, and I think Rogers in a way only tumbled to the real importance of this third thing later on, but the ability to be in a relationship where they could really be themselves, even if that meant acknowledging very painful and difficult feelings, and very painful difficult weaknesses, and that at the same time as they felt able to be more honest themselves, to sense that they were with a person who would be similarly honest. Who wasn't actually in some curious way hiding behind something, in the way that they'd had to hide behind something for so much of their lives. But here perhaps was a person who was prepared to be a person, and not as it were a professional behind a white coat, or somebody who was continually using something to duck behind.

So from that we get the classic core conditions of the person-centred approach. A relationship characterised by a high level of acceptance, a determination on the part of the therapist to exercise empathic understanding, and a willingness on the therapist's part to be himself or herself a genuine person. But it seems to me that what we find in all that really is a very practical, pragmatic response to the needs of clients. Let us provide precisely those things which have been lacking and of which so many people have experienced the antithesis.

What is the 'model of wo/man' that lies behind Rogers' approach?

He's a person who experiences reality in his own unique way. If you want to put Rogers' thought into a philosophical tradition, it must be really in the tradition of phenomenology, mustn't it? The emphasis is really upon the uniqueness of personal experience. Rogers himself once wrote a paper where he suggested that there were as many realities as there are people. And that should be our starting point. Which means therefore that this individual has a subjective reality, and it is that subjective reality which is actually going to condition his or her ability to find a way through life. Therefore although I think the person-centred approach is sometimes almost ridiculed for being so lightweight, theoretically, it does have some very important theoretical underpinnings, and they are quite crucial. The notion that a person operating from his or her subjective reality will begin to build up a sense of self which is determined, to a very large extent, by the experience that he or she has, and particularly the experience of the interpersonal relationships which he or she has. And in person-centred therapy one of the core theoretical constructs is the notion of the self-concept: that if a person actually has a poor self-concept, thinks badly of himself or herself, then it is very likely that things will go awry, either because they will begin to act out that self-concept, or because they will try in many, many ways to disguise that from the external world and become more and more disintegrated.

The ideas about human development behind person-centred therapy are really very important. How is it that some people apparently do develop strong, and healthy and usable self-concepts, which can enable them to make something of their lives, and others do not? And find themselves really crippled with a sense of self which undermines them in almost everything that they do. Well I think the person-centred approach has got a lot to say about that, and again we can see the kind of work that a person-centred therapist is doing, as an attempt to create a new sort of interpersonal environment where some of those things can be put right.

For me as a therapist, certainly, I come to recognise the magic moment. The magic moment for me is when a person goes across an invisible line which divides a basically self-rejecting attitude from a basically self-acceptant attitude. Where that self-concept moves just that little bit from 'I am basically a pretty invalid person', to 'I am basically a valuable person.' And I know as a therapist, I know that moment, or very often I know it. That's one of the great things about this work for me.

Some people criticise client-centred approaches for only dealing with relatively 'healthy' people ...

I certainly believe it's unfair, for a number of reasons. One is my own experience of actually working with people who are extremely articulate and also extremely confused, and you can get those people in universities just as much as you can outside, so I'm thinking of both. And the sure knowledge that I have, that if I can be with that person in the ways that I've described, then gradually they do begin to get a handle on what is happening to them. But many need a great deal of patience, a great deal of time.

So I can draw upon personal experience, I think, but in a way even more importantly for me is some of the recent work that has been done by a man called Garry Prouty, who, using very much person-centred principles, has been doing remarkable work with psychotic people in hospitals; work which is now being developed in Europe, in Belgium particularly. What basically is going on there – Prouty describes his work incidentally as pre-therapy, something that has to happen before therapy can itself begin – is actually giving this psychotic person that deep respect, that deep empathic responsiveness in a way which can enable the psychotic person to feel eventually in relationship with self and the other.

Now clearly I can't describe the methodology completely, but what I am saying is Prouty's work is based entirely upon the person-centred approach and its underlying philosophy. That if you can actually use that philosophy and use that approach very specifically with people who seem to be out of touch with reality – whatever that means – then movement will occur.

Do you actually tell clients that you will be the opposite of what they've previously experienced in their relationships?

I don't think I would be saying quite that. That would be making a claim of almost godlike proportions, and I certainly won't be making that claim. What I will be saying is that I'm hopeful of offering you a kind of relationship which you probably have not had the opportunity to experience before. I can't make up for all that damage and all that deprivation, of course I can't do that, but hopefully I can get you to the point where you can begin to believe that a different kind of way of being is possible for you. That's a rather more limited objective, but it's an important difference.

Having said that, however, I would acknowledge that there is inherent in what I've been saying a fairly colossal sense of responsibility. Because a person-centred therapist has not got a vast array of complicated theories to disappear behind, hasn't got a well-developed professional persona to use, there is inherently more of the person of the therapist at stake within this enterprise. Therefore for me what is absolutely critical in the person-centred therapist is that he or she has attained to a pretty high level of self-acceptance.

Now that is not something which is necessarily always constant. Clearly all of us have our dips, but if we have our dips, there are ways of hopefully remedying that fairly promptly. But if the person-centred therapist is not himself or herself, deeply self-acceptant, then there can be all sorts of trouble. Because there can be a kind of need gratification going on. 'If I can really win this client's love, if I can really be for this client somebody who is really almost of the order of God, then I'll feel better.' And that's where the danger begins.

So as a trainer of person-centred therapists, the thing that I'm most concerned with is how far is this person who is training for this work, himself or herself self-acceptant? And if they're not, then much has to be done.

How do you find out?

I think within a training group situation, a person who has not actually achieved a modicum of self-acceptance very quickly becomes apparent – apparent to themselves and apparent to others – because they're continually having to withstand the interaction in depth with a number of people. It's impossible within that training situation to somehow conceal from yourself the fact that you are still deeply self-negating. And it's certainly impossible for you to conceal that from others.

You've talked a lot about 'love' ... In therapy what might that actually mean?

For a person to feel loved and therefore, in my case, for me to be able to offer love. What does that mean? What does it mean for me to offer love to a client? What it means for me is – can I convey to this client, because I truly feel it, and if I don't heaven forbid that I should try, but if I truly feel it, can I convey to this client that he or she is a person whom I consider to be of infinite value? Simply that. That's what I mean by love.

You're not expecting any reciprocal feelings?

Not at all, not at all. But there is another issue there, and this is very interesting for me as far as notions of transference and so on are concerned. It seems to me that one of the things that many human beings very much doubt is their own capacity to love. Many people who come into counselling and therapy not only believe that they can't love, but actually believe that when they try to love they are damaging and destructive. I would say that that characterises a substantial minority of people coming into therapy. That not only do they feel somewhat unlovable, but they also feel that when they try to love all they do is wreak havoc. They destroy.

And therefore it's very important for me that if a client is clearly feeling warmly disposed towards me, clearly is beginning to regard me as a person of great value, that I do not reject that. That I don't try any way to minimise it, because if I do that then I'm giving yet another bit of evidence that their loving is defective, and unwelcome and injurious. Therefore I want to be prepared to accept my client's love, if that's what he or she is experiencing.

Now as far as transference is concerned, clearly there are times when we don't see each other aright. When we are seeing in the other person, probably somebody else, or an amalgam of other people from our past. For me as a person-centred therapist, if I begin to sense that I am being perceived as someone other than I am, my major task will actually be to unearth that and look at it, not in any sense to encourage it or to work with it, but to unearth it and face it. 'When you say that to me, or when you respond in that way to me, I sense you are not really seeing me at all. That's how I feel. What's going on, do you think?', or whatever the appropriate reaction might be.

In detail, what happens when someone comes to see you?

I'll attempt a response to that. I think in a way the process that goes on is probably recognisable from client to client, but in many cases that process will be a very rapid one indeed, whereas in other cases it will be very long and drawn out. But to try and respond to some of the detailed questions ...

I usually operate with two chairs. We usually sit not exactly facing each other, but at a slight angle from each other. Because if people are facing each other, then it's rather difficult to escape each other's gaze, it's rather important that people can feel free as it were, not necessary to look you in the eye, or even to have to look at your body. So slightly angled chairs, but two chairs. But I always actually make a point at a first session of enabling the client to choose whichever chair he or she wants.

I don't have my chair, and that for me is quite significant, and it always interests me too that different clients choose different chairs, and in subsequent sessions I often have to remind myself 'Oh yes, so-and-so likes the left-hand chair, whereas so-and-so likes the right-hand chair.' That's actually for me quite important. A sense that this is a situation where hopefully we can be working together, and where I haven't predetermined everything. I mean by predetermined, *I* sit in that chair, and that in a curious way sets the wrong tone.

Now in terms of duration and so on, it depends so very much, I think on why this person is hurting. Because if somebody who is basically a pretty self-acceptant and functional person has gone through a really rather nasty experience – they may for the first time in their lives have failed something, for example, or there may have been some traumatic episode – then that particular person is going to need probably a very brief space of time, during which their basically healthy view of themselves, which has been to some extent shattered, can regain what we might term its normal equilibrium.

Therefore, working in the university, for example, I think where quite a number of young people do experience sudden and at the time fairly catastrophic events – this ghastly mark they've got for this essay which they thought was really the tops, or a broken love affair or whatever it may be – now painful and difficult as those things are, and very disruptive of effective living, they can fairly quickly be integrated, and therefore the person is going to need that sort of relationship which I can offer for probably a fairly brief period, as they come back into terms with themselves.

Whereas another person who is bringing the woundedness of 25 years of rejection, of not-understanding, of inauthenticity, of conceal-ment, that person may well need rather longer. When I say rather longer I mean two to three years. So I'd like to feel anyway that I'm prepared to accept my client where he or she is. And that is clearly going to cover a multitude of different situations.

What actually goes on? Very little talk ...

Well I think that the best way of trying to respond to that is to say this – that person-centred therapy as far as I'm concerned is essentially the giving expression to attitudes and beliefs. I believe certain things about human beings. I believe certain things about what can happen to human beings, given a particular kind of relationship. There are certain things which I believe, there are certain attitudes which I've described as the acceptant empathic congruent attitudes, which I feel are effective.

Now how I'm going to give expression to those attitudes, how I'm going to deploy them, is going to vary enormously from client to client, and that's where the awful caricatures of the person-centred approach come into existence. Because there is the notion that somehow you can apply those attitudes in a kind of mechanistic way. But clearly you can't. If, for example, somebody comes to see me and I'm the sixth therapist they've tried in the last five years, clearly I am going to be very different in my way of conveying to them the sort of attitudes that I want to convey, than to a person who's never been to a therapist in their lives before, extremely frightened about having crossed the threshold, and therefore is probably going to need an enormous amount of reassurance that they haven't done the most foolish thing in their lives.

So it's very difficult to actually tell you what will happen. But I think I can say that what I'm going to try and do, initially anyway, is to enable this person to feel that they've come to a safe environment. But the way that I'm going to convey that this environment is a safe one will depend very much upon my client, because I could say something to one person which would actually enable them to feel really much safer – the very same thing I might say to another person and far from making them feel safe it might actually make them feel unsafe. I'm talking here particularly about the sophisticated client. Because, for example, if a sophisticated client comes and I say something like 'Well I'm really wanting to hear what it is that concerns you. Perhaps we can begin by you giving some notion of what it is that's brought you here', now that, for the first-time client, may actually be very reassuring, it may make them feel that they're not somehow going to be now diagnosed and have lots and lots of questions thrust at them. For the sophisticated client that may actually feel like 'therapese'.

You're trying to get inside someone else's shoes ...

Yes, certainly. What I'm trying to find out is how this person experiences reality, and particularly how they experience themselves, yes.

Do you separate insights from the Rogerian approach from other therapeutic traditions?

No. But I'm pretty much on my guard against a kind of unthought-out eclecticism. I think the person-centred approach can easily be contaminated in a way which deprives it of its essential quality. With the notion that somehow we must add this or add that so we can become perhaps more effective or proactive, there is a great danger there that it can actually undermine the whole approach – which is essentially to trust the client, given the appropriate conditions within the relationship. I think it's very easy to kid yourself that you're introducing something for the benefit of the client, whereas basically what you've done is to lose confidence and trust that your client is actually capable of finding his or her own way forward. So I'm against an unthought-out eclecticism.

But having said that, I do believe that human beings, in terms of a growing sense of their own value, need or can use all sorts of different forms of nourishment. That's a word which means quite a lot to me. It's a word in fact that originally I picked up from George Lyward, who I mentioned right at the beginning. He was very keen on the notion of nourishing people. Which means, therefore, that for some people with whom I'm working, I discover that their view of themselves and their view of reality indicates that a particular kind of nourishment will be for them very sustaining. And that may result in my drawing on some of my other interests and some of my other understandings, in response to this particular client.

I find it quite useful, obviously from my own, I suppose, Christian understandings, to think of people essentially as spiritual beings. And if I conceptualise a person as a spiritual being, or essentially as a soul, then it may well be that there are forms of nourishment which are really rather critical to that person's wellbeing. As a person gradually begins to develop a sense of self-worth as opposed to self-denigration, then with that evolution comes very often a new searching, or a new yearning almost. It's almost as if the person begins to sense 'there is more to me than I ever thought there was. Up to this point I had really considered myself to be a pretty useless character anyway. Now I'm beginning to discover that perhaps I'm not so useless, perhaps in fact I've got quite a bit of value. Then I can dare to begin to think further. Who am I really? What am I doing here?' All sorts of questions of meaning begin to arise. The point where a person begins to feel some self-acceptance, they can dare to ask these other questions. And I think very often do. One of the things that I certainly experience as a therapist, and Rogers himself talks quite a bit about this towards the end of his life, is that sometimes within the therapeutic relationship there is a sense of being in touch with an overarching reality, which seems to be greater than the sum of the two people present. When those moments occur, they're nearly always recognised by both counsellor and client, in my experience. We can't just ignore them, we have to consider them, and that's pretty important too.

Who talks when, and to what degree?

I think that changes as therapy proceeds. Again it's very difficult to generalise, but I'll attempt to generalise. I think that somebody who is badly damaged, who's not really had very much chance to discover who they are at all, then initially in therapy the therapist is going to be doing a very difficult and sometimes very sophisticated task of empathic understanding and acceptance. So that essentially the client is doing most of the talking, although sometimes I think – again with true empathy, true empathy can sometimes be quite complex, and therefore the therapist will actually be making at times quite lengthy utterances, because what they're trying to convey to the client is that they are understanding the complexity of the experience which the client's undergoing. So I'm not saying the therapist will be confined to ten words each time, but basically most of the verbal input will be coming from the client.

But as time goes on and there is a real sense that there isn't a monstrous power imbalance in this relationship, as the client begins to feel an increasing sense of identity, an increasing sense of worth, then it may well be that the counsellor or therapist is contributing more. Because there isn't the risk that by offering things coming from within the self of the therapist, the client will feel somehow overpowered, done out of his or her own identity. So I think in a long-term therapy we can talk of a movement from a basic safety into what I would describe as a form of intimacy, where the client is actually more and more willing to give expression to his or her inner reality, to a third phase which I think I would deem to be mutuality. Where it is possible for these two human beings to be in an equal kind of relationship and where, therefore, the contribution of the therapist becomes increasingly significant.

Are you always aware of what your relationship with your client may be doing to their partner?

This is an enormously important question isn't it? And becoming increasingly important too, with the notion of third parties sometimes actually – in the States anyway – taking out legal action against therapists. My answer is yes, I want to be very alert to what is going on within the total life of this person. On the other hand I am not going to start asking lots and lots of questions about that, but I am certainly going to be alert to that. My experience is that most clients after a while, if there are things which are going on with other significant people in their lives, that automatically becomes part of the therapy anyway.

If a person is actually coming to me from an obviously fairly complex family situation, perhaps a wife is coming and it's quite clear that there's a husband and several children in the background and all the rest of it, I may well quite early on in the therapy address the issue of change – that he or she clearly is wanting change. If that change occurs then that's going to create all sorts of things for the people who are near. And – have they thought about that?

Interestingly enough, I do this as a matter of course when people are coming for training. Somebody wants to train to be a person-centred therapist, and we go into this in great detail. It has only struck me in the comparatively recent years, that these issues which are so important for trainees are actually incredibly important for some clients. That they need actually to look at that and to take that on board.

Your other question is – do I have other people in? The answer to that is – yes. If the client feels that that would be helpful. I've had an example of that only in this last couple of weeks, working with a student here. Where at his request, we have had two sessions with his father present. Very important, very moving sessions. But that was the client's request. If I feel myself an overwhelming sense that it could be helpful and useful for this client to have another person present – and this might well happen where a marriage relationship is involved – if I feel that overwhelmingly inside myself, it won't lie down as it were, then I will voice that and look at it with the client. That doesn't happen all that often. But if it does, that's what goes on. But then of course, it will be the client's decision.

Do the clients ultimately always have to 'help themselves'?

That's again, I find a very tricky question, because it seems to me that human beings by definition are relational creatures. So in a sense, yes, I suppose we all have to help ourselves, but the notion that a person does that, as it were from a kind of vacuum, seems to me to be absurd. That very often, helping ourselves means actually making the very most of the relationships which are available to us. So that if I understand myself as a relational being, then helping myself will always be within the context really of the relationships which are available to me.

Have you any thoughts on 'false memory syndrome'?

It's something that we're actually talking quite a lot about. And I think it would be fair to say that we exercise a great deal of caution. Now the reason for that, well there are many reasons for it, but I think in our particular tradition where a great deal of focus is upon subjective experience and subjective reality, then we know that one person's reality will not necessarily be another person's reality. Therefore we are actually responding to this person's reality rather than an objective reality. So it is very important that we move with caution for all sorts of reasons, but that would be the pivotal one.

'False memory syndrome' ...

Yes, I personally have thought quite a lot about it. Are you asking me do I believe that it exists?

Well I think my view is that it is certainly conceivable that a person has a very clear conviction that such and such a thing happened, and it may not have happened. On the other hand it seems to me that very often when that occurs, that's not the end of the story. Because why is it that the person has arrived at this particular memory? That is often to do with what we might call the emotional climate which was experienced.

So very often what we're actually hearing about is a very real emotional situation which has been converted into particular activities or incidents which may or may not be true. But that there is something in the recall of the emotional climate, I would say certainly in my own experience, almost every time there is truth in that. In other words, if I may just illustrate that, a person may have apparently a clear memory of having been violently physically abused, by somebody. Now that may or may not be the case – what certainly will be the case is that with that person they experienced a great deal of emotional violence.

Can we talk about 'burn-out'?

Yes. Well it's a very pertinent question of course for me, because I've been doing this work now for 27 years. Quite a stint. I thought to myself quite recently, that I could probably half fill Carrow Road [Norwich City Football stadium] now with clients. It's running into many thousands, and so it's a very pertinent question.

In a way, I believe in my particular tradition, there is more likelihood of sustenance within some of the therapeutic work than there is in some other traditions. Insofar as what we were talking about just now as mutuality does arise with some clients, and there is in that very much a sense of nourishment for the therapist. But clearly that can often be in very short supply. Therefore what for me is enormously important are my colleagues – and I would never dream of working in a single person practice, all my experience really has been working within a team, and that for me has been absolutely critical, so that's really terribly important.

But then for me personally we come back to this business of nourishment. What kind of nourishment do I as a person need? I think I have to be really very astute about ensuring that I don't put myself on starvation rations. I think the kind of nourishment that I need will be rather different perhaps from the nourishment that another colleague needs. In my own case, for example, it is absolutely fundamental that I continue to be nourished by creative literature.

It is an essential for me that I continue to read poetry, that I continue to read novels, that I still go to the theatre. That feeds me. Curiously enough so too does the speaking of foreign languages. That in a curious way nourishes me because it takes me out of myself, or shows me a different part of myself. And of course fundamental for me is my own religious discipline. I could not conceivably have done the work that I have done over 27 years if I wasn't nourished by, particularly the Eucharist in the Christian tradition, and by some of the other very important ingredients which come to me from Christian practice. So that is fundamental for me.

I think most therapists that I have had close dealings with do begin to sense when they're not performing well, and it's usually a concomitant of exhaustion. That most therapists that I know begin to recognise when they are not any longer able to give that attentiveness. When they cannot be properly present. In our tradition, because there is so little you can retreat behind, I think we become very aware of that, that we

are wandering, that we are not there, and that our empathic responses
seem continually to be totally wide of the mark. So yes, I think people
do know when they're beginning to perform inadequately.

How is it possible to 'empathise' with so many different and varied clients?

I certainly think that it's important for therapists, probably of any persuasion, but certainly in my persuasion to be open to new experiences,
and open to meeting new people. Certainly from time to time I effect a
little discipline on myself in the sense of trying to meet people whom I
wouldn't normally meet. That's where my languages again are very important. But in other ways too.

For example, for me it's been very important that I have never
driven a car. It's important to me for a lot of reasons. One, in this
sedentary profession I think I would have died by now if I was going
round in a car. The second thing is because it exposes me all the time
to public transport, and that for me is actually a very important thing.
That I'm meeting bus conductors and people on the bus, and I'm going
around in trains, and things like that. It keeps me alert and aware to all
sorts and types of humanity. So it's for me almost a professional issue
that I don't drive a car.

I think the other thing is that clearly what we're talking about here
is the capacity to develop, really, one's own imagination. And the imagination is obviously developed in all sorts of different ways. Again for
me, through literature, and so on, is a very important way of doing it.
I'm very intrigued incidentally how many person-centred therapists are
also very much involved in responding to literature. Many of them are
poets. My own chief colleague here has a Doctorate in English Literature. And I don't think that's coincidental really. It's something to do
with the exercise of the imagination, which clearly is closely allied to
the development of empathic ability.

Some people denigrate therapy, others want to see more of it ...

I think why quite a number of people denigrate therapy is that they
have been one of the persons who's actually been caught if you like, in
somebody else's change process. What we were talking about just now.
The husband who's been left or whatever it may be. I think there are a
lot of people who feel that they are the third party that's been damaged, and they are actually enraged. And when people are enraged they
can become really very, very abusive. I think there are, however, some
clients who've had a very bad deal. I think abusive therapists do exist.
I'd like to imagine that they are in a very small minority, but I think
they do exist, and when people have had that sort of experience again,
they are not only enraged, but also very hurt.

So I think that's one of the reasons why there can be a denigration of
therapy. I also think curiously enough, that it's very often when something

is obviously growing in strength, and therefore obviously in effectiveness, that it attracts criticism. It's almost as if the light inevitably attracts the dark, if I may invoke that rather curious image. But I think there is a bit of that going on.

When you ask me, 'Do I want more of this activity going on?' – I'm not so sure about that to be honest. I think if I'm really honest, what I would hope for is that gradually as a species we become more empathically disposed towards each other. That we take really seriously the fact that we are by definition relational beings. Therefore I would like, personally, and this is a hobby horse of mine, to see something happening at a very much earlier stage within our educational system. I would really like to see empathy on the curriculum, however ridiculous that sounds. I believe that essentially, counselling and therapy are personal education of the profoundest kind. But that if that is so then there must actually be a place for them in the educational arena in a much more general way. So that's what I would like.

Under what circumstances – if any – do you turn clients away?

On those occasions when I find that something is touched in me by a client which makes it almost impossible for me to extend to them the kind of relationship that I want to. Occasionally I will meet somebody who for whatever reason I find it impossible within myself to offer that level of unconditional acceptance which is necessary.

Can you elaborate?

It doesn't happen very often, but it's usually a person who is absolutely determined that somebody else should take over responsibility for their lives. It's a curious inversion of the authoritarian personality. 'You must direct me in what I'm going to do. Tell me what I must do.' And although in some cases I can actually understand that, I can empathise with that and gradually we can begin to relate, I have met a few people where that seems to be such an intractable response to life, that I find it impossible to maintain the necessary acceptance of it. I can't work with them.

I actually also have grave difficulties these days with the issue of abortion. That's a comparatively new one for me, and it's come almost entirely through what I now myself believe to be incontrovertible knowledge of what goes on for some people within the womb. At the point at which the human foetus becomes a sentient person. And I've had some very profound experiences in that area, and therefore it makes it increasingly difficult for me to be able to offer myself in the way that I would want to with someone who's seeking an abortion. But I make that very clear.

Your thoughts on paying for therapy?

Well a few comments on that. Certainly in my private practice, I do believe it to be the case for some of those clients, that the fact that they're paying for it enables them to feel very much more empowered in the relationship. In my particular tradition that's a good thing, because it means that almost from the outset we have a sense of a co-operative undertaking, and I like that. In other words it gives them not only a sense of their own power, but it also increases their motivational energy to get on with the work.

Having said that, I've also had fee-paying clients where those things really do not happen. I've had fee-paying clients who seem to be caught in as much of a dilemma about their motivational energy for being there as some of the people that I see within the University. So I don't buy the notion in fact that if you're paying then you will somehow put your heart and soul into it in a much better way than if you're not paying. I've certainly had many, many clients over the years who clearly are not paying, who have put themselves into this particular work, body, soul, and spirit from the moment they start to the moment they finish.

I personally prefer on the whole, working for an institution. Even in my private practice I work in fact under a charitable foundation where the client does determine the level of fee. We have a standard charge, but if the client can't afford that then we negotiate with the client what they can afford.

Could you think of a client, recently, and describe their changes?

Yes. I'm thinking again of an anonymous person, clearly, who had embarked upon a university course and arrived here looking dreadful. When I say looking dreadful, I mean dishevelled clothes, unshaven, all the appearances of self-neglect. It was clear that here was a person who felt that he had in a curious way arrived in the University almost under false pretences. That he got in through the back door. He wasn't properly qualified with his A levels, and now he was being rumbled. That he didn't really have the capacity, that what he had hoped would have been a kind of salvation for him was now really the reverse – it was making him feel even worse than before he came.

As I worked with that person gradually he became very much more able to face the past sense of rejection, and adverse judgement. He began to experience not only from me, but also from one or two of the faculty in the University, that he was actually regarded with some honour – even though he wasn't performing particularly well at that stage – gradually a shift began to take place within him. And I suppose the first signs of that were actually in his physical appearance. That he did actually begin to shave rather more regularly. I always remember the day when he actually arrived looking really as if he'd turned up for an interview. I didn't make any comment on it, and from that day onwards, he was dressed in a way which was markedly different from when he began.

It's a long story – that particular person remained in therapy for the whole of his first two years, and a little bit into his third year – but suffice it to say that the University community had a very large share in that person's therapy, and that's one of the joys again of working within an institution. Because you can actually help a person in the other relating that they're doing, and begin to help them see where in fact they are being really accepted and respected.

Do you hug, touch clients?

Oh yes. I think touch deprivation is one of the terrible things that many people have experienced. If they're not touched, they often have a sense of physical repulsiveness, and therefore it's not only in my particular tradition perfectly in order to touch people, but sometimes in fact it's seen as really extraordinarily significant that a person can feel that they are indeed touchable. Clearly I will always check this out with my client. I wouldn't just do it. Or if I find myself spontaneously doing it, I will always check out immediately afterwards whether that was all right or not. But yes, I feel that touch is very often a way in which we convey to a person that we value them and that we understand them. Thinking about empathy, for example. Seems to me a touch is very often very much more empathic than two garbled sentences.

CHAPTER 4

Transactional Analysis

Charlotte Sills

Charlotte Sills is a London-based psychotherapist in private practice. Her particular interest has been in bereavement and loss. She is the author of a number of publications, including many concerned with Transactional Analysis.

Can you talk about your background – as it relates to your becoming a therapist?

I think – in my past – I've always been interested and fascinated in human beings and why they are the way they are.

Something significant in my life was my school – the last two years of my schooling – after having been in a co-educational grammar school, my parents sent me to a convent in Belgium, which I, at the time, completely dreaded and thought a terrible idea. It turned out to be a wonderful idea. Not a bit like the convents you hear awful stories about. There was a nun we used to call *chere-mere* – the reverend mother. If people were feeling low they would go to her and say, 'Chere-mere I'm depressed', and she would sit down with them for an hour and listen to their problems and encourage them to express their feelings. The idea of paying attention to people's psyches and offering emotional help was very much in the fore-ground and I was really affected by that. I think that was probably my first major introduction to the idea of living in a community where people tried to treat each other in ways that respected each other, took account of feelings and paid attention to communication. So that was a significant influence in my school life.

Have you always been a therapist?

No, I did a variety of things in my youth, and then I got married and I had my children – I was teaching French actually when I started to have my children – and then after I'd had them I was thinking to go back to work, and I certainly didn't want to go back to teaching French. I didn't think that was useful to most of the young people where I was teaching.

I wanted to do something that would be part-time – my children were little – and I saw an advertisement for a bereavement project that was being set up. And I thought 'That's something I could do. Talking to people about being bereaved is something I can do.' So I contacted them, and got involved as a bereavement counsellor, and then trained as a counsellor. I ran the bereavement project at Hounslow Social Services for many years. During that time I trained in TA psychotherapy.

Can we talk about the main ideas of TA?

Well the originator of TA was a man called Eric Berne, who was Canadian and moved to the US. He trained as a doctor like his father, then trained as a psychoanalyst. Then for a variety of reasons broke from the psychoanalytic tradition and developed his own ideas, which were based on his own observation, his training and experience in client work, his experience in developing his intuition and, no doubt, the spirit of the age. He developed his theories and called them 'Transactional Analysis'.

He was very concerned with the fact that psychological theories should be made available to everybody. They shouldn't be a bag of expertise that the therapist and the psychiatrist has and keeps in their pocket in a smart way – superior, unbalanced power. He was all for making the theory available to people so that they could use it for themselves – very keen on self-responsibility. He believed that people could take responsibility for themselves, that they could think for themselves up to their full potential, and that they could change. They could find out what they were doing and change it if they wanted too.

So he wrote all his theories in very simple, very accessible language – people have probably heard of ideas like ego states: the Parent, Adult and Child ego states. Now the idea of Parent, Adult, Child is actually very complex and subtle, and if you go into it in depth you realise that actually TA is a sophisticated object relations theory. It incorporates some of the Freudian ideas of drive theory and so on, but also a lot of the object relations ideas of the importance of the relationship in forming the person.

So if you go into it in depth it's actually very complex. However, Berne and the people who came after him, found ways of putting it in a very accessible way so that anybody could understand it. And one of the disadvantages is that people come across these quite simple terms: Parent, Adult, Child, games theory, script and so on and they sometimes think it's simplistic. I feel quite passionately that it isn't simplistic, in fact TA people have done themselves no favour by selling it as a sort of simple pop psychology, because actually it's a very serious useful tool. So that's that little homily from the pulpit. [Laughs]

So he used very simple ideas, concepts, words. Encouraged patients to read the books. He was very keen on changing people fast. He was also quite cerebral, quite analytic, and most of the things he wrote about originally were cognitive. It was the people who came after him that developed the more affective side. He was very concerned with the cognitive and behavioural: you look at what you're thinking, look at what you're doing, and those are the things you change. And people like Bob and Mary Goulding, who studied also with Fritz Perls as well as Eric Berne, founded the Redecision School of Transactional Analysis, which they sometimes used to call Gestalt TA, because it used a lot of the Gestalt principles of 'here and now' and phenomenology, and many of the Gestalt techniques of two-chair work, heightening techniques and so on.

They brought a whole other dimension to TA which was working more with the Child ego state. Eric Berne had always talked about the child from our past – known as the inner child. What we call the Child ego state is in fact a number of ego states, but we are talking about experiences from the past. They're archaic states of being: feelings, attitudes and behaviour. A state of being which for some reason was not fully integrated into our here and now living. When something happens that reminds us in some way of that past, we trigger into the Child ego state. What the Gouldings developed were all sorts of ways of working with that Child ego state in the here and now in order to resolve or 'deconfuse'.

There were other developments in something called the Cathexis School of TA, whose proponents were developing a way of working with the really more severely disturbed clients. Then in more recent years a lot of the theorists in Europe and America were interested in developing some of the roots of TA, some of the psychoanalytic and object relations roots, and also integrating newer ideas from self-psychology.

What do you think is unique about TA?

Some of the things that I've talked about are – I don't know if they are unique but they are special – simplicity, accessibility, self-responsibility, some of the philosophies. 'I'm okay, you're okay', which is the most awful glib way of putting one of the most important things in the humanistic tradition, is this idea of two separate human beings accepting and respecting each other, even if they differ from each other, even if they're really furious with each other. It's an existential position that we might aspire to, we don't always achieve all the time. It's similar perhaps to Carl Rogers' unconditional positive regard, or Buber's I-thou dialogue. These ideas are what puts TA into the humanistic tradition rather than the analytic tradition. It has many of its ideas and concepts from the analytic tradition, but it's humanistic in philosophy and beliefs.

Finally, the other thing that I think is extraordinarily special about TA is that it is an integrative approach. It has theory, and methods of application and practice to deal with intrapsychic phenomena, understanding who we are and what we are inside, where that comes from, why we are like that: all that intrapsychic understanding of the structure of personality. It has then a way of understanding how that inside becomes outside, how and why we behave on the outside because of the inside. There's all sorts of theories and ways of working to understand that. It has a way of understanding and analysing relationships between us and other people; when they go well, and why they don't, and how that relates to our past, how we are affected by the environment and so on. And it has a whole theory of communication. So it really has an enormous amount of different aspects, intrapsychic and interpersonal approaches. It does, I believe, integrate cognitive, affective, behavioural, and to some extent physiological and spiritual as well. Though those last two areas are not so well represented.

What happens when someone comes to see you?

Do you want to know what will happen if someone comes to a TA therapist, or to me personally, because they're probably slightly different. Or maybe somewhat different.

Speak for yourself ...

Yes. Well. I'll give you a little bit of both because I do have a slight bias probably. Someone comes to see me and the first and most important task, I think, is for me to make contact with that person and develop some sort of rapport or relationship in that first session. Also one of two things will probably happen. Either the person will come because they're in a state of distress, which is often why people come to therapists – they've come to their wits end and they phone up. So then I think my job is to set a container, to use a bit of a jargon word. It's a sort of an attempt as far as possible to provide a safe boundary and space. I make very clear that we're going to meet for such and such a time, I've already explained all that on the phone anyway, that'll be the boundary. So they know the boundary of time, of space, any fee they might have to pay and so on. I try to provide a safe enough space for them to just sit down and tell me why they've come. Very often that will take quite a long time, and I will really just listen to them, and not start asking too many questions.

The other thing that might happen is that they're not distressed at all, and have come to therapy because they're interested. There was one client of mine who said once: 'I want more of myself.' She'd been in a TA group for a year and she'd discovered some things about herself she didn't know; she said, 'I have started to know myself. Now I want more of myself.' I thought it was a wonderful thing. So in that case we would just get on with the exploration. The other thing I'd obviously do at the first session, and perhaps towards the end of it, would be to take some details – enough history, so that we have enough information to go forward.

I would also – being a TA therapist – be looking to make a contract, and this is where I say I differ from some TA therapists. Some TA therapists feel very strongly, as Eric Berne did, that there should be an extremely clear contract from the start, or as near to the start as one can do without being rude! It would be extremely abusive to say: 'Stop crying, sit up, now what do you want from therapy?' Would be not very nice. But as soon as this was feasible, they would be going for making a contract. And some people would make quite a tight contract – What do you want from therapy? What do you want different in your life? What would have to change for you to get that thing? How would you have to change in order to get that thing? They would fine it down and refine it down, so that, with the client, they would translate somebody's original desire to be, for example, less depressed and have more friends, to exactly what they were going to do to get those friends, and then with some more exploration what they would have to change inside them and in their behaviour in order to be the sort of person that got friends, that sort of thing.

Now I don't make contracts as tight as that, partly I think because of natural personal style. Some people really like working with those tightly pre-thought-out behavioural contracts and some don't. And partly because I always think of the book by C. S. Lewis called *Till We Have Faces*, the whole phrase is 'How can we come face to face with the gods, until we have faces?', and I think the same thing applies to contracting. How can I tell you what I want until I have met myself, until I know where I am now? Most people don't know where they are now and why they are now. I don't believe in asking them to say where they want to go before they've found out who they are now.

So I would tend to leave the contracting until a bit later. However, I would make some sort of a contract. I would make the contract – 'Okay, well let us agree to meet. This is what you're saying your difficulty is, that this is roughly what you're wanting – you're depressed and you don't want to be depressed – that sort of thing. We'll agree to meet weekly and let's meet for so many sessions and then we'll see how and where we are going.'

So we'll make some sort of a mutual commitment. Contracting is a very important part of TA. Eric Berne introduced it because of the philosophy of equality, as far as possible, of power and expertise. The belief is that the client knows what he or she wants and has the right to ask for it, and it's not up to the therapist to be smart-assed and say, 'Oh no I think you really ought to be working through x, y, z.' The client says what he or she wants, the therapist thinks, 'Am I competent to help this person? Do I think I can offer what they need? Yes, No.' If I do, I offer to work with a person. Berne says somewhere, something like: 'I run a therapy shop, this is what's for sale in my therapy shop, do you want it?'

I didn't realise how person-centred TA was.

I like you using the word person-centred, because I think that the person-centred relationship should be at the heart of TA therapy, that all TA therapists and counsellors should start with that person-centred relationship, and that all the other tools, techniques, concepts are used in service of the process. The relationship should be a respectful relationship, embodied in the TA concepts of 'I'm okay, you're okay' that we talked about, and of empathy and respect for all the ego states.

Berne talked about autonomy as being the goal of TA therapy. Autonomy is the attainment or reattainment of three capacities: awareness, spontaneity, intimacy. It's awareness of myself, my senses, everything that's going on around me, fully – not distracted by fixated ego states or whatever; spontaneity – the capacity to respond to the world from any part of me and not be repressed in any way (I'm mixing psychoanalytic words with TA words here), or limited by fixed ways of reading; intimacy – which is the capacity to meet another person, share my thoughts and feelings without games and with honesty and openness.

It seems to me that this is the definition of congruence that Rogers describes, and that we have the same tenets that Rogers talks about – congruence, empathy, and unconditional positive regard at the heart of TA, in the same way as the person-centred people do.

So how long might therapy last?

How long it might last is a variable feast, and I think also should be negotiated with clients. I think because we counsellors and therapists are very, very interested in analysis and understanding and all that, we can be led to think that long-term therapy and counselling is good for everybody. Whereas I think an awful lot of people don't want that, they would like reasonably brief intervention – they want to get on with living their lives and get on with doing it more effectively, they don't want to spend years analysing themselves. Having said that, some people really do want to take the time. Sometimes people need to, depending on what their particular problems are. For some people it's important that they take the time to make a relationship with someone and share themselves with someone, for perhaps the first time in their life. That maybe can't be done in just a few sessions. So that they need longer term. I think it's very important to negotiate that with the client and not to launch into long-term therapy when actually perhaps eight or ten sessions would be excellent. And TA's a marvellous tool, I think, for short-term therapy. There are lots of very good concepts which can be used immediately.

So, but, what would I do? Yes I would do a lot of listening. I would do a lot of listening and, I hope, understanding and, I hope, conveying that I was understanding and therefore inviting the person to listen to and understand themselves. Depending on who the person is, I might teach them some TA concepts, and when I say depending on who the person is, there are some people who really use the theory wonderfully. So I might say, I might lend them a book, for instance, or I might – I've got a white board on the wall in my room – get up and draw something. There's lots of diagrams, a very visual theory TA. Draw something, teach them a bit of TA, because some people really like that, it makes them feel empowered, it gives them hope, they feel a bit confident. They think: 'Oh, right, I understand. That's what I'm doing.' If they've got a handle they can use, that can really help people to feel more in charge of their lives.

I've got two clients at the moment, to whom I teach some theory, and they both take it in immediately. And they come back the following week: 'I really thought, and I did it differently with my husband. And he said this, and I realised that, and I did it differently.' They find it really useful.

Could you give an example of such 'teaching'?

Right, well, for instance what I was just thinking of then was that I recently taught ego states to a client. Now in order to tell this story, presumably I have to teach ego states now, do I?

I've got the time if you have.

Ego states, is the idea that we have different states of being as I was referring to earlier. A whole load of different states of being. The one that we are in, and that we hope to be in, which would be a healthy state, is in the here and now. When I am in the here and now, responding to you in the here and now, as if it was this date in 1995. I would call myself in an integrated Adult ego state, which would mean that my feelings, and thoughts, and behaviour were appropriate to now. They're appropriate to a woman of my age and stage in this room with you now, and I'm not unhelpfully limited by my past, my script, and so on. So that would be the ideal thing. I wouldn't be shutting out my past, but I would be integrating my past, and all the influences on me.

However, we have other categories of ego states, which are called Parent and Child. Parent ego states are the states of being that we introjected from parents and parent-figures when we were young. So the idea is that from the moment we're born we are experiencing the world, the world is doing things to us, treating us in certain ways, treating each other in certain ways. And babies have a fairly limited range of people that they see, so for the first years – the early few years of life – we are swallowing whole the experiences, and the way that people are treating us. When we are very small babies we probably are not seeing a difference between ourselves and the other person, so that the swallowing in of the impression of my mother becomes part of me anyway. The theory is, and I think it's true having watched babies, that they're not yet clear about their identity. It is interesting to read Daniel Stern and others these days writing about babies' developing sense of self.

In the first few weeks and months, a baby will introject the mother as part of himself. And then even later on, we continue to introject our mother. Even though I know she's separate from me, I introject her because that's what I learn from, that's my experience of life, that's how people are. Then later on in life, coming back to the present, I might – triggered by something that happens outside or inside me – get into a Parent ego state whereby in a sense I become my mother, or my version of my mother at least. I'm influenced by what I've learned from outside. It isn't an integrated Adult ego state, it's not something chosen – 'Yes I've learned this from my mother but it's also me, what I want to be, this is me in the here and now.' I just flip and become a Parent ego state, in the way my mother, or my father, or my teacher, or my minister, or my big brother or sister, whoever was significant when I was little.

Some of TA therapy is about sorting out how we are still influenced by our Parent ego states, and whether we still want to be. Some of it would be useful, but some of it won't.

So there'll be Parent ego states, and then Child ego states, which are the states of being, as I was saying earlier, that we retain from childhood. Unresolved states. Feelings, attitudes, and behaviours from childhood that we can 'drop into', as it were. Something happens in the present that, perhaps out of my awareness, reminds me. For instance, we're sitting here talking and suddenly the scene is reminiscent of the day I was in an interview with my headmaster who was grilling me about did I cheat in my science exam. And I might drop suddenly into that state of being, that eleven-year-old child, or that five-year-old child, or two-year-old child, whatever the incident is, and feel, and think, and behave, and I'll even have the look of a child from the outside. I'll get all embarrassed and nervous and shy, won't want to answer your questions, and so on.

So anyway I taught this to my client – the idea of the Parent, Child, and Adult, and how obviously our partners have Parent, Adult and Child as well, and that our communications can go awry. She had been talking to me about a bind that she got into with her husband, where she wanted him to give her praise, and support. There's a way that we can draw two sets of ego states and draw the communication between the two people with arrows indicating the ego states involved. You draw the overt communication with a proper arrow. So there was an Adult to Adult arrow, which was: 'How did you think I did in my talk?' But there was a dotted line arrow. You draw the arrows with dotted lines when they're the unspoken messages. And she also sent him an unspoken message which was: 'You don't think I'm any good, do you?' So when the husband responded, Adult back to Adult, 'Oh, fine. I thought you did fine', she actually went into a sulk and sulked for the next six hours, and her husband was a bit surprised about that. Because of course her dotted line was saying 'you don't think I'm any good' from her Child ego state to his Parent, and she experienced his 'fine', as meaning 'not very good' – from Parent back to Child.

Eventually, she's been in a sulk in her Child ego state – 'nobody appreciates me. I try and work hard. It's just like when my mum and dad never praised me, and they always praised my brother instead, etc. etc.' – and he has been all this time feeling aggrieved because he thought he'd been quite supportive and there she is in a sulk. So he snaps at her, 'Oh, for God's sake, pull yourself together' from his Parent to her Child, so that in the end she gets the put-down that she was expecting. So I talked to my client about this, how we get into Parent or Child ego states, and we talked about how it had come about. She didn't say to him, 'I'm feeling rather unsure about this, so could you reassure me?' She just casually said,

'What did you think of my talk?', and he said 'Fine'. And we talked about how he probably felt pressurised, because even though she was feeling needy in her Child he might have even experienced her from a Parent ego state. Making some demand on him or something. For whatever reason he didn't end up delivering the goods, but ended up getting cross with her. Anyway, the following week she came back and said: 'I did it differently with my husband. I wanted reassurance from Ben about something and I said "Will you tell me some things I did well today. I need to hear it from you."' And he did and they had a nice time.

You mentioned 'scripts' ...

A script is a life plan made in childhood. It's certainly not unique to TA by any means, it's an idea that's embraced by many psychological approaches I think, and has been proved by all sorts of bits of research. Did you see the programme on television *Seven Up*, where they interviewed the children at age 7, 14, and 21? At seven they were saying, 'I'm going to be a farmer', and sure enough they were. Or, 'I'm going to be a spaceman' – he ended up working in space research.

The idea is that in the first few years of life, while children are quite vulnerable and impressionable, they 'decide' in a sense – it may not be a conscious, cognitive decision – but they decide partly consciously, partly affectively, partly viscerally as it were: their whole body decides what's going to happen to them. What their life's going to be like. This is partly because they have very limited information. We're brought up by our family, and we don't have the information to compare what happens in our family with another family. Partly it's because children are very small and their parents are very big, and little kids are under tremendous pressure to obey orders from parents. They like to please their parents and they want to be loved, and they don't want to be abandoned. So for a variety of reasons children are very able to be influenced, very susceptible to being what we call scripted.

Which means that they have experiences, from the moment they're born they experience the world, they experience on the inside – inside their bodies and their minds – and they experience what the world is like around them, what other people are like, how they are treated, what's important in their family. As far as they're concerned, their family is the world. So what's important, what they're supposed to say, what they're supposed not to say, what they're going to get – what we call – 'stroked' for, what they're going to have attention paid to them for, what their parents are going to be pleased with, what their parents are going to be not pleased with, and so on. They think this is the world and they say: 'Right, I'd better not ...' be or feel or act a particular way, and they learn to shut down on a part of themselves. The classic example is the little boy who gets told off for crying – 'Don't be so soft.' He says to himself, 'I'd better not be a cry-baby', and learns not to cry. That would be part of his script. Another example of an early decision: 'I'd better please Mummy, because look how happy that makes her, and how much she loves me, and look how I can make her eyes light up if I'm sweet to her, and put my arms around her and how that light dies if I'm angry. I'd better always be very nice to women.' And so on.

So the script is a life plan that in those first few years, up to about seven, mainly, the child decides upon. 'That's what life's like, that's what I'm like. Yes, I see, other people are like that, but I'm clearly like this. If this is how people treat me, this is how people will always treat me, I expect. This is how I will treat them', and so on. Not in those clear words, of course – although occasionally people do recall having made such a clear categorical decision. Often the 'decision' is unconscious, and developed over time; yet there is a way that it can be called a decision none the less. Then the decision becomes lost and the resulting behaviour becomes ingrained habit and feels like the 'only way to be'.

So you point out to people that they're now doing things not out of choice.

Absolutely. I say 'Pull yourself together, stop doing that ...' [Laughs] It would be lovely if it was as simple as just pointing things out. But people hold on to their scripts because they believe it is the only way of being. And it is the way they have learned to manage the challenges of living and facing the unanswerable questions. It usually takes time for the old patterns to be gradually dissolved. There is a story that Adler was once asked: 'What do you do if you think you've spotted something that a person is doing and you know that it is script and that they're not doing it out of choice, but they haven't seen it yet? What do you do while you're waiting for them to see it?' And Adler said: 'Chew the ends of pencils.'

I think particularly if we're interested in why people tick, we can often quite quickly think: 'Aha, I see what's happening here, this person's got this script, and that script. They need to be aware of that.' It's very important, very slowly and gently to explore people. For a start we might have got it wrong. It's important that we follow their truth rather than ours. Secondly, what is most powerful for the person is to develop their own awareness at their own pace.

But yes, broadly speaking you're right. One of the major things is to heighten awareness and have people become aware of who they are today and how much of that is influenced by the past, or habit, or a desire for attention or whatever it is. So that people realise where these things come from. And that alone, that awareness, can bring about enormous change. It really can. Just by people saying: 'Good heavens, I've always done it that way, I don't need to.'

Presumably you think about how the changes in the client might be affecting their partners ...

I do think that we should take it very seriously if we're ethical. I think somebody once did a piece of research that said if one part of the couple is in therapy for very long – a year or two – then one of three things will happen. Either the partner will go into therapy, or the person in therapy will leave precipitately, probably when things start really threatening the marital system, or they'll split up. I don't think it's ethical or right to lightly do things that are going to split up relationships. I suppose I believe also that couples have an enormous amount to learn from one another. Now give me another six hours, I'd wax on to another hobby-horse of mine. I believe, talking of scripts, that the person we choose to marry, or live with, is going to be somebody who's going to have a blend of two things. One is they'll have enough of the things like our mothers and fathers and brothers that there is a risk that they'll reinforce our scripts by treating us in all the negative ways that we were treated as a child. Then we could prove to ourselves: 'Yes, I'm the sort of person who will always have this happen to them.' However, the second thing is that they will also have enough qualities which are different from our family's to give us the opportunity for change and growth.

That's why I think people are so brilliant at intuitively choosing their partners. The other extraordinary thing, or perhaps not extraordinary thing, is it'll be the same for the partners. So that's why people fall in love with each other and they think: 'You're my other half.' You *have* met your other half. You met them; they could fulfil your script and they'd be your other half. Yet there is such an opportunity for learning. We marry the people that we have to learn from – the qualities they've got, or the facets they've got which we need to integrate. If we can hang in there and love and respect each other enough, and share our difficulties, and share our scripts, we can learn to change. There's a man called Harville Hendrix who talks about accommodating our partners' hang-ups in a way he calls 'flexing'.

For instance, one partner might say: 'I really hate it when you do x, you shouldn't do it.' And the other partner could say: 'Don't be so silly, you're being paranoid or passive/aggressive', or whatever, nasty words they use. Or the first partner could say: 'I know it's a hang-up of mine. You are not wrong to be doing what you are doing. But I really hate it.' And the second partner, if he or she was 'flexing', may say: 'Okay, as an act of love, I'll stop doing x, not because it's wrong, because it isn't, but out of love and generosity.'

Harville Hendrix's idea is that this act of love, of accommodating the other person's hang-ups, will stretch you in a way that coincidentally will push the boundaries of your script and help you to grow in important ways for you. Equally if your partner will flex to accommodate your hang-ups it will stretch him or her. Meanwhile you're struggling at the communication and you're learning from each other. Of course, sometimes marriages really do need to finish, they're very destructive. But very often marriages have such a lot of good, exciting, growth opportunities.

So going back to your question. I am very aware if my clients are in relationships and have families. I try to be respectful to the not present spouse, and – while not losing sight of the fact that it's the individual who's my client – try and bear in mind what might be happening in that system. How is the client going to be changed, and could he or she do it tactfully or usefully, sharing with the spouse and getting their support and so on?

Can we talk about those numerous issues surrounding transference ...

The transference and countertransference exists as far as I'm concerned in pretty much every relationship. In a way it's a healthy form of transference that when we met in the hall today, and you put out your hand and walked towards me, I assumed you were going to shake my hand in a friendly way, because that's what people in my past have been going to do when they put out their hand and walked towards me. If I hadn't transferred my past learning into the present, I'd have thought, 'I wonder what that fellow's doing with his hand stuck out?'

Fairly simplistic, but I think it's true. Unconscious transference is everywhere. You remind me of my father, for example, and I respond to you as if you were him, and I actually sometimes induce you to treat me like my father did, which is the standard complementary transference or countertransference. I think that happens in all relationships to some extent, or some of the time. And it will happen particularly in a therapeutic relationship, because you're actually inviting your client to go deep into his or her feelings, and thoughts and psyche, and to surface all these things. Also you're offering them a very intimate relationship in which their thoughts and feelings are prized, and in which your entire attention is upon them. That's a really very special relationship that they might never have had in their lives. Maybe they might have had it as children, but very few of us have that sort of prizing. So it would be very strange if it didn't stir up all sorts of feelings.

Much of what a TA therapist might do would be gently to help the person understand what they were doing and why. 'You thought I was angry with you when I wasn't and then you got angry with me. In your life now, you quite often think people are angry with you. Maybe they're not either. How do you treat them when you think they're angry with you? Do you get aggressive yourself? You're surprised that people back away from you when you're aggressive, and I must admit when you were aggressive with me just then, I wanted to back away.'

So it is about learning from what's happening, helping the person to become more aware, and perhaps therefore changing their behaviour. Starting to think 'Good heavens, do I expect people to be aggressive when they're not?', is again an increase of awareness and insight.

Having said that, I think some transference/countertransference – some of the material that Kohut writes about transference – seems to me more a description of a need rather than a transference, because it's a need often for something that didn't happen. I think that happens in a therapeutic relationship, and we need to allow that, the importance of that relationship and the failures we're inevitably going to make, and the being with our client even when they're disappointed with us. I think that is working in the transference and countertransference in a way that's very productive.

TA has wonderful easy ways, nice business-like ways of doing things. We have a concept called games, which is effectively a useful way of analysing the manifestations of transference and countertransference in life. I treat you like this, so you treat me like that, and then I respond like that, and Bob's your uncle, I've repeated a pattern exactly, and I end up saying: 'How has that happened again?' It's the repetition of what's happened in childhood. So analysing the game would be analysing the transference and the contertransference behaviour and how it ends up eventually with what we call a cross-transaction, and everybody feeling bad or uncomfortable in familiar ways.

A man called Jack Dusay said there are four things to do with games, which is like saying four things to do with transference and countertransference. Either you can 'expose' it: talk about it, say this is what's going on; or you can ignore it; or you can 'play' it, which means you would allow it to develop, so that it is so clearly in the room that the person really understands what is happening; or you can change the game: 'play' something different which alters the system and means you take on a different role in relation to the other person, for example, competing for the 'victim' position with someone who is determinedly passive and helpless.

So why did I bring that up? I think something about wanting to keep the polarity, wanting to hold both ends. On one hand taking transference very seriously and believing that it can be a wonderful therapeutic vehicle. Sometimes I do not aim simply to help someone see that they are being affected by transference; sometimes I allow it to develop if I think that it is going to be useful. On the other hand saying: 'Let's not get too precious about it, it happens, it happens all the time, you can do this, or that, or the other.' People can be aware of what they're doing, they can take charge of their lives, let's not make too big a deal about it.

You asked me – was I afraid of clients getting dependent on me, or me getting dependent on them? Well, I shouldn't get dependent on my clients. If I am in regular supervision and I think all counsellors and therapists should be, this would be something that could be monitored and avoided. You can feel very loving towards people – but getting dependent would be a very different kettle of fish.

Clients do get dependent on me. And I suppose if I'm strictly honest, there are times when I might feel some reluctance, because this is a long commitment I'm making, will I be big enough or good enough to cope? This person is going to be quite dependent now. I might feel like 'Oh, crumbs, it's quite a big burden.' Generally though, if you're feeling very burdened by dependence, I think you're probably in a game. You're taking too much responsibility. I think clients are entitled to become dependent on their therapist, and it's up to the therapist to draw boundaries and make agreements, contracts if you like about how available they're going to be in terms of time, and whether the client can phone up, and that sort of thing. Because in terms of emotional dependence, that's all right, that's what we're there for. There's a man called Bob Resnick, he's actually a Gestaltist, who talks about the boundary between human beings as if it was a sort of a wall. And I find if I stay on my side of the wall, paying attention to that person but always knowing that they're on that side of the wall, I feel fine. What they're doing is their business and it's their responsibility. And I have made a commitment to be there for them, but on my side of the wall. I've found that difficulties like trying to make people better and them not getting better, are usually because I've forgotten to stay on my side of the wall. I'm leaning over, reaching over on their side and trying to change them, instead of respecting them enough to let them live their own lives. And also respecting myself to know that this is my side of the wall and that's all mine as well.

How different are male and female clients?

I do think there is a difference between men and women. I think Jungians are right. The Jungians talk about the feminine functions and the masculine functions; the feminine being feeling and intuition, the masculine being thinking and sensation. It's not universal, of course, not everybody can be categorised like that. And all women have thinking and sensation functions too, and all men have feeling and intuitive functions. But I do think that they're right, that there is a difference. Recently there's been some research where they injected some chemical into the bloodstream so that they could take a picture of the brain while they were asking people to do a certain number of tasks; work out a problem, make a list, make a rhyme up and so on. And the women used the right side of their brains, and the men used the left side of their brains. Did you hear about that research?

Yes.

Isn't it amazing? They actually took photographs.

So how does gender affect the work?

I think with any client, we will take their personality into account. Their personality and their particular strengths. You remember earlier I was talking about the fact that some people really like to have the theory and use it for themselves, and some don't, and if you try to teach them theory, will feel profoundly unheard and ignored. They just need you to listen to them for a while. So that's a difference in type, and we would of course have to take male and female – whatever our client is like – we would have to take into account. And there is always the dynamics of male and female clients and therapists. You don't ignore the fact that one of you is a woman and one of you is a man. Obviously that might have more relevance for some people than for others.

Are there people you feel you can't work with?

Yes. I work from a consulting room in a private house. While I have medical backup – doctors and psychiatrists that I can consult with or refer to – we don't have the facilities for offering the support that somebody with quite a lot of disturbance may need; what in TA we might call a not very strong Adult. Normally I see people weekly and I see them at my home. I also do a lot of supervision and training, and I run the TA Training Programme here at Metanoia, so I'm quite busy. So my clients have to have enough Adult to be able to make a clear contract with me, and to be able to contain themselves enough in between the sessions, so that they don't become too distressed to function. Having said that, of course I'm fine for people to ring me up if they feel they need extra support, but that is different from being permanently available. So those sorts of clients I couldn't take on in my practice.

There are also some sorts of clients whom I might easily refer to other people, because I didn't think the particular problem was a strong area of competence of mine. Or occasionally I might recommend someone to a different form of therapy; for instance, some form of bodywork or a transpersonal approach. It also depends on my caseload and the sort of demands it is making on me at any one time.

The client in distress ... what problems do they bring?

It's quite often a cluster of depression or anxiety, perhaps, and self-worth issues. Or it could be relationship issues, either marital or 'I've had a series of relationships, they've all gone wrong and I really don't want to keep doing this.' Or, 'I don't seem to get on with people, I'm not popular at work.' This sort of thing. Depression is surprisingly common in Britain, and then the problem might be described as 'I'm very unhappy, and I've been like this for ages and I want to feel happier in my life.' Or simply: 'I can't stop crying.'

What do you think are the necessary skills a therapist should learn?

I think there are various areas. One is to have the capacity and be able to demonstrate the capacity to make that relationship that I was talking about earlier; to be able to meet, listen, understand, empathise, respect the person's culture as well as who they are, and also share oneself when it's relevant. All those things to do with making a containing therapeutic relationship.

Then I would expect a TA therapist to know how to use the theory in a way that isn't mechanical. A colleague of mine talks about the 'TA trolley', because TA has a lot of really useful concepts and techniques, but it can be used like wheeling in the TA trolley and suddenly introducing a TA technique into the process. It's like at tea time; you're chatting to somebody and then you suddenly whack a piece of Battenburg cake off the trolley on to their plate. I think the important thing is to use those theories within the relationship relevantly. Integrate the tea, the cake and the conversation.

So there's the body of theory and how to use it, there's the knowing how to have a relationship. Then there are personal attributes, which we were talking about earlier. At least an attempt at or willingness to be what TA calls autonomous – to be willing to be aware and examine oneself. Willing to be in a relationship, to be spontaneous, willing to be intimate where possible.

The ability to assess, to be able to step back from being in the relationship and use one's assessment skills, and think, 'What might be going on?' So that one can offer information or interventions or even confrontations that are useful.

A colleague of mine, Maria Gilbert, says that she thinks one of the most important things that therapists ought to be able to do is to make an intervention which they can explain. They can say 'I'm doing this because I think ...' They might not at the time. They might simply respond spontaneously. But then afterwards they should be able to think about it theoretically: what they're doing and why.

She says that you should be able to make that intervention, and then notice what impact it has, what effects it has. See the response, take account of the response, and then be flexible about your next intervention accordingly. So that you think: 'The client didn't seem to understand, so I'll let that go. Or they looked a bit agitated, perhaps this is not the moment to push it, or perhaps this is the moment to push it. Or I've missed him completely, something else is going on for him.' Essentially, you take account of the feedback that you're getting from your clients.

How do you monitor your performance? Some therapists admit they drift off ... lose concentration ...

I think we should definitely, as therapists, monitor ourselves. I do try to but I also do know that feeling, and I guess that my clients and supervisees will say 'We know it too', when they see me not being so completely focused, because I'm a bit over-tired or whatever. Having said that, I personally don't have a large clinical caseload, because I do a lot of supervision and training. So that there isn't a danger of me getting burned out from just seeing clients, and clients, and clients. Which is possible coming to the end of the week, having spent all the time seeing lots of people. It's something called encounter stress, I think. It's a new buzzword. It comes from your focusing your attention all the time on other people. That can be a problem for some therapists though not for others. Personally I enjoy the variety in my work.

The economics of therapy ... is it a problem?

My thoughts about the problem of money. I think it is a problem. People say that it's important that people pay something for their therapy, however small an amount and that's probably right. It's some-thing about focusing the commitment and facing them with 'Is this important to me?', and if it is, increasing motivation. If you've paid something, you're more determined to get something out of it. It's also a way of trying to ensure equality in the relationship – a mutual invest-ment of resources. I think that's all true. However, the social question is a different one, which is very difficult. There are many people who simply cannot afford to pay and the provision of therapy and counsel-ling on the National Health or low-cost clinics is still inadequate. We've actually just started one here (at Metanoid), I'm pleased to say. The people for whom those services cater are often people with the most need, and so therapy is still mainly the luxury of the people who have money. Although I'm not saying that they don't need it: people of every type and group have psychological problems.

Do you support the recent 'professionalisation' of therapy? Have you thoughts on this?

I do. I think TA is actually acknowledged worldwide as having one of the best systems of monitoring of accreditation, and of monitoring and accrediting the trainers and supervisors of TA too. So that there really are standards. Each country where TA exists – it's an international network – has it's own training standards committee, and there is a training and standards committee overall. I'm very proud of it.

The clinical accreditation involves several things. A 60-page disserta-tion, including an account of oneself as a practitioner, a theory section and a very substantial case study describing work you've done with a client. That's one part of the assessment. Then there is the requirement of several hundred hours of supervised practice, with the supervisor submitting reports, really monitoring the work. Then the oral exam: an hour to an hour-and-a-half. The person has to take along tapes of them working and a Board of Examiners listen to the tapes and ask what the thinking was in working this way, and why they've made particular interventions. So we really have a very careful accreditation system.

Actually I think accreditation in Britain is improving enormously, as I'm sure you know. Until recently there weren't any checks on people who wanted to set themselves up as therapists, which I thought was shocking. Clients were not protected against incompetence or wrong treatment. Sometimes money was wasted on long courses of treatment which were inappropriate. Now there is a lot of self-regulation by psychotherapists as a body, and I hope that ultimately it will become part of the law. There is one problem. I don't want to lose the concept of the gifted healer, because I think there are some people who are very gifted although they don't have a lot of theoretical knowledge. Yet they're good people and they're naturally healing people, so it would be a tragedy if we lost them. I don't know what we can do about this as a profession. Generally speaking though, I think the UKCP, the BPS, the BAC and other organisations are really taking standards seriously now. It's ethics that's the most important. I really believe that if a person is an ethical and careful practitioner and sits in a room with another person, and listens to them, and does his best to understand and so on, no harm can come.

Why are the English so reticent about therapy?

I think it's an interesting question, why in Britain particularly, or is it just Britain? We've had a long tradition of stiff upper lips; one doesn't talk about one's problems and so on. That must be part of it. Perhaps there is also the historical factor: the tradition in the old days of treating our mentally ill people really rather badly, locking them up and submitting them to all sorts of terrible procedures. A stigma became attached to mental illness and everybody hustled up the other end of the health continuum and said: 'No, no I'm fine, please don't associate me with people who have to be locked up.'

Do you touch clients? Hug them?

Some forms of TA involve personal contact – always very carefully contracted for. In the ordinary way I personally don't touch my clients very much. I might with clients that I know very well; I know that I have a very good relationship with and I'm not worried at all that there's going to be any misunderstanding or difficulty. Especially, we have to be sure that there isn't any issue for them about being touched, associated with abuse or something like that.

Actually, I also think that touching can often be a way of comforting a feeling away, and actually in a way avoiding contact; replacing one sort of contact with another sort of contact. If you were my client and you were sitting and you were telling me your distress, and you could see me, if you looked at me, you could see me listening and really being with you, I think that that is probably more useful to you than if I came round out of your line of sight and put an arm around you, and comforted you. So that you get the 'there, there', but you don't get me, a separate person witnessing and empathising.

Somebody once said 'the challenge' – when we feel the desire to hug someone – 'the challenge is to put that hug into words', and I think that's right. To convey from one person to another, that attitude.

Have you encountered many cases of so-called 'false memory syndrome'?

Personally – not that I'm aware of. False memory syndrome is a very interesting and difficult topic. And the BPS and UKCP have recently done some interesting studies on it, and some very interesting results have come up.

The implication is that spontaneous memories are unlikely to be false. Now having said that, of course, we don't have any verbal memories under the age of about two. We haven't got the neural pathways. Also even after that our memories can be jumbled and we can run several memories together and think it happened all at the same time, or we can mix our memories. Memories are likely to have some truth or experience with the truth, but the memory may be locked in our bodies, as it were, and therefore any intellectual construction must be tentative. And it has certainly been proved very clearly that you can implant a memory in somebody else, by telling that something happened so confidently that they believe it did happen. Somebody in a vulnerable state is particularly available to that.

So basically I think therapists have to be very careful, and I think therapists are. Most therapists are scrupulous about avoiding suggesting things to a client. Of course, every time we respond to a client, we are influencing them in some way by what we nod our head to, or the sorts of questions we ask. One of the things the UKCP paper pointed out was, if you say, 'and how do you feel about that', to someone, you're implying (a) that someone has a feeling; (b) that they should know what it is; (c) that they should be willing to say what it is (d) that it isn't a thought, and so on and so forth. So that we are subtly or unsubtly influencing our clients all the time. But I guess that's inevitable. Humans are subtly and unsubtly influencing one another all the time anyway, therapists just have to be that bit more careful because of the power in that relationship.

Freud stressed the importance of 'love and work', didn't he ...

Yes. That the outcome of a successful analysis would be to love and to work, and to get used to ordinary human misery, rather than hysterical despair. TA agrees to some extent but would put it differently. The ideal would be what I was talking about earlier, about autonomy. That I and the person, my client, would be able to be in the present moment in a real relationship with each other, an integrated Adult with a capacity for awareness, spontaneity, and intimacy. And that's what we'd aspire to, and [laughs] if either I or my client can get to that state we'll be very happy people. I suppose realistically if we can get to that state some of the time that is great. Calling therapy successful depends on what a client comes with, and what they want to change. If the client feels generally better about themselves, or it's clear that they're functioning better, or that their life feels better, and if they accept themselves warts and all, that's good. Nicholas Spicer, a Jungian analyst, says that the goal of analysis is for the client to feel that they live in a world which makes sense.

Have you thoughts about 'emotional literacy', especially as a subject being taught in schools?

Yes. Like it was in my convent school. More than that, I think – and I'm passionate about it – that TA is a brilliant model for introducing to schools, because it's simple. We've got a big TA in Education movement in Britain, and in the autumn our first educational TA trainer is getting qualified, and I hope she's going to do a lot of training. She already works a lot with teachers and parents. What I would like to see happening is for a TA101 to be introduced in schools. That's an American term meaning an introduction to TA. It's a two-day course introducing all the major concepts. For each one there are exercises where the person applies it to themselves and their lives. I think all schools should have TA101s taught in them. Perhaps in the fifth form. About that age. Also basic concepts could be introduced earlier down the school, so that in the primary school the children and their teachers would become familiar with the ideas of emotional literacy and good communication. I think it would be brilliant. It would put all us therapists out of a job! That would make me happy.

CHAPTER 5

Psychoanalysis

Peter Lomas

Peter Lomas is a psychotherapist who has a private practice in
Cambridge. He is the author of a number of books, most
recently *The Limits of Interpretation* and *Cultivating Intuition*.

How did you come to be a therapist?

Well I think a religious background comes into it. Because part of that
religious background contained the view that it was important to be
caring to people in general and it could have led me into the church,
but it didn't. It led me into medicine. I would care for people in that
kind of way. I don't think that was the right work for me. I'm not
particularly good with my hands. I was interested in the broad basis of
science, but I wasn't interested very much in the intricacies of the body,
or anatomy, or physiology. As I began to see patients I soon realised
that I was much more interested in how they ticked with their minds,
them as people.

Now that was one thing. The other thing was that, for various reasons
that would take us too long to go into, I was an anxious child – suffered
quite a lot from anxiety – that continued into my teens, and I didn't know
how to handle it and I just put up with it. But I realised that I did suffer a
lot of anxiety. Then I came across a book in the university library by
Freud. At this stage I was very much into medicine and science, and I was
very uneducated in a general cultural way. I didn't grow up in a family
where there was a lot of culture around. And I borrowed this book.
Actually I had quite an embarrassing tussle with the librarian, who seemed
to think I wanted it for a 'dirty' reason. 'This is a university. These books
tend to get defaced', she said, 'these kind of books.'

Anyway I was rather impressed with this book, and I fought my way
into finding one or two others, and I found a psychoanalyst in Manchester – there were only two at that time – and I found one and I had an
analysis, which I now realise was a pretty strictly Freudian one, but I
didn't realise at the time. I feel it helped me up to a certain point, and
I got the idea then that I would like, if possible, to do that kind of
work myself. But there was a snag that I found in working with very
disturbed people – even in the course of medicine I would pay visits to
mental hospitals and see quite a number of disturbed people. I worked

in neuropsychiatry for a while. I found they disturbed me, so I thought 'I'm not really going to be able to do this particular kind of work.' Anyway I decided to pursue the matter further. I was at that time in general practice. I came to London, where I thought 'That's the place to get a training.' And I went to an analyst – Charles Rycroft – and I said 'I need more analysis for personal reasons because I get this anxiety. But I would hope eventually to train.' So I had some analysis with him, and then we both came to the conclusion that it would be okay for me to train, and I trained. At the Freudian Institute. For better or for worse. So that's really how I came to it.

What kind of tradition are you from?

Well I'll start by talking about the lineage which I must confess I'm not quite clear about, and can't be precise. I can only talk about the areas of influence which are fairly clear, but what comes from more deeply within me I'm not so clear about. I do suspect that it's things in early upbringing to do with the ideals that were set before me and my religious back-ground, that more or less unconsciously had a big effect.

But I did find myself, even when I was training, questioning the dogmatism, and the rigidity of the technique. Even though I had an analyst in Charles Rycroft who was not as rigid as many. But there was a pretty strict regime all the same. I felt there was not enough freedom. I think it is in my nature to question, and it is in my nature from somewhere or other to be a bit of a rebel in the sense of not taking what is offered for granted, but questioning it.

The first influence I can remember was coming across an article by Martin Buber, which was not in his books. I'd never heard of him or his books. It was in a psychotherapeutic journal, and I thought, 'This puts a new dimension on things.' And that got me interested in existentialism, and I read *I and Thou* and other books, and I began to feel that this was a language which was more apposite to what I felt was the work I was doing. It talked about people, it didn't talk about systems and bits of people, and egos and ids and things. It seemed to be my experience of life.

There is quite a contradiction between the simplicity of the message of the existentialists – what seemed to be the simplicity, taking away all this theoretical stuff and saying: 'It's me and it's you, it's I and it's thou.' But they were as full of jargon and as intellectually contorted as anybody else. I mean you can't get much more contorted than Heidegger and Kierkegaard. But I put up with that as best I could.

Another great influence on me was reading the work of the Americans on so-called schizophrenogenic families. Gregory Bateson and people. I read those articles when they first came out, and they were a revelation to me, and I realised – again from my own experience – I could see things in me and in my family which were not covered by the Freudian way of thinking at all. It opened a new dimension.

Then I read Ronnie Laing's book *The Divided Self*. He, although I'd

not met him, had known who he was, and went to the same analyst as
myself which I think you will know, because you know about him, and
who his analyst was. And I realised that he used to come out of the
door as I was going in ... [Laughs] I now think – I wonder what sort of
a shape that Charles was in because I imagine Ronnie was a very
demanding patient. He is a great challenger.

Anyway I read the book and I wrote to him and we met. And I
had in the meantime written a paper myself, which I read to the
Freudian Institute, in which I'd expressed some of these ideas. And
Ronnie asked me if I'd go to his group and read this paper, and I
did. We were sort of very pleased with each other – to see how close
the thinking had been. I joined with his group and we used to talk,
and we did some work. I joined in some of the work that was being
done on so-called schizophrenic families. I think what I got from
Ronnie, perhaps, was not so much intellectual insight, because I'd
already got that from reading existentialism and from reading these
American papers, which were the source of his inspiration – I think
those two mainly, although he was better read than I was in that
field – but the encouragement from his nerve, of his drive; that he
was prepared to tackle anyone or anything. But I left the group
because it became fairly clear to me that this was a group in which
there was a leader – a guru – and satellites (maybe putting it in a bit
of an unkind way) but that's how it seemed to me. And it's not in
my nature to be a satellite. So I left. I think I'm the sort of person
who has to work in his own way, and I think partially too because I
felt that my field really was one-to-one, rather than families. I wanted
to get what knowledge I could out of families, but I didn't have a
drive to make my career in family work. So where does that lead us?

At that time I was working at the Cassel Hospital, Richmond, which
was a therapeutic community, and gave me a lot of experience – I really
regarded it then as quite a tough place. You were into the middle of
things. I think I learnt a lot there, but of course the orientation there
was quite different to the way I was thinking, particularly short-term
therapy, and emphasis on technique, and on brief therapy, where one
designs what one does before one starts. I don't believe in that kind of
way. More and more, I have come to believe in something growing
between the patient and therapist, which is unique in itself – that there
is no one technique that one can apply. And one has to learn what is –
as in ordinary life – what is the best way of being with somebody, and
that is very different to the way I see so much of contemporary psychotherapy, even in the analytic field, let alone the cognitive field.

Just before you came I was doing a supervision. I seem to have
incidentally a bit of difficulty in knowing even how to formulate what I
do. When I say 'doing a supervision', I feel a bit uneasy, as if I do the
supervision to somebody, instead of that we have a conversation and
talk. Just as I wasn't very keen a few minutes ago on talking about
'patients'. I have no other word for it: I don't think 'client' is any better,

but you can't just say 'person'. You have to say what you're doing. And I haven't found a way that satisfies me of saying what the relationship is or should be as I see it.

And we were discussing this question of 'was there a theory of psychotherapy', and she spoke about someone who had been saying that she thought one just did it out of oneself, and that that had made her feel uneasy, that there must be more to it than that. And we discussed this and I found it very difficult, succinctly, to formulate my position. Which is that there is no one technique, there is no one theory, there is no certainty, that one is uncertain from moment to moment about the right way to do it. But that doesn't mean that one hasn't got quite apart from everything else in one's life – in particular from the work of therapists who've gone before us – broadly speaking, in the analytic field – that one hasn't got some very valuable ideas from them.

If I have to think of one idea which I can't imagine I would have thought of myself (not being a genius), that idea would be transference. Because even if one speaks of defences and resistance as Freud did and was so central to his thinking, that's in a sense – although he formulated it so well and in such a useful context – that is not a new idea. We have always known that people feel uncomfortable if you tell them truths that they don't particularly want to hear, and I think an enormous amount of psychotherapy is using to the best of one's ability in a very facilitating context, one's experience derived from every area in one's life where one has tried to learn what people are like – to try to understand them, and to try to find the best way of working with them and being with them.

I think psychotherapists have elaborated this, much of which is – I'm hesitating again over what is the right word – one could say common sense, but that's a very dodgy concept because it can include ideas which are current in a certain culture, but are very unnatural. Or one could use the word intuition, something that is part and parcel of what one has learnt in everyday living. So I think that a student is best served by being exposed to the ideas of therapists who have been in rooms with people for hours and for years, and done their best to think of ways of helping them and understanding them. Provided what is expressed in the literature is not taken as gospel, as certainty, as a formula for doing it.

What happens when someone comes to see you?

What might happen, I think, is that I respond with a mixture of the conventional psychotherapist – the way most psychotherapists I imagine work and the way I was brought up to work – and to be as spontaneous as I can be. To be as informal and as spontaneous as I can be, in the hope that they will see me as another human being like themselves. Not someone who is taking up a detached professional stance to them or looking at them as though they were a specimen. So I suppose I try to be with them as near as I can. To be how I am with people in ordinary life who come to me – a neighbour might come to me and say 'Well look, my husband's just walked out on me. What shall I do, Peter?' And I try to respond, I suppose, in the kind of way in which I would in those circumstances. I'll not stand back too much, and start to think of their infant development or start to think 'Well I mustn't give anything of myself away', or 'I mustn't answer their questions about myself.'

On the other hand I am aware that they have come to me as a professional. Rightly or wrongly that does make a difference. I think some of it is probably okay, and some of it is probably not okay. The not okay bit, I think, is that I feel a little bit constrained by that. I feel I ought to be a bit more proper somehow, than I would be in ordinary life. I don't mean that they expect me to wear a tie and a pinstriped suit, but in some sort of way, and in my manner perhaps, they would not expect me to be too chummy. And I think I do, unconsciously, respond to that.

But a more reasonable way, I think, is that I feel that someone has come to me not quite like the neighbour next door who's come and we have a cup of coffee, and she says 'My husband's left me.' I don't feel I'm necessarily taking on the problem in quite such a major way, that if a neighbour comes, I hope I would do my best to say something useful and perhaps do something useful. But my neighbour will not be expecting a lot of me in ordinary circumstances. I am one of the people that she knows that she feels she can perhaps talk to. I happen to be there. Whereas with a patient I'm taking on something big, usually, not one-off consultations or short-term things. Most of my work is long term, and when a patient comes I feel that I'm – not to put it too grandly perhaps – I'm taking on a life. I'm taking on their basic being, and I might be doing that for years. I don't want to rush in at the beginning to be rash, and that, I think, curbs my spontaneity which in part is not good, but in part perhaps is inevitable if I'm going to be cautious in the beginning. I don't know this person. I don't quite know how disturbed they might be and so I will be more silent, more reflective than I would be in most situations. And I'll listen to their story.

I think that's for the most part appropriate, and I think that's what they want. They've come – in the first place at any rate – for someone who will listen to them. As regards the practical arrangements, I suppose I'm fairly orthodox in that I feel comfortable with the Freudian 50 minutes. If it goes on much longer than that I begin to get a headache ... [Laughs] Shorter than that doesn't usually seem long enough. So the people who come to me usually get the 50 minutes, unless there's a specific reason for them not to.

I like to see people two or three times a week, if I can; depending on what they've come for, depending on their circumstances, depending on what they're willing to do, what they can do, time available, money available, and so on. I don't see people more than three times a week, except during periods of crisis when it might be necessary to see people five times. But I no longer believe in the magic five times a week of orthodox analysis. But I do think that three times a week gives quite a lot of continuity, and one can usually work better with most people. I feel fairly easy with twice a week. I feel uncomfortable with once a week, but sometimes that is all people can manage. And I have people who come once every two months.

Do you talk contractually with patients? And spell out what therapy is all about?

I don't much go in for that kind of conversation when I meet people. I think, largely because people have got to know – certainly in Cambridge perhaps more so than in many places – roughly what psychotherapy is about. What the formula is likely to be. The people that come to me usually might want me to tell them what to do. But I think a lot of them expect – have read or heard enough about psychotherapy – to have got the idea that psychotherapists try to help people to understand themselves rather than give them directions. So I don't think on the whole I find myself spelling things out, other than making the times and arrangements, and prices and this and that. But of course it is different with every patient. And if it were appropriate of course I would say things like that. Just as if it felt appropriate, I wouldn't necessarily even in the first session just feel that my job was listening. I might make an interpretation. I think with many people who come for the first time, now I come to think about it, I don't necessarily just listen. I do something which is perhaps a bit like what you have in mind. I will try to discuss with them why exactly they are coming, and whether it is a good thing, and I might challenge them on that. And that might involve my speaking about what I think are the limitations of what I'm going to do or what I can do. I certainly make no promises.

Do you discuss dreams with your patients?

I think that with most of the people that come to me, I do encourage them to talk about their dreams. I don't rely on dreams, and it wouldn't worry me if a patient never had a dream.

I think it would be very unusual in a long-term therapy for me not to talk about the patient's relationship with me in the room. Which merely amounts to something rather similar to talking about transference. I don't mean I would necessarily compare with everybody the experience in the room with the experience of this person as a child with her father and mother. I very often do it just as analysts usually do it, but I don't regard that as necessary. I do regard it as very important to talk about what's going on between us and how we are with each other, which could be formulated in other ways in terms of transference and countertransference. And I say to them, very often, something like: 'Well you tell me about this thing in your ordinary life which keeps cropping up. Don't you think it might be useful to see if it crops up here, because then we can see it more clearly and more convincingly, and I can see it in action?' And I will look for it and point it out if I can see it.

Now one could think that I am looking for the transference, but I don't necessarily formulate it in those terms. I don't feel it's always necessary to trace it back to a childhood thing. Because I think it can be very useful to deal with it in the present and say: 'Look, you have seemed to have the habit of acting in this kind of way. It doesn't seem to do you any good. Let us look at it. Why? What is it in you that makes you act in this way against your own interests, and which does unpleasant things to me?', or whatever it is. 'What is it that makes you turn me into a god? What is it that makes you despise everybody, including me?' That kind of thing.

Well I might trace it back to childhood, or I might not.

How do you square the Freudian and the existential ...

Well I'm not actually conscious of a problem, when you put it to me like that. I'm not conscious of that being a problem. Because to me the here and now includes the conscious and the unconscious, and if it seems relevant to guess at what people are not quite aware of or what they're hiding, I don't have to think of myself as a Freudian, reducing something, as the existentialists say a Freudian does, to 'What's happening is merely a transference that's going on, that what is really important is what happened when you were six.' I don't think of it that way. What is important is happening now, and if we can get some help from learning about the past, well good luck to us. But to me the relationship is basically, except in perhaps a very sick person, is essentially a real one. And I think that to think of it in terms of merely a repetition of the past is, I think, detrimental to the patient's sense of their own reality, the sense of their own worth. I think they can easily feel they're not being taken seriously. One can question a patient, one can challenge a patient, but I don't think one should dismiss the fact that the patient is in present-day reality and what they say and do is best taken seriously, as having an effect.

You don't make promises ...

I tell them what I would hope to do. In fact it may be all implicit, it may not need to be said. Intuitively they know, they hope that I will do my best to help them, and words needn't be said. And I will say: 'Well, it seems a good idea', or 'Let's try', or so and so. I do find myself with certain people giving my misgivings, and I say: 'I'm not sure I can help you. You seem to be very settled in your ways. I'm not sure you want to give up your ways. I'm not sure whether you're prepared to face the trauma, the anxiety, the uncertainty of change.' And I might say 'For that reason, I don't feel I would want to try to help. I would like to help, but I don't feel enough hope to be able to help you to do therapy.'

Or I might say, almost with misgiving, 'but if you're prepared to try well so am I.'

But with most people I rather take the attitude: 'Well, let's meet and see how we get on. And perhaps it will emerge whether this is worth doing or not, or whether I'm the right person for you', and so on.

What qualities should a therapist have?

Yes, well, I think that is a very difficult question. Because a therapist needs to have in the room certain qualities that I would call 'good'. I think that a philosopher would probably use the word 'virtuous', but it's not an everyday word. Because they are qualities which are, I think, potentially healing to someone in trouble. And they would be things like wisdom; capacity to care. Care in two ways – one is being responsible in the professional way to go on doing it, if one has committed oneself. To go on doing it even if one begins to hate the patient, and still to have some kind of professional responsibility. But I think also care in another sense, and that is actually to care about the patient in one's heart, and that is a very difficult thing either to claim or to have – because it is saying, 'I am a good person, I am a caring person' – when we all know that therapists are just as bad as anybody else as people. And it's a rather difficult thing to say to a student, 'You've got to learn to care.' How the hell do you teach a student to care?

But it does include caring, because for the people that come to me it matters to them enormously whether I care for them. I've hesitated a bit to use the word 'love', although it is a word they would use quite often. 'I want you to love me.' And I think therapists can love their patients, but it's such a dodgy word, and it can be so misinterpreted, that it's a word that I think all of us feel uneasy with. Because it's not being in love nor is it saying 'I want to live with you', or 'I will take you home', or 'look after me', and there are clearly limits to it.

But I think one can feel with a patient one has come to know over a long period of time a great deal of warmth. And I think that matters to the patient, because it encourages them to feel that they are valued by somebody who's seen them, in a sense, in their nakedness, and who still cares about them. I think it encourages them to feel that the therapist is likely to do his or her best. I think in actual fact it's important, because I think if one cares about a patient one is likely to try to do one's best.

I had someone come to me for supervision recently, whose patient was in a deep practical predicament, which was a mixture of her own psychopathology and something that someone else was doing to her which was very cruel. And I could see that this therapist was deeply concerned, and at one point she said 'There's got to be a way.' Now that gave me the feeling that the therapist was going to try very hard, not in any loose or soppy way, but in a rigorous way to do everything she could to get this patient out of this jam. She would think about the theories, she would if necessary do something unorthodox. Something that might even put herself at risk. To help this person. Now that's caring. I think that is one of the qualities. And there are many obvious ones.

One needs to have a degree at any rate of integrity. One must have a degree of patience. Once again, one can have too much patience. One can be too passive. One could be shouting at the patient, it's not usual but sometimes it might be the only way to get through to them. So that these are all what I would call good qualities, quite apart from the intellectual quality, if you like, and the interest and capacity to absorb ideas in the psychotherapeutic field from other therapies, from teachers, from books. To learn whatever they can about therapy and about areas related to therapy. So that an individual therapist would, I would hope, learn about family therapy, which would add a new dimension. And would learn about sociology, anthropology, whatever things – religion – that might have a bearing on the intellectual side of it.

Now the problem for me in thinking about this is – how can any therapist claim to have these kind of qualities? Okay, it's no problem that they have the learning from their particular discipline, which Joe Soap in the street hasn't got. But I appear to be saying that they must have virtuous qualities, which are important. Which of course a therapist cannot claim to have any more than Joe Soap in the street. The only way I can think about it is that it is a setting in which it is easier for the therapist to care for somebody in distress than in most settings in life. There are other settings – two people who live together and love each other, who would care in a deeper way than the therapist would.

But in most settings one doesn't get the time, one doesn't get the quiet, one does not get the therapeutic drive in the other person who is turning to one, who is prepared as much as they can to lay themselves bare and naked. Trusting that the therapist, because he or she is a therapist, will not betray that confidentiality. I think that every therapist, I'm sure, would agree with me that there are people who come who attack one, who manipulate one in such a way that it is very difficult to be good, to be virtuous, to not in some way get one's own back on them. Consciously or unconsciously, in some subtle way, one is so angry that it is difficult probably not to want to actually hurt the patient.

I don't mean physically. I cannot at the moment, think of a therapist who's told me that he or she has hit a patient, but I wouldn't be surprised if it happened. But I would think that's rare. But there are easier and more subtle ways of just putting a patient down. So I don't mean that a therapist is always acting virtuously, or is not sometimes provoked, but I do think by and large it is a setting in which however the other person behaves, the therapist is in a better position than most to behave well, to behave decently. That is one of the ways in which I think one could think of therapy as a moral pursuit. There are other ways, but that's one way.

Where do the 'hurts' that people suffer from originate?

Well ... [Pause] ... I'm hesitating because it's quite obvious that there is such a tremendous variety, it's rather difficult to think of a patient who would stand as a paradigm model that one could talk about. I don't know that anybody knows the answer to the nature/nurture problem. I don't know how much children are born into the world in a way in which leaves them ill-equipped to deal with it. To me that is a bit of a mystery. I do think there can be misfits, in that children are born who are okay as far as one knows. They're as okay as anybody else. But they may be born into a family or a culture where there is not much of a mix, not much of a fit. And then there will be trouble.

I think there are probably some people born who are perhaps an exception, perhaps exceptionally sensitive. Which is potentially very good or very bad. Quite often it might lead to creativity, or quite often might lead to trouble. What is more obvious is when one hears stories which on the whole I am inclined to believe have a lot of truth in them rather than to dismiss them as just pure fantasies as some writers do: the stories of childhood where it does seem to me that things have happened to the child, either out of ignorance in the parents, or cruelty in the parents, or the tragedy of life. The parents don't choose to die when their child is two years old, but they might die. And things have happened which do seem to account for some of the troubles that people bring me. But that doesn't mean to say that when someone comes to me, I think, 'There's a bad parent behind this.' Well, some- times I do think that.

Over the moral issue, I think that the question is: 'What am I as a therapist trying to do with such a person?' If the person is incapacitated I think that the first thing to do is a bit like first aid. The first thing to do is to stop them bleeding. Just as a doctor may go to a patient who is bedridden and help him to get out of bed. Now his thought is – to put it in a very simple way – to get that patient in good enough shape to be able to get out of bed and eat his food. And that doesn't seem to me to quite fit into a moral issue. This seems to me a matter of common sense. If someone has fallen down on the floor one goes and tries to pick him up.

But there are many patients who are not, as it were, the equiva- lent of being bedridden. I think most of the patients who come to therapists who work independently like I do, and not people who are sent to mental hospitals, most can, in lesser or greater degree, func- tion. Some can function perfectly well, but there's an emptiness inside. And some function not very well, and don't sleep well, and can't make good relationships, and so on. And I suppose one way of just simply looking at it is to enable them to function better. But I'm not quite content to leave it like that, because what does functioning better mean? If this person is, amongst other things, doing destruction of some kind to other people, does functioning better mean enabling them to destroy more effectively? Or does it mean making them able to be happy, but still continue to do their destructive thing?

So I think that I would add to all this that one is trying to make them, amongst other things, into better people. I would not be content to do therapy with somebody who is sadistic. Or a child molester, who would go away quite happy, but still be a child molester. I would feel that I had failed in some sort of moral sense. I failed with them morally, that they had not become morally better people. They have not – to use a biblical phrase – they have not cast out the evil. So I would think part of the aim, or one way of looking at this idea, is to make people better people. I think that's very difficult to say in a way that sounds intellectually respectable. It's not the way that psychotherapists speak. It sounds like old-fashioned preaching. It makes me sound like a priest. I don't pretend to be a priest, and by and large I don't even pretend to know what is best for people. But like everyone else I have my own ideas, and child molesting is not one of the things that I would choose to endorse.

There is one way of looking at it, I think, which does rather fit in with the psychoanalytic way. That is that although psychoanalysts don't speak of this in moral terms, I think they do try to enable their patients to become less narcissistic. And a lot is written about that. To get – from Freud onwards – to get rid of the omnipotence. To get rid of the Kleinian greed, and so on. Now in a sense these can be spoken of in moral terms. The ordinary way of putting it would be, to get rid of selfishness, to get rid of vanity, to get rid of all the sins which the religions speak of. So I think there is hidden even in orthodox analysis, a hidden moral aim, but it's not one that's on the whole talked about in everyday work, when therapists talk to each other.

Do you have 'proof' that people get better after seeing you?

Ah, I have no proof. When I say 'I have no proof', I have no proof that could convince anybody outside this room, I mean outside myself. I don't do any statistical studies. If I have any way of trying to prove to other people the value of what I do, it is either the very personal way, in which if I am able to help some people they will tell other people, or if in my writing I can say – without giving anything that the scientists would think of as proof – I can produce some kind of argument or some kind of description of something that I have experienced which might make some people think, 'Well there's something in this.'

But for myself, I just hope I'm not fooling myself into thinking that most of the people that come to me go away in somewhat better shape than they arrived. If I didn't believe that, I wouldn't do the work. I'm not trying to claim that that happens to them all, but it happens to enough of them to feel that it's worth doing.

How do you monitor your work?

I think that happens spontaneously rather than that I have a plan, a monitoring plan. I think it just would come to me – 'Look I'm stuck with this patient, should we stop? What am I doing wrong?' Or the patient might, if you like, do the monitoring, and say 'Look, I've been coming such a length of time and you're not helping me.' Patients monitor me as well as I monitor myself, and will sometimes be specific about it and say: 'Well, I think you're doing it wrong this way.' But it's more likely to be a general comment that they don't feel they're getting on too well.

Occasionally I get jolts from outside – Cambridge is a small city and there's a lot of gossip, and people know each other and so on. This area – not the whole of Cambridge – but the area in which therapists work, I do hear things. I particularly hear things about patients from outside, because several of the people who come to me are in training. They're in training in the same group, this is the Cambridge Society for Psychotherapy, which we now speak of colloquially as the 'outfit'. I see some of the people who are in therapy with me in the group, which is difficult for them and is difficult for me, and has its disadvantages. But it also has its advantages. Because I hear about some of my patients from other patients, and sometimes a patient will say to me 'Look for Christ's sake what you're doing with Judy. Had you not realised that she's doing this and she's doing that? Have you not cottoned on that she's got a severe Oedipus complex with you?', or whatever.

So I get that kind of monitoring more than probably most therapists. It just happens to be the position I'm in. And it can sometimes be quite chastening. Or sometimes someone will say: 'Look you're doing very well with so-and-so, she's really blossoming.' I say 'she' because most of the people that come for therapy these days seem to be women. I don't know quite why that is, but most of my practice now are women. It wasn't always the case, it wasn't the case in London when I worked, but it does seem to be now.

What are your thoughts about the 'registration' process?

I am appalled by it ... [Pause] ... I am not sure whether we wouldn't be better without it altogether, and risk the fact that there will be a few charlatans around, doing bad work, which is a very disturbing thought, with no control over them, and I think it is very understandable that the profession and the public want to avoid that at all costs and want to have a register. And I think that a register is inevitable. Indeed, it has already happened. I do not think that people realise how dangerous it is and how careful one should be with it. I think the register should confine itself to ethics, to have the power to make sure that certain therapists who behave very irresponsibly to their clients should be struck off this register.

But I think one should be very careful about what is considered irresponsible, because therapists can do very strange things with their patients which might seem irresponsible to somebody outside. And I have sometimes been told that I have behaved irresponsibly to a patient. I don't mean in any obvious way that's going to get into the *News of the World*. I don't mean in that kind of way. But in some kind of way which has I'm sure been perfectly all right in the circumstances between me and the patient, and where I've actually written about it with the patient's permission – disclosed it – I have been told that that behaviour is quite irresponsible.

So I think one's got to be very cautious, but I think that the control, the monitoring of the training of therapists is very destructive of creativity. I have first-hand experience of this, because I'm a founder member of the Cambridge Society for Psychotherapy, and we are very unorthodox in our methods of training. We don't have a training committee; we don't have examinations for people to pass at the end. We're very unorthodox in all kinds of ways. And that might be good or that might be bad. But we try to make it a place where the student has as much responsibility for themselves, as much freedom as possible, and as much opportunity to think for themselves, and be creative – that is our aim. I think despite the sort of in-fighting that goes on in every organisation, I think we have largely succeeded in creating this kind of thing, and we now have trained therapists who seem to me to work well. But we have had to submit ourselves to inspection by the UKCP. And we have had more trouble; have spent more time over trying to make ourselves acceptable – because we feel we have a responsibility to students to train them so that they can practise, and to practise they have to be able to register. So we feel we've got to fit in.

I think the greatest threat to our creativity is the register. That's my own view. I'm not giving the view of the group as a whole. I think there is far too much belief that there are people, centrally placed, who know what is right about how psychotherapy could be done – how particular groups should work, and how particular students should be trained – because I feel students are unique individuals who will learn best in their own individual ways.

Just for example, I think it is absurd that it should be laid down that students see their therapists for a certain length of time. Now I think a therapy should have the length of time of a piece of string.

CHAPTER 6

Personal Construct Psychology

Dorothy Rowe

Dorothy Rowe is well known for a number of best-selling books including *Breaking the Bonds* and *Time On Our Side*. She is a personal construct psychotherapist and works in London.

Can you tell me a little about your past?

When I went to university in 1948, I intended to read English and History, because those were the subjects that I excelled at in school and I wanted to write. But when I got there I found the English and History courses were not very interesting, and I had already covered a lot of the work. But I had to take a fourth subject in the first year, and I took Psychology. And that was the subject I did best in, so I just went on and majored in that. But then I had to teach, because although I'd won exhibitions at the university that didn't pay my upkeep, and so I took a Teachers College Scholarship, which forced you into a bond. You had to teach for five years afterwards. So I was four years at University and then I did a year as teacher trainee, and then I taught for nearly three years, and by that time I was married and expecting a child, so I left. Then when Edward was about two and my husband was starting his own legal practice, I went back to teaching. When I went for an interview with the Board of Education, when that Board asked me if I had thought about becoming what was out there called a School Counsellor – an Educational Psychologist – I said 'Yes', because I wanted to get back. So for the next two or three years, every year, they asked me whether I'd want to do that training – it was a whole year. And I didn't want to do it, because it was nine to five, with a lot of travelling, and I had a small child. So I had to stick to half past nine to half past three. And somewhere close to home.

But I was teaching in a girls' high school, and teaching 1D and 2E, which was pretty hard work. On the third year there, when I discovered that the English mistress still refused to give me a senior class I wanted – if she'd given me a fourth or fifth year to teach History, I'd have been happy, it would have balanced all of this other dreadful stuff. So I thought 'I can't go on doing this', and I accepted their offer, so I spent a year doing this training, and that was lovely. I really enjoyed it, and the kind of issues that we were being given to consider – all of it was falling in place. I meant to say that I had to do a lot of writing, we always had to write essays and things. So I became a School Counsellor, and that involved a lot of travelling – it was a big geographical area, and my office was my car. I kept all the files and everything in the boot of the car.

So I was learning to do interviews and observe people, and talk to people in a way which few psychologists would ever do nowadays, because I'd talk to children on school verandas, and then I went to their homes and sat around having cups of tea. Then I became – some of the counsellors were specialist counsellors for children with different special needs – and I became a specialist counsellor for emotionally disturbed children. But I felt that I just didn't know enough about it – certainly our training wasn't adequate to cover that. So at night I did my Diploma in Clinical Psychology.

By this stage, my marriage was breaking up – yes about two years after we split I was doing my Masters Degree at the University of New South Wales, and corresponding with Monty Shapiro at the Maudsley about a really tremendous change in research practice. He was the only one who'd done it. Then, all psychological research still had to be done with vast numbers of people – if you didn't have a thousand subjects, it wasn't proper research. And I knew that – getting these nomothetic results was all very well for articles in the *British Journal of Psychology*, but these results had no relationship to real life, to real problems. And Monty was starting to develop some techniques for looking at the individual. So I was corresponding with him about that. One night I came home, found a letter from him, and he said 'Why don't you come to England? There's lots of jobs over here.'

So I thought 'Well I can't go, I haven't got any money.' I was divorced by then, getting money out of Ted was very difficult. So I looked through the papers, and I'd been working for the Education Department for some years by then, and so I'd built up superannuation and long-service leave, and under the rules I could draw that in cash. So what I had then was enough to pay our fares to England – Edward, my son, and myself – and then when I got here I found that there was a job going in Sheffield where I could work fulltime, get a full salary, and do a PhD, and you couldn't do that back in Australia. I was the only person who'd ever applied for that job. There were many more jobs than psychologists, so I went to work in Sheffield, where Alec Jenner at the – you know Alec – and he was very biological and absolutely certain: he was that much [gesticulates with fingers] off discovering the biological basis of mood change. He was going to make this discovery, win the Nobel Prize, create a cure which would reverse this change, and we'd all live happily ever after. He had an enormous amount of money from the MRC, and he wanted to have as many researchers around him as possible. So he suggested I should look at psychological aspects of people with regular mood change. And I'd still be waiting – there aren't such people – but that started me talking to people who were depressed, and he also collected manic people. I've met more manic people than most psychologists ever do. They're fairly rare, but he had hundreds of them there. In psychology then, all the tests we had were reliable, that is if you gave a person one twice, you always got the same result. So we didn't have any tests that measured change. I'd heard this word 'repertory grid' and I went to a lecture of Pat Rabbit, who is a Professor in Liverpool now, and he talked about repertory grids. Then I went to a summer school at York University, run by Don Bannister, Fay Fransella, Phil Salmon and Millar Mair, and so that was how I discovered personal construct theory.

So personal construct theory ...

... personal construct theory. It just seemed to me like coming home, because that's what I knew life to be like. You know how it's always said that if you're going to be good parents, you must be consistent in your approach to the child. That is the worst advice you can give parents. What you should do for your children is show them that different people see things differently, that everything can be interpreted in different ways. I just grew up with that because whatever happened in our lives, my father interpreted it in an optimistic way. My mother interpreted it in the blackest most pessimistic way, and my sister interpreted it solely in terms of what was in it for her. So I had these three very clear sets of interpretation, and of course I had my own interpretation. I can recall the instances throughout my childhood and teens, where I would talk about this and get myself into terrible trouble, that I shouldn't be saying these things, pointing these things out. Just simply, that different people see things differently. The reason – unless you've met me through Personal Construct International Conferences, because they have them every two years – you wouldn't have associated me directly with construct theory, because I usually only mention in passing that that's what psychologists call it ...

I think you're seen as the respectable face of 'popular psychology' ...

My colleagues see me as the unrespectable face ... [Laughs] ...

What happens when patients come to see you?

Well the framework I work in is simply this. We get ourselves into difficulties if we believe that what we see is reality, and that what we think – the way we see the world and interpret ourselves and interpret the world – is fixed, that that's the way it is, it's reality. You're born into the world which is just a stage set, and you come out on the stage and you play your part on that stage, and then you go off. The stage is real and everything is as it's been described to you. This is of course one way that most children are brought up. They're told

that there is one true way of seeing things, and if you don't see it
like that you're mad or bad, if not both. We're very ignorant of the
way we operate as human beings. The way in which we're structured
physiologically. So when somebody starts to tell me their troubles, I'm
aware that they're talking about what they see is something fixed and
unchangeable. So what this person needs to discover is that what
they're talking about is not reality, but their interpretations of reality.
So in the course of the conversation, and once we've got past the
stage where the person is telling me things, and I'm listening, and
when we've got to the stage where we're getting to know one another
fairly well, then I'm starting to say things which imply that there are
alternatives, other ways of seeing things.

The example that I always give, because it always comes to my
mind, and it happened with just about all of my depressed clients – was
that you get on to the topic of talking about your mother. I'd discovered that depressed people have only one of two sorts of mothers. Their
mothers are either angels or witches. Absolutes. And they're sacrosanct.
Whichever. If they're witches you didn't say anything terrible about
them, because they know what you're thinking, what you're doing and
they'll punish you. And if they're angels, well you'd just feel so guilty if
you ever criticised them. So I would talk a bit about my mother and
not say 'Oh you think you had it bad, let me tell you about mine'; I
would just drop in a few little stories about my mother, and my stories
were often just as horrendous as the stories they were telling, but I'd
put in the context of laughing about them. At first the person would
just be going – terrible shock – you can make up jokes about God, but
you don't make up jokes about Mother. Then after a while they may
move to the position of: 'Well everything about my mother is totally
serious, but Dorothy can joke about her mother, that's all right.' Then
after a while they realise, and we probably discuss this – yes, this would
be something which you'd actually talk about – because I would have
told the person that I come from Australia, because the English always
want to know my accent. So we'd discuss the thing about what do you
do with your mother. You can hope that she'll change and go on hoping
to the day she dies that she'll change – some mothers do change, and
become much nicer and more understanding as they get older, but lots
don't; they stay fixed in their ways. So if your mother isn't going to
change, what can you do? Well one remedy is to put as much physical
space between you and her as you can, so we look at that possibility,
but that's not open. So the other thing is you can't move away from
her, how can you deal with her when you know that when you hear her
voice on the phone or when she comes to the Sunday lunch, you're
going to go into a state of nervous anxiety? So the other alternative is,
instead of being frightened of her, why not just feel sorry for her? 'Poor
fella', the aborigines say – somebody who's sad, but who you can laugh
at. And so if you laugh about her idiosyncrasies, and not let them get to
you, then you've found another way of dealing with your mother.

So by the time you've gone through all of that discussion, extended over many weeks, the person is starting actually to experience the fact that while there are many things in life we can't alter, we can always alter how we interpret those things. In my experience, once a person actually understands that – really takes it in – that's the end of therapy.

So you believe in the Freudian '50 minutes'?

Well. I explained to you earlier that I started off as a psychologist using my car as an office. Until I went to England I had no experience of actually doing therapy in a room – a room which was mine, which I actually controlled. So all the skills, the techniques, the habits that I'd acquired were ones which weren't dependent on place. Having your chair in a particular spot and so on. They were certainly not time-bound, because a lot of important things would go on when I was transporting a child from one place to another, or I'm talking to a woman in her kitchen and so while we're talking about how hot it is something else gets said, and she controls the time because we're having a cup of tea or something. So I never felt that was very rigid, and when I was working in Sheffield I'd go for a walk with the patient or we'd sit in the garden. Then in Lincolnshire – public transport was practically non-existent in Lincolnshire – and so, for a lot of people, getting to the hospital where I worked was such an effort that, for their sake, I'd have a two-hour session, once a fortnight or three weeks, rather than hourly sessions.

So I found that there wasn't a lot of point in having anything more than two hours, because I got tired after that, and I would just say that to the person, 'We won't talk for any longer than that.'

A lot of people complain about the conceptual absence of 'emotions' in PCP ...

Yes, well, it shows people's ignorance. I'm always explaining this to psychologists. They say: 'What about the emotions?', and I say: 'A construct is something like – I hate my father. Now is that a purely cognitive construct?' In any case, emotion is meaning. When you have an emotional response, even though, even though it mightn't be a verbal thought in your conscious mind, your emotion – that is your expression of the meaning that you have given to something. Emotions just don't arise, they always arise in response to something. So emotion is a meaning. A thought is a meaning. A feeling is a meaning, everything is a meaning. We're meaning-creating creatures, that's all we do. All we ever know are the interpretations that we create.

I haven't read Kelly for years, I didn't read much Kelly – I read him once – he does go on. It was said years ago, Epictatus said 'It's not things in themselves which trouble us, but our opinions of things.' And there's a wonderful poem by Xenophanes where he talks about all we know as a woven web of guesses – wonderful.

Personal Construct Theory is quite straightforward, isn't it?

It's always a struggle to express it to people who've had their minds cluttered by psychological theory. It's very straightforward talking to people whose minds are untroubled by tertiary education. It's obvious once you think about it. It's just obvious that each of us has our own way of seeing things, and necessarily so. You can't get inside another person's head. Our thoughts are always private. Once you become aware of simple things like how you see, then you realise that what you see is what you've learnt to see. And the old saying of, 'If I hadn't seen it I wouldn't have believed it' – it ought to be the other way around: 'If I hadn't believed it I wouldn't have seen it.'

The problem is that the two ways of regarding – if you put the interpretation way of understanding against 'you open your eyes and you see reality' – those have been philosophical ideas that have been argued down the centuries. But it no longer is, if only my psychologist and psychiatrist colleagues would read some simple up-to-date physiology. The work that Oliver Sacks does – he's got beautiful ways of explaining – the difficulties his patients have, because of the way they're constrained in the way they construct the world. And Susan Greenfield, who's just published her book *Journey to the Centre of the Mind*, which again is all about all you ever know is what you've constructed.

So it's not a philosophical argument any more. This is the way we are, we can't ever know reality directly.

Are there any particular issues that are especially amenable to construct therapy?

Well you see, all therapy is construct therapy. Construct theory is the over-arching theory that encompasses all the theories, because all the theories depend on, they're all about meaning. I know Freud always rejected this, but he was busy explaining how children interpret what happens to them. That's one way of explaining it. Jung explained how people interpreted what happened to them – and the behaviourists would like to think that they're totally objective. But a reinforcement is a reinforcement only if the subject interprets it as a reinforcement.

Is there a developmental aspect to all of this?

See what happens to us in our first years, we're busy interpreting – actually we start interpreting before we're born – and we make such major interpretations of life and of things that stay with us for the rest of our life. In the first couple of weeks you create the structures for seeing depth and distance. If you've missed out on certain things, then you won't see it. Colin Blakemore demonstrated this in the experiments for which he now gets persecuted, with those kittens. If they spent their first six weeks in a box which only had vertical lines in it, they didn't see horizontal planes.

So a lot of the interpretations that we create in early childhood stay with us until the day we die. We go on using them. Then there are lots of other interpretations which can stay with us if we don't realise that we ought to consider them again. Whenever we create an interpretation we try to make it the best interpretation we can given our experience and knowledge at the time. And of course as a small child you don't have much experience and knowledge, and you can only draw on what's so far happened to you. So if your mother is prone to say to you: 'Oh do be quiet, you're making me ill. I'll just die if you don't stop that noise', and then she dies – well, you must have killed her, mustn't you? You have no other experience to draw on. If you don't look at that in later life and think, 'Oh well that was why I thought that then, but of course I'm older and wiser now', and draw another conclusion, if you don't consider your interpretations then you have to go on living with them and the consequences.

If the behaviourists' model of people is of a 'ping-pong ball with a memory', to quote Don Bannister, what is PCT's?

Well for me it's that what you are, your sense of identity, your person, your sense of existence, is the sum total of all the meanings. So that you are your meaning structure. Often when I talk about this I have to say something which isn't true and say things like 'You create meaning', but the truth is that you – your meaning structure – creates meaning. And the task, the ever-present task is that even though you can never know reality directly, to keep yourself safe you need to try to get as close to reality as possible. So you need to think about your interpretations and you need to test them out. Kelly talked about 'man the scientist', and that's really what you need to be doing. If we're unwise we just live in a world of fantasy, and we don't ever test out our interpretations.

Can we elaborate using, say, sexual abuse stories ...

There are a number of people who had sexual experiences when they were children, but they were in circumstances where they didn't feel too threatened by the other person, and it wasn't a real big power thing. So the experience was one which fitted into their meaning structure without too much difficulty. The interpretations of sexual abuse which cause people in adult life problems, are when they interpret it as a feeling of 'there is nothing I can do to control my life, other people come and control me, I'm helpless. I am intrinsically sullied by that happening. The dirt that is inside of me, on me, myself, my soul can never be washed away.' There are lots of children who have had the experience that something's happened and they're confused and intrigued by it, and so they go to an adult to find out. 'What was that that happened?', and then the adult flies into a great rage, or gets all het-up and upset, and it's this second adult that causes the problem. Because up until then the child was just curious – when you're a child lots of strange things happen, and you see peculiar sights ... [Laughs] ... but it's when the adults go into their outrage performance that you start to get frightened and feel that something has gone wrong.

I remember when I was a schoolgirl, riding home from the beach, and some chap in an open-top car stopped me to ask the way, and got me to come a bit closer and he was exposing himself. I felt quite shaken by it. I was annoyed because I'd been caught out, I should have had more sense. But it was just like the annoyance you feel when your sister or playmate tricks you, and you think: 'Well I should have been brighter, why didn't I think of that?' But as I rode home, I knew I would not tell my mother because the performance she would put on would be so horrible, so hard to deal with that I would just deal with this memory myself.

So it's the interpretations, and whether you carry them forward. I've met a number of women now who've suffered a terrible amount of sexual abuse as children, and who have got together and shared their experiences and who've gone on and become extremely strong and powerful. There's Kate Toon and Carol Ainscough up at Wakefield, have been running these groups, well at least they start off running the group and then the women gradually take over. The day I went to visit them, half a dozen of these women had just come back from the prison where they'd been talking to men in for sex crimes. I almost felt a tinge of pity for these chaps. Having to meet these formidable women. Because they now had it all together. They had transmuted what was an interpretation which was very destructive to them into an interpretation which had made them very wise and very strong, gave them an immense sense of power.

What role does the unconscious play in your scheme of things?

Well it seems pretty obvious that you can't hold everything that you know at the time in your conscious mind. So a large part of your meaning structure is there busy being itself, but it's not in your conscious mind. Because you can only hold a little bit in your conscious mind, and at any rate, consciousness is very 'gappy' as Daniel Dennett calls it, bits and pieces come up, and if you hold interpretations like 'it's best not to remember nasty things', then of course you'll be busy not remembering nasty things. Because that's one of the rules that your meaning structure's operating on.

Are you at all eclectic? Freud, Skinner ...

Well these are all alternative interpretations. A good interpretation, a good theory is one which accounts for the facts and is a good predictor. Now back in my Freudian days, I found that Freud's theories, particularly his and Anna Freud's work on the mechanisms of defence, I found that was very helpful in understanding what people were doing, and seeing patterns like the way in which certain people preferred repression rather than isolation. So that part of his theory had good explanatory value. But in terms of prediction and advocation, it wasn't much use at all. It helped me understand but there was no way of putting it in some kind of form that was of use to somebody else.

Whereas some of the stuff that's well-established now in behaviourism, is very applicable with things like the principle of partial reinforcement. I sometimes use those words because people like to hear these funny jargon words. But explaining why you go on doing something which they know harms you. So I talk to people about how they'll go on being depressed, because there's something in being depressed from which you get a benefit, a reward. It's very instructive to say to people: 'What advantages do you get out of being depressed?' They come up with some wonders. I did a series of workshops on self-confidence for business women who said they lacked self-confidence, and I'd say to them right at the beginning of the workshop: 'What are the advantages of lacking self-confidence?', and they'd come up with some really good ones. 'Well if I lack self-confidence I get lots of good compliments from my husband. Lacking self-confidence, I don't ever have to do anything I don't want to do.' Then I explain it's the advantages that you're not prepared to give up, that's why you hang on.

You mentioned earlier the stage you thought when the time was right to end therapy ...

I don't think the time is right. It's when somebody who's been coming to see me every Monday afternoon for two years without fail, and who has complained every time I've gone away on holiday, and who one afternoon when I'm getting out my diary to write in the next appointment, she looks at hers and she says: 'Oh, I can't come next week, I've got a hairdresser's appointment.' Therapy's complete – we're now just having a chat.

Some therapy goes on a long, long time ...

I wonder what's been going on in the therapy all along, because I know with some of my analyst/Jungian/therapist friends and colleagues, their relationship with their client is as important to them personally as it is to the client, perhaps even more. They don't really see themselves as a passing guru at some stage in that person's life – as a teacher who might be of some use, might have something of value to impart, at that particular time for that person. Sheldon Kopp sums it up very well out of his own experience; you know this or shall I tell you the story? He started off as a very bright psychologist from a very crazy family. He went into therapy as a psychologist, asking 'Why do I feel so miserable? Why am I such a horrible person?' And after some years, he discovered that he wasn't a horrible person, that he just felt like that because of the terrible things that had happened in childhood which he'd explained in terms of 'I am a horrible person, and my good parents love me.' So he came out of that therapy feeling that he was a good person, and therefore being good he would get his reward. So he went round doing good to people for a long while. And knowing that by doing good and being good, nothing bad could happen to him. Then he got this terrible brain tumour. So he became very depressed and he was saying: 'Well I've been good, why has this happened to me?' So he came out of therapy with the answer, and the answer is: 'Why not?'

So this is the state that people come into therapy, saying 'I'm an intrinsically bad person, I'm in misery.' The therapist then can help them discover, give them permission to actually look at their childhood and be critical of their parents. Now a vast number of unscrupulous therapists use this as the way of keeping people in therapy, because if you want to go on, you can spend the rest of your life feeling bad about the terrible things you've experienced ... [Pause] ... a lot of therapists do this, so every week it's a matter of the person saying how upset they are. This gives them a wonderful excuse: 'I can't help my mad behaviour. I'm a love addict, or a sex addict' – the whole recovery movement – you never recover, you're always in recovery, and the reason you eat too much, or smoke too much, or drink too much, or shop too much is because of your terrible childhood. It's a wonderful way to make money as a therapist.

Can we talk about the idea of transference?

Can I just go back and finish what I was telling you about, because I was talking about people staying in therapy, and talking about their childhood. The only way they can free themselves from this is for the therapist to help them come to the 'Why not?' Everybody has a bad deal. We don't live in a just world. You've been unlucky. The fact that you've been unlucky in the past doesn't mean you have to be unlucky in the future. You can be lucky, you can be unlucky – it's a matter of chance. If you want to see the world as a just place where goodness is rewarded and badness is punished, you can spend the rest of your life feeling bitter and resentful, because you haven't got your just rewards. Or you can have the courage to see the world as a place where things happen by chance and you can be unlucky, you can be lucky. And when something bad happens to you, well that's bad luck and you bear it the best you can. And when good things happen to you, you just enjoy them: you don't have to bury them by feeling guilty or feeling that you don't deserve it. Now to help a person get to that understanding, all I would do was to use those kinds of interpretations as we talked about this and that. This way, I'm just letting my client grow up, and I'm not hanging on.

I've always seen my job as a therapist is to enable the person to enjoy life, to use the opportunities that are there, and to be able to do that a person needs to think well of himself, and needs to be optimistic.

If as a child you have a mother who regards you as a wonderful person, and who views the world in an optimistic way, then you've got lots of strength to go on and face your own life.

Transference, countertransference ...

The therapist should be able by their own growth and wisdom, to be able to take a stance where they neither want their patient to get better nor not want their patient to get better. Where they don't just operate on the construct 'patient better/patient not better'. Because if you want your patient to get better, your wanting will stop that person from getting better. Because whenever – and this is necessary – in order for the meaning structure to be able to defend itself against all the other meaning structures who want to impose their ideas, whenever we think somebody is putting pressure on us to behave in a certain way, our immediate response is to say 'No'. It's only later on that we sometimes say 'Yes'.

The poor old politicians have this problem all the time, whenever they want to sell us a set of ideas, and advertisers have the same problem. So if your patient is picking up that you have a vested interest in him getting better, then the patient will be resisting and wondering 'what's this all about?'

Do you tell clients/patients what you can and cannot do?

Yes. It'll come out that I haven't got a magic wand or a magic word; that we can look at these things together and try and work out something which can be useful; that it's not for me to say 'this is where we must go, this is where you have to end up', because I don't live that person's life, that person has to live that life.

Should therapists themselves have had a troubled life?

Well, it's pretty hard to get to about 30, and not have suffered one way or the other. One advantage of being a therapist, when you have disasters occur to you, you can always think 'Well at least I've learnt something' ... [Laughs] ... That's one of the advantages. I think there needs to be a desire to see things clearly, and I know that there are a lot of therapists who are quite happy to or want to work in ideas that aren't very clear and structured, and I think 'Well okay, that's how they want to operate', but I don't think that helps other people because they don't know what's on offer. And the way in which words are used – I'm always encountering people who are telling me about how important spirituality is. I will say: 'What do you mean by spirituality?', and no two people ever give me the same interpretation. The one I liked best was the one about all the different spirits that are around – 'Oh, that's an interesting spirituality, yes.' But spirituality lately has acquired the connotation of virtuous. So if you talk about spirituality you seem to be a very virtuous and deep-thinking person. But it's very vague, very vague.

How do you measure success in your work?

Well, whether something's successful, the conversations you have, the only measure of whether they're successful is if the person thinks they are. My friend Jeremy Halstead has been doing this research for a long while now, and he's part of the David Shapiro team at Sheffield University. Jeremy has been giving his clients questionnaires to fill in after each session and such. He found that people were very clear as to whether they feel they've been helped and what's been helpful. That's the only measure. They have to live their lives. A lot of the people that I saw in therapy in Lincolnshire, I saw them for a long time, and a lot of them I've kept in touch with. So I've got long-term outcomes, and the one thing that's very clear is that people end up doing things that I would never have predicted them doing. Things that wouldn't even have crossed my mind that they would do. Because once a person really grasps that you've got choices about how you interpret, and then choices about what you do – then they make all sorts of choices, amazing choices.

Not a lot is known about the social organisation of construct psychology ...

When you talk about personal construct theory, or personal construct psychology, it's a very diverse group, and I've always divided this into three groups. Three groups which became very apparent right from the earliest days of having International Conferences.

First of all there are the Kelly men and women. They carry the little red book of Kelly around with them, and you always know whether they're a Kellyian, because every article they write either starts with an epigraph from Kelly, or begins with the words 'As Kelly said ...'

Then there are the 'gridders'. The people who only feel comfortable when they've reduced human experience to numbers.

Then the rest is just a rag-bag of individuals who go off and do all sorts of interesting things.

Can we talk about keeping files/records, things like that ...

Well, like most people, I just love it when somebody tells me a story, and my dad was a great storyteller, and he could make up stories. So the best days of my childhood would be Dad telling me a story. So for me to have a job where I was actually paid to listen to people tell me stories, I think 'This is wonderful.' I've often heard therapists have discussions about keeping notes and keeping records, but I never wrote anything down, except when I transmuted it into stories into my books, because – for one practical reason I didn't want to put on paper stuff which psychiatrists could then call for – if I didn't have notes nobody could read them.

Then the other thing was I didn't need to have notes, because I remembered. When the sessions were week to week, or fortnight to fortnight, a person would come in and he'd have the agenda of what he wanted to talk about, so I didn't need to draw up an agenda. When that person started to talk, even if I hadn't been rehearsing the details of this person's life – but once he started to talk, I'd recall all the relevant things. When I left the Health Service in '86 and went to Sheffield to live, I thought at that stage I would have to do private practice in order to have enough money. So I started doing some private practice, but what I disliked about it was that I was no longer part of a group. I didn't have any other colleagues to go and talk to. Not necessarily about what went on in therapy, but just not having other people there. When after a couple of years I realised that financially I didn't need to do it, I just stopped doing it. The other thing was I had been responsible for people since I was born – Alice Miller, in her book *The Drama of the Gifted Child*, talks about 'the child who right from birth is expected by the mother to mother the mother', and so makes this great leap forward in that kind of intelligence. I was just tired of supporting people, and by that time my son didn't need any sort of support, except sometimes he'd ring up and tell me his problems at work which I was interested in and I thought: 'That's all I want'.

Some people say that working-class people are not amenable to 'talking therapies' ...

Well on the verbal thing, what I've found working with working-class people in Lincolnshire, many of whom had extremely limited education, on most topics they might find it difficult to discuss/express, but once they talked about themselves they had all the vocabulary necessary and they had the most wonderful metaphors. You'd hear the metaphors when they were describing an experience, then you could talk about that metaphor: 'Oh that felt like such and such, yes. I've always seen my father as this great big bear of a man who's coming after me to get me.' That's no problem: we're all very, very good at talking about our own experience provided we feel the person we're talking to is actually interested.

[Then] on the paying for it. Well, I just see this as being an irrelevancy, because the NHS people were paying for it, they pay their taxes. So they certainly weren't getting it for free. But the way things have turned out now it means that so many people can't get therapy. A couple of weeks ago when I was in the States, I was at the 10th Anniversary Conference of Depressed Anonymous there, and the two counsellors that I was talking to, the organiser and his assistant, they were each having terrible problems in their own finances because they knew that the people who needed their help couldn't afford to pay them. They just couldn't see a way around that. They really didn't want to spend time with paying clients when they knew there were so many people out there who desperately needed help.

You see there's such a lot of people in the States now who don't have health insurance. The dreadful thing that's happened in the States is that psychologists are now locked into the DSM4 [*Diagnostic and Statistical Manual of Mental Disorders* 4th edition], and they have to fit their clients into that mould. It's all very well to say: 'Oh well I just do that for the insurance form'; you actually have to think about it, it becomes part of your own construct system.

Should there be ethical guidelines in therapeutic work?

I think we can certainly have guidelines, but I think it starts with the person's own feelings. I think we should recognise the dilemma that a client comes to you because the client hopes that you have the power to make things better. So the client projects power on to you and a lot of therapists are very happy for that to happen. So the therapist, in my way of seeing it, and Sheldon Kopps' way of seeing it, is to say: 'No, I don't have that power.' I think that we should be very careful when we interfere in other people's lives.

Will registration help?

Yes, it has a value, for the clients. Because it means if you suffer at the hands of a therapist there's a legal form of redress. So I think that's good. But I don't think it has any advantages for the therapist, except one that I don't approve of: the struggle for power. This enterprise for registration – it's gone on for how many years, about 15 years now – and when it started the psychoanalysts said: 'Well, of course we're the only ones who are properly trained. So we're the only ones who can be registered.' When they were hammered on that position, they then came up with: 'Well we're the ones who should judge whether other people should be registered' ... [Laughs] ... That's the position they're trying to hold on to now.

Now there's all this business of people trying to get more and more therapists into their groups. Someone wrote to me quite plaintively a year or so ago, and asked me if I'd join the personal construct group, and get registered under that umbrella. She didn't tell me at the time how much that was going to cost me in money, because the smaller the number of people the bigger the amount of money you have to pay out. So I'd have been much better joining the behaviourists, I think. Financially better ... [Laughs] ...

So many people worry about whether they're being good therapists, and they look at other therapists to measure that. They don't look at the people they're actually listening to. Which is the only measure.

Should 'emotional literacy' be taught at schools?

Can you give me a definition of emotional literacy? ... [Laughs]

Well ... [Pause] ...

I'll bet you got that from Susie Orbach. I think there's lots of things they could teach, like – as small children we learn very complex ideas on the basis of marks on paper being given certain meanings, and the basis of music and maths, and such. But we're deliberately not given an under-standing of physiology and the way in which we each create our own individual structure. Because anyone who understands that simply doesn't become a good, obedient child, and doesn't grow up to be a good, obedi-ent citizen. So if we did have courses on emotional literacy, or whatever, they'd set up norms. You're allowed to get angry legitimately but not illegitimately, whatever that might mean. This is what people ought to feel, and if you don't feel that then there's something wrong with you. All these courses in self-esteem that they run in the States, and which is just so phoney because saying things isn't the same as feeling it, knowing it.

Are your books more about 'self-help' than anything else?

I started off writing about depression because I sat in case conferences and worked on wards and saw the terrible, dreadful cruelties inflicted on people, and part of the cruelty was the way in which they weren't told anything. They were told lies, lies. And they're still told lies. When I was at this Conference in Louisville, a psychiatrist gave a talk about his work with depressed people, and he talked about chemical imbal-ance and how this scientist had discovered it. So I said, 'Now I happen to be an Associate of the Royal College of Psychiatrists and I always read their journal. Now this research you were quoting about chemical imbalance ...' So we had this little discussion and he backtracked com-pletely and said he told people they had a chemical imbalance because he wanted to give them hope. That rubbish is still going on.
   So I wrote about depression to give people the information, so they can make up their own minds about what they want to do. It's a way of undercutting the powers of the state and the church that want to keep us in misery, for their own benefit. And giving people, helping people to see that they have got choices.

What are you up to these days?

Trying to get this house straightened out ... [Laughs] ... What I'm doing specifically is, I'm about to do an update of *Depression – The Way Out of Your Prison* because Vivienne Ward of Routledge has asked me. For the last nearly three years I've been going round getting people to talk about how they interpret money. And that's fascinating. So I've got to write that book, I'm supposed to hand it in at the end of the year, but I haven't got that far.

Money and distress?

Just money generally. I've been talking to money men. Everybody's interested, so you see I've been talking to the money men, the men – futures and options, and derivative traders and so on. And they all want to know about fear. They get really interested when they discover what I do, because they want to know why does the market move? The market doesn't move, it's the people who buy and sell. So why, why?

CHAPTER 7

Humanistic/Transpersonal Psychology

Paul Taylor

Paul Taylor combines numerous traditions and techniques –
many from the East and some mystical – in his London-based
psychotherapy practice.

Can you talk about getting into this kind of work?

Well the background is, when I was a child, I was into History and at
the age of five and six was copying out dates in Ancient History and
was very much attracted to Greece, Egypt and India. I was fascinated
by the film directed by Alexander Korda – *The Elephant Boy.* I felt I
had something to do with India. Also when young, I was very involved
with Shakespeare at about the age of ten and eleven and read Shakespeare plays; as they broadcast them on the radio, I read them. I
eventually became involved in acting and the theatre.

During my acting career and going to drama school, with the work I
did on the body I definitely had what we call a Kundalini wakening – a
Shakti awakening about the age of 18 – when I was listening to Mozart's
Flute and Harp Concerto; all of a sudden the head went back and I
experienced a kind of spiritual ecstasy. I was starting to be interested in
meditation about that time. The yoga teacher said: 'Keep your head level,
let the eyes go up, no rolling back of the head, let the eyes go up here to
the third eye.' Of course, my eyes at that level, because of the restlessness
of the mind, were very, very jumpy!

Slowly through my twenties, I looked at different yogic disciplines.
Then at the age of 28, because of a rather hedonistic lifestyle, I contracted psoriasis and was unwell, but was still into yoga. I had left
working in the theatre by then and started living in the mountains in
Wales in a very isolated house, which, with a friend, I restored. I think
many people in the early '70s took to the hills, to live and find a more
natural lifestyle. I kept bees, kept a garden, and there was no electricity
in the house; spring water – we built a well, a bore well – a very much
getting back to the earth and to the roots.

I think that for me was a part of male initiation – that thing of
building your own house as a man was a very important step for my
consciousness. I think many of the basic initiations into masculinity
seem to be done only through competition; the football field and the

pub. This is not enough. Because of the male consciousness being blown apart by the First and Second World War, with that a basic lack of trust happened with the masculine principle; men not trusting men. Our fathers after the War withdrew emotionally from life and their sons. I was born in 1947 so I felt that very strongly. My father used to say reading the paper: 'Do as your mother said, I don't want any problems here.' When I was in CND in the late '70s, doing the kind of Ghandian-type of protest – sitting down and getting arrested – I went to jail actually for a week, which was very interesting; I learnt a great amount, going 'inside'. My father said: 'Well, it's up to you lot now, I've done my bit.' It's that withdrawal of the masculine, after the War, from collective responsibility, a withdrawal from life. Last year during the D-Day com- memorations I said after much thought: 'Thank you, Dad, for fighting the war.' There was a silence; then he said: 'No one has ever thanked me before.' It was a deep reconciliation between us.

So Wales was very much finding my masculine strength through the elemental earth energies. Then, after that with the psoriasis, the illness, I realised I had to make a big step and went to India. I went on a yoga teachers' training course in Southern India. All of a sudden my lower back erupted in boils as part of the purification process. This was very much what I call the cleansing of the hereditary miasm – the hereditary physical traits releasing themselves through the yoga. However, on the yoga course at that time, nobody could really deal with that type of problem. Somebody on the course said: 'Go into town, there's an old man there, and I am sure he can help you.' And that's when I really met my Teacher. His name was Dr Padmanabha Pillai. He was able to say 'this and this, then this, then you do this and this.' He just hit the nail on the head all the time what I should do. He said, 'Go around India for eight months and come back in a year's time. If you're cleaned up I'll take you further on the development with your yoga.' He was very much of the style of Guru Kula Vasa – living in the house of the teacher, not a big organisation. He only had two or three students around him at a time. He practised a very deep massage, and certain yogic techniques, which made sense of the yoga: of all the odd bits and pieces that I'd worked on. So I went around India. I went up to a place called Badrinath, in the Himalayas, which many Indians try to do a pilgrimage to. This place is to help release the energy of the ancestors. This is the basic personality structure, the conditioned structures that we have: physical, emotional and mental.

I had an amazing experience of releasing toxic energy there. I remem- ber my eyes pussed and I couldn't see for three days. Just a whole lower chakra, ancestral release. The three base chakras are very much to do with the ancestral energy. I came back to England after eight months and had some tests. I was very clean and cleared up; the psoriasis, everything had healed. Then I went back and spent six months with Padmanabha Pillai in Kerala. During that time he really took me through what we call the subtle world dimensions. Connections to his dead teacher in the astral; deep meditation experiences for six months. In the end I was connected to a lineage called the Siddhas. He then said: 'You are now ready to teach and channel.'

So I came back to England and started working in Wales. I'd met somebody in India, another homoeopath, because I am also a homoeopath, and we started a practice in Wales together. What had happened in India was that I had understood the yoga of India through my teacher. However, I was very fascinated to understand what was the esoteric inner tradition of the West. So where was it? Where were the traditions which talk to knowing thyself and healing oneself? That inner tradition seemed very lost. It was very clear that in India their exoteric – that means the external religious structures – never persecuted the inner, internal tradition of yoga. It was always able to coexist.

When I was in Wales I was surrounded by many Jewish women. With my colleague, Annie, we invited a man from the Wrekin Trust called Henry Brown who introduced me to the Jewish Kabbalah.

This, I began to realise, is our western inner tradition. It's the inner tradition behind Judaism, Christianity and Islam and is also the connection between Sufism, Gnosticism and the Jewish tradition of 'Otz Chim', the Tree of Life. I began to become very interested in that, and I studied it with Henry for about a year. Then my Indian teacher came to England; he did a course of Yoga Therapy at Cambridge University. We took about 40 ill people, and with doctors and using his methods – there's a report in the *Alternative Medicine Journal* on that – we had a great success. He went to Wales, Devon, Scotland and London. When he left he said, 'You stay in London and work in London, because this is where the centre will be, where people will come and see you.'

That happened in 1985 and – well, I never looked back – I never looked back from when I first met him. A whole transformation took place. His Yoga was one of ease, of gentleness and certainly not one of competition. He took all the competitive side out of Yoga and the conditioning that we have about competing with each other spiritually and on other levels.

So I came to London and started practising. Then, suddenly something happened with the Tree of Life and the Judaic tradition. What my work has been to do, is to pull the Yoga of the West with the Tree, and the Yoga of the East together. That seems to have been my destiny. I worked in London for a couple of years – 1985, 1986 – and then started collectively working with the Tree and the Yoga. I formulated a small circle from my practice. The numbers doubled in the second year, trebled, and then another teacher arrived, and we've had a seven year cycle with a collective called the 'School of the Tree of Life'. An inner esoteric teaching which is not advertised, nothing is written, it is verbally taught.

I was born in the West, and my destiny lies here. Therefore, in finding the western tradition I've been able to link and bridge, as before that I never felt comfortable in western society. With this tradition I've been able to make that bridge. It's very interesting, a friend of mine called

Nasser who actually teaches Yoga here, he was a trainee bridge-builder, he's Iranian and he said: 'Paul in Iranian means bridge.' I felt very much this whole thing of bridging the eastern and western traditions. I feel I've been very gifted and blessed in being able to do this work.

It seems the lineage I've been connected to are my guides, as I have no earthly boss. Their direction and backup that I've had from them has brought about the 'School of the Tree of Life'. It is now in its second seven-year cycle and – as in all energetic things – has gone through a period of creation, preservation and breaking down for transformation, a destruction. The school is actually now going through a new period of creation. I am very much a great believer in the seven-year cycle, and that's what much of my work with individuals is based on.

What do you do, you think, that is different from other therapists?

Well, the thing is I don't know. With my connections and my teacher who has now died, I've not felt the need, I don't over-investigate what other people are actually doing out there. I've just been on a journey with this discipline and I felt, because of the connections I have made with it, I'm incredibly contented just to channel and be with that. So, I am not very versed in what people are doing out there. At first, when I started in Wales, yes, I was. There was that competitive thing 'what am I doing?'; that insecurity in my development. I've become very confident over the years of the approach I take and the results that are rapidly achieved with people.

Okay. How would you describe what you do?

Well, many people come through that door at the age of 28. And what I start explaining to them, and – can I explain this to you? They come in and of course they have an agenda, so to put them at ease I will give them a little bit of my agenda first. Then they can respond to that accordingly. Basically you take the Chakra system. It's all about the personality, the soul and the spiritual connections of the soul to the spiritual Source, the creative Source. So, I would talk about the fact that your soul has been attracted through the love-making of your parents, the energetic field of the parents to make a descent into life in order to discover itself. So the soul is drawn to the seed of the father and the womb of the mother. It enters – that is the consciousness of the parents, as a reflection of one's own soul consciousness – as we make this descent into life. The level of parental love being a reflection of the level of love developed in the soul. The parental conflicts seem also to be a reflection of the conflict of the soul karma of the individual. We come to earth to resolve this conflict. Many of us are attempting on an inner level to be resolving the parental conflicts, bringing conflict to resolution.

We talk about the third eye – pituitary gland – as we make this descent on the line of the spine, through the vagus nerve and the endocrine glands that seem to formulate first at birth. So we make this descent through the third eye, through the throat chakra, to the heart, which is the resting place of the soul. Then the solar plexus develops, then we become a sex, either male or female, after ten/eleven weeks in the womb, then we come out into earthly reality after nine months of inner development.

So we have made this descent into life. The vagus nerve which connects these centres is the core of our inner life. So there's the pituitary gland, the mind – the consciousness. The throat – the thyroid – creativity and communication and metabolic rate. The thymus – which controls locked emotional memory recall; the immune system; the gland of the child; and the centre of the centres, the Being part of ourselves. The adrenal glands, the energy power of will – what you genetically inherit. Then the split into one sex or the other, the prostate and reproductive organs, with sexuality very much to do with self-image and the survival mechanisms, the libido. Then finally, out into the world. What I tell people is that it's about the exploration of those levels and the opening up of that potential. So it's about ascent of potential, the journey back. Looking at the Tree of Life – the descent from Kether – you pick up your father's seed, your mother's womb; you carry certain soul awareness, because I do believe in the philosophy of reincarnation – the evolution of the soul over many lifetimes. The positive karma, the positive thing which we have learnt and then the negative burdens, the inner conflicts which we are here to resolve into greater consciousness, truth and an expansion of love. Then the establishment of the heart – the seat of the soul – which resonates the space of Being. Then the ancestral energy; the male hormones – the female hormones; the split into sexuality; and then out into the world.

So it's about the journey of life, our expansion of potential and healing of the soul in life. What I would say to the client in therapy sessions: it's about that journey back; it's about remembering in order to forget and become empty once more, a process which creates a space to be who we are. Only then are we truly happy. So the consciousness remembers the process that the body holds – it has 72,000 nerve cells – and each of those cells has a cellular memory of the past. So, why are we unhappy? That possibly is within that cellular memory, there's a burden or there's a trauma. It's about releasing those traumas so we can make the ascent, the return to the source of life, to God.

So, I very much see 0–7 years of the life, the first seven years the aura is connected to the mother. Many women know that at about seven years, there's a whole transformation/change where the child becomes more independent from the mother. And then 7–14 years, where the child is inclined to go out into the world; discover the world. The role of the father becomes much more apparent at 7–14 years, as the child is directed out – school, etc. Then at 14 years, puberty, from 14–21 years the development of the sexual fantasy – the attraction, the orientation as a sexual being. By 21, what we call the ego – the conditioning – is totally formulated, and people quite often think they are red hot by 21 years and they know it all. But they find out – during their twenties they go through certain experiences – as a reflection of this conditioning, that possibly who they are and what that conditioning is are two different things. The split between the ego and the soul becomes more apparent. It takes Saturn 28 years to go around the Sun, and Saturn has nine moons, symbolic of the nine months of the gestation period. This represents very much the planet of the mother. So at 28 years people almost feel they are back in the womb – they have to face that first seven-year cycle, they have to face something about the early traumas, the early consciousness of themselves. If we don't work that out at 28, 35, 42, 49 and so on through the seven-year cycles – because through these cycles you are confronted with the inner self – and that's the period when great upheavals and transformations take place. If we don't confront these inner things, we become more and more split; we can become ill later on.

I quite often say: 'Unless we face the enemy within ourselves, the pain in ourselves, we don't really heal the soul.' What many people do is to externalise the internal enemy. We go into blame. We blame the parents, we blame society. We don't take responsibility for our pain. We'd rather face a troop full of enemy soldiers, where we've externalised that enemy, than face the pain in our own consciousness. Love has many, many dimensions; multiple dimensions, including the pain within our own hearts. It's very simple if we are willing to confront our fear, our grief, our anger. Deal with that and be responsible for that! Become conscious of its nature! Why are we holding suppressed feelings against our parents, against society, against our teachers, against ...? We quite often project that enemy on to the people we love, and have relationships with. So we very much have become a 'blame society' not taking responsibility for the Self. We can only be truly happy if we can heal the relationship with the parents and then we can have successful, happy relationships, because there is so much projection on to partners from our conditioning. We don't seem to be able to establish very happy relationships particularly in this period; with the basic fracture that's happened between the masculine and feminine principles, reflecting the deepening split between the Ego and the Soul.

Then ...

After I've talked a while with the client, I would then set an agenda according to where I felt their whole vibration to be, where they were coming from. I would have some ideas. Within the first ten/fifteen minutes of talking – I just talk ad hoc – I seem to hit off on their agenda somehow. This connection is quite quickly made. That's the intuitive part of my work. Then I will ask them 'Well, why have you come here?' and they will start saying perhaps: 'Problems with relationships, I keep following a similar pattern. Every two years I seem to start a relationship and every two years I finish it.' Then I will possibly say, 'Well, what is your relationship with the parents?'

I really start going into, very quickly, the relationship with their mother and father. What has happened in that process? I might make some observations, like a man who – I'll give you an example – a man who had a relationship that lasted three years. The third year he seemed to reject the woman he'd been having the relationship with. It was quite simple, at the age of three his mother left him. So he has deeply in his psyche, in his cellular memory, 'I am going to be rejected at three years', as a reflection of that. So I suggested to him as he'd just split with his girlfriend – this came up in the first session – that we have to look at that abandoned child at the age of three. What you're doing is you're rejecting your partner before she rejects you because you expect to be rejected in the third year of the relationship.

That's a very simplistic thing but it hit off on something immediate in him and from there we started our Yoga therapy relationship. He then asked, 'Well, what do I have to do?' I said, 'You have to heal the pain of that rejection and stop projecting it on to everybody that you're having a relationship with.' So he went back to that woman and got the relationship together and eventually married her. He was working with me during that time. We were overcoming the fear that he was going to be rejected. That sounds very simplistic, but in the first session that resonated something in him.

I then draw six columns and say, 'This is your homework.' Having convinced the client that their process is to become conscious of the parental laws and the formation of their personality through the genetic, ancestral, myths and conditioning, I get them to draw six columns: negative feelings – past, present, father; positive feelings – past, present, father; negative – past, present, mother; positive – past, present, mother; negative – self, past, present; positive – self, past, present.

We discuss a little of that in the session, and they go away and they work on that. Also, I get them to look at the 'personal law'; that is attitudes given to them by parents, relationships, relatives, work, school: for example, my father was told 'little boys should be seen and not heard'. He was an introverted man and whenever people came around he headed off to the drinks cabinet, or to the garden, because his little boy – he believed – was to be seen and not heard. This was a value maxim, this was a personal law of his. He woke up to this at 60 and began to confront that. He had colluded with my mother so she'd done all the talking, she'd done all the socialising for him. He began to be heard. So we worked on that personal law, becoming conscious of the laws he had been given; enabling him to break with those conditioned patterns through self-awareness.

Then, the client, in a second session, comes back to me, and we start really investigating those negatives/positives, and personal laws. Within two or three sessions we can get to the root of some of the personality problems that the person has. We are either like the parents, negative/positive: the masculine psyche identifying with the father's negative/positive; the feminine psyche in us identifying with the mother's negative/positive. We are either like them or we compensate for them. We swing to the opposite of them and quite often go into rebellion mode. So if the mother was very talkative and chat, chat, chat, and the child is very introverted, the child will go very silent. If the child is extroverted in its nature, the child will go into competition with the mother and just be fighting for air space.

That's just an example of these polarities on the male/female psyche as seen through the conditioning of the parents. Then we will start going into the way the parents loved, because the next part of the personality agenda is to do with co-dependency. The co-dependent is to do with the victim, persecutor, rescuer syndrome as seen through the way the child perceives love and the way the parents loved. The relationship to love with the parents. What we do in adult relationships – quite often we're playing out a parent/child syndrome, instead of having an adult coexistent, interdependent relationship.

So, I also start covering the nature of addiction – of course people have many ways of escaping from themselves through alcohol, sex, drugs, food, even using spirituality. People can even use Yoga and meditation to escape from who they are. I do not allow that. By discussing co-dependency I am also preventing the client from becoming co-dependent on me. I learnt that one pretty quickly. Although I am helping a client, and I'm taking them into the nature of their child and their conditioning, with covering co-dependency, I'm getting it clear they can't become co-dependent and over-reliant on me.

So that's a fourth, fifth, sixth session as we build into it. Also at this point I'm using homoeopathy, starting to give them homoeopathic remedies. Perhaps I've covered through a session the Bach Flower Remedies and asked them, 'Are you like this? Are you like this according to the Bach Flower Remedy Diagnosis?' I am also making an analysis of them homoeopathically. I treat them homoeopathically on very high potencies, using the psychological and emotional diagnosis I've done through the parental law, through the negative/positive parent work. The homoeopathy is shifting things on another level.

That's the early sessions. Then on top of that I teach them a grounding exercise. One of the great exercises my teacher taught me was a breathing exercise of using a throaty voice, which re-stimulates the vagus nerve; the nerve which connects each of the centres, the central core nervous system. In stimulating that nervous system, I'm connecting the person up immediately to their centre. At the same time, each breath is re-birthing this centre and bringing itself into life and grounding them. Because it's such a simple exercise – as most people can't do three hours meditation a day; they are at work, have families, they have relationships – but they can do this one exercise, at any place and at any time. It's very useful.

Part of my work is helping people into life. People have many unconscious death wishes. They don't want to be here in life. It's a painful experience for some people, but a joyous experience on another level. We've got to arrive at that happiness and joy. And so much of my work is about grounding them, rooting them. At the same time examining reality; what they are doing in the world. Examining their survival mechanisms, their self-image, their sexuality, the 'I' of themselves. Then, examining the emotional seat, their energy power and will. If the psyche is split between the heart and the head, the will to do is weak. So this joining, 'Yoga' means to join – union – joining a person to themselves, connecting themselves to their centre, to the heart, the seat of the soul. There is a point in the heart, it's like the centre of the sun, the centre of any revolving body, a centre of stillness, a centre of knowing. The soul and the soul nature – this is where we get into the controversial area of reincarnation – according to a person's evolution, to where they're at. I do have methods whereby I take people into that soul journey and help them understand. The whole thing – birth/death – the way we come in and the way we go out.

If you believe in the theory of reincarnation, the way we die and the way the soul then sums up life's experience at the moment of death: 'Oh, that was a waste of time, nobody loved me. I'll never be loved', and out the body they go. Well, obviously they haven't reconnected to the love of God at that point. That is not the will of God. The will of God is for us to become conscious, expand consciousness, expand truth, expand love in life. To celebrate God's creation and life. That's where I hope to be able to take my clients, to help them discover that for themselves. I'm a facilitator, I'm a teacher, I'm a Yoga therapist. That is my intention. That's to do with the heart and the soul.

Then their creativity and communication. Fears around that, around being successful. What they are doing in life? Are they fulfilled? Have they found their destiny? Because unless we find our destiny, we are not truly happy in what we're doing. Then the mind and consciousness. The mind and consciousness are divided into four. One: the consciousness – the seer, the viewer; two: all the thoughts – the chit-chat; three: the discrimination – the choices we make, the 'yes' and the 'no'; and four: the ego, the conditioned mind. With this witness consciousness being the overviewer of the second, third and fourth parts of the mind. This is known as 'squaring of the circle'. I often say 'the wise person stills the mind and allows the unconditional love to be connected to the heart, the centre of centres, and at the same time, also to connect to heaven, to the higher potential of ourselves.'

Then, ultimately, the top Chakra. Our relationship to spirituality. As God and life are synonymous; unless we really have come to terms with life, that relationship with God is very tenuous. I find a lot of people blaming: they don't like life, they don't like God. They have a hidden agenda with God. Of course they have a conditioned agenda through religion with God, and their conditioning from their parents or whatever has been placed on them in their culture. Each individual has to find their own relationship to God, and that is different for every one of us.

God is beyond mind or thought; it's a sense of the presence of a field of energy. A sense of awe. It cannot be mentally defined; only sensed and experienced. This is to do with the esoteric way of 'know thyself'. Coming to terms with our life and God. That's the process. The Chakras are the potential. The Tree of Life and its structure is our journey of return to the Source.

What is very sad in religion – I feel religion has lost the ability to teach about life, these things, these stages, these cycles. What happens when a woman gets pregnant? People are not really taught any more about the philosophy of life or the science of the soul. That's where I contribute in teaching people; understanding cycles, pregnancy, what happens after you've had a baby – what you're going to feel. People just come into these stages in life on a very unconscious level. There's no structure or guidance. Sadly, because of the disharmony in religions and the antagonisms, some people are saying: 'We're right, you're wrong', people are alienated from that. However, they still need to find themselves. I feel, part of my role and the whole role of therapy that's now being set – the discovery of 'knowing thyself' is a very key one; the discovery of life's structures.

I also go into sexuality, self-image, the shame and the guilt felt around this area. I go into the subtle nature of the feminine G-spot and its connection to satisfactory orgasm. Many men are disconnected from the knowledge of their own prostate gland. The lack of understanding and of the function of the prostate gland and ignorance of this area causes much illness and problems later on in life for men. There seems to be disconnection for our deep masculine understanding of the nature of spiritual and sexual ecstasy.

Is it always you teaching the client?

No. I receive and listen then respond to what is appropriate. As I said, I have to adjust my communication according to their process. I have talked about my basic philosophy. Of course, a woman who's got a backache, might come for homoeopathy only. That backache is a reflection of something psychological and emotional, it's to do with support. The way she might be supported or support herself. So some people just come on that physical level. If they do, I will get to the psychological and emotional causes of that quite quickly. Then I suggest a process for them, that they could follow – possibly diet, Yoga classes. I'm very much for people actually working on their physical body and taking responsibility. Although I don't teach Yoga *asanas* now, there are three or four classes a week here and I will send clients to other people who can help them on the physical level.

I'm always giving people the slight nudge. Nudging them a little further. I don't nudge them too quickly as I used to in the early days. I have become more experienced; I've been working now for 14 years with people. I just seem to be able to hit it more on the level to give them the appropriate directive nudge! I am directional in my work. I don't just let them sit here hour in and hour out and chat on. I'm definitely suggestive to what they can do to facilitate their process, to involve their souls, to engage themselves deeper into life.

I have been influenced by Jung, the anima and the animus. I see that as a reflection of the left and right pillars of the Tree, and the ida and pingala in Yoga – subtle channels of the left/right sides of the body – the polarities. Without those polarities there's no movement, there's no frisson, there's no evolution. There has to be that tension, but at the same time I give people a sense of their centre. Many people don't have a sense of their centre.

How long might the process take?

One moment or many lifetimes! It is Jacob's ladder and there's a definite step-by-step process. I've mentioned the first two steps – co-dependency and relationship with parents. Then, what? Many people in our society are emotionally repressed, because we've been told as a child, especially for little girls: 'Don't be angry, you can cry, but don't be angry', for little boys: 'Don't cry, but yes you can be angry. You can express that.' Everybody has a certain suppression of emotions and that's very much held in the solar plexus. So many people are damping down their potential of their power, their will, many people are locked into fear. This is all to do with the breath. If it's fear, we hold the breath. If it's anger, it's a 'rrrr'; we don't think these feelings, we feel them in the body, whether it's grief or the rhythm of joy. Thus, after a while, they will lay down on my floor, I will put a blanket over them and start a Yoga technique called *Bastrika*, which means the removal of emotional ghosts; a process of connected breathing.

I will begin to support them in their breath rhythm. Now the breath has a direct connection to this cellular memory and the unconscious. What I am supporting a person to do is to breathe out on the exhale traumatic emotional memory. So I start a client doing connected breaths. Then, I do group cathartic workshops with the School. Possibly, I will introduce them to Yoga and to the School for them to work collectively when they are ready. People behave very differently in here on a one-to-one than when I see them collectively within a group. That will be to do with the collective conditioning they have had with school, work, etc., different behavioural patterns happening.

So I like to see people work with me individually, and then collectively. Many have a fear of people. That's when cigarettes come out, that's when the suppression comes out. You go to a party and all of a sudden a new person walks in the room and people immediately light up out of fear. Of course, much of my work is to try and get people out of their destructive, addictive patterns; off smoking, off alcohol. Addiction is a reflection of emotional repressive patterns; an inability to let go of a craving and replace it with spiritual longing. I don't use sledgehammer techniques, but slowly just work with the breath releasing suppressed emotion which is locked in the body. Clients can only bring up what they can bring up in their time and space.

There's bodywork. Bodywork can be to do with massage, acupuncture, cranial osteopathy, which I might send people to. It's interesting; I can send clients to other people, but they also seem to end up coming back here, because I am part of a thread of their growth. I am very clear. So I'm able to get people to be very clear of a through line, working through personality into their being, who they are, to the soul. Then, taking them further along the journey, through reincarnation work to their soul law, and possibly clearing some of that so they can eventually connect to spirit and become empty once more to receive God.

In other words, I believe we've evolved from this creative source called 'God'. We are an aspect of that creative God force. I believe within the soul's evolution we are returning God to God. A very fine writer of the Tree of Life called Warren Kenton, 'Halevi', said that God got bored on a Sunday afternoon – and God was this pure consciousness, and exploded Creation of which we are the physical evolution. I particularly see that in evolving ourselves. God evolves us. So we are evolving God; in the physical mandala of this Universe from the sun to Pluto. This is a reflection of our own inner consciousness and of our own physical reality. Returning God to God. The descent and then the ascent; a journey home.

Do some of your clients not want to take it that far?

Ah, that's to do with the nature of their unconscious or how much their soul is burdened. A space has to be given to that. What I've perceived, I might work with somebody for a year then that relationship which has eluded them is there all of a sudden. They end up in a relationship and they end up married and happy. I no longer see them. I feel that people in good relationships mirror each other deeply, so I become redundant. My mirroring is no longer required. What has happened in their relationship? Their parental conditioning, because they've become a mother, their own mother agenda has come up on a deeper level. They've become a father so their father conditioning has come up on a deeper level. I'll find them knocking on my door and perhaps wanting a joint counselling session. The mirror has become cloudy. I do much joint work with people now, which is very exciting. It's working with the couple. They've come to a point where they are not communicating, they're blocked off and resistant to each other. The love they have shared has opened up their heart. Perhaps to the point of soul pain. They can't progress beyond that pain together. So they return to me who – already knowing their background – can help once more.

Again I am working very much into life, into the realities of life, into the realities of relationships. People sometimes become stuck on some level, so they can't evolve further at this stage, that's quite difficult. Some people's development isn't entirely with me, so they have to move on, especially as far as their spiritual process is concerned, to disciplines which are nothing to do with me. I'm very much located Middle East/ India. Some might have a connection with North American Indians on a karmic level, on a soul level. They might be attracted to African culture. Aborigines – well, I do have a connection to – but I don't have very much connection to Japanese and Chinese cultures. It's not in my soul experience. This is what we call the soul *samskaras* memory. I remember one woman, working with her for couple of years, and all of a sudden she entered a deep relationship with Islam. That's where our spiritual development broke off. I've taken people to certain levels, but I am not totally their through-line to God. They break off into other areas. It's the nature of the unconscious, this area of the unknown. I deeply believe when people talk about the perfect teacher, the perfect master, it does not exist. The spiritual teacher is only there to facilitate the growth of the inner teacher within the soul of the student at certain stages.

Even Christ on the cross showed his vulnerability and humanity in Gethsemene: 'Why have you forsaken me, I don't want to do this. This is going to be painful. Why have you put me in this situation? Why have you forsaken me?' A crisis of faith on the cross, revealing his pain and humanness.

There's that area of unconscious in us all. I do believe that God, the creative force, is always ahead of us. The unconscious is God's carrot stick to draw us to the knowing of God. Always one, two, three, four steps ahead of us. As the teacher, I'm a mediator as part of the client's evolutionary process. Each individual has, as I said, their own relationship to that creative force in their own destiny with that. They must find that for themselves.

You don't train people obviously ...

Yes, in fact, I have trained people through the 'School of the Tree of Life', through the work of that and through the Yoga. Yoga teachers emerge from the work and what I did with my original teacher, so passing on that knowledge of my teacher in India, and his lineage. Great friends and relationships have also been my teachers. Life is the teacher. Teachers definitely come out of the methods that the 'School of the Tree of Life' has evolved. If I'm working with somebody, and they are a trainee counsellor, they might pick up some of my methods, they will use them. I'm free with those methods, I don't set a course, I don't charge people for it. The information is free and they take it and do what they have to according to their soul growth. Within the school there are four or five teachers – or is it seven? – who have emerged from the School and are out there communicating aspects of what I've taught. They are having sessions with people, they are using the breath, using the series of breathing exercises I was taught, using the conscious breath. What I've not done, is written a book and I don't intend to at this point. If I did write a book it would be autobiographical: how all of these things have transformed my life; something very personal.

What my teacher taught was part of a verbal tradition. Actually, some of the teaching of the Tree and of the breath are only to be taught verbally. They are not to be written. So, that answers that question. There are some people who are following these techniques.

Now your second question?

The necessary skills of a therapist?

At the age of 28 I went back to my parents, I'd had a deep fracture with them in my twenties – part of the rebellious period, the breaking with them. Then I went back, and began to put the relationship consciously together on a very deep level. And from 28 to 35 I worked on my relationship with my own parents. Everything that I teach, I've done and experienced myself. I teach from that point. My parents are my friends; we have a wonderful relationship with each other. It's not a duty thing, but now a deep, deep understanding of them and myself.

The first step that every therapist should take is to heal the relationship with their own parents. Then, from that, they can begin to have successful relationships with other people on an intimate level. Purification. I don't smoke. I don't drink. I treat my body well. I'm 47. I'm not an indulgent, hedonistic person like I was in my twenties. With bodily and psychological purification, my senses are sharp, I see, I feel, I hear, I smell, I taste, I touch. That heightening of the senses through Yoga means that one's perceptions are very receptive to whoever's sitting in front of one. Those disciplines are very necessary. I would never go to an acupuncturist or a therapist who smoked because I feel they would be pushing back something. They are in a state of repression and I don't want their lack of purification transferred to myself. It's the criteria which one holds oneself, a blending of theory and practice. I've been working for 14 years and never had a day off work. I've never been ill and that's important in itself. It's keeping myself physically, mentally and spiritually fit for the work. I also give myself good breaks. I work six weeks on, and then have a week off, and in those weeks off I go to nature. Every year I spend three weeks in India and have this incredible set of massages. In fact the people who do these massages are visiting now and we are doing this type of massage as an extension of my practice here at the moment. The criteria is to love thyself and really nourish the soul. I give 100 per cent to my clients and 100 per cent to myself. I'm not going to run myself down. I'm not needy of my clients. I don't need anything from them at this stage now. Earlier on I did, I wanted acknowledgement, I wanted to be considered, 'Oh, isn't he a wonderful person.' In wanting that I wasn't getting the acknowledgement anyway, so I came to the conclusion that I just needed to love what I was doing and I have continued to love what I am doing. If I stop loving what I'm doing – I'm finished. People will not accept me sitting here in this chair.

What does the healthy person look like?

Good skin. [Laughs] And clear eyes!

Mentally healthy ...

Yes, consciousness. Consciousness, an awareness of themselves, an ease in communication in all levels. This knower, this overview. Watching what you're doing while you're doing it. Conscious of what you say, feel and do. Coming to deeper levels of truth. Being receptive and creative, a reconciliation of opposites. It's Yoga, it's the union of 'That'. Feeling comfortable, at ease. Disease/ease. At ease in reality. At ease with one's sexuality. A freedom of emotional expression. No toxic guilt. Confident – a self-image which is projecting the being of oneself. The 'I', 'I am what I am.', 'Thou art that.' Blended as a unity. The 'I', the ego is balanced, neither low self-esteem, nor high self-esteem, no hubris. Balanced and working with the am-ness, the being of ourselves. That working with the higher self. Some form of identification with the creative overview, the Creator God.

If a client feels they've got enough, but you don't, is there any real conflict?

No. If they've got enough, they won't make another appointment. I attempt to resolve things, but sometimes I just let people go. If they've missed an appointment or I sense they are getting restless, I let them go. I don't ask any questions, I don't push it. Some therapists chase their clients, I don't. I'm not inclined to. I learnt that in the first seven years of the School, through some very tough lessons at the end, some people move on, people move through this. Where they have gone, I don't know. Some keep in touch, some don't.

Of course you do build up attachments to people, and I have to say some of my clients have become friends, because of the level of consciousness we're resonating at. I'm not looking for that at the beginning. It will take many years before that personal thing happens. I used to be too open on that, but I've actually become more detached and it's a little more difficult these days for that to happen. There's one woman who has been working with me for quite a while, and we have become very, very close friends. They're older people, they're people I love. In their twenties people are very competitive. They are too close to the competitive values they've been given, the survival mechanisms. As I get older, I just want to be with individuals who aren't moving on that personal level. Therefore people of my age, I've become very happy with them. They've given up that competitive aggression; they're contented, they're successful, they've achieved what they've had to achieve. I don't know if this is relevant for your book, but I'm beginning to mix with more successful people in the world who've reached a level of accomplishment and are not competing. On the ego level there is competition, but on the soul level there's none.

Can we talk about money? [Laughs]

I have been reasonable with finances in my practice, partly because I feel everything I need has been given to me. I own this flat and was very successful with previous things that I did. I was an antique textile dealer and showed antique textiles in museums and galleries. I had a collection of quilts and shawls, oriental carpets, all that type of thing, which I later sold and that left me in a very comfortable position. So I have been incredibly reasonable, which has given me an access to all levels of society. People say, 'Oh, why don't you go to Harley Street? Why don't you charge £100 an hour?' and all that bit. No way.

I have certain spiritual, political and social principles. I started at £12 for two hours, 14 years ago, and it went up slowly. Last May I was charging £30 for two hours – that's £15 an hour. I give two hours. I'll tell you why: when clients come in here, they've got their own rhythms from outside. They come through the city. By the first half-hour they are beginning to relax; by three-quarters of an hour we're getting somewhere. By the first hour they're beginning to open up emotionally, and that first hour, hour and 15 minutes, we're really getting places. Then bringing it to resolution, I need two hours a session, and that's long. However, my clients find that worthwhile. They even come from all over the country sometimes, to have a session. I have just gone up to £35 for two hours. I've kept my prices reasonable, because I have all I need on a material level. I have my home. I have a friend with a beautiful house in the country I go to. I don't have to own it, I have my holidays. Four or five of us hired a yacht in Turkey, £25 a day each, for a week. The people own the yacht, it's their responsibility, I don't need to own the yacht. I have a car. That's it. I also contribute to a charity in India concerning social change and development, returning in some way what India gave to me.

As for timing sessions, if something's on in here and we're over the two hours, I cannot cut that person. That is going to damage them. I would be abandoning that person in their grief, at that moment. Sometimes my sessions will run into another person's session and he or she will have to wait. Generally sessions have a beginning, middle and end, some sort of resolution, otherwise that person's in limbo. I don't allow people to live through therapy, like three sessions a week. One a week and then one every other week, because I need time to let the homoeopathy work through. I must give space to that person to allow things to happen in their life from a session and let them experience things. They then know they are going somewhere with me, as we're on a journey together. I only see four, five or six persons a day. Because I don't travel to work and start at 8.30 a.m., I can finish at 8.30 p.m. I can do a twelve-hour day, ten-hour day, or eight-hour day. I give myself a four-day week, sometimes a three-day week and have a long weekend.

Do you have contractual type talks at your first meeting?

No. I'm inclined to set the pace, because I'm very directive and trust in the synchronicity of our sessions together. That's where I say I'm a teacher, not totally a therapist. It's interesting: a therapist. T-h-e-r-a-p-i-s-t, the rapist, if you look at it. What one is doing is stripping off the layers of the onion to get to the core of the centre. I see myself as a facilitator for the individuals to discover themselves. I'm mirroring objectively their process. It depends on the person and what he or she wants. Yes, I can teach about male initiation, the laws of cause and effect, etc. There's much I can teach. It's a teacher–student relationship rather that a therapist–patient relationship. It's slightly different. It's a school. I'm part of a school. Of course, it's all to bring that person, as I've said, to their inner knower, to teach them to listen to their inner voice.

I can have a thousand truths about somebody, but I don't utter them. It's not always appropriate. Somebody might have been abused – but my way is to get them to come to that point of recognition. Yoga stimulates the memory. As I said right at the beginning, it's to remember things in order really to let go and forget it. If it's not remembered and it's in there it's a burden for the person.

Quite recently, there was a woman who'd definitely been sexually abused by her father, and she stated it; she knew it. So I did go along with that. You have to be very careful about transferred suggestions. Therefore, I have to wait and be patient and allow the person to discover it for themselves. There is something else, apart from the breathing work. The very advanced clients, I will suggest they go in my bath and breathe underwater with a snorkel. This takes them back to their birth memory and early unconscious memories, especially to the subtle transferences from the mother. This is particularly beneficial to mothers in order for them to clear their own birth trauma, so they don't repeat this when they give birth to their own child. Many people have a fear of water, that's fear of what happened in the womb, and just out of it. That is again part of the regression, the remembering in order to forget. Thus, some clients end up in my bath: they breathe, they do it for themselves, and they bring up their own unconscious process. Then I will suggest possibilities of a cause and effect from that session: 'This could be a possibility; your mother could have felt that, your father might have responded like that. You as a child might have felt and reacted like that.' I'm not into manipulating archetypes. There are some people using archetypal work – Warrior, King, Queen – I'm aware of the archetypal potential in people, but I don't want to become over-suggestive of that. I do visualisation work, dreamwork, analysing dreams, visualisation work on the Tree, whereby they are doing it; I am not doing it for them. I'm just facilitating a process where they can come to a point of self-recognition. I believe in giving space for people to discover their own archetypes, their own destiny.

So any of these techniques you'll use when you think it appropriate?

Yes, according to the needs of the person. I have many arrows to the bow which I can fire. All this, I've experienced myself. I've done visualisation work, I've done dreamwork myself, analysing my own dreams. There are one or two of my colleagues now in the School, if I have something going on, I will go to them. At the end of last year I was a little angry about certain things that had happened in the School so I went to one of my colleagues and I did the breathwork myself, and breathed out my own anger. I have an accumulation, I have my own process. Part of my work is keeping myself clear. I have three or four people I completely trust. So I am continually working through a process myself with these people.

Some therapists doze off when they're with their patients ...

Because of the Yoga training, I have very good concentration. I feel that's why people come here, because they do sense during the two hours I am completely with them, moving with them. Yes, it's what I said early on, listening and being with somebody. If they respect me enough to come and pay me £35, travel across London, spend that time with me, I am certainly going to be with them. No, I don't wander. By the way, I do tell my clients, 'If you've got anything with me, please bring it up. Please challenge me. If I've said something which is rankling you, disappointing you, ring me please, and let's talk about it', because I want to keep the transferences to a minimum. Of course some clients have a problem where they don't say what they feel and some can come back six months later and say, 'You said that six months ago', and I say 'Yes, let's look at it. But it's six months ago, and I am not with that now.'

My teaching is to get people to respond immediately. 'Respond in 24 hours to something, please.' I do have an amazing memory. I write down some notes, but a client can come back and all of a sudden, because I've been with that person before, I can remember their process. I can remember who their parents were, etc. I've been gifted with that. I feel that's part of the Yoga training of my twenties and thirties, and what I continue to do now.

But I see you keep records ...

Yes, my record keeping here is to write down what is important, what I would consider as a cause and effect in their case. Sometimes I give my clients the notes to read. I rarely look at it. Once it's written down, something's gone in here about it. [Points to head] That's how I used to learn when I was a kid. Write it down and then I'd remember it. So I've conditioned myself to do that. Of course, I don't remember everything, but basically I've got a structure. I feel successful, I've never stopped working, I've never advertised. It's all done on recommendation. If people stop coming through that door, that will be the end of my practice. I will never advertise.

Why?

I don't have to. [Pause] I always have the appropriate amount of work according to my own growth.

If people stopped coming, and it wound down, that would mean I would really have to look at myself and re-evaluate my position as a teacher. Was the work I was doing irrelevant? Wrong? Possibly close the whole practice down, go on a retreat for a couple of years and re-evaluate myself. I nearly had to do that last year, but it didn't come about. That was something to do with the School. I needed a rest as well. The spiritual lineage gave me a break! I had less clients last year for the first time in over 12 years. It dropped off a bit. I went through a process myself, re-evaluated myself and bounced back this year and I'm busier than ever.

The English are supposed to find it difficult to talk about themselves ...

Well, you see, this thing about England. I have a different sense of this country now. There's a wildness in this country. I go to the theatre. I went to the theatre last week. I love theatre. I saw a woman sob from the depths of her soul on stage. Don't tell me we're not a passionate lot. Don't tell me we're not an emotional lot. I'm an embodiment of my own passion. And there are quite a few very passionate people in this society. There's repression but there's repression in every society.

We say: 'The Italians? They have easy access to the emotions.' I have found there are repressive elements in all societies, repressed elements in all individuals. There are repressed elements in what we consider the most passionate societies. So this whole idea of a view of this country as a repressed, emotional society – yes and no. That's how I perceive it.

With the growth of the feminine consciousness this century – suffragettes, women into Tai Chi, Yoga in the '60s, therapy in the '70s, their growth as therapists in the '80s – they have moved light years, very quickly, from the oppressed states of consciousness of the past. At first my practice was 80 per cent women. Gradually, over the years, more and more men are coming through the door. They are recognising they need help. They cannot do it alone. It's something that the male has been conditioned to. 'If you can't sort it yourself, you are no good as a man.' Gradually, those men – they do not want to be Saturday fathers any more – they are beginning to want to make their relationships work, they are beginning to want to work it through. Because of the insularity of family and family relationships, there are no mediators in society. If I was going to put another name to my work, I would say I was a mediator. A mediator definitely between couples; because there's that objectivity, I am not subjectively involved in their relationship. More and more men are sitting here, businessmen are coming through that door. This is a great delight, it started very much in the '90s. This is to do with the War. This is to do with the damaged male consciousness after the War. I believe in this society we've been incredibly passionate as men, but the War suppressed

that. The effects of the War were enormous on the consciousness of men –
and women – but more on the male and the effects of this on subsequent
generations. It is so exciting at the moment that the men are coming to
investigate the inner self.

*I was going to ask you whether people always had to help themselves, but I
think you've answered that.*

I always push people back on to themselves so they can learn to do things
for themselves. They do homework. I support, but I want them to learn to
support themselves. I give them a phone-in-time between 8.00 and 8.30
a.m. and they can discuss things then. I am available. I go away at Christmas for three weeks to a month. I've prepared them for it generally. I
don't give them high potency remedies at that time. Many people are
working with me, and in the School there are other teachers who they can
relate to. So I can go away.

Remember I was telling you about that psychic ... about Danette Choi?

Yes, Bob, you've just mentioned a very interesting incident about a
psychic area. The woman in France, you went to see her and she said:
'You were an Indian politician in the eighteenth century.' Now, this
psychic awareness of someone else. People do channel, they do have
deep insights and I respect aspects of that. There is, however, a certain
percentage of that – ten, twenty per cent – which is wrong. I am not
willing in my work to take that risk of a psychic projection on to
somebody that could be wrong. I really want people to discover it for
themselves, because they have the knowledge within them. They have
the aspect of God within themselves. So I find it dangerous and it
makes people lazy to give them answers all the time. It has got to come
from within. 'The Kingdom of God is within, look you there.' A good
spiritual teacher facilitates a person to discover what their own reincar-
nations are themselves. I might suggest something, I don't want to
pronounce it because I would be wrong. And I don't want that karmic
burden of being wrong myself, so misguiding others in my work.
    We're talking about spiritual teachers, and I don't believe in any
'isms'. There are great traditions, and I adhere to the great traditions
and out of those there are many fine teachers. But if any of those
teachers say, 'You must belong to this religion. You must belong. You
must become this.' That might be in denial of what your inner knowing
is. I don't believe in conversions. I believe in the 'I', the 'I am what I
am', and 'thou art that', the ultimate identification. The spiritual teacher
is to facilitate that journey. It's all in the breath. The breath is the
essence of life. Bring the breath into the body, spiritualise matter, and
from that you build your own Heaven on Earth. If one individual does
it and emanates that spirituality in their life, then if more and more
people do it, the world will become spiritualised.

At this point in time many great religions have developed and I'm a friend of all religions, but there's now enough organised religion. What we have to do is take religion back to the essence of the individual and re-evaluate those philosophies to suit our present age. The Will of God is moving all the time, it's in perpetual motion, it is not static. So, the spiritualisation of ourselves as individuals must be in constant movement as in the breath – an expansion and contraction, a going out and a coming in. I'm afraid religions get stuck in dogma, they get stuck in laws, which possibly are not appropriate for the present time and the present evolution of consciousness. Science has moved the physical world forward. So we must now move the spiritual world forward and develop the science of the soul and awareness of life to create balance between the material and the spiritual worlds. It's all a matter of being able to access movements of cause and effect. It's not static.

The other thing is, if I said, 'I was a shaykh, or a priest, or I was this or that', I define myself in certain terms. Those terms can make me a superior to my clients or to the people I'm associated with. So I just want to be known as Paul, all the time. I am what I am. I hope my clients accept me as that, as I accept them in my process. On another level, some clients come here and have taught me things about myself. If I set up a superior position because of the spiritual knowledge I've attained, I create a separation from humanity. I don't want to do that. I want to be present with people and develop relationships with clients which move towards equality. I call it adult communication. After I've taught and shared for a while, we can then move to a level of equality, having an adult, interdependent, coexistent relationship. We share our knowledge and experiences together. From every client I also learn something in the process and can release something with them. It's a two-way process in the end.

It's the most difficult path to take in the world. As I said before, we'd rather externalise the enemy than face the enemy within. Of course one of the difficult parts of the work is people's resistance to themselves, to their own pain. The fancy footwork games that get played around that, of people not wanting to confront their inner pain, confront themselves. I find sometimes that part of the work gets tiresome and trying. I'm attempting to nudge it along, but they are unwilling to go with it. This possibly is another area where the client and myself separate. It's a natural process. Sometimes it can be a bit hairy, but there it is: taking a risk.

Do you separate psychological knowledge from spiritual knowledge?

No, I think this society creates a lot of separation. Cancer is an illness of separation. In our structures we give our children to the schools; the political body to Westminster; the spiritual body to the Church; our physical body to the doctor, and expect others to take responsibility for these areas of our lives. Spiritual life is taking total responsibility for oneself and one's evolution.

It's all Oneness. Politics, social structure, spirituality, the individual – it's one flow of energy. Definition, compartmentalising, separation – all create disunity. Today I will move through a political, social, economic, spiritual, emotional, psychological agenda. It's all one, it's all one flow, and I'm not going to allow my mind to separate or compartmentalise any of that flow. With the four Worlds of the Tree – physical, psychological emotional, the world of energy as the soul of being, and the creative force and Source – it's all One. There's still a great need for the large spiritual organisation, for people to feel that they belong to something. But then ultimately on the spiritual path it's about belonging to your Self, freeing that conditioned child within one's self. We have come from that source as a child. So empty, we can return as that unconditioned child to God if we evolve the soul. Returning God to God. My teacher very clearly put it in a very powerful moment working with him, he said: 'Be happy, do service in the world and die consciously.' He himself did have a conscious death, he read his pulses regularly. He realised by reading the pulses the energy in the liver and spleen declined. He was 82 years old, and for an Indian man that is very old. Then, within two weeks, he woke up in the morning and said: 'I'm leaving at 11 o'clock this morning', and that's the ultimate state of Yoga; the state called *Samadhi*. He had a conscious death at 11 o'clock that morning. So: 'Be happy, do service and die consciously.'

In 1993, I worked in the School with a group of men in a meditation circle and at the end I wrote this:

I believe it's in the nature of the human soul to go beyond itself to return to the Self. I believe it is in the nature of the human soul to go deeper, beyond its depth of pain, its grief, its fear, its joy; to return to the centre of the Earth. To return to the stillness of the womb of the Earth, the primal dung of the cow goes deeper than we do.

I believe it is in the nature of the human soul to transcend its need for love and its inevitable soaring to the awe of its completeness. The primal dung of the eagle flies higher that we do. I believe it is in the nature of the human soul to go beyond mind and its consciousness and return to the eternal Oneness. The being to return to the eternal source. Rest awhile and come into the body of its Self. The completion of the longing for Thee.

CHAPTER 8

Cognitive-Behavioural Therapy

Brian Sheldon

Brian Sheldon is Professor of Applied Social Studies at the
Royal Holloway College, University of London and also is a
cognitive-behavioural therapist in private practice.

How did you become a therapist?

I trained as a psychiatric social worker in the old days of specialisation,
and became interested in a wide range of psychological ideas, but only
the psychoanalytical model was taught on my course. I became aware
from private reading of a number of criticisms of this approach both at
the level of logic, from people like Sir Karl Popper – and at the level of
outcome research – Eysenck's material, for example. Also by chance I
attended a lecture, at the University of Leicester one evening, by Professor Meyer, who carried out one of the large experimental studies of
counselling effectiveness then being conducted in the United States.
These were large scale, very well put together studies, of long duration,
fairly good service exposure, yet producing 'nil-nil draws', or deteriora-
tion effects in their subjects. Trying to get such studies on the agenda
of my course, and wondering why this empirical material was not being
taught was not easy. It produced some fascinating 'antibody reactions'
from people with the psychoanalytic *idée fixe*, I think I shall call it. I
suppose there's something slightly perverse in all of us, so that if one
meets defensive reactions, it drives one harder to look for the reasons.

*How would you describe what you do? What happens when someone comes
to see you?*

If you were sitting in one of my sessions from the beginning it would
strike you as fairly atheoretical. In other words the behavioural part of the
cognitive-behavioural title of the kind of work I do would not initially be
very visible. This is because I believe in attempting a broad-ranging assessment to start with. So I ask clients fairly directly what their difficulties are
and I try to get a view of the aetiology of those difficulties, the history of
the causes. I am particularly interested in first onsets. What was happening at the time difficulties began? In other words I focus on the learning
history. Questions that I try to get answered early on are: Was this person

always like this? In other words are they temperamentally predisposed in any way to the difficulties that they have? One usually finds that in anxiety states and often in phobic reactions, that there is a predisposing temperament and personality there. So I ask about childhood, which might confuse some people who are expecting something more Skinnerian. I try to get some idea about how this person came to learn the reactions that may now be causing them problems. I put across the view that we can learn *anything*, and that we don't always *look* to learn things, but by association and by covert processes of reward, we are often shaped into patterns of behaviour which later become troublesome to us. So the key issue is: 'how interested is the client in unlearning these connections – both emotional, Pavlovian-type connections and problems derived from power of habit and of reinforcement?'

Sometimes I look a bit more broadly and try to uncover patterns in families, or in relationships and marriages, which may unwittingly support some of the problems with which people come.

I am not eclectic in the usual sloppy sense – eclectic often meaning simply 'do what comes naturally to me and ignore all other evidence'. I am a cognitive-behavioural therapist purely on empirical grounds. I used to find the ideas of R.D. Laing very satisfying and interesting, I couldn't find any support for them in research. The biological material on schizophrenia came forward, these theories and findings cannot both be true. Therefore I gave him up, and I think that's the kind of affiliation we need to have with theory and research – to be 'good friends' with theories, not to 'fall in love' with them. I think that's one of the problems with the analysts. They have these dark secret relationships with their belief systems. I don't have one.

So, to return to your question, I'm quite general to begin with, and later on we get down to (and this is where things start to look behavioural) a priority list, a target list – patterns of behaviour, or thought, or feelings. Things that people seem motivated to change, and we start conducting little experiments together. That's how I work.

Could you give me an example?

Since the evidence is that, generally speaking, people are either going to improve reasonably rapidly, or they aren't going to improve much at all, I tend to create an expectation of around twelve sessions. I'm not dogmatic about that. I have a client at the moment who used to be quite depressed, he's now improving steadily. As far as I'm concerned, he's probably okay now, he doesn't need to see me really. I put this to him gently and quietly discover that he is not keen on changing the relationship yet. He wants to see how he goes for a while. I'm happy to do that with him. But typically I think I create an expectation that there should be some change within an estimated timescale. I think this contributes to the effectiveness of the behavioural approach.

The work I do can be exemplified in a couple of cases I could talk about. The first was once referred when there was concern of excessive physical punishment to a child by his mother. He was being beaten, largely as a result of his behaviour at school. He'd been to two schools – and they'd both thrown him out for severely disruptive behaviour. He was described as 'disturbed' and various psychiatric terminology was beginning to be used by staff. The first thing that I did was to get a look at his behaviour in the situation where it occurred – and I think this is where behavioural approaches are really radically different from talking therapies. Behaviour often occurs within particular contingencies, so you need to get a look at those contingencies and what prompts and what reinforces that behaviour. To cut a long story short, this boy was being reinforced by attention. This was in short supply at home from his single parent mum and largely absent father. Whenever he was behaving in a challenging way, he was responded to by teachers. For their own skin's sake they had to. The rest of the time, they tiptoed around him and ignored him. They called it 'a sleeping dogs' approach. He'd occasionally wake up and 'bite' them, though. He'd hit other pupils, and so on. So we tried to reverse these contingencies. We tried to find a way of getting everyday attention into the boy's life, routinely. The last thing the teachers wanted to do was to be nice to this child when he'd been awkward with them only an hour ago. So really it was a pattern of teacher behaviour modification which we devised. The child's behaviour changed quite rapidly by the reversal of contingencies, with some important social consequences for him.

Now that's one kind of approach in behaviour therapy, another would be the more personal one-to-one work. I think I should make a point here. There is a danger with the importation of cognitive ideas (they are important and they are logically consistent with the approach) but there is a danger that we head off down the primrose path towards purely talking therapies again, which have proven so ineffective in the past. So I would describe myself as small 'c', big 'B' – cognitive-Behavioural therapist – there are others who do it the other way round. I do almost no straight, talking therapy.

The next case example that comes to mind was that of a young woman who had been in a psychiatric hospital and was diagnosed as schizophrenic. In fact she had been assigned about half of the disorders in DSM3R in her life. She was a crushingly shy individual, and had almost no eye-to-face contact with anyone. She therefore felt cut off. She would hardly speak at all, just occasionally in a very, very quiet voice. I did some work with her using closed-circuit television, trying to get her used to the look of herself in safe, benign circumstances. This work contained an element of 'desensitisation' – a very important therapeutic device. The cognitive element was to challenge her rather catastrophic views about how she looked, and what people thought of her. She was a resident of a hostel, and if at night (she went out very little) it was perfectly quiet, she would believe that this was because people were lowering their voices to have a critical conversation about her.

She'd feel very upset about this. If, however, she could hear loud voices, particularly laughter, she knew that she was the cause and the butt of it. So you can imagine as a cognitive therapist that you have to get at the illogicality of the mental set that implies that 'whatever happens in this building is about me', 'That people therefore spend 24 hours of their day concerned about me and my behaviour', when the reality is 'hardly anyone ever sees me'.

So we had to do some rethinking. We tried to address the implausibility of that, the illogicality that anyone would devote their life to the tormenting of another person for no particular reason. This seemed to have some gentle effect, alongside the main element of the approach which was to practise slightly more assertive behaviour with others – little tasks, little tasks, little tasks. Such a person is never going to be completely rehabilitated from such a condition I think, but certainly I think that the approach made a contribution to making her life more bearable. She now has a flat of her own, goes out, and has one or two friends.

Do you think that your approach is best focused on people who definitely have problems that they come to you with, or do you think that the approach is something that 'the mentally healthy' can benefit from?

My position is that I would wish to concern myself only with moderately-to severely-encumbered people. Now it's possible not to have a formal mental illness and be psychologically troubled, or to be on the fringe. So I wouldn't turn anyone away simply because they don't have a label from a psychiatrist. But at the same time I am not one of these trendy people (there are a lot in social work) who talk about 'mental health problems' and don't distinguish between the various diagnoses. Because these *are* illnesses, they are formal, genuine, illnesses. They may have a social component, they may have a psychological component, but they are not just labels or social misunderstandings. So if I am working with a depressed person I am always aware of the suicide risk, and I also know that it is most likely to manifest itself when recovery begins. I think it's important for therapists to know that and not tinker about, but to behave responsibly and work collaboratively with medical colleagues.

As to whether it's a good idea that therapies are available for the mentally healthy, or the 'worried well' you could call them – yes, by all means. My only concern is that the analysts have shifted their ground from being a very clinical profession to being something closer to applied philosophy as the outcome studies on their clinical work have got on so very, very bad. Therefore I think they have decided to change the name of the game, and now they are saying, 'Well it is really about developing oneself as a person' which is much harder to measure – although there are ways! I think it is a way of getting off the charge of ineffectiveness. After five years of analysis something quite visibly different should occur, surely, with that amount of technical investment, that amount of money?

How would you summarise the philosophical and conceptual background to cognitive-behavioural work?

Dealing with the behavioural component first. Human beings are learning animals. From the moment of birth we are in interaction with an ambivalent physical and social environment. Things get 'stamped into' our repertoire as a result. Some things we try don't work, they get 'stamped out' of our repertoire. So we all have this rich and highly individual learning history. We can learn useful things, pro-social things, we can learn (in exactly the same way) antisocial, problematic, self-defeating classes of behaviour. Therefore I think any view of cognitive-behavioural therapy should start with the work of Pavlov on how we learn emotional reactions – emotional connections with things, then move on to reinforcement principles. The other element is recognising that part of the learning equation is selective perception. We all look at a different scene or set of events and pull something different out of it. The more we know from the study of perception, the more active and 'constructive' that faculty is revealed to be.

So putting the cognitive component alongside the behavioural component, one would also wish to look at how people typically interpret given stimuli. Some people see a threat where others see no threat. A group of people to me implies very little threat, in general – a lecture audience these days, very little threat. For other people, such situations are paralysingly threatening. What they perceive in the situation is therefore of concern. And there is no doubt that people often perceive in a very self-fulfilling, problem-confirming kind of way.

A further element in the equation is modelling. We can also learn by observing behaviour in others. Children, if brought up with daily exposure to aggression, are likely to practise it themselves. Therefore the question is, are there alternative role-models available for people? As a therapist you are also a role-model – in my case, I hope, a model for problem-solving behaviour. One of the most important things I do with individuals is to get them to look logically at the origins of their difficulties and how they might practise a different way of behaving and thinking.

If Skinner and Pavlov are the figures on the behavioural side, are there figures on the cognitive side?

Aaron Beck springs to mind immediately. I am very fond of his work: for example, Beck's direct style of interviewing, beginning a first encounter, with 'Why do you want to end your life?' This, for me, is the only sane and logical way to begin a therapeutic encounter with someone who is threatening suicide. It is the most important question. Any other question is a tiptoey irrelevance, and introduces the element of surreality which is often lampooned in the media regarding therapy.

I remember reading, as a student, 'Changing Man's Behaviour', in particular the stuff about aversion therapy, desensitisation, and so on. Are the major techniques now, the same ones?

I think aversion therapy has practically disappeared. It had some unwholesome associations, in that it tended, like most things that cause one's ethical hackles to rise, to be used with very few middle-class-fee-paying people. It tended to be used within the public system. I think there are some ethical worries about that, and I think some ethical worries even if patients request such a approach. There are other better ways – more effective – ways available. The evidence on aversion is that it is not very effective. Remember that also Oliver Cromwell put a stop to bear-baiting for the sake of the baiters – I take the same position.

Is there a group of techniques which all cognitive-behavioural therapists would use?

A number come to mind. First of all there is the idea of looking for contingencies surrounding a pattern of problematic behaviour – what maintains it, that is an interesting question. In a relationship difficulty it is often more interesting to know what daily cues and rituals maintain a pattern of awkward and happiness-destroying behaviour, than it is to know exactly what the events were on Jubilee Day 1977, said to have 'caused it'.

I have a client at the moment who is depressed and is under considerable stress at work. His reaction is to keep his head down – it is understandable. He's been made redundant on several occasions before. He keeps a low profile, he tiptoes around the place, and says little or nothing. He accepts exploitation on some occasions. In his heart he knows it's wrong, and it is, to use his own phrase, 'poisoning him inside', but he does it. He occasionally, when the lid blows, has a very aggressive outburst which might seem to support Freudian notions, but doesn't in my view. What I aim to do with him is to get him to make a small 'down-payment' in *initiating* something, anything. I would like to encourage him to experiment with this environment. What would happen if, instead of keeping his head down and hoping not to be noticed, he tried a little bit of initiative in a controlled way, in a relatively safe bit of his environment? The hope is that such bits of new behaviour get reinforced, and that he learns that he doesn't have to tiptoe as a way of life. So rearranging contingencies, or even, as in this case, trying to get the client to do it, is important.

Another major principle in behavioural work is undoubtedly the idea of exposure to threatening stimuli. I saw, some time ago, a young woman who had a persistent and life-destroying – as far as she was concerned – fear of vomiting in public. She was a young woman, and it was ruining her social life. Her life in general as a result. I asked her how often this had happened – vomiting in public? She said: 'It has never happened.' There's an interesting cognitive component. 'It's never happened, I just fear it will.' So partly it's fear of fear. The approach used was not exactly systematic desensitisation, but had some elements of that. Relaxation first of all, imagining completing small tasks which challenge the fear of vomiting. Sipping iced water on the fringe of a group of other people, for example; having a meal with a close and understanding friend, would be steps number one and two, and exposing oneself to the reduced threat of that set of stimuli by staying in the situation long enough for anxiety to come down would also be important. So she did that in a kind of hop, skip and jump, exposure-therapy sort of way. One can only stay anxious so long, and therefore if one is exposed in a graded, professionally responsible way to the stimulus, it will eventually cease to have its effect. So a lot of work is done with fears and phobias, using such approaches. I have also done modelling work. I have helped a group of psychiatric patients about to be discharged to re-enact the little dramas that they foresee lying in wait for them when they get home. Things such as people putting on those special voices reserved for the mentally ill. Being treated like children, as some older people are. Being avoided, having suspicious looks shot in their direction. People talking behind their hands. The old business of the stigma – sadly, still there – of mental illness, and what to do when you get back home. How do you deal with friends and neighbours, and if you have a job – workmates? How do you do that? So we practised it in a group, in a fairly supportive group setting, with a little TV camera. We practised the kinds of encounters they were going to have with people, and tried to work out in an experimental way what the sensible reactions to such difficulties should be. The answer normally was something mildly assertive and direct, rather than coded or avoidant. Social skills training is still an important element of behaviour therapy based on the work of great figures like Albert Bandura.

We're not just plastic people, are we?

Plastic in one sense, but not in the other. We have between our ears thousands of miles of nerve fibres, coiled up together in such a way that it gives us great adaptability. We *are* plastic people in that we have enormous plasticity in our relationship with the environment. Lower animals have one or two basic big reflexes. Sometimes they work. If I were a hedgehog I'd want to rethink my big reflex at the moment. Since Mr Daimler met Mr Benz it's become a bit of a loser!

Human beings have this capacity – since nature could not foresee the conditions into which they might be propelled over time or distance so we were endowed with this enormous capacity for adaption. The problem is that sometimes the reflexes delivered to us by evolution – aggression, an ability to associate one thing with another so that a strangely quiet clump of trees sets hearts racing – those kinds of things, can go sour on us, can turn against us in such a way that we become afraid of things we don't really need to be afraid of. Other people, maybe; any dependency, anything. So just as you can learn something very useful, you can learn something very self-defeating too.

The view I am trying to put across, the view of people encapsulated in this model, is that we are learning animals and so we can learn something different if we find it 'pays off' more for us. Social co-operation now pays off for human beings, and therefore it is people who are aggressive and individualistic who are now regarded in pathological terms. It might once have been a winning combination.

What is your response to those people – Rogerian, Maslowian, all these humanistic psychologists – who think that somehow the behaviourist approach demeans human dignity?

I think human beings have capacity for fulfilment and for greatness. Few of us get there; few of us get to Maslow's final stage of self-development – only people such as Nelson Mandela, Alexander Solzhenitsyn, people like that. I think Alexander Solzhenitsyn got to be the kind of truculent, dogged, liberty-loving, brilliant writer that he is largely by learning – possibly with a little genetic push behind it. I think that Maslow and Rogers are the products of the contingencies that shaped them into two great humanitarian psychologists. I think – it's a bit like wanting to deny the law of gravity to deny the power of learning – it won't stop people falling. People *will* learn something. We should do our best to ensure that they learn things that are likely to bring them happiness and not cost other people too much.

If we all agree that, yes, we want people to learn things that are pro-social rather than antisocial, then the next question is, of course, who decides?

Behaviour therapy got itself a bad name in the 1960s, when it was used in large institutions, particularly closed ones. When *Clockwork Orange*-type, *1984*-type, fantasies about what was going on were not entirely unjustified. Those patients, in large token economy schemes – chronic schizophrenics normally – should have been brought back into social life in a different way, I think, rather than simply paid tokens for numbers of 'units of speech'. But there were some successes, too.

I have seen group schemes work wonderfully well with challenging behaviours in children, the kind of challenging behaviour that is going to get them locked up if we are not careful. I think that people who wish to produce profound changes in other people in a kind of 'look, no hands' way are deluding themselves. If you learn that aggression pays, or if you don't modify the basic aggressive instinct and are dangerous to other people and continue to clash with society over a period of 30 years, the idea that a gentle, pleasant chat with a talking therapist will work, is self-deluding – it only happens in *The Waltons* I think, where people say 'Gee I never saw it that way before' when coaxed into change over the supper table! In therapy you need something equally powerful to the contingencies that set up that behaviour in the first place. If clients are to unlearn, 25 years' worth of behaviour, or even ten years' worth, or five, it's likely to be hard work. I think the idea that you don't have to take some extraordinary precautions to have influence with people is a silly one. I am very direct about it. I am very direct about involving people in change, and saying: 'This is what we should do if we are going to prevent you getting locked up. Will you try and help me as much as you can?' If the answer is 'Push off', I try and find the lowest common denominator goal that they are interested in.

Do you think that people's early childhoods should be of particular interest to therapists?

It is useful; I am quite fond of this medical term 'aetiology', the history of the cause. 'When did the spots first appear?' is the equivalent in medicine. 'And the day before that, nothing?' 'When did you first feel this sudden sense of panic when you went out of doors? And before that nothing, ever?' I think that gives you an idea about the site of the causation. But no, I'm not particularly interested in early childhood events. Early childhood events are of course formative. What you learn first, particularly pre-linguistically, is very powerful, and we tend to learn in concordance with what we already know and can do. Therefore childhood patterns in general can be of interest. When you try to unknot something, somebody in this case, you pull back and see where the tangle starts – it's quite interesting to give patients a view of the early origins of their difficulties, but not *especially*, because you can only produce change in the here and now. We live in the here and now. And doing something different has to occur in the here and now, so we have to focus on that.

One final thing on this topic, I think the therapeutic professions in general, people in general, grossly underestimate the difficulty of producing change in human behaviour – particularly by verbal means alone. I don't know about you but I am *full* of insight. I go to my bank manager, and he tries to persuade me not to live beyond my income, and I say: 'Gee I never saw it that way before!', and I go away and my behaviour quickly comes under the control of CD shops and book stores. We also *under*estimate the extent to which one can change feelings and thoughts by changing behaviour. If people start to behave differently, they often feel differently about themselves, and they think different thoughts as a result. So I think this idea that we need first of all to change the cognitive map – or in the case of the Freudians, the tangle of repressed feelings – then the behaviour will change, is too unidimensional. It is much more mechanistic than what behaviourists do, which is to say 'test the reality of this fear that you have; go out and do it, it will go away after a bit. I bet you if I stand there with you for a couple of hours you won't feel fear, let's go and try it.' And so thoughts and feelings alter as a result.

There is no evidence of symptom-substitution anywhere in the literature. People talk about it because they have steam-age views of how human beings work. That if you block off one exit port, that it will have to come out in another way.

Very few therapists mention the brain. In your work, you don't avoid that, do you?

No, because that is what people have, super-computers made of meat. We have brains and if you know a little about the brain, its enormous complexity as an organ, its enormous plasticity, then you don't really need to have 'ghosts in the machine': it is a pretty 'ghostly' piece of machinery in itself. So when people talk about behavioural approaches being 'mechanistic' they reveal their scientific ignorance. No, I am very happy with the idea that people have *brains* and that mind is a reification of brain activity. Though I *feel* I have a mind and I can enter a discourse with you about 'changing my mind' and so on, I think I am really using the term metaphorically. I think 'mind' is the product of this immensely complex organ at work.

Can you tell me how you would face notions of the unconscious in your work?

Much of our behaviour is unconscious. There are two ways to look at this: first, we are often unconscious of the contingencies which trigger our habitual reactions to things. Some people, for example, when faced with stress, take action, any action, and they are unaware of the commonalities across a range of situations where this impulsivity is not a rational or useful response. They don't know what triggers them, they don't know what 'cues' them, they don't know sometimes what the hidden reinforcement value is even. A lot of our behaviour is unconsciously formed because we are not aware of secret sources of pay off, or of hidden cues, which nevertheless are processed by the brain at a subliminal level.

The other use of the word 'unconscious' that I am happy to accept is the idea that much of our cognitive processing is at an unconscious level. I can say to you now, 'notice your breathing', and that will have quite an effect upon it. It will come off 'auto-pilot' and on to 'manual control'. A lot of our behaviour exists at this level. People do things – some useful, some good, some bad, some awkward, some self-defeating – entirely without knowing why they do them and they therefore behave 'unconsciously'; 'unwittingly' might be a better word.

So what is it about the term 'the unconscious' that you won't allow?

Our heads are not hollow, it's dark in there, it's fleshy. So where is the unconscious? This non-detectable place where all our deep, dark desires are kept under control – where is it? How is materialism transcended?

My biggest objection to psychoanalytic principles like the unconscious, like fixating stages of development, is that: (a) there isn't any evidence for them; and (b) most people you talk to have never experienced anything of the kind, but it makes no difference to the people who hold the views. Since we have all 'repressed' our anxieties. Millions and millions and millions of us – Chinese, Moroccans, Italians included – who have entirely different family traditions, have all repressed these dark worries, and can't remember it any more. Unless of course we pay huge sums of money to people to uncover them for us – with no guarantee whatsoever of a successful outcome. Now all this seems to me to be surreal beyond the dreams of Salvador Dali.

I remember there was a debate in the '70s and they were saying: 'Okay Behavioural techniques work, but it is just because the therapist is a kind person.' How do you approach that subject?

I think that to a very considerable degree in therapeutic work 'the medium is the message'. In other words, one of the most potent sources of positive reinforcement is likely to be the therapist. This is so in teaching too. But then you can be a nice, approachable, but hopeless teacher. It is also possible to be a clever and effective teacher at one level, but an unapproachable person. Most of us who think back to the good teachers that we knew remember a combination of technical effectiveness, approachability and humanity in these individuals. So I think yes, the contingencies in the relationship are a very important source of motivation for change.

Presumably some would say despite whoever Brian Sheldon is or isn't, his techniques work. Or don't you think that's true?

I think it is unlikely. It depends on the circumstances. I think I could run a classroom management scheme by phone using mediators. It wouldn't matter all that much as to whether I was liked.

As an empiricist I have to acknowledge the (reasonably good) research showing that certain kinds of therapeutic variables – warmth, empathy, genuineness – as well as the kinds of things which one would wish to display on ethical grounds anyway, are also quite potent forms of influence. There is no doubt too, is there, that if we like people and get on with them and regard them as professional and reliable and stable individuals – somebody I would like to be a bit more like maybe – then we are open to influence much more readily. I think therapy is about *deliberate* influence, and we shouldn't wish to deny this as some people do.

I have seen Carl Rogers interviewing on video tape, he is a most engaging man, he is one of my favourite interviewers to watch, I like him. However, his constant batting back, again and again and again, of requests for advice seems to me ludicrous. It becomes ridiculous after a while. I agree with the idea – I incorporate it into my own work – this idea that people have to take charge of themselves, but some people need a bit of help with that. Some people need a bit of advice first. They don't want to engage in verbal ping-pong games. The therapists go home in their cars. The people with the problems are left with their screaming kids, their worries, and it seems to me that occasionally 'Why don't you try this?' is a perfectly good and plain piece of human interaction.

What kind of qualities do you want to instil in trainee therapists?

Number one: good therapists, whether they are social workers with other roles and responsibilities, or psychologists, or psychiatrists in training, need to be quite clever. Yet we have a culture within which everyone imagines they would be a brilliant therapist if they only had a lower mortgage payment and a bit more time. Which I think is why some of the helping professions are held in such low esteem here compared to other cultures.

Now why quite clever? Because I think, particularly in respect of cognitive-behavioural work, untangling the complicated patterns of learning that people have been through, and working out an individually-tailored and consistent and logical answer to those learning patterns, takes quite a bit of cerebral activity, alongside the emotional activity that we have been talking about.

I think the second thing you need is for therapists to be prepared to go out into the rain. I think one of the reasons that behaviour therapy doesn't catch on with some professionals is that it is an 'awkward' style of practice. If somebody has a fear of supermarkets, you end up in supermarkets, not talking about them in warm consulting rooms. Clients who have certain kinds of difficulties have to be seen in the evenings or if their difficulties occur in the middle of the day in the classroom, at school. So this is not therapy by 'remote control' where you talk in one setting and hope that this magically generalises to another. The phrase I always use to try to get this point across is, 'No-one ever learned to swim by attending seminars on it.'

You mentioned earlier, you won't turn people down. But presumably there are some people for whom you consider the work inappropriate?

Beware of the therapist who says that his or her approach is good for everything! I think, however, that since we are talking here about an applied branch of learning theory, and learning is such a central human activity, its claims to be good across the range, and probably better than other approaches for many conditions, are more plausible. There are, however, some settings where its clinical effectiveness is in dispute or there seems to be limited evidence in effectiveness. Multiple anxiety states, for example. There is no doubt behaviour therapy does better with single phobic reactions. This doesn't mean that we should abandon people with generalised anxiety states, but we need to make sure that they are medically treated alongside this approach.

I can think of a few types of cases ... delayed recovery from bereavement, for example, where I wouldn't automatically think of a behavioural programme. I can think of some cognitive components that might be of use, though; for example, getting clients to say to themselves that feeling angry about someone that they are supposed to feel a sense of loss about, and loving towards, is okay, is part of the human condition. 'You feel abandoned.' There is the concept. I can also think of one or two principles of reinforcement that would apply, because getting a person who is stuck fast in mourning for a lost loved one, gradually expanding their sphere of operation, even though they don't initially like the idea, is essential at some stage. Try to arrange a benign circumstance. Scheduling pleasant events for people who, for example, are depressed.

In a case I am dealing with at the moment it is the most important element of the whole programme. Talking to yourself in a different way when the 'Oh no, I don't think I will bother' reaction comes on. Try it, and take a deep breath when you start to find it pleasurable, and noticing that you are finding it pleasurable. In other words acknowledging the little pattern of reinforcement that is present in the new circumstance.

So I think some elements of learning theory probably apply to most problems, but to varying degrees.

Do you think that it is in any way beneficial for a therapist to have 'suffered' to be an effective therapist?

I certainly think that there are some people who come forward for social work training on the basis of their own experiences, who turn out to be too damaged. In other words they have too little left over from their preoccupation to be able to help other people. So I think therapists need to be reasonably 'whole'. They should be stable, their life not too chaotic. If they have got themselves together after a period of disintegration, maybe they can be better therapists because of this. It is not a necessary condition, certainly, of good therapy. But then I think that people who have lived very narrow lives probably make poor therapists. There is a kind of American, hi-tech behaviourism which I just do not like the sound of. It is too 'squeaky-clean', too 'clap-happy' for me.

Human beings are strange animals, and there are deep aspects to what they have learnt. This idea that you just tune somebody up with a little more assertion, something like that, it seems strange to me. Self-knowledge is important I think, and also occasional sharing with clients of comparable circumstances from one's own life. I am working at the moment with someone whose marriage has folded, a vulnerable individual, interestingly with a history of loss, and here is another confirming instance of his own unlovability. We are talking about his thoughts, which border occasionally on 'ideas of reference'. Since his collapse he has noticed so much unhappiness around him, which is the selective perception tendency that we all have at work. Everything that comes on the radio tugs at his heart-strings. And I remember saying to him: 'I have lost people myself, and I know that feeling, that the world is conspiring to remind you of what you are trying to overcome.' And I think that is perfectly okay. A little self-disclosure, different from 'So you think you have got problems?' approaches, can humanise therapeutic encounters.

There is a trend, it seems to me from my travels – a move – which started in the '60s but is increasing, towards what they call transpersonal psychology. What are your thoughts on that?

I want to ask a question of them: How do you know? That is a good question to ask Freudians, too. How do people *know* what two-month-old babies think inside their brains? Both good questions to start with. To move the discussion on to an older example of the same thing: how did Melanie Klein know that they are having these thoughts? In terms of developmental psychology, well beyond the level of their cognitive development.

Another good question to ask proponents of any approach is: 'does it make a difference?' In other words, 'do people who go through/are exposed to this, improve in some way, in some detectable way?' So again, the outcome problem. And the only way to settle the question is lots of placebo-controlled random-allocation controlled trials. Nothing would please me more than to know that a mixture of sage and carrot juice will prevent cancer if you drink it every day. I just want a random-allocation controlled trial or three, scientifically done, by reputable scientists, to put the matter as far beyond doubt as it can be, and then I will drink it myself, and argue that it should be available on the National Health Service. I don't care what it is if it works, within ethical limits. Many of these 'transpersonal' therapies are rooted in sloppy thinking.

What are your feelings about the ethical issues surrounding therapy in general? Have you applied your mind (sorry, brain) much to this?

I think all behaviourists, whether cognitive-behavioural or otherwise, come across ethical questions very early on, for a number of interesting reasons. One is that they quickly learn that what they are doing will very likely make a difference. So the fact that this approach works rather well concentrates the mind on how the process of helping is to be managed. Because if you have influence, and you are aware that you are having influence, you have to ask yourself 'influence for what?'; 'And by what right do I have this influence?' A particular problem I think is working with young people who are in a different power position to oneself. Yet, in extreme cases, sometimes I think we have to bite the bullet and do what is good for them, since they are as yet unable to make good decisions for themselves. Either because of their condition, their state, their upbringing or their age, of course. Sometimes you have to do the best you can for people. So I am not an ethically queasy person. I think most of the discussion about ethics that goes on is defensiveness on the part of professionals. I think we should worry a lot more about our own ineffectiveness. There is a big ethical question there. As we sit here talking there are hundreds and hundreds of people talking to therapists who are rather unlikely to change any aspect of their feelings or behaviour. So effectiveness is a very important ethical issue. 'First – do your patient no harm', said Hippocrates to his student physicians and if you can thereafter, do them some good.

Can it be said that some of the so-called therapy which has taken place in the field of child abuse has done no harm to people? We have all those scandals – Orkney, Cleveland. The collective mind set; the dreadful interviews that one can hear on the tape-recordings of their interjections of these children, who no matter how often they insisted that they had not been sexually abused, it is implied to them that they indeed had, but had repressed it. Some very large ethical questions here.

Interestingly you tend to find ethics discussed in books on cognitive-behavioural therapy more than in any other field. Most books in this field have either a good discussion of this, or a chapter on it. This is not true of all approaches.

I can think of some things that I have done as a therapist which I wish I hadn't. They were mistakes. I have ignored things, I have not seen things. I have been lied to, and feel in retrospect I should have detected this. If you evaluate carefully then you learn from these mistakes – because you can see what results you are getting.

What are your thoughts about the economics of this enterprise?

Because of my background in social work I am very keen on these cognitive-behavioural approaches being used in the front line, with the poor, marginalised, troubled people of this world. That is the particular contribution that social workers can make. Social work is a very interesting test-bed for this therapeutic approach in least propitious conditions. We can reach the parts that other therapists don't reach. Many don't move out of Swiss Cottage, they don't move out of their consulting rooms. They treat the comfortably well-off. I think that's ethically dubious and regrettable. It is not something that I do, neither do I charge high fees. If I think someone can pay a little – quite a small amount in effect – I will take it from them. I don't kid myself that it necessarily helps them, in the way the Freudians do. I simply save it, and the next person I meet that has no money, gets it for nothing. But then I am an academic, I have another source of income.

Do you think the UKCP is going to help the British come to terms more with the fact that therapy is a useful kind of enterprise?

I rather like the attitude of scepticism towards therapies that the British have. I share it. I too want evidence. On a recent visit to the United States I was taken aback by the amount of time that people – people in bars, people in cafes – spend talking about their personal development. It seemed to me unattractive. It seemed to me a waste of life, since most of the problems they were talking about seemed to be trivial. So, I rather like the healthy scepticism of the British, and I hope it doesn't change.

The difficulty of belonging to one large organisation which is promoting therapy is the amount of compromise that different groups have to accept – I am sure the analysts feel it too. In the early negotiations (I was President of the British Association for Behavioural and Cognitive Psychotherapists at the time of these negotiations for registration), it was basically a trade-off. The analysts wanted written into the rules an apprenticeship of I think something between three and five years. That suits the way they train their people. We thought it entirely unnecessary. We, on the other hand, wanted written into the rules the idea that you should practise the therapy only if there is good research support for that approach, which they found a rather threatening idea.

So I think the danger is that we end up with an anodyne 'cones hotline' equivalent, charter and mission statement, obsessed approach which is so bland and meaningless that everyone just ignores it. So I think probably I would be in favour of stronger sub-divisions to suit the different approaches.

Just getting back to the Freudian approach again, why do you think it has held sway for so long?

Sir Peter Medawar refers to the 'dark, visceral appeal' of psychoanalysis, I think its mysteriousness, its initiation rites for people wanting to train in it, the idea of becoming a therapist through personal suffering and confrontation of one's own complex desires, fears, worries, and so on. This is an attractive idea. It is a more dramatic view of the human condition. I think also it is a way of looking at some basic concerns of human beings. The struggle for good and evil inside all of us. We are still left with some of the impulses which were once useful in our long evolutionary history. Viciousness, doggedness. We are the most aggressive species on the planet. That needs some explaining in our daily lives. I think it is perfectly rational to see how in evolutionary terms a naked ape like ourselves; not particularly strong, not equipped for killing, no big teeth, no claws, nothing, would develop another way of domination, of getting our supplies. Aggressiveness plus co-operation. The twin forces. Now if you look at that in terms of impulsive aggressiveness, and also the twin attribute that we have for co-operation, love, living in family units and so on, you can see the evolutionary origins of both of these together. If you reify them they sound rather like id and super ego, don't they? The best and worst of which we are capable. How we would like to be versus how we sometimes are by instinct. So I suppose what I am saying is, I can see how they have a plausibility, these ideas, the notion that we are driven from within by these forces.

At the turn of the century this new, risqué brand of psychology must have been fascinating. Its concern with sexuality which the culture had, on the surface at least, suppressed for a long time was suddenly out in the open. So there is that. People like something mysterious, and I am afraid the stuff that I peddle doesn't have the benefit of much mystery. I am simply saying: 'Practise something different. You will probably like it when you have done it!'

If the empirical research suggests that there is limited evidence for the efficacy of psychoanalysis, is that an ethical question by allowing people to continue to go to people without necessarily improving themselves, or is that just people's free choice?

I think free choice to the extent that any choice is free. But the mass media could do more to delve below the present position on therapy that most journalists adopt; 'different things work for different people'. The therapist saying 'I do what works for me.' Levels of evidence that are purely subjective, such as, 'I have helped a number of people. I see the changes with my own eyes.' I think in this culture we are more scientifically illiterate than this. We allow standards of evidence in this field that would never be allowed in medicine or even plumbing. But there is an anti-intellectual, anti-scientific revolt going on throughout the whole western world. The 'wackier' the therapy, the more you can charge for it in the United States, and something sober and empirical is less attractive to people in the short term.

I have had a number of patients who have been to see me a couple of times, and I think have been expecting something more exotic than they were getting, and have left. I think that raises the question about the reinforcement contingencies of the therapeutic relationship. Some people will pay for other people to listen to them, and sometimes people want to come and tell you of their patterns of lying to themselves about their lives, in the hope that you will confirm those for a fee. So, they are unlikely to come anywhere near anyone who is going to say 'If you have a profound fear of birds, with this approach you end up in an aviary.' You have a fear of flying – you end up on an aeroplane.' That can be very threatening. 'If you have a fear of social encounters, you are going to be out with your therapist meeting people – which is the very thing you fear – but will come not to fear.' Tough stuff.

How do you monitor your own performance with people, and when do you know when it is time to take a break?

All people who are employed in the helping professions can become desensitised to the strong emotions which are coming their way – think of social work and child abuse and neglect. Think of psychiatric social

work: you are confronting misery day in, day out. It does lead necessarily to a certain distancing. I think a certain distancing is important.
What we were all taught about 'controlled emotional involvement'. Now
if you look at the phrase 'controlled emotional involvement', there are
three words there, and the 'control' one is important but the 'emotional'
is also important and the 'involvement' word is also important. I am
more worried about students who *lack* emotional involvement with
people. And there is much in the present organisation of the public
services to encourage a managerial, tick-box approach, where you never
actually get a chance to talk to people about their real fears and
worries. 'Virtual reality social work', I call it.

An extra pressure that comes on behaviour therapists, I think, is the
level of organisation that is required to make the approach work. It has to
be very consistently done. Sometimes the nature of a problem is such that
you have to be there for blocks of time – you cannot see people who are
being aggressive at school in a counselling room somewhere else for about
50 minutes a week and hope to change their behaviour. You have got to
be in the classroom, with the peer group – if they will let you in. Now that
doesn't fit into most therapists' diaries. It is another reason, I think, why
there are more comfortable kinds of therapy to practise.

With this approach, too, you can fail visibly and clearly in front of all
your peers. The goals are clear. The great contribution of behaviour
therapy to the helping professions has been a close evaluation of results:
either through research, where we have an unrivalled tradition, or through
single subject designs. In other words, manifest evidence of change is the
touchstone of effective therapy. That means that if you are not helping
someone, it will be clear to you and also to everyone else. So we need a
climate, I think, within therapy where it is better to fail early and clearly
than to go on for a long time, and then use some loose phrase at the end,
like 'I think he has come to terms with his worries', to justify it. In some
therapeutic approaches I think it is very difficult to see, given the kinds of
loose and intangible goals they set for themselves, how it is *ever* possible
to fail. You can always say: 'At least all this anger is out in the open now',
as the couple you are counselling fall fighting to the floor in front of you.
So what would a bad result look like? It is something that you have to be
willing to confront as a behaviour therapist.

*Some of the people I talk to say this issue of what they call 'emotional
literacy' should be on school curricula ...*

I am worried about recommending that *anything* else be added to the
National Curriculum. But I think education for life is a very important
thing, particularly given the emotionally impoverished circumstances
within which some families bring up their children these days. I am not
talking about single parents or dual parents, you can be brought up as an
emotionally literate person by your mother on her own in circumstances
of relative poverty, and, if the emotional circumstances are right, grow up

into an emotionally mature person. Similarly you *can* be damaged within a '2.2', 'Oxo advertisement' type family in just the same way. I think this idea that we leave to chance the complicated skills that people need in order to get on with each other and to live happy lives, is rather strange, particularly with the disintegration of some of the structures of society that we could safely leave this to in the past.

But the danger in recommending interventions is that it will be done via a non-intellectual approach to emotional development. In other words it will be done in a 'let's all sit round' kind of 1960s way, and will bring itself into disrepute. It will have little meaning for the children. If you talk to teenagers, schoolchildren, they are very strongly interested in questions about how to get on with people, of the same sex or a different sex; how to get on with adults, these strange creatures who make their lives a misery from time to time. So if it were soberly and soundly managed it would make a very interesting contribution to the development of children, but I fear it wouldn't be.

I am particularly interested in preventative schemes for teaching young parents how to cope with behavioural problems in their children. These do not come out of nowhere, and the idea that babies just grow on their own is a peculiar idea I think, perhaps a peculiarly British idea – that if you feed them occasionally, and pat them on the head occasionally, then they will grow up okay. That seems to me to be leaving an awful lot to chance. We ought to be equipping people with at least the basic skills of parenthood.

Wouldn't it be interesting to see more non-stigmatised courses on how to manage disciplinary problems with young children, for people who wanted to come to them. Preventative schemes, broadly educative, with a bit of practical work built in. Most of the reasons for foster placement breakdown are behavioural problems. Most child abuse begins – apart from the very dramatic violent act done by someone outside the family – by discipline going wrong. People start on a cycle of violence – hitting – and it gets out of hand. So I think prevention is a vital part of the therapeutic endeavour.

CHAPTER 9

Existential Therapy

Ernesto Spinelli

Ernesto Spinelli teaches at the School of Psychotherapy and
Counselling, Regent's College, and is the author of numerous
publications including *Demystifying Therapy*. An Existential
psychotherapist, he has a London-based private practice.

*Can you just tell me a bit about your personal background, particularly as
it might relate to how you eventually started in therapy?*

Sure. I began studying psychology at McGill University in the late '60s
and obviously at that time, one of the big areas of interest and concentration was the boom and rise of humanistic psychotherapy and humanistic
psychology. And quite frankly at McGill, psychology was dominated by
behavioural psychology in the guise of Professor Donald Hebb who was
one of the main bulwarks of that area. So this was like a tremendous wave
of something completely new and exciting, and it fitted in with the times,
and all of those things.

So a group of us actually managed to get a course organised in
Rogerian approaches, and we had somebody who had trained with Rogers,
and initially we began doing experiential work on ourselves and so forth,
and that eventually turned into a kind of training programme, which lasted
for just under a year. At the end of which we all came out of it thinking:
'Oh yeah, we're practising psychotherapists now, we're humanistic psychotherapists.'

And so that was in one sense my first interest in psychotherapy. I
continued to do that throughout the last year at McGill, and then when
I first came to England in '71 as a postgraduate at the University of
Manchester, I was doing some seminars and courses that were not in
my official area – which was actually child psychology – but in my kind
of subsidiary area, which was in humanistic therapy and psychology.

So my first real involvement was in the humanistic field, and looking
back on it, while it was a tremendous buzz, it was also I think the first real
exposure and inkling I had to a sense of the tremendous power that can be
generated in psychotherapy, and the potentials for its abuse, which has
become a continuing theme in my work. But in any case, after a while I
became – particularly since I came to Manchester, where the ethos in
psychotherapy was much more classically psychoanalytic – I began to

study much more psychoanalytic work than I had done prior to that. I mean I'd read some Freud and so forth, but nothing to any great extent. It was not, as I say, it wasn't part of the times.

By about '73, when I moved to Guildford, to the University of Surrey to do my PhD, I'd pretty much left humanistic psychology and psychotherapy in a spiritual sense; I'd become very disenchanted with it. I'd begun to see great obstacles in what was being done, even though in a sense that was really a boom time for it here. You had the rise of various programmes that were humanistically-oriented, particularly around London. You had people – I remember there was a group calling itself 'The Travelling Humanistic Circus' going around to different places. And of course at Surrey, John Heron was there and he'd been doing this long project [The Human Potential Project].

So I moved out of it at the time that it took off here. And I moved more and more towards psychoanalytic studies. And I began to, obviously, read a lot, and eventually decided to start training as a psychoanalyst, which I began to do at one of the principal centres in London.

I lasted just over a year. It was quite a negative experience. I found the whole training process really quite dogmatic. I thought the lectures that were being given were really superficial, particularly when it came to other approaches to psychology and psychotherapy. Most of all, I found the actual experience of being heard and interpreted in a psycho-analytic way as being tremendously off-putting. It was an interesting experience because reading the material felt like something – that you were being enlightened or something. There was something really excit-ing and interesting and open to all kinds of possibilities of understand-ing oneself. Actually experiencing the process was completely different ... [Laughs] ... It felt much more like being pushed around and manipu-lated and abused, and all of those things. In some ways I feel it's a continuing problem, that I think a lot of people continue to be attracted to the material when they're distanced from it, and they read it as an intellectual way of understanding psychic processes. But when it actually comes to the lived level, I think – I mean maybe I'm biased in the sense that the kind of people I speak to tend to be people who in some way or other are dissatisfied or disillusioned with psychoanalysis, but never-theless that's my experience. That there is a real gap between that kind of detached reading of the stuff and the lived experience of it.

Quite honestly, it affected me quite badly, because I realised that I had invested a lot of my – not just my intellectual energy – a lot of my personal sense of my aims, my ambitions of the future in that approach. And to a large extent, I think I was left floundering. 'What do I do now, I can't commit myself to this because it doesn't feel right.'

So what I did, like many other people do, is I stopped any kind of attempt at continuing training for the time being and began teaching. I thought that maybe by teaching I would actually learn something as to where I wanted to go and what I wanted to do, and as it happened the main thing that I found myself teaching was actually psychoanalysis.

So for a few years I taught it, and I'm sure I convinced a lot of students to whom I was teaching it that I was an ardent and convinced psychoanalyst. I think I taught it well enough and accurately enough, and was able to present the viewpoint in a fair way. But there was an ambivalence about it, because it was still very much, 'We're talking about it in this intellectual isolation, we're not talking about it in the sense of what it might actually be like to be a client, or to be a psychoanalytic therapist.'

So through that teaching coincidentally I was then asked to start to teach a course, initially in humanistic psychology and psychotherapy. I agreed, if the focus of the course was actually not looking so much at the wide variety of approaches that fall into that area, but if the focus of the course was really on the underlying philosophical assumptions that invest humanistic psychology. And I think I said that because I didn't really know all that clearly what these might be (I knew in a vague sense what they might be), but because I wanted to know, I thought of it as a way of being paid to do your own studies.

It was accepted, it was agreed that I would do that, and very early on in preparing for the course, I was reintroduced to philosophies, primarily Husserl and Heidegger, that seemed to me to be crucial to the kinds of assumptions and ideas that the humanists in some ways both understood, and more importantly misunderstood. I became fascinated by the wealth of stuff that existed both in philosophy and in psychology, which of course as an undergraduate and as a postgraduate I'd had little snippets of, but nothing to any great extent. And of course, one of the main figures that we'd had, who we'd associated with phenomenology in some strange kind of way, was Laing. This was not a return to Laing so much but more a – my first experience of studying Laing in a much closer way than in that kind of 'pop' sense that we'd done as undergraduates. Little by little I became more and more convinced that there was a wealth of material within the existential phenomenological framework that was tremendously valuable for psychotherapy. And at the time – I'm talking now about the early '80s – I didn't know anybody who was practising or applying these ideas in psychotherapy other than, obviously names like Laing and the Philadelphia Association.

So it was very much a kind of isolated training. I've never trained officially in existential or phenomenological psychotherapy, probably because I wouldn't have known where to go, and partly because I think my own character was such that it was something that I wanted – initially at least – to really focus on in a much more private fashion.

What I began to do was to then go back to practising, and to start to see where some of the applications from material that I'd been reading could be put into the psychotherapeutic arena, and in a sense what the result might be. So I was carrying out experiments really, hopefully fairly humane experiments with my clients. I learned a great deal from them, because initially even though I was attempting to work phenomenologi-cally or existentially, the whole method I had was really from my psychoanalytic training. So I was trying to do a kind of 'psychoanalysis that wasn't'. I think that I was probably quite confused and probably communicated confusion to my clients, who, in many cases, provided me with tremendous insights as to how to clear up that confusion. The most important of which were the ones that were about basically them saying to me 'Look just hear me out, hear me accurately. Listen to what I'm saying, without you jumping in and taking that material and transforming it into some other kind of thing. Just listen to what I'm saying. Give me back what *you're* hearing.' I think that was a crucial moment for me in the sense of actually letting go of a lot of the baggage of psychotherapy, and in doing so finding much more of a sense of engagement with people, which was exhilarating, but also frightening.

Is there anything in your personal background, do you think, that might explain some of your motivations to want to do therapy or do you think that's irrelevant?

No, I don't think it's irrelevant. My attitude towards therapy is that it's largely overblown in the sense that it's presented as an elevated thing that only special people can do. My experience – certainly personally speaking, but also in talking to a lot of other therapists – is that in many cases it's more the result of a process of elimination. It's more realising all the things that you can't do, and discovering, 'Well here's this one little thing that maybe I can do', which is to some extent partly listening. But I think more than that for me, it's just having tremendous curiosity about people's lives. About how people are, and think, and consider themselves and the world.

Now for me, that curiosity initially was very much aligned to a fantasy I had which was of becoming a film director. That was my great love, and I was too much of a coward really to pursue it to any great extent. For various reasons it just didn't happen. But I think what interested me about being a film director was that it was a means of presenting a canvas of life. I was fascinated by – again being a product of the '60s – those films of the '60s that were in a sense not so much about stories but were about character, were about an examination of individuals and of relationships in their lives. Like didn't really end anywhere, they just went on and on and it was interesting. And it seemed to me that that was something that I had some insight in, some ability to empathise with, but I think it largely boils down just to curiosity – I'm just curious about the way people experience their being – not because I want to change it or because I think that I can offer something to them that necessarily will make their lives better, but because I just find it interesting. I'm an observer.

In that sense it was a natural progression for me to say ... 'Well if I can't do that, and yes, well, I could try writing' (again the idea that psychotherapists are all failed novelists – I think there's probably some truth in that as well). But it just seemed like one of those things that could appease this curiosity, and which would also allow me to employ whatever minimal gifts I think I have. So it's not out of some great exalted thing. It's just more out of 'I can't do much else', to be honest with you.

How do you conceive of existential therapy being different from other therapies?

Well, I think the first thing to be said is that it's characteristic of existential therapy that the various individuals who practise it, who label themselves as existential therapists, probably each practise it from their own idiosyncratic standpoint. So although there are underlying similarities and connections that we can all agree upon – and maybe we can talk about this – it's also important to recognise that there are important individual differences. So the way I might practise it and how I understand it, may be partly in agreement with my colleagues, but also is likely to be in some points of disagreement with them.

Part of that is due to who influenced you at the philosophical level most significantly. And because existential therapy really has a number of significant voices at the philosophical level, it could Kierkegaard, it could be Nietzsche to some extent, it could be Husserl, it could be Heidegger. I think those are the main philosophers. Then clearly those voices that influence you the most will direct in a way the focus, the attention, the style if you will, of what you're doing. So there's that kind of divergence that appears. The other is really, 'Where do you come from?', academically or intellectually speaking, that has led you to the point where you're practising existential therapy. As I said to you, my background is in psychology, and so in that sense I practised from a much more psychologically informed way, than perhaps those who have come into it, again either from philosophy, or indeed from psychiatry or from sociology or social work. So again, there are these different influences.

For example, if you were to work with me, by and large we would be sitting face-to-face. I think that's probably something that is largely common among existential therapists. But I think those are superficial things that I know psychotherapists get very het up about, but it's silly I think ... [Laughs] ... Perhaps the most important thing about it is that we would be engaged very much in mutual discourse. It wouldn't be, for example, as passive on my part as a therapist, as you might find in more classical psychoanalytic approaches. Equally the discourse wouldn't be like in cognitive-behavioural approaches, where I would see myself as the one who is in some way or other taking the role of the teacher, or who is trying to extract from you those things that are irrational about your thinking and so forth.

So that although the cognitive-behavioural therapist would be quite active in dialogue, it would be from a position of, as I say, teacher/educator: 'I will give you homework.' As an existential therapist I wouldn't presume to take that position. My interest would be to engage with you – again as I said largely from the standpoint of wishing to make an attempt accurately to enter your world of experience. So in that sense, my interest would not be in trying to discern from my standpoint what I thought was wrong with you, or what could be changed, or how you might live life in a better sense. I would hope that to some extent those questions might arise for you, and that you would then explore them should you wish to. But I would see my task largely as being engaged with you in a way that would allow both of us to view your 'experience of being' far more clearly than perhaps you had done so in the past. And what assistance I might be able to lend would be in making comments or asking questions that would challenge in the sense that they would force you to be clearer about your messages, your statements to yourself, about your experience. That would be as far as I would think I would feel right in going.

That, I think, is a crucial difference between existential therapy and many other approaches, largely in the sense that it puts me as therapist in a much more precarious and open position than, say, a psychoanalyst or a cognitive behaviourist, or even a humanistic psychotherapist. In the sense that I'm kind of abdicating to a large extent the tricks of my trade. I'm trying not to engage with you as a superior or a more stable, or a more aware human being, and instead of that I'm trying to say 'Well, what I'll attempt is to respond to you in a way that – I give you a glimpse of how I try to be you.' That can be quite genuinely disturbing. Disturbing in the sense of your experience of being may actually be quite a disturbing experience, but disturbing also because it puts me as the therapist in a much more defenceless position than if I were to say to you: 'Well I'm going to be your interpreter, or I'm going to be your teacher, or I'm going to be your mirror.' I think it opens the engagement to something quite different. I think that's what makes the approach both highly attractive to people – again in a kind of distanced sense – but which also, in applying, they realise how difficult the approach is, and equally how scary it can be for them. How it opens them, the therapists, to a confrontation with the biases and assumptions that they hold about themselves as being therapists, or what they're supposed to be doing as therapists.

So we would in some ways engage in conversation that was focused upon the exploration of your experience, and it would be an attempt at a descriptive analysis rather than a more analytic analysis which would seek to go behind your statements, or beneath your statements, and try to extract from those that which was implicit in either an unconscious or a symbolic sense. I would agree with the idea that much of what we say contains implications, but I think those implications are at the conscious level rather than necessarily at an unconscious level. So my task would be really to assist you in making that which was implicit much more explicit. Not by saying 'This really means something else, that you're unaware of because it's down in your unconscious,' but rather 'it means *something* and I think you know what it means, but let's be clearer about it.'

For example, a client comes and says 'I feel depressed.' Well depression can range from clinical notions of what depression is to 'I'm feeling low, I'm feeling miserable today.' And so, as a stupid example, that kind of statement contains a lot within it that is implied. But I don't know what *you* implied by that statement – I might know what I would think, what I would mean by it – so it would be my task to say to you: 'Okay, tell me more. What's it like to be this?', in the hope that in doing that both of us would get a much clearer sense of what was contained in that word that you used. So much of the therapy is really about *disclosing*. Disclosing to oneself views, opinions, biases, statements that one keeps largely unexamined. That's one kind of disclosure. The other kind of disclosure is the disclosure that will occur between the two of us. What are we disclosing about ourselves in our dialogue with one another? And what does that say, with the focus on you as the client about the way you are; not just here, but maybe how the way that you are here expresses a much more general stance towards life. Again that does allow for many clients a confrontation with themselves which can be very powerful, as powerful as any other psychotherapeutic confrontation. But hopefully one that allows them to feel that what confrontation is being generated, is being generated by them rather than by the intrusions or the statements from on high of the psychotherapist.

What are the major strategies, concepts and indeed material that you deal with?

I think generally speaking the concerns lie around questions of choice, freedom, responsibility, temporality. What do all these mean? They're points that focus around how each of us constructs a meaningful existence. Within that is contained those points in our lives where meaning seems illusory, where we don't seem to find meaning in our lives. And we search for it, or the meaning that we hold seems to evaporate upon us for one reason or another. So these questions of freedom, and choice, and so forth are questions that fundamentally are about issues of being or existence that are universals. And in that sense which each of us – through our construction of meaning – in some way or other deals with, copes with, makes sense of. We might make sense of them by, for example, restricting the amount of freedom that we allow ourselves. So we might live life in a meaning-filled fashion that says: 'I am restricted by forces of culture or forces of genetics, or forces of environment or whatever.' And therefore I find myself in a position where I've abdicated to a large extent the sense of responsibility for what I'm doing. I'm not responsible for these things because of my past, or because of my parents, or because of this or because of that. And in that sense the existential approach seeks to explore first of all how these broad terms are actually lived by each client. How the client has constructed a meaning, a *lived* meaning of such things as freedom, or responsibility, or choice.

As I say, largely to see initially: 'Okay, this is the way that the client is in the world. This is the meaningful relationship that has come into being.' Now from that, hopefully, what can happen is that by examining and clarifying it one begins to see that there are points that don't fit. Where there are gaps in the meaningful structure that has been developed, and that these are exposed so that there are contradictions here or there are gaps, or there are mixed messages being given which again are largely at an implicit level. If we make them explicit, what happens then? Does it allow the meaning of being of the world, as lived by the client, to be affected – either in a sense of acknowledging it: 'Yes I actually chose this way of being', or alternatively, looking at it and saying: 'Well actually this meaning doesn't really quite fit. I think it's more complex or there are other things to it.' So in other words it opens up more possibilities.

So these philosophical terms become employed in a very practical, lived sense – 'Tell me about how you are' – and within what you will tell me undoubtedly are questions about your relationship to the world, to others and to yourself, that involve these questions of the amount of freedom that exists for you, where the notion of time in the sense of your view of your own temporal life is. So where does the notion of death come for you? How do you deal with that? How do you make sense of your own temporality, and so forth? Now I want to emphasise that as a therapist I wouldn't at some point come to you and say 'Right, today we're going to talk about death.' They would be things that hopefully would emerge from our dialogue, and that would come from you, and again I found that initially they come in an implicit fashion which only requires a very small amount of clarification for the client to then look at them.

These are the crucial concepts that would emerge in the whole process. In one sense they might emerge from *dreams*, so I wouldn't want to give the impression that as existential therapists we wouldn't talk about dream material. We would do if the client, for example, came in and said 'I had a very interesting dream', or, 'Unusually, I dreamt last night.' And we would treat that experience in the same way as we would treat any other exploration of experience. But what would be avoided – going back to the terms you used, like transference or of the unconscious, or whatever – would be all of those terms that in one way or another unnecessarily mystified both your experience of your own being, and which mystified my function as a therapist, and which mystified what we're doing together. It would be much more straightforward.

Now I often find that clients use words like 'unconscious' or whatever, or they might say, 'I wonder when transference is going to begin', or things like that. And I will respect their use of those terms in the sense that I will try to find out what they mean by them themselves. But I think it is unnecessary for me to employ them in a way that supposedly helps me to understand – to a large extent they're useless terms, and in some ways misleading.

So that's in a broad sense, we would be looking at those universals of human experience that are experienced at – let's call it a conscious or a lived level, rather than we would have to hypothesise as being at the unconscious level, like, say, the Oedipus complex or whatever. So the concerns would be about conscious life. Now my own special interest, and I suppose the way that I fashion my clarification of clients' experience has over time been largely built up around the construction of the self that clients – all of us – generate in our attempt to make ourselves meaningful. What interests me about it, is that it seems to me that the self-construct reveals very clearly to all of us, first of all the self that we believe ourselves to be and implicitly the self that we have denied or that we believe we cannot be, or we shouldn't be, or we mustn't be. And reveals in that sense both what might be called 'sedimentations' – those things that we feel to be absolutely unquestionable, or crucial about the construct that we have – and those 'dissociations', those elements of non-self, denied-self.

It seems to me that many of the problems that clients present us with are problems largely of sedimentation and dissociation of the self-construct, in the sense that many issues are about people having experiences – whether at the lived-at level, the behavioural level, or at the thought level – that do not fit their construct. So, for example, if I considered myself to be 100 per cent heterosexual, let's say, as some clients I've worked with do, and at some point or other in my experience I find myself being attracted to another man. This is a tremendous challenge to the construct that I've sedimented. My sedimentation is 'I am only attracted to women', but my experience is 'Here I am, I'm attracted to a man.' How do I explain that? Now typically, I think, the way we explain it is to deny the experience, to cut it off in some way from ourselves, to say: 'This is not mine, it somehow comes from something else.' Now that something else could be something supernatural, it could be something chemical – we find all kinds of explanations to detach or dissociate that experience.

What I'm getting at is that many of the issues that I find myself working with with clients are issues that are about having experiences that do not fit the construct, and the consequent attempts to explain those experiences in a dissociated fashion. So: 'It wasn't me, I wasn't being myself, or I was possessed, or I was this, or I was that.' In the exploration of that, what you're then attempting to do with the client is to consider those possibilities that emerge when you seek to look at this experience from another meaning standpoint. What if it wasn't dissociated? What if it was saying something about you, and your experience? What then happens? It seems to me that that's a largely phenomenologically-informed way of looking at things, and that phenomenology, in investigating anything, rather than try to close it up, actually opens it more and more to potentials, to possibilities.

It seems to me that a lot of what certainly I do in therapy, is allow people to consider that those things that have been sedimented or closed may actually be much more flexible, much more open to a variety of ways of interpretation. Including, of course, the self-construct. So in a sense it's an exploration of the construct in order for it to gain a greater flexibility than it may have had beforehand. Now this can be deeply, deeply disturbing, because it seems to me that to attack any point of a self-construct attacks the whole of it. If I change any little bit of the sense of self that I believe myself to be, I'm really changing the whole self. So it seems to me that it's something that a therapist needs to approach with a great deal of caution, and a great deal of sense of responsibility as to what could be taking place. We know all too well what happens when the therapist adopts the position that that's the best thing that can be done, or the most important thing that can be done. Havoc is created, not just in the client's life, but more importantly in the various relations that the client has. If I go through this dramatic process of self-reconstruction, what I might tend to do would be then to say: 'Oh, that self that existed, that lived with this person, or had these children or had that kind of job, that's all denied.' I go off and I become somebody else.

And it seems to me that that creates as many problems as it might offer initial solutions. It raises that inherent contradiction within it. I'm assisting you in one way to question things, and in your questioning it may provoke dramatic reconstructions of meaning. Both meaning in terms of your relations to others and meaning in terms of your relation to yourself. Yet at the same time we have to do it in such a way that those relations that currently exist must also be respected, and don't provoke a denial which is all too similar to what you're doing already.

Because of the emphasis on conscious choice and the here and now, presumably if a client talks about a sexual incident or a childhood pattern, you're quite happy to talk about that, but presumably your emphasis is not on those incidents as explanatory concepts, but about what the client will consciously do about that now. Is that basically it?

Yes. Obviously clients, and many therapists, treat the past as being a crucial component of their current experience, and I think they have every right to. Where existentialists would disagree with other approaches is in the notion of the causal connection between the past and the present. And equally and maybe more importantly that the past is not somehow a fixed structure; that the past that you remember today is saying something about the being you are today, rather than saying much about who you might have been then. So in other words it seems to me that the past is tremendously open to constant reinterpretation and in that sense the past, existentially speaking, is really much more connected to the present and indeed to one's future aims and ambitions than perhaps other approaches would have us believe. So to use your example, if the client comes to me and says 'In the past I was abused in some way or other', it seems to me that what's crucial is what is the sense that you are making of that experience now, today? How do you use it to explain who you are, who you can't be? How do you use it to explain the obstacles in your life, or the weaknesses that you experience in yourself? So it's not about going back to it and reliving it, I don't think you can do that, but what I think you *can* do is to be clearer about how that event is expressing something about you today, and about who you want to be *now* and equally who you want to be in the future.

If sexuality is the organising principle of Freud, is it meaning then for existentialists, rather than existence?

In my understanding of it I would agree with you, I would think that it is the construct of meaning of our lives, and the recognition within that of how the process is ongoing and how it's a completely plastic process. That it's a tremendous illusion on our part that we can somehow capture meaning and encase it in something that is not going to change, that is not going to alter. I think many of us try to live our lives in that way, as though we *could* capture our meaning or another's meaning and say 'Right, it's now hermetically sealed, it will be like that for ever.' It's just impossible.

Is there a person that existential therapy is far more suited to? Are there kinds of problems you feel somehow fit a little easier with this type of therapy?

I think they are good questions to ask. Some people have written that certain clients probably would gain most from existential therapy. The kinds of things that they have said are, either people who are in a very precarious position as to their existence – they're either contemplating suicide or they've been suicidal – or they're in that meaningless void that you sometimes get into where things are very uncertain. Equally they've suggested that people who have moved from one culture to another might benefit most from an existential approach, because again it's about reconstructing meaning and reconstructing yourself in an alien environment. So it lends itself very much to multi-cultural or cross-cultural approaches to therapy. And indeed a number of my students are particularly drawn to it because they were or are themselves from other cultures and societies, and they find that this approach is the one that allows them the most means of exploration, as opposed to others.

Another suggestion that's been made is that it's effective with people – oddly enough – who are not terribly intellectual. One of the critiques that's often made is that it's a terribly intellectual and head-based therapy, but in fact in some ways those people who are most intellectual perhaps would tend to avoid the examination of experience. They would want to examine what experience might be like in an abstract sense rather than in a lived sense. So there are these ideas around that. My own experience is that I've worked with a tremendous range of people. At the moment I only work privately, because I have a very limited amount of time with which to work with people. But in the past I've worked both privately and in the NHS, in GP practices, which I found to be a tremendously useful experience, because I was getting a totally different clientele. I was working in a largely working-class area of London, and was working with people who in other circumstances – either financial or even at the level of knowledge and awareness of counselling and therapy – would never have had the opportunity, might not have even contemplated the idea of engaging in therapy. And what I found was that the approach lends itself tremendously well to examinations of issues, primarily because it doesn't seek necessarily to go beyond them or underneath them. *It takes people at their own level.* And it says: 'Okay, let's work with what's given to us rather than what we might want, or what we think is important.' Now it seems to me that the restrictions are not so much with the client but with the therapist. It's the therapist's biases and assumptions as to what he or she can do or can work with, or under what conditions work can take place. I think those are the crucial elements rather than necessarily the kind of clientele that one gets. I think psychotherapy as a whole is dominated by these kinds of superstitious beliefs, generated by therapists and by their theories, as to what the necessary essential conditions for therapy to take place might be.

Do you set some set of goals in the beginning with the client, and relatedly, when does it end? Is there a moment of enlightenment or what?

When I first begin a contract with clients, what I do typically is to initiate a very short-term contract of six sessions which is a kind of 'let's see how we work together' time. Sometimes it might happen that the issues or the problems that the client initally came to me with, if they're very specific, over the period of six sessions the client says: 'I've dealt with this now, I don't want to come back. It's not that I don't want to see you, I've dealt with the issue.' But in most instances, it's a means for us in a strange sense to start to get to know one another. To consider really whether it's an enterprise that we want to continue to engage in, and in most instances for the client, it is; it's a recognition of 'Do I really want to commit myself to something that is in one sense usually much more open, and I might not know how long this will last?' Some clients will ask, very specifically ask: 'Can we have a time-limited process? I want to commit myself to a series of sessions, whether it's ten or 20 or 50, but at the end of that I want to be clear that it's finished.' And I'm quite happy to accept that, largely because my goals are about attempting to explore the world with you. So in that sense, if we spend 50 weeks or we spend 150 it makes no difference. So I have no expectations that in some way or other I can provoke independently some kind of beneficial change or effect in you. *I've no idea what I do that you might consider to be meaningful or helpful.*

I'll tell you an anecdote that I think captures that, that I've used quite a lot with students. A number of years ago I had a session with a client, which was one of those sessions where you come out and you think: 'Oh God that was really exciting and so much was said', and so forth. And the next time I saw the client, the client came in and sat down and the first thing he said was 'God that session last time was really so amazing, I got so much out of it.' Then he said 'You know, I don't remember a thing that you said or that I said. The only thing I remember is that at one point you made this gesture with your hand [it was kind of a chopping gesture with the hand] and *that* captured for me absolutely the crucial points of all of the problems that I've raised.' Now I had no idea I'd made this gesture, but that was what the client took from me, that was the significant thing, and it had a tremendous effect upon him. Now I can't pretend that I know what you're going to take from our interaction that is going to be meaningful to you, and I think it's really false of a therapist to make that assumption. So in that sense it seems to me that all I can do is to engage with you, and somewhere along the line maybe this gesture or some word I say, or whatever, is going to strike you as being meaningful. But I have no way of predicting that.

To go back to the time thing, I know you want to know about this. In one sense, one of the things that existential therapy argues is that really therapy doesn't in one sense end. First of all, one of the things that we believe is that perhaps the most significant things that happen in therapy are likely to happen outside of the sessions, rather than in the sessions themselves. Again that's hard for a lot of therapists to swallow, because it takes away a lot of our sense of mystique. So in one sense it's really what happens outside of the sessions and what the client then brings back and relates about *being in the world* that is important. Equally, when, for one reason or another, formal sessions come to an end there is the recognition that there is always the possibility that in six months or a year's time, two years' time, five years down the road – assuming that the therapist is still alive and practising, whatever – that the client may well want to come back. And that's not seen as a failure of the therapy. It's just seeing that the client has reached a point, at that point where the client has decided, 'This is good enough for me at the moment, I've got enough here to deal with. And who knows? Maybe at some point in the future, new issues will arrive that I want to discuss with you.' So in that sense, the idea of things coming to a final, complete end are treated with some degree of scepticism.

On average I find I tend to work with clients probably for about between 24 and 36 months. It's that kind of range. Now within that obviously there are clients that I work with in a very short-term way, and there are others that I've been seeing for four or five years, something like that. But on average I would say that that's the kind of time that I tend to work with people. I tell that to people when I first see them, that on average this is what tends to happen. So that they have a sense of, again, what they might be committing themselves to.

*One always assumes that a lot of people who come to see existential thera-
pists are concerned with problems of life and death. What if a client believes
that suicide appears to them to be the most appropriate option? How do
you deal with the ethics of those kinds of things?*

At that level I would say my view is that the client has the right to make
that kind of decision. What I would hope is that we would have the kind of
relationship whereby that thought, that possibility, could be discussed
openly. Not necessarily with the idea that it's being discussed so that I can
talk you out of it, but it's being discussed so that we can see really what
you are telling yourself about it. What the idea of committing suicide
actually allows for you. What does it provoke? What are the implications
of it? And if at the end of that your belief is still 'It's the right thing for me
to do', ethically speaking, personally I don't feel I have the right to intervene. Now there is a problem in this, in that increasingly there are legal
issues as opposed to ethical issues being presented to therapists. The more
therapy becomes a recognised profession, the more these ethical questions
become translated into legal issues. So, for example, in America at the
moment in some states, therapists are legally bound to inform on their
clients if they are contemplating suicide, on the grounds that the therapists' licences might be taken away from them. Increasingly those kinds of
issues are being presented here in the UK. So, in one sense, I'm sure the
time will come that if one wants to practise in a capacity where one is
recognised as a professional psychotherapist, there will have to be com-
promises made in the sense of having to say to clients: 'Look we can work
together and we can talk about all kinds of things, but you need to know
legally what the conditions are.' I don't know how helpful or beneficial this
will be. I think in some ways it will create tensions in the relationship that
might otherwise have been resolved. It might actually paradoxically promote suicide or violent attacks, or whatever, rather than alleviate them. I
don't know, I'm not sure. But it is a problem.

*Before I move on, can I just briefly get you to clarify something for me.
Very briefly, how would you conceptualise the difference between what you
do and cognitive therapy, which again is about looking through someone
else's eyes?*

Well I think there are several differences. First of all from a cognitive-
behavioural viewpoint, most cognitive behaviourists come into therapy
with the idea that the problem that the client has is in some way
irrational. That there's a great deal of irrationality. And they will try to
promote a notion of rationality. I can't tell the difference to be honest
with you. I think in many cases those things that seem initially to be
irrational, when you explore them a bit they contain an inherent rationality to them. That's part of the divergence and the sense of 'If I
pretend to know what's rational and irrational about your way of being,
then I can teach you, I can tell you "This is how you should be, these

are the kinds of tricks that you can do to become more rational."' If I
make it far more questionable as to what is rational or irrational in your
way of being, then I can't teach you any more. The most I can do with
you is to help you to clarify those things regardless of whether they're
rational or irrational.

*Using the classical psychiatric language, what range of people can you not
see? Or doesn't that apply ...*

In spite of his being ritualistically torn to pieces by his profession, I still
think that Laing has a lot to tell us about working with so-called schizophrenics or psychotic cases. I think there's a tremendous amount more
to be done and to be learned in doing that, and I *do* think that it is
largely therapists' limitations on themselves as to what they feel they
can and cannot do that determines that. I didn't train as a clinical
psychologist, and my experience of working with severely disturbed individuals is perhaps more limited than clinical psychologists. I did some
work in hospitals as a graduate student and there I felt that in many
cases the dominant view of madness was very much a mythology, that
there is a great deal that you can do and that you can learn and
understand from individuals, at the very least when they're in a position
of being willing to talk with you and when you are in a position of
being willing to listen to them, without immediately imbuing their statements as being crazy or irrational or whatever. So I do think that the
approach can be applied very successfully with more severe cases of
mental disfunctioning.

Or are you more of a political animal than most therapists?

Oh God. Maybe with a small 'p'! The question of subjectivity is deeply
questioned by phenomenology in the sense that it argues for a kind of
inter-subjectivity. I only raise that because it seems to me that it immediately places the client and the therapist in a position where they
cannot talk about themselves in this isolated framework, that they are
relational beings. And that therefore everything that they say about
themselves is in regard to the various relations that they have to the
world. Both in terms of their immediate family relations, and friendships
and so forth, and to the world in the broad sense. So those things *of
necessity* come into the process of existential therapy in that that's
where meanings are generated. That's how I constuct meanings of
myself. It is always in terms of where I am with regard to others.
Where I am with regard to the division in my self-construct that I was
talking about earlier. So in that sense I think this is one of the important distinctions between this approach and many of the humanistic
models, where I think quite rightly the charge of solipsism has been
presented to them. Now it seems to me that this model is very anti-
solipsistic, it doesn't allow that – in everything that you tell me about

yourself, you are making implicit statements about others and the relations that you have with others, and the relations that you have with the world. It is very important in our dialogue with one another, to bring those statements to an explicit exploration of others, both out there, but also, more importantly, of the therapist as the other. Everything that you tell me you are saying to another, and therefore what's it like to express oneself to *this* other? And as the therapist, how do I represent the others in your life?

I think that this is a kind of twist of notions of transference and so forth. I'm here as a therapist, as an individual talking to you, and we engage in a particular kind of relationship. But at the same time, in your expressing yourself to me, I am a representative of that which is not you. And in that sense we can gain a great deal by simply examining for example how it is for you to express what you say to me. What's that like? And to yourself? And what's it like for me to hear it, and to respond to it, and so forth? So I think it's absolutely crucial – the politics in that small 'p' sense, is embedded in the whole approach.

Is there anything from any other traditions that you can use as either strategies or techniques, or is everything that you need subsumed within what you call existential therapy?

I think it would be tremendously arrogant for me or for anybody else within the existential approach to say, 'Well we have the knowledge, we have the truth, what all these people are talking about is irrelevant.' But I think there is a distinction to be made – and this goes back to really the first thing we were saying – about this conflict or division that I experience between, on one hand, finding that there might be very interesting things in the literature, say of psychoanalysis, as opposed to the experience of it. It does seem to me that there are possibly interesting insights that can be brought from other traditions to the understanding of what the existential issues might be and to the understanding of what therapy might be. But that's in a very different realm of discourse than practice, and it seems to me that it is important to make that division. I am informed by my theories, I live them in one sense. But at the same time it seems to me that I also have to acknowledge both the usefulness of those theories, and also the hindrances that those theories might provoke in my listening to you. I have to remain at a level of scepticism with regard to them. I would think that maybe that's one of the things that distinguishes (again), existential therapy to other models in the sense that, I think that as a bunch, as a whole, existential therapists tend to be far more sceptical, far more cautious about making vast statements of truth and knowledge than other representatives would do. We're willing to go so far as to say: 'Look, what we are concerned with is the exploration both of that which is unique and individual to each person, and also the possibility of extracting from that those things which may be universals of our human experience.

And we think we may have extracted some universals, in the sense of these questions about freedom, or the sense of the notions of death and the possible anxieties surrounding death and so forth.' But there are very few. They're the types of things that don't require a great deal of extrapolation and analytic interpretation. They're there and they do seem to be multi-cultural, and they do seem to occur regardless of class, or gender, or sexual orientation, or culture, or whatever. So in that sense we are dealing with things we can feel to some extent have a universality about them, but even so, they're few and far between. As opposed to other models that try to *impose* universalities, really on very dodgy grounds.

Every tradition has its case studies, and existentialism is saddled with Ellen West. Can you give me a brief account of any case of yours which explains the way that existential analysis has come to bear upon the way that they've changed their lives, or changed the way they see it?

Let me give you an example – it's quite a short one, and I use it in the *Demystifying Therapy* book as well. I had a client who was very much involved in socio-political causes, was very involved in ameliorating conditions, looking at poverty and so forth. First of all she came to me with a personal issue which had to do with her relationship to her partner. But as she talked it became more apparent to her, and to me as well, that the kind of lifelessness that she was experiencing with her relationship with her partner permeated the whole of her life. Where it was most crucial was at the level of her work and her commitment to her work, and what she found in discussing this was that her intellectual commitment to *the cause*, the rightness of what she was doing, hadn't dissipated. It was that she was somehow increasingly feeling herself to be detached from it and that this was deeply problematic. Now we explored this, and at one point what emerged for her was the realisation that she had been to a very large extent *driven*, from very early on in her life, to do good deeds. This was the concept, the position that she had created for herself: 'I am the kind of person who must do good things.' What she realised was that her whole life, her whole involvement with causes came from this 'must' position, this 'have to' position. That in a sense she had no choice in the matter. To consider not doing it would have been in one sense life-threatening to her. Now through the course of dialogue what she was able to do was to acknowledge for the first time that those things that had been 'musts' about her position, actually were open to some degree of choice. That she could conceivably say to herself 'I've done enough, I've done far more than most people have done, so I could conceivably stop. I could start looking at myself and focusing on the issues of my own life.' Not that that happened. What happened was that she switched from a position of 'I must do it' actually to 'I want to do it, I'm actually choosing to do it.' That didn't change her work one iota, but it changed her whole attitude towards her work. It changed her relationship to it. Again she discovered, maybe for the first time, her actual involvement with it. She, in no longer having to do it but wanting to do it, was able to invest a meaning into the work that had been lost to her. So it didn't change anything, it didn't change her life; she continued to do the things that she was doing, but it changed the whole relationship that she had to her life and to the specifics of work. What provoked that change was that switch from a position of 'I had no choice in the matter', to 'I do have a choice and this is what I choose', and that was tremendous for her. Now that also had its implications for her personal relations as well, but in that particular sense it was a movement that was a recognition of a greater degree of freedom, without taking away any of the responsibility that she had beforehand. The crucial element was a reconstruction of the meaning in the relationship that she had to her work. Equally as importantly, it had to provoke a reconstruction of her sense of who she was. 'I no longer have to be this person that must do good deeds. I'm a person who does do good deeds and I like doing them. But it's very different.'

How do you respond to the sceptics, from the mild sceptic – the man on the street who says 'this is all a waste of money' – to the Jeffrey Massons?

Well first of all I think that largely I acknowledge the sense of, certainly the person in the street, I'd acknowledge the sense of scepticism that they have. I think they have every right to be sceptical. I think there's a tremendous amount that psychotherapy's been allowed to get away with, that it shouldn't get away with. It's promoted this mystique of knowledge. It's promoted this idea that we do know a lot more than we do, *and it's false*, there's just no basis for it. So I think at that level the person on the street has every right to be sceptical about what is possible from psychotherapy or through psychotherapy, and what is not. At the same time it does seem to me that even if we're acknowledging that scepticism, part of it may lie in the false assumptions as to what psychotherapists can rightfully claim to offer to people. If my claim is, 'What I can offer you is an engagement with you whereby we explore your sense of meaning construction in the world', it may not seem like much and you might say to me on that basis 'I don't want to pay you £30 a session, or whatever it is, to do that.' On the other hand you might well do, and you might find it beneficial. So in that sense I think it's very important for therapists actually to be much clearer than they have been about what they can rightfully offer and what they can't offer. Now with Masson it seems to me that what he's done that's been constructive, is to raise the whole question of the unnecessary power and authority that therapists bestow upon themselves, and I think he's quite rightly pointed to infringements and abuses of therapy. I think in some ways, in some cases I would say in an unnecessarily polemical fashion. But, it is going back nearly ten years since he wrote *Against*

Therapy, maybe that was necessary then, and it certainly provoked a lot of discussions. So I think he has to be acknowledged as having actually said something of importance. Having done that, however, it seems to me that where I disagree with him, and a couple of years ago he came and he talked to the Society [the Society for Existential Analysis] here and we had a debate about that, is this whole idea that he has that if there is a power relationship then of necessity it's negative and it must in some way or other be bad. Now it seems to me that I don't know of any relationship that is not a power relationship. I think we have to work with that rather than pretend that we could have, in any kind of relationship, a strictly egalitarian relationship. I don't know of any such thing. What I do know is that power exists in the therapeutic setting; that the therapist has power that perhaps the client doesn't have, but equally the client has power that the therapist doesn't have. And that in one way or another the relationship that we engage in, is one whereby hopefully we can know more clearly how and when to use the power and authority that we employ in a way that is useful – not just to me nor just to you, but to both of us. So I take issue with Masson, not so much in the general critique that he makes, but in the specific factors that he then presents. I think they're naive, and on that I think we would have a parting of the ways. But I do think that he has had an impact which has been largely constructive. It's forced psychotherapists, unfortunately from a voice from outside, to actually consider and contemplate much more carefully what power they might be employing that is unnecessary. Now my own sense is that even though this has been initiated there's still a great deal to be done with this question ... [Pause] ... So I think the problem lies in the fact that however much therapists might say 'Yes, yes, yes, we want to deal with the unnecessary power that we might be expressing towards our clients', I think unfortunately that the theories themselves are imbued with those tremendous potentials for abuse. And again I've tried recently to point that out in picking up the three main models – the psychoanalytic, the cognitive/behavioural and the humanistic – and in pointing out where I think the theories themselves are problematic, in terms of what they provoke. Now obviously that has not made a great many friends for me, because what the implication is – the problem is so fundamental that it requires a reassessment of your whole theory, mate, as opposed to the kind of superficial things that we might do about whether we *tell* the client to 'Lie on a couch', or *invite* them to do so. It's not those surface things that are fundamental to the problem of power, it's deeply rooted in the theories.

Because of your approach, are your tempted, or are you involved at all, to engage in residential work – like Ronnie did with Kingsley Hall?

Well I think there's a lot that still needs to be written about and understood about that social experiment that Laing engaged in. From what I know of it, it tells us as much about areas of failure as it might tell us about areas of success, and I think that there were things that perhaps went on in those settings that may have been right for the time, but may no longer be acceptable. And I think – reading some of the later interviews that Laing did, particularly when he was asked questions about the kinds of social experiments in Italy, of opening up the asylums and to some extent, the madness that's taken place here in the UK – my sense is that he himself had become quite critical of some of these projects, and that looking back on it maybe Kingsley Hall informs us as much about the unforeseen problems of such things as it might tell us about the benefits of them.

Personally speaking, I have to say that I'm not as gung-ho about therapy as others who might wish to take that up. I certainly would be very much in favour of carrying out investigations at that lived level of these kinds of social relations and social settings, but at a personal level to say 'Yes, that's something I personally would like to do', my honest answer is 'No'.

Do you know much about what happens to one of your patients' spouse or family when they're undergoing work with you? Do you ever by implication say: 'Well bring your husband or wife in and perhaps the three of us should talk.'?

Right. Yes and no. Yes to the fact that, again I think it's part of the generation of an open relationship that clients will feel perfectly free to talk about the issues that they are having in their relationships by the fact that they are coming to see me, and the questions and the concerns, and so forth. It becomes quite an important means of exploring those relationships, by saying, 'Well, how do you deal with it, do you tell your spouse what's talked about? Do you keep it private? What does this relationship mean to you?' And again it raises one of the things that is a central process in existential therapy, that it's a process of, in discussing something with the client, there's a constant movement both outwards and inwards in the sense of the client making the statement and considering that statement in terms of the client's general relations, but also bringing it back to the specific relationship of him or her and me.

In doing that, what emerges is that the client brings in aspects of other relationships to this relationship. And quite often, because this relationship is important to them or is meaningful to the client, the client will talk about it in terms of how it is lived or expressed in other relations. So yes, I think it's a very interesting and important thing and it's something that quite understandably the other partner or the other members of the family – I would be surprised if they didn't feel some degree of questioning or 'What goes on in there? What is he or she telling them about us?' I think it's a very useful thing to explore.

Now with regard to your second question, I wouldn't bring in the other partner to the sessions, because my contract is very explicitly 'I'm working with you.' I'm working with you and it's for you to bring in those other relations as you wish, in the sense of our discussion about them. But actually to bring someone else into them creates a very different kind of process. Now I do work with couples, but if I work with couples it's from the very beginning. I don't work with them starting out with an individual and then the partner coming along. It's a very different process that takes place.

Do you have many thoughts about the notion of false memory syndrome?

Yes I think again it's one of those things that comes out of assumptions about the mind and memory and about the unconscious, that I would have a great degree of scepticism about. Clearly in some cases it also brings out the more questionable aspects of therapist manipulation of clients clearly by imposing meanings upon clients. Now even in those cases where this doesn't happen, and clients for example will say 'In the course of things I've *now* suddenly remembered having been abused as a child' – it seems to me that what the whole repressed memory syndrome stuff has tended to do is to then lock clients into that experience. It's as though they then say: 'Oh, this is clearly so crucial, and can only be understood in one way that we must just dwell on it and just stay in it and relive it as a past experience.' Now my sense of it from the existential model is, first of all, that my experience with clients who've been abused is that the meaning that they construe from that varies significantly, for some it's the most crucial incident in their lives, for others it's a very different kind of experience. For some it's very painful, for some it's guilt provoking, for some it's almost like – it's something that happened. And so to take an experience that is open to a plethora of meanings and experiences, and to say 'There's only one correct meaning, which is that you have been abused and this is terrible and you must feel awful about it', I think is very problematic. So that's one thing.

The other thing, as I say, is that from what we were saying earlier, it seems to me that the client remembering the event now is saying something about himself or herself now, and what remembering that event now is allowing them or is expressing about them, rather than again bringing it back to what it might have done to them then. So it's a very different way of tackling it.

Is it inevitable in our culture for a patient to want to see you as the provider of solutions?

Absolutely, and it would be both absurd and irresponsible of me either to pretend that such things didn't happen, or to in one way seek to say to the client: 'Look you must never allow this to happen.' It happens. Clients might express it in terms of 'You are the most important thing, the hour I see you is the one meaningful thing in my life at this point', and I think I have to – it's what I say to my students – the important thing for you to do as a therapist is to believe and accept that the client believes that. The danger is when *you* start believing it. That's my commitment to you, that I'm going to work with your system of meaning and beliefs, and if you say to me 'I think you're the most important person in my life', or, 'I think you're the most attractive person in my life', or whatever, regardless of what I might think of that statement I have to accept that what you're saying to me is meaningful to you. Equally in that acceptance I then have to, as I would with anything else, say to you, 'Now tell me more about it.' Rather than seek to avoid it or try to get you to deny it, or convince you otherwise or whatever. I've got to deal with that as with any other statement that you give me. So I see it as being no different from your coming to me and saying: 'I believe that little green men control my life.' In the same way that I might respond to that by saying: 'Okay, tell me about them. What are their names; how do they work; who are they; what do they look like; are they here now?' In the same way I would have to treat material that was about me, or your experience of me in the same fashion. Because you're communicating something that is expressing your stance, your position in life. And if I avoid that, or if I say, 'No, no, no, no, that we don't talk about', then I'm making claims to offer something to you that I'm not offering to you.

One thing that's always amazed me is that very little has been written on the social organisation of therapy in, say, Britain. Do you have strong feelings about that?

Yes, very strong. Sometimes I feel really embarrassed and ashamed to be associated with psychotherapy. Particularly what's going on now. As you probably know there are two organisations that are attempting to professionalise psychotherapy. There's the United Kingdom Council for Psychotherapy, which holds most of the training organisations in the UK, and presents really all the broad orientations to psychotherapy – psychoanalytic, existential, cognitive-behavioural and so forth; and then there's this kind of splinter group, which is the British Confederation of Psychotherapists, which is made up solely of psychoanalytic organisations. *Some* psychoanalytic organisations.

Now what's happening at the moment is that there's a real political battle taking place between these two organisations as to which one is the right one, which one *rightfully* represents psychotherapy, both in the UK and in Europe as a whole. My view of it is that some of the things that are being done to try and sway things one way or the other are more along the lines of the kinds of things that one might see in religious schisms than what one might hope to find in a profession that was, supposedly at least, knowledgeable and slightly influenced by the desire for knowledge and a broadly scientific approach.

I think it's horrible. I think that there are cliques and clubs within psychotherapy that have existed for the last hundred years or so, since psychotherapy came into being, and I think it's about time that some of these clubs started to get questioned. For example if you look at advertisements for postings in the NHS in psychotherapy, what you find typically is that it's made explicit that 'The only kind of psychotherapist that we will consider is a psychoanalytic psychotherapist.' Now my question is 'Why?' Has anybody ever shown that psychoanalytic psychotherapy works any better than cognitive-behavioural, or existential, or whatever? The answer is 'No'. All of the research that's been done indicates very clearly that all of the therapies by and large work pretty much at the same level. There's no clear indication that any one approach is more suitable to clients, or more successful in outcomes, or whatever. Yet there is this tendency to promote or to elevate one model – let's be clear, the psychoanalytic model – as being the great model. Why? I think in many ways this is a model that has the greatest number of inherent problems within it. I personally think it's a dying, if not already a dead, model. It's proven itself to be increasingly behind the times in acknowledgement of such things, [as you yourself said], the whole social ramifications of it, the psychological understanding of the individual, and so forth. Yet there is still this notion, even held by many psychotherapists, that really in the end the only true psychotherapists are those that are psychoanalytic in trade. I think that's total rubbish.

So I think there's a lot in psychotherapy that leaves a bad taste in one's mouth and I welcome to a large extent over the last few years the criticisms that have been forthcoming about psychotherapists. Largely by, finally by, for example, clients who have said: 'Enough of this, I think that what's happened to me is just not right.' So there have been organisations built up assisting clients actually to examine what has happened to them in psychotherapy, and which are – I don't see them as destructive to psychotherapy – I see them actually being very constructive. And I think the psychotherapists themselves should be much more involved in dealing with such organisations, and in listening to them, and in listening to the issues that come out. There's a tremendous division between psychotherapists' views of what is crucial and valuable in therapy and client's views of what is crucial and valuable in therapy. I think psychotherapists who claim, by and large, to be listening to their clients should actually start to listen to them a bit more ... [Laughs] ... Particularly about their experience of psychotherapy.

There is some research that suggests that training is largely useless in the sense that therapists are born rather than made. I don't know, I think it's too tentative to arrive at any conclusion about that. My sense is that I do think that perhaps the crucial thing is this question of curiosity, and it seems to me – I've used the analogy of therapists as actors, particularly as method actors – it seems to me that if there is something that is crucial for the therapist to be able to be or to engage with, it is a flexibility of being so that the therapist is willing and able to attempt experiencing life as the client does. In that sense I think the therapist is like a method actor who is told: 'Here you are, be this person. What do you invest this person with? How are you in trying to become this person?' Now clearly in doing that the therapist's own experiences, and personality, and so forth will still be there, you can't get rid of them, but nevertheless there's a disengagement from that personal hold on oneself that allows the flexibility, allows an openness that says: 'Well actually I could consider what it might be like to be the kind of person who engages in behaviours that I personally would never contemplate, but I would like to imagine myself being this kind of person.' Now I think that takes quite a lot for a therapist to do, for anybody to do, and I think it's perhaps far more rare than we tend to think.

I think that – the way I understand it – is what Laing was suggesting. I think this idea of attending to the client – that for me captures what I've been trying to say – that it's about really attempting entry into that world, and being willing to do so, and actually being excited in doing so. People sometimes ask me: 'Don't you ever get bored in listening to all these problems and so forth?' My answer is quite genuinely: 'No, I don't get bored, because it really is an exercise that I enjoy. It's being given the opportunity to live other lives, or to attempt to live other lives, and I find that tremendously fascinating.'

You mentioned earlier, you worked in the NHS, do you have very strong feelings about how money affects the whole process?

Well, when I was working in the NHS the people weren't paying money, not directly anyway: they were paying it indirectly through their taxes. But I didn't find that there was any difference in the degree of commitment or significance that they put on to the process. So in that sense I think it's another myth that's built up, because it's a way for therapists to get away with charging the fees we charge. Now I do think that it's not a question of money so much as a question that the money expresses something far more important which is this idea of commitment. How can the client be committed, express a commitment to the process? And I think in a way it's crass to say 'Paying money is equivalent to commitment.'

I do think clients should be invited to offer something, and I don't mean something simply restricted to money. They might be prepared, for example, to offer some time in terms of working in an office, or doing things. For example, I know in some MIND centres that people who are clients volunteer to do gardening, or whatever; not because it's therapeutic, but because they enjoy it. And it's something that they feel they're contributing back to the organisation.

I think that idea of people contributing something back is very important, and I think it's false to simply equate it to money. And I do think that particularly in community social settings, that sometimes the assumption that people are victims and don't have anything to contribute can be quite problematic. I'm not saying that people should be required to contribute, but I think there should be an invitation made so that if something can be offered, and is desired to be offered, then people will do it. I think in many cases people will take it up.

The final question I'm going to ask you ... I've been amazed over the years, how old some therapists are. Do you have any thoughts about the length of time one should spend doing this?

I think one of the very few attractions of psychotherapy is that it doesn't end at retirement age. For some therapists that's really supposedly when you're at your peak. So I would hate to impose an ageism on it. At the same time it does seem to me that the danger – and this is something that many therapists have said, and I agree with them – the danger is when the whole of your life is spent doing therapy. I think that's bad for clients, and I think it's just as bad for therapists. It's a very solitary experience. Unless you're seeing a supervisor, and even then the idea of what you're doing is so secret and so shrouded in secrecy that I can't but believe that it provokes a psychological mind set that is not terribly constructive or beneficial to anybody. The way that I deal with it is that, whereas I can foresee myself hopefully continuing to remain sufficiently interested in it to continue past the official retirement age, at the same time I would hope that I would also be physically capable also to be involved in some capacity with some other training or academic establishment – where I would be confronted constantly by students who would, I hope, challenge me in the views I held, in the practices I did.

In other words, I think it's necessary to have a lifestyle that allows for contact with a world that is clearly interested in what you're doing, but is also willing to say: 'Now, let's talk about this, let's consider it, let's focus on it.' I've found that those therapists who do manage in some way or other to maintain this dual world are the ones who are least likely to suffer from burn-out, and who continue to remain excited, intrigued and open to their profession.

CHAPTER 10

Gestalt Therapy

Peggy Sherno

Peggy Sherno is a Gestalt therapist working in London
and Hertfordshire.

Can you tell me how you got into therapy in the first place, as a therapist?

I got in through being a client. I don't know how much detail you want.
I didn't know anything about anything in those days. I was experiencing
physical symptoms, heart palpitations and all sorts; I had this uneasy
feeling that there was something wrong in my life. I went to see a
woman who lived locally at that time who was a Gestaltist, and worked
with her and picked up from there gradually.

I did more and more work – individual and groups – with her. After
a time I stopped going there as a client and became an apprentice
really. That was my root. So it's a very ad hoc training, as trainings
were in those days.

*What happens when someone comes to you? What might they come for, and
what happens when they walk in the door?*

Well the first way the client usually approaches me is via the phone. So
I'll get a phone call and I'll get a very brief idea of what the person's
interested in, and I'll suggest that we meet for an hour's session, which
is an initial session for us both to get a sense of what this person is
wanting from therapy, to discuss whether Gestalt is a very promising
way of them achieving that. Get to know each other a bit to see if
there is a basis of some kind of rapport which might build into a
therapeutic relationship; discuss things like my fee, and all the other
contractual requirements. At the end of that hour we usually – well it
depends – quite often we can say there and then, 'yes, go on' in which
case I go on and do six more sessions, and then review again.

My criteria at review are, 'Is the person feeling satisfied with this
process? Are they getting something out of it?' Unless there's something
which is worrying me a lot. But usually it's a question of whether the
client is engaging in the process. Because if they're not then I may not feel
so comfortable about going on – that it might not be useful for them.

Sometimes a person isn't very clear, and if a person has not got very

good boundaries or is humming and hawing in some way, I would perhaps
suggest that they go away and ring me within 48 hours or something like
that, to give them a bit of time to make a decision which they'll stick with.
Because in this therapy, consent is really important.

Can you elaborate on that?

Well, I'm very fortunate because I work with people who come to me
wanting something for themselves. I don't get referrals from organisations
where people have to go and see the therapist, or whatever. So I don't
have to deal with that kind of resistance, and in that I think I'm very, very
fortunate. What I'm looking for is clients who become interested in how
they function, in learning about themselves, so that eventually they can
take the tools into their own hands and, whatever blockages or difficulties
they've been having, it feels as though they steer their own way. At that
point, the therapy can finish.

So essentially for me it's a co-operative endeavour between the
therapist and the client. That's not to say that as a therapist I might not
be challenging if that seems useful to do, or necessary to do, but it's
within the larger container of an understanding that this is a mutual
endeavour for the benefit of the client.

Again for the uninitiated, what might happen if someone comes to see you?

Well I spend quite a lot of time doing what I call 'ploughing the field'
which is seeing what's there. So a client will usually come presenting a
problem of some sort, a particular thing which has brought them
through the door. But I'm often not particularly interested in the problem. It's one of the things that I need to find out. 'Is it the problem
that the client's really interested in?' and that's where they want to stay,
that's the focus they want to retain, they don't want to go into the
whole wider area of 'this problem is a symptom of something, it's not
the thing which is important in itself'. If a person really does want to
attend to a particular problem, then I will work differently than with
someone who I think is actually just coming to get themselves through
the door, to do some wider and perhaps deeper exploration.

One can differentiate a bit between oneself in counselling mode or
in psychotherapy mode. So I spend a lot of time 'ploughing the field',
seeing what's there, and also I take a lot of time to begin to build a
relationship. I don't think it's a good idea to ask people to start to dig
into themselves and to arrive at the kind of point of, 'Oh my god, I
never knew that about me', until there is a sufficiently strong relationship in which they can support that. So I go slowly usually, and in fact
I'm quite suspicious of people who want to rush in and tell me the most
intimate details of their lives right off. I wonder about that. How good
they are at really taking care of themselves. A kind of 'spilling out'.

I'm looking at different areas all at the same time. I'm looking at the focus of the person's work as an intra-psychic event, I'm also looking at what's going on between the client and myself, all the transferential stuff. Contact is key in Gestalt. Gestalt starts with the notion, the very obvious notion, that we're always, all the time, in relationship with an environment – physical, emotional, intellectual, psychic; probably elements that we aren't very consciously aware of all the time. It's what happens, it's the interaction between a person and their total environment, which also of course has the time dimension to it as well. Which is where we work.

So I'm looking at them, their intra-psychic universe, I get a feel. Some people live in a universe which is very brittle – it's either they're right or they're terribly wrong. You get to feel the tension that living like that produces; get a sense of how they create that in themselves; get into the Gestalt polarities, 'top dog, underdog', and I don't know how familiar you are with these terms. We can come on to all those.

So I'm looking at what goes on between – the contact between the person and the rest of the world – with me as the other person in the room as a focus. That gives me a tremendous amount of information about whether, for instance, this person is basically a monologuist in the world or a dialoguist. Whether there is an interchange or whether there isn't.

Might you talk a lot, or listen a lot?

I do both. I think I'm quite interventionist and I think that especially in the first two or three sessions, people come and they're actually very nervous, they're quite scared. They may hide it, but people feel put on the spot and I think that by my asking questions or by my reflecting back what I've heard, or expressing a very ordinary kind of human interest really, I want to settle them down a little and help them feel this is a relationship they can trust. That I'm not suddenly going to do something frightening or they're going to find themselves out of their depth or whatever. So I take a long time to build up that trust and support, and safety. Because it seems to me the necessary foundation for people going on doing other stuff.

What makes Gestalt therapy unique and different? For somebody who doesn't even know the name of Perls ...

Right. Well Gestalt is a German word, which has no direct translation into English, I believe – I'm taking all this on hearsay because I don't know any German. But it's supposed to have some kind of meaning like 'a configuration, a meaningful *whole,* an assembly of parts of which the sum is more significant than the parts'.

So we'll just come back to the idea – I'm always in context. Right from the moment I was conceived, I develop in a context, in an environment. And Gestalt is, I think, extremely optimistic in a way, in that it's partly based on the notion that human beings – unless people are born with brain damage or something or other – have the innate capacity to interact constructively and productively, creatively and fluidly with the environment. This is not about people being happy all the time, because of course that would manifestly be nonsense, but it's about people being able to do the best they possibly can for themselves, in the circumstances they find themselves in.

It's the process in Gestalt which has the awful name of 'organismic self-regulation'. One of the things that I like about Gestalt is this basis in what seems to me to be a very obvious biological observation and principle. In that way, we're the same as trees, or animals – we can all do this. Human beings, obviously, are at a much more sophisticated level. The work is in the interaction between the person and the totality of their field. Field theory is the thing that's coming strongly into Gestalt now. When Gestalt started, and with people like Perls, there was this tremendous emphasis on the 'individual'. It was the 'I do my thing, and fuck you' business, you know. 'I take total responsibility, and I don't need anybody ... ' Gestalt principles haven't changed, but the emphasis has changed an awful lot. And now we're much more interested in that part of Gestalt which is actually informed by field theory, which is very aware of the interdependence of everything.

So what I'm looking at is how much healthy organismic self-regulation is available to a client, and how much they have become stuck in worn-out ways of dealing with the world, which would inevitably have been learned by them in the early years of their lives. Of course that will depend on the nursery they were born into. As well as whatever genetic inherited characteristics they've brought. All of that stuff. So in Gestalt we never deal with the person just as an isolated individual – it's just not possible. We're always looking at the totality of them in the field. I suppose my job is to help people to become aware of their own blocks to free-functioning. By 'free' I don't mean it's self-centred, more and more the emphasis in Gestalt is on the I–thou relationship and the success of that. The success of the relationship between the individual and the world.

You were saying the principles still remain the same although the emphases have changed. What kinds of concepts and principles are central to the Gestalt tradition?

Well the one I've been talking about is the central one. That the individual is always relating in a context, and it's the relationship between the individual and the context which is the focus of Gestalt work. Another principle is the one that lies behind the sense that you and I both sitting in this room – we're having totally different experiences. Everything that you bring being you, and everything that I bring being me, and what we're about here means that you are selecting from the totality of what's going on that which has meaning and excitement for you. That is your Gestalt figure. So there is the importance of a person's ability to create Gestalts.

So you're interested in whether the tape recorder's working, and that I'm going to talk some sense, and whatever preoccupations you have, and so on and so forth. One of the bases of Gestalt is the idea that experience is subjective, that there is no ultimate truth about truth, or existence, or whatever. Each one of us is in a continual act of creation. You're creating your truth right now; I'm creating my truth. They're not incompatible, they're simply different. So another of the Gestalt principles is the tolerant recognition of difference. Seeing that as an enrichment rather than as a threat.

What people tend to come across is something called 'the Gestalt cycle of awareness', which is something that was devised in the United States by people like Miriam and Erving Polster – the Cleveland School, which was a way of describing Gestalt formation. Now Gestalt formation – a Gestalt is that which has interest for you or for me, out of the combination of my self and what's going on out there. The usual kind of example that is given very basically is that I can be sitting here talking to you, and suddenly I realise I'm feeling very thirsty and little by little my thirst becomes much more important to me than my sitting here talking to you, and I go through various stages: becoming aware of my thirst, whether I can do something about it; mobilising myself to go and do it, get a drink of water; drinking it, and the experience of my thirst diminishing. Then my attention, my being, is free for the next focus of interest, the next Gestalt form.

That's a very basic level, but that can happen on any kind of level, which is I think one of the reasons why Gestalt doesn't, unlike psychosynthesis, for example, have theories about spirituality or the higher consciousness or whatever. I assume that if spirituality is an innate part of being human, then some humans will become interested in that about themselves and will follow that interest. That's where they'll go.

What level of concepts are things like 'top dog', the popular notions of Gestalt?

Well, they're very useful. Taken out of context they can be abused, become techniques. In Gestalt it's very important that techniques come out of an understanding of the total situation, not be applied mechanically, or whatever. So 'top dog' and 'underdog', well, I talked about Gestalt's notion that we have an innate sense of doing the best for ourselves in the world. What we look at is how that process has become interrupted. Say you are brought up with an extraordinarily strict father and mother, and you had to always mind your 'p's and 'q's, and if you didn't you'd be punished. Then you'd pretty soon learn that you couldn't just say whatever you wanted, what was on your mind. You'd get slapped down for it. You couldn't rush up and ask for a hug.

So – children are immensely quick learners, aren't they? And so they modify those innate impulses to contact.

So how would you begin to describe and enumerate the techniques of Gestalt?

Well, just continuing from what I was saying. What I would become aware of was that the person had probably developed a 'top dog', a 'top dog' who would say 'You mustn't do that, that's not allowed. Don't be so silly. Grow up now. Be a big girl. That's not nice. That's not polite', and so on and so forth.

On the other hand probably there would be what we'd call the 'underdog' who doesn't want to be dominated by 'top dog' but doesn't know how to stand up to 'top dog', and so snipes and sabotages. People can get enormously taken up with this internecine conflict, which can go on and on and on, for years and years and years. It's my job to help people to become aware of that inner conflict, to surface it, to work with it, to deal with it, and to transform it. So that instead of the client experiencing themselves at war with themselves, they experience themselves working – going down the same track.

That can happen in any kind of combination. Polarities is an important bit of theory in Gestalt. We postulate that people do comprise lots of polarities, and it's very handy when it comes to working with a client. For example, if you've got somebody who presents like a really good little girl, butter wouldn't melt in her mouth, and she never says anything nasty about anybody, and she just is so grateful for everything, you can bet that there's a vicious brat around somewhere, but entirely out of the person's consciousness. I say 'vicious brat', I don't say that judgementally: what I'm saying is that I perceive that I have in front of me a person who has actually cut off half of their resources, the resources for direct aggression – aggression is not a dirty word in Gestalt, it's that impulse which leads you not only to pick the apple off the tree, but also to bite into it, and then chew it, and all the rest of it. The idea is to restore to somebody the full panorama of their possibilities to experience aggression, or strength, or anger as positive resources rather than as things to be denied. Shut away at any price. If you like, we're working to restore the wholeness of the personality – no, scrap the word 'personality', that's not a good word in Gestalt – the wholeness of the person.

Group techniques are well-known in the Gestalt tradition ...

Well, it depends. I doubt if there are many Gestaltists now working in the old Fritz Perls' 'hot seat' way, in which the work actually went on between Fritz Perls and one participant, and the group were there kind of as witnesses – they weren't involved, they were audience witnesses. That sort of thing. We're interested now in group functioning. So again, rather as I take a while to lay the ground work of a relationship with a client, I do exactly the same with a group. I don't start to do heavy pieces of individual work with group members until it seems to me the group has got itself to a point where it's really ready to support and contain that. So I would be attending to interpersonal function, much more than to individual function until I feel that's been adequately dealt with.

The pros and cons of groupwork versus one-to-one work ...

Well, for people who are in training with us we require both, because when people can do both it's absolutely dynamic. I think that for people to go into groups they actually do need to have quite a high level of self-support. They need to feel fairly okay in themselves, so more fragile people I would recommend to go into individual work, certainly initially. In Gestalt we always balance challenge and support. There's no value in putting people in a situation where they are so overwhelmed with fear, or embarrassment, or shame, that they can't thrive on it. There's no point at all.

Presumably the emphasis on the 'here and now' is still strong?

Oh yes it is, that's central. Well, if you think that you now, me now, we're the sum of everything that's happened in our lives. So that the way we're communicating would encapsulate everything there is to know about us, so as Gestaltists we can begin with the here and now situation. Gestaltists, hopefully, are trained really to see, and really to hear, hear not only the words but the music of the voice. The kind of delivery, the richness around the layers of vocabulary. Whether the person is giving a message with their eyes, as well as with their voice. There's a tremendous attention to the phenomena, to the data in the room. And from that, with experience, you can begin really to tease out how this person functions.

I do it in the present. I don't think that you have to go back and attempt to clean up past relationships. It may be important for a person who, for instance, as a child has been frightened by a parent and has therefore shut down their aggression; it may be important at some time to have an 'as if' encounter with the previously frightening parent. The client now bringing with them their resources as an adult, and the support of the therapeutic relationship to experiment with taking back their aggression and anger, and telling it directly on the 'empty seat' to the parent. By doing that – of course the past situation is what it was, you can't change that – but it changes the person's sense of who they are, and what is possible for them *now*. It's all right to be angry, the ceiling doesn't fall in. I, the therapist, do not throw them out – 'don't darken my doors again' – all that sort of stuff. So it's like an enormous psychic risk to take back those parts which have been split off.

Does each therapeutic encounter differ from other ones?

Every therapy is different. For some people what goes on in the relationship between themselves and me – which is where the transferential material would surface – maybe that's important; that may be what the therapy is about. I look for the person who is willing to engross themselves, to become interested in who they are and what's going on. That's the criteria for me.

Presumably you just feel sorry for those who can't do it ...

Well, it's not that people can't, some people have very good reasons for
not doing it. It may be that they're too attached to the persona they've
developed to keep themselves away from all that stuff, and that's fine. I
respect people's resistances and choices in that matter. That's perfectly
okay, and I don't feel sorry for them. Generally, with people like that I
will leave the door open, and say 'If you want to come back and do
some more, give me a ring.'

Are certain problems especially suited to Gestalt work?

Well, you see, you're talking about problems, and I tend not to talk
about problems, but to talk about processes, the processes whereby
people function. So I would rephrase that to say: 'Are there processes
of functioning which are beyond the assistance of Gestalt therapy?' I
don't know, I'm not very experienced personally outside the field of
your ordinary walking neurotic. Though from people who have experience working with people who have a great deal of disturbance, there
seems to be usefulness in Gestalt, given that Gestalt, remember, is
about contact. It's about how the person makes contact, both within
themselves and within the world that they live in. That's always useful
in working with anybody. And of course you'd have reservations, you
wouldn't go into working with different aspects of himself with somebody who has a tendency to schizoid episodes, because the problem is
trying to hold himself together, not flying off into pieces. So there again
you work very, very steadily with just a basic ordinary grounding in the
possibilities of contact.

What do you think are the necessary qualities of a therapist?

A therapist is somebody who can see, and somebody who can hear –
can really see and really hear – and who is able to absorb phenomena
about the client and allow that to find its own shape. So a therapist, for
me, does not immediately jump to conclusions about a person. The
initial stages of a therapy are explorations and getting to know, and
sounding the depths, exploring the country.

Well therapists must certainly have a good enough understanding of
the basic theories of Gestalt in this instance, so that they can begin to
talk speculatively to themselves about how they see this person. 'This is
a person who I perceive does this in Gestalt terms, whatever it might
be, they interrupt themselves at the point of mobilisation, so Bob knows
what he wants and he knows where he is, but he stops himself from
actually going out and getting it, isn't that interesting?' So a therapist
needs to be very interested.

A therapist needs to have enough self-knowledge, to have done
enough self-work so that they are aware that if they are getting, as it

were, emotionally caught up in responding to the clients – what that's about, where that comes from in them, and how much it's useful and valid to bring that back into the therapy. Obviously it's important if dealing with the kind of client I was talking about before who is really trying to work something out by challenging the boundaries, and who can be very irritating. To become irritated is not productive. You need to stay very cool with such a client, and keep feeding back what's going on. So therapists need to know themselves well enough to be able to maintain that therapeutic stance – being aware of their own reactions but not becoming reactive in the therapy.

I think therapists need to be very human, by which I mean each needs to have a head, and a heart, and a body, and a spirit – if you want to use that word – and be aware of all that in themselves. Have overall interest and compassion in the human condition really.

How much is physical contact a part of Gestalt therapy?

Well, I mean Gestalt therapists would say that they would do anything that would further the therapy. There's a lot of debate about touch at the moment and that's partly because the whole profession of psychotherapy has become very alarmed because of registration and litigation. Psychotherapists are not licensed to touch in the way that a physiotherapist is. So that's one side of it. And it varies a lot among Gestalt therapists. I have colleagues who very, very rarely touch at all. I leave that open for myself as an option and especially with people who are very long-term clients, and in what you would call regressive work – people who have needed to go back to a very, very young age in order to retrieve themselves, and then grow again in a happier, more successful way. I will give the support of a hug or holding.

Most of the people I see are long-term people, and over time we go through a tremendous amount together, and I will perhaps just touch an arm, or if somebody says 'I'd like a hug', I probably will unless there seem to me very good reasons, intrinsic to what's going on in the therapy, not to do that. Like if I think that a person is asking for a speedy hug at the end of the session to make everything all right, whereas it would be much better if they left with something that they needed to pick up next week. All those judgements go on all the time.

And groups?

In groups? Well in a way it's much safer to touch in groups because it's public. I will do, but there are other considerations there, because in a group you have all kinds of considerations, like sibling rivalry – almost inevitably in a group I become to some degree a mother figure. Although I don't foster that, I don't – but I am – and the group members become the family, the siblings.

I actually find I don't touch people in groups very much. I don't know if there's a theoretical underpinning for that, it's just that I do much less one-to-one work with people anyway in groups. I'm interested in the group as a whole. I don't have a rule about not touching people in groups.

Do you draw from other traditions?

Oh we draw from lots, yes. I like the – I was going to say the freedom of Gestalt – it seems to me to be based on extremely sound principles that make tremendous sense to me. The methods open for Gestalt therapists to work with are limitless, unless they're against the law, or dangerous, or something like that. I can talk about dreams with someone, someone who creates images as they speak, I can work with their images. Someone who is visual, we can draw. I can use anything, theoretically. It's tailor-made to the person I'm working with and to the interaction between us. Repeat your question again?

Well, another one ... remind the reader what the goal is ...

Well, to restore fuller functioning to the person. In the most successful therapies I think, the people go out with a heightened degree of awareness about themselves – and also they become the owners of the toolkit. They don't need the therapist, because they know about the internal conflicts and dialogue. They have such heightened awareness that they can pick it up. What's that old Marxist thing? – 'You give the tools of production back into the hands of the worker' – it's that. So the goal of therapy is to end therapy. It doesn't mean to say that a person stops their therapeutic work. If life is always changing we all need the tools, but the idea is for the client to have the tools rather than the therapist retain them as some kind of mystic apparatus.

Monologuic, Dialoguic ...

Well that's a term special to me, it's not a Gestalt term actually. But one of the ways that I think about people. I think: 'Do these people really have dialogue with the world? Is there that flow of energy and interest between themselves and other people who are in the world, or are they essentially in their glass bubbles, monologuing?' You can tell, if you're sitting down with someone, if someone's actually talking with you or if they're just talking at you. Very important. And that's the kind of data in Gestalt which is absolutely crucial, because it tells me so much about this person.

The earlier question was about drawing from other approaches ...

Oh, that's right. Well Gestalt is an amalgam of approaches: Freudian, existential, phenomenology, field theory, Reichian stuff, to name the main ones. What we do in our training is to input quite a bit on developmental theory, because Gestalt doesn't have a developmental theory as such. It does in the sense that we observe that a child will deal with the world in a very different way than someone with an adult body. There's a lot of interest in Gestalt on the shifts that go on in the person from the infant who can only suck and drink, to what happens when the infant gets teeth and learns then that they have something to bite with, they bite off, and spit out what they don't like. There's an enormous amount happens when a child develops teeth.

That's the nearest thing I think Gestalt has to a developmental theory. You can read up on that if you want to. So every couple of years, what we do is to ask people to do a very brief baby watch. It's not a formal thing like you get through the Tavi [Tavistock Institute] or something, but just to spend some time with a baby, noticing how that is, and how much communication is possible from a small being that can't speak, that has got a minimum control over its environment. We can talk about people like Winnicott and Stern, also the object-relations people and Freudian ideas. So we think it's very important that our students are equipped with that kind of contextual information, and can use the insights from other therapies.

Are there approaches you find offensive?

Well I don't care much for therapies where the therapist does things to the client, runs a programme on them. I'm worried about this whole thing about brief therapy. It's terribly the vogue, and GP counselling practices are being set up on the basis of half a dozen sessions or a dozen sessions. And I think that's okay if that is perhaps seen as an assessment time, and the client by and large is then referred on for longer-term therapy. But I don't think that does happen. I think that doctors probably in their ignorance or lack of experience, genuinely think that something of significance will happen in six or twelve weeks. I'm afraid that they're going to become totally disillusioned, and they're going to chuck the baby out with the bath water and say that counselling therapy is no good. 'We tried it; it didn't work.' An aware client coming in with a particular thing might benefit very well from six weeks, but I imagine the kind of people in doctors' surgeries who find their way to counselling – long-term depressives or whatever – it's a nonsense, and I really do fear for the consequences of that in the long term.

It's important, isn't it to stress the importance of the 'here and now'?

Well the implications are that you don't necessarily have to do all that archaeological digging. You don't have to dig into what's called the unconscious. We tend to talk more about what's in awareness and what's out of awareness in a person. The unconsciousness is not something that figures in Gestalt terminology or Gestalt thinking. The promise of it is that, if I

become aware, doing a session with you – you're my therapist – and I
become aware of 'God, yes, I've got this awful voice in my head, every
time I want to let my hair down or something – "You can't do that, you
haven't finished your work yet. You can't even do that on a Saturday
night" ... ', but I've learnt something about myself and I can then turn my
own attention to this that is going on inside me, and work with it. I can do
it now, I can sort it out now in my life. I might be interested in where that
came from. I might have to be interested in where that came from if the
valency is still so strong, somewhere back in the past.

I think Gestalt's very optimistic, because we do assume, and it's
based on experience, that people can change. You've experienced that.
You change out of experiencing, out of – the Gestalt proceeds by
experiment. In the therapy room I will set up a little experiment,
maybe; slot it into what the client can cope with. An experiment is
talking to an empty chair perhaps. It is a device which can be used in
different ways. It can be used as a way of having a client sitting in one
chair, facing another chair in which they, as it were, put their own
projections. That is, if I'm an employee I might be very scared of my
boss who I perceive as being totally sophisticated and powerful and
wonderful. The boss may indeed be all those things, but what's interesting to the therapist is the way that the person who is the client, who
presents as a mouse, is clearly projecting; that is, disowning their own
wonderfulness, their own power, their own glamour or whatever it is,
and putting it in the person of the boss over there.

So the work might start off looking like employee/boss, but it actually
comes to be an intra-psychic exploration of how this person has managed
to split themselves up and lose contact with the resource of their wonderfulness, so to speak. By having the dialogue, the confrontation between
those two aspects, what happens is that the relationship changes. So
where the person was split, this can now change. In the dialogue the client
might discover how it became necessary for her to do that, if at the age of
seven she came home from school and said, 'I've won this prize', and was
told, 'You mustn't blow your own trumpet, you mustn't be conceited.
Little girls are not nice when they're conceited', and prolonged messages
like that. You learn after a while; you get the message.

So they can reclaim it, and it's not just done at a head level, but it's
done at a total level, because the whole thing is enacted. Psychodrama
is very close to Gestalt in this. By entering, by engaging in the different
kind of aspects of the self, the whole person becomes informed and the
whole person is changed by the end of the dialogue. Someone can walk
out with a true sense – maybe their chin's up a bit or their shoulders
are back a bit – that they leave not quite the same person as they
arrived. If they don't retain it, that's all right because they can remember they've had the experience, they can come back into therapy and
repeat that. And gradually shift that familiar sense of self.

An experiment's not to prove anything, an experiment is open-ended:
'Let's see what happens if ... you never could be angry with your father,

well let's bring him in and see what happens if you're angry with him now.' That's only after enough work, so that it's okay for the person to do that, they're not too frightened.

Do it with an empty chair, yes, so that might bring in the father. The father might be dead; intra-psychically he's still very much alive, so the person has the opportunity to rework some situation, some relationship. Give him- or herself some experience – we don't know what's going to happen.

What might happen?

Well, the person might, as it were, put the father in the empty chair, and the person may become totally tongue-tied and say: 'I can't, I'm too frightened. I can just see his eyes glaring at me as he always did, and I'm shaking like a leaf.' So then I would immediately – or could – back away from pursuing the experiment to becoming interested in what was happening to the client, and I would go with that. The client's not yet ready to have the encounter, they need some support for themselves before they're ready to do it.

Or the client might start to talk in a low voice to the father about how hard it was, and then the voice suddenly gathers pitch and volume, and the person becomes more and more involved, and the body gets involved, and before you know it they're standing up, and their voice is bellowing, a fist comes out, and then they might say: 'God, I didn't know I was so angry. God I feel good.' Then you can go on to integrate that, give it some time to settle into the person.

What are your thoughts about transference?

Well we understand transference, from the basis of projection. We certainly acknowledge that transferential projection exists, and we'll work with it as necessary. But we don't foster it. Because we work in the now, with the totality of the now situation, we aren't dependent on trying to establish that old parental/child situation. We don't need to do that. What I will try to do is to work to dissolve the transference as it appears. So the Gestaltist stance would be much more likely to become aware of the transference, feed that awareness back to the client, and as far as possible dissolve it; that is, by not cultivating it, by not playing into the kind of construct that the client wants. So not, for example, obliging the client by being the heavy parent or whatever.

That's not to say that it's ignored, but just to keep pointing that this is an as-is situation, the client is turning me into an authoritarian parent. That's not who I perceive myself to be. However, that's obviously the client's experience, and isn't it interesting that the client seems to do that. What purpose does that serve the client? Do they have a choice about that? Are they in some way invested in being a mutinous child in the world? What's it like when I *don't* become irritated and lose my temper, and start wagging my finger? So that's how we'd work with it, or I'd work with it.

And countertransference?

I don't know if there's very much to say about it, we just remain aware of that possibility. Which is why we think that it's essential for trainee therapists to do a lot of individual work. All our therapists do years of individual and group work, so hopefully, if they are people who, for example, need strokes, who need people to love them, who need to be thought the most wonderful therapists in the world, that will be caught and addressed before they're let loose on the client population.

I'm not saying that all dependency's about that, or all counter-dependency's about that, but that certainly can be one of the hooks. The other one of course is money. We're a lot of us here in private practice. Has this person really finished, or could finish the therapy? Is there any possibility that you might be holding people long-term because you actually want to safeguard your income? So we try to look at it on all kinds of different levels.

Therapy ends when the client no longer needs it?

Better rephrase it: that when somebody leaves therapy, I hope that they're taking with them some of the tools in the toolbox. Not the complete kit, I don't suppose, and anyway I think people need some-times that outside person to help.

Well, I think for me when I'm lucky – which is to say that when something external doesn't intervene in the client's life, like a sudden lack of money, or a need to move house to another part of the country. When the therapy can go its full course – I think it becomes apparent to the client and myself at some point that the therapy has reached its fullness. That Gestalt is complete, and it's appropriate to stop. That's the most satisfying way of ending. Then we'll take – I often work with people for three, four, five years and we'll take a considerable period of time, by which I mean maybe as long as two or three months, con-sciously addressing the fact that this work is going to end and this relationship is going to end. Trying to leave as little unfinished business around as possible, for both of us.

At other times a shorter-term therapy can finish, and we'll both know in the moment that the person is satisfied, that they have done what they came to do. It's happened, it's worked. And it's time to finish. They might leave after one more session. Complete in one more session. Sometimes something will happen. A client might – this is current for me at the moment – somebody's financial situation has altered, and there may be other things going on there too which we are certainly addressing, but I think there is a reality. Gestalt is very reality-based. We know that people can't always make their £25, £30 a week for years and years at a time. So with this person – and this person has benefited from the work that they've done – I will leave the door open and say 'Well if you get back on your feet again financially, and you want to come back, let me know.'

I will usually, anyway, say to people 'If you want to come back and do some more work at any time, let me know.'

Analysts often say that paying for therapy makes the client more committed ...

Well I've changed actually, I would have gone more with the analysts. But I've changed because a friend of mine recently set up a counselling service here in Hitchin, which is free to the client. I was very dubious about this. And I think sometimes it does make a difference in that people who perhaps find the counselling situation strange and would take a little while to get into it, might take one or two sessions and then just buzz off, because they haven't invested any money, so they've got nothing to lose really. But the counselling service has been running fully, properly, for a year now, and it seems as though overall it actually doesn't make any difference. The people who get committed, who really get involved in the process, stay. So I don't know.

I have to earn a living. So I'm very clear that my charge refers to what I decide that I need to earn in order to make a reasonable living. So that I'm not worried about money. It relates to how much I charge for my time, rather than what goes on in that time.

Do you do 50-minute sessions?

No. I do an hour. And sometimes I'll go over a bit. I try to stick pretty much to that time, but sometimes I'll go five minutes over, or sometimes more than that if somebody in the course of an extended therapy hits something enormous a quarter of an hour before the end of an hour session. I'm certainly not going to cut them off at the exact hour; I'll go with them, until they've gone through whatever it is and have come out the other side and are ready to go back into the world again. So generally I keep to an hour-ish ...

What for you are the major ethical issues in your work?

Well I think the whole thing is based on a respect for the client and a respect for therapeutic work. So that things that you've already mentioned – the possible dangers of countertransference, which blatantly can be manifested by emotional, or financial, or sexual abuse of a client, but there are much more subtle levels than that.

I think one of the things that we are very concerned about, talking about in the training, is power within the relationship, but in a much more broad sense than just those very obvious things. So I don't go down the line of saying that there is equality in the relationship. I say there isn't, because therapy works really when the client empowers the therapist – at the start. I think the relationship between client and therapist at the end of therapy is going to be very different from that at the beginning. There should be a sense of equality then, I think. Because the client has dropped a lot of their transferential things and has empowered themselves, they no longer need to empower the therapist, because they've re-empowered themselves in an informed and experienced way.

So power is important, and we get down to the minute details like – in a session if I talk too much because I like the sound of my own voice, that's an abuse of power, because sometimes to intervene with anything said at all is much less helpful to a client than just to let the silence go on a bit.

You mentioned UKCP ...

Well I think it's a juggernaut that's started rolling. The organisation I belong to is a member of UKCP, the Humanistic and Integrative Section. I think we joined just the year before the constitution was ratified. What do I think of it? I think that so long as UKCP stays with its basic principles, which are to seek to establish really high standards, and at the same time to respect and foster diversity within the profession, then I don't have a quarrel with it.

So long as it remains a democratic organisation. There are stresses evident in the profession around power and status. Some groups have broken away from UKCP to form their own organisation. I find the work that the HIPS section does immensely valuable and appreciate the opportunity of getting to know and work with other humanistic practitioners.

How do you self-monitor your work?

Well I know my stamina quite well by now, so for instance, I won't see more than six people in a day, unless I do something silly. But I prefer five, five is comfortable. I suppose over a week I see about seventeen, eighteen individual people. Some of those are supervisees, not therapy clients – and I run a training group and do tutorials and do other management stuff. We work in term times, so I have good breaks at Christmas, Easter and in the summer. I have three weeks at Christmas, and three weeks at Easter, and a block of four weeks or so during the summer. I generally know when I've had enough, and I just feel 'I don't want to be here doing this. I've lost my appetite to speak in Gestalt terms. I no longer – I don't want to be there – I want to be doing – I'd rather be whatever for instance the bumper sticker would say.' Obviously, because of what we've been talking about, the basis of Gestalt being effective organismic self-regulation, it is a bit daft if Gestalt therapists burn themselves out – we're supposed to be able not to do that. So I make sure that I don't work too many weekends during the year, and that I have enough time off on a daily/weekly/monthly/yearly basis, so that I don't get sick, and I'm actually still interested in being with the client.

Its efficacy?

Well, I have personal experience. I was a client in therapy, I've gone back into therapy in the last few weeks. I have the evidence of my own experience with clients, and their own say-so. Working means people discovering that they are not who they thought they were, or have been told they were. It's like breaking out of the clay mould: 'Wow I can do that!'

Would you like to see our 'society' embrace therapy more than it does?

I hadn't thought about it. As you speak, the first thing that comes to my mind, as a block to that happening, is the role that the media play – television and video and all that stuff. I have the sense that society may be coming much more passively sponge-like. Willing to sit in front of films, and whatever, and take in rather than be more actively engaged in the processes of their lives. So long as that's so, I think people are not going to be interested in or have a clue about, or perhaps even have the emotional energy for, the hard work that self-knowledge is.

All life is a bit of a struggle ...

It's part of being human in this world, yes. Struggle in Gestalt terms is very positive. We would consider a spoilt child a child who has had everything on request, has never had to struggle, because unless a child struggles they don't discover the resources that they have. They don't grow their muscles. They don't discover that they can find other ways of achieving what they want. They don't grow up. They don't have to engage with the world.

In the old days Gestalt work was coupled with self-absorption ...

Yes, it certainly has been portrayed as being that – a very narcissistic view. Human beings are social animals. Are we tribal or herd – we're tribal, aren't we? So we have an interest in the tribe. It seems to me that one of the things that people display is our social responsibility or social interests. What I'm saying is that what we work with is what interests the client. Now if a client is entirely narcissistic, that is, their only interest in the world is the world as extension of them, as possible gratification of their need, then I think that's skewed. So I would work specifically to help that person begin to have an experience that the other person, usually the therapist, actually is a discreet individual with thoughts and feelings and a point of view, and whatever, and can the client tolerate that, assimilate it, and begin to shift themselves?

You mentioned Paul Goodman before, didn't you? Paul Goodman is being published again, and he was always a very, very strong influence in Gestalt. Have you ever read *Growing Up Absurd*? Well he says it all there, doesn't he? It's no good just trying to work with a person, a person can't change unless there's an environment that can support them to change. It's an interchange. The environment changes with how the individuals in it function. So we're absolutely interdependent.

When a client is changing do you worry about how their partner might be feeling?

Yes. That can be one of the difficulties, because 'I' is a convenient fiction, it lets me know who I am when I get up in the morning, it also lets you know who I am when we get up in the morning. So if one person in a couple is in therapy I do pay a lot of attention to the effect that that's going to have on the couple, and where is the partner in all this? Is the partner feeling threatened and defensive? Or is the partner welcoming the change and changing themselves? I very rarely work with couples. It's not a choice, it's just that I don't seem to attract couples very much. But I am acutely aware of the other person. What effect does the factor of the therapeutic relationship between me and you, have on your partner? What's going on? There's a triangle here. So I try to remain as broadly aware of that whole web as possible. I always bear in mind that I only see – and if we're talking about your wife – I only see your wife through your eyes, I don't know her. So I have to work with that as well.

CHAPTER 11

Neuro-Linguistic Programming (NLP)

Annie Keller

Annie Keller runs seminars and sees individual clients at
NLP International base in London. She combines many
techniques including NLP and hypnosis.

*Could you talk a bit about how you got interested, in the first place, in
therapy?*

Well it started when I was in my early teens. I went to a spiritual
healer, because I had a bad back, and I used to play a lot of tennis at
the time. I suddenly got what they said was fibrositis down through my
shoulders. I was in real pain; standing up, sitting down, I was in pain
whatever way I looked at it, and I stopped playing tennis. The doctor
said that it wouldn't ever be better. I thought: 'No, you're wrong, you're
wrong, it will be better and I'll make sure that it is.' So I started to go
to different people. I went to a spiritual healer who managed to get rid
of most of it, and later on started to do the Alexander technique,
meditation and pilates technique a bit later on.

With the spiritual healer?

Not with him, not with the spiritual healer, but I started to do lots of
different things in order to get it better. And eventually in my teens, I
went to an NLP/hypnotherapist. She was an absolutely amazing woman;
she was extremely creative with what she was doing and just brilliant.
After about a year of being with her I felt that I could do a lot of what she
was doing, and had in my mind that I would quite like to use that, what
she was doing, *myself*. I also had wanted to be a performer since I was a
kid. I knew at an early age that I wanted to be (1) a self development
trainer; and (2) a performer.

I knew that, knew what my path was. So I went to this woman and
then she suggested to me: 'Why don't you do something like stage hypnosis?' So I thought, 'Oh, that might be interesting', and started to train with
a man in Brighton. The guy who took me on and I remember when I first
went to him he ripped me to pieces mentally. I'd been meditating for years
and he thought I was too much up in the sky. Then he waited to see if I
would come back. And of course, the next week I knocked on his door,

and we started training. Now we started training in observation, observing people on the streets. So if somebody was in a telephone box, who were they talking to, depending on their body language. If two people were walking down the street together, what was their relationship, depending on how far apart they were walking. If somebody was by themselves, what was their spouse like at home, depending again on their physiology. What might they potentially get when they're older, depending on how their posture was, how they walked or moved.

So I started training with that and decided very early on not to be a stage hypnotist. But he was teaching me NLP skills, and lots of observation skills, among other things – giving me therapy – he was totally unpredictable. I never knew what would happen from one day to the next with him. Then I found an NLP practitioner training, here in England, and then followed it on with a Master practitioner training in the United States. I then came back here and assisted on a practitioner training, then went back out to the States to assist on other practitioner trainings, with the Andreases. The reason why I wanted to train in the States is because I find the Americans much more open, and also I wanted to train with the best. The people who had introduced it.

So I then did a trainer's training with Robert Dilts, and meanwhile, about a year in between that, I had started setting up my own seminars here. I have to backtrack a little bit because before doing NLP, after training with this man in Brighton I did some other self-development seminars, called the 'Outlook' seminars, which are still going on and are incredible personal development seminars. So I spent many years not just doing NLP, but doing other trainings and seeing other therapists as well; quite a mixture of people. One woman, who did a mix of Gestalt and her own methods, was an American Indian. So from my teens I was doing bodyworks and therapy due to my one driving factor. If I am totally true to who I am, and all the defence mechanisms, and all the superficiality that has been built up for protection and safety from childhood is let go of, and I am who I am totally at all times with all people, whoever I'm with, then I can do and have whatever I want. That was my driving force, my total driving force.

And eventually I set up my own seminars and started with very few people ...

NLP means neuro-linguistic programming. Where does the 'neuro' actually come into it?

The neurology is what we see, hear, what you feel, taste, and smell. I don't know why they thought of that name, really. I think it was out of the blue – 'Okay, let's call it that'. And actually it's quite an off-putting ...

Yes, like the word 'programming' ...

Horrible, horrible. 'Programme' is just horrible, it's a horrible word. I often don't use it. I just say 'Neuro-Linguistics (NLP)'. I agree ... Natural Learning Processes would be so much better.

Can you explain what NLP is?

NLP's principal co-founders – Richard Bandler, an information scientist, and John Grinder, a professor of linguistics – define NLP as the study of human excellence. In the early '70s they met at Santa Cruz University, and joined forces to research the question 'What is it that makes somebody excellent at what they do while someone else can do the same thing and not be so good? What is it that the excellent person does in their brain?'

They studied three therapists. They studied Fritz Perls – Gestalt therapist; Virginia Satir – family therapist; and Milton Erikson – hypnotherapist. Three therapists who consistently produced positive changes in the lives of other people. They sat in on their sessions, observed their body language, listened to their language, and aimed to discover 'how come the clients trust them straight away? What is it that they do? How come they have incredible results?' From there they went on to study talented people in other fields – managers, negotiators, athletes and artists – to find out what these individuals did to get their outstanding results. Out of that came the modelling process of NLP. And from that, Richard Bandler and John Grinder plus other people like Robert Dilts, the Andreases, and many others, have created and continue to create new processes to expand the field of NLP.

And it has expanded to many areas. There seems to be a process for every issue, whether it's a behaviour, habit, belief, identity, or spiritual dilemma, including dealing with phobias, allergies, co-dependency, grief, trauma, unwanted habits and behaviours, and a more recent addition to the spiritual/identity aspects of NLP, 'The Aligned Self' which was created by the Andreases.

There are, of course, also the communication skills, use of language and body language when working with someone. Rapport is number one and looking at the questions 'What do you want? What are your outcomes?' brings me to the difference between NLP and other therapies.

We focus on what the person wants. We may focus for a short while on the issue and it is early on that we shift it to 'What do you want?' (You were talking about psychotherapy.) Obviously there are different types. All are different and in some the person comes in, they chat, and they talk about their issues, and then they go home. They've talked about their problem, but has the issue been cleared? It's probably forced them to think a lot more about it which can be okay to an extent in terms of insight. But as we think about it more and more, it creates the problem more and more in our brain. The more we think about it, the more it comes up. Doesn't it? People go on going to the therapist because the issues are constantly there for them and they are still reacting to the memory of the experience rather than the experience itself, as that is over.

With NLP, I don't ever see anybody more than six to ten times. It gives people skills to use for themselves. This is why I went into it, because it allows you to become master of yourself. At some point you don't need to see a therapist any more, you know the skills which you can use. You've got the skills, use them for yourself. Because it's a sort of co-dependency going to a therapist all the time. It's great if you need some guidance for a while, that's fabulous, that's progressive. But to be going for years to a therapist is co-dependency.

What do you do when somebody comes to see you?

That's a loaded question.

I simply want to know the 'basics' ...

Well, it really depends on what the issue is. It is important that the person feels comfortable. I then ask how I can be of service to them. Then the issues obviously come out, whatever they happen to be. Usually it's around identity. As I spoke about before, about not feeling totally – and not being totally themselves. Who they are. Feel that they cannot contact who they really are inside. They know they're in there, their real selves, but it's like they can't contact this self. Child spirit, whatever you want to call it. In order to be themselves, fully one hundred per cent.

And then there's also the desire to change behaviours and improve relationships and communication with self and others. But I start by asking how I can be of service to them and somebody will talk for a while on what the issue is. Then I ask: 'What would be a successful outcome/result? What would you like to have happen by the time you leave this room today?' So then already we are focusing their mind on what they want. Then we deal with that. I give them a certain amount of time to tell me what the issues are. Some people obviously need to talk a bit – and it's very early on that I switch round to 'What do you want?' And then once they've told me what it is they want, I work accordingly. Now I don't use just pure NLP. NLP has been described as anything that works. It's other things: it's intuition, it's a mix of therapies and ways of thinking, *and it works.*

What are the core concepts of NLP?

NLP, like any subject, has a set of underlying principles. The first is, 'The map is not the territory'. A map is a distorted view of reality if the map is our thoughts and feelings and the territory is reality. We respond to our thoughts and feelings about reality, not reality itself, which is good in many aspects as it means it's possible to get a better map, that is, a better way to think and feel. Another principle is that the mind and body are part of the same system. If you change your mind about something your abilities will change. Change your posture, breathing and very likely at that moment your thoughts will change. A third principle is if one person can do it, anyone can do it. For example excellence and achievement have a structure that can be copied. If we learn to use our brains in the same way as exceptionally talented people we can possess the essence of that talent. A fourth principle is that experience has a structure. For example, the way in which memories are arranged in our minds determines what they mean to us and how we will be affected by them. Change the structure of the memory and we will experience those events in our minds differently. And a fifth principle is that people have all the resources they need. Our brain sees inner pictures. They can be fuzzy or clear. Inner voices can criticise or encourage. Any feelings we've had in our life, like confidence or will, whatever it is can be transferred to where we want it and need it in our present and future.

What do you actually do if someone has a phobia?

NLP looks at how the brain works, and if we understand how the brain works, say for example, somebody has a phobia. Now a phobia has been caused mainly when they were younger, or at some particular time when somebody has connected a physical emotion/feeling with something in the environment. So see a spider – feel the fear. The visual and the feelings are connected. Now every time that person sees a spider it's as if they're associated again in that experience. What we do, or what I will do, is to disconnect the visual and the kinaesthetic.

NLP works on the senses, the mind understands the senses: what we see, hear, feel, taste and smell, and there's the sixth sense. However we focus on see, hear, feel much more, because in the western world those are the three main senses.

If the mind only understands the senses, then the shifts need to be with the senses.

Okay, and a co-dependent problem?

Somebody who's co-dependent, 'What is it that they get from the other person? What part does that person fulfil for them?' It may be their creativity, confidence or drive, or a mix of things. So they can't do without that person, because they fulfil their creativity or drive, whatever it is. So my aim is to allow them to realise their own creativity and drive, so they don't need that other person to fulfil those criteria.

What do you actually do in the work?

Obviously there's hypnosis in terms of the language that I use. There's a lot of ... we do it moving, standing up, not actually moving, but they could be standing up, imagining the other person is over there. Another pure NLP example which might assist you is called time-line therapy. Somebody who's had a particular incident when they were a child which hasn't left them. Imagine that there's a line on the floor which is their life. We're standing up, so I'll imagine we're standing up, and this is something called your time-line, which is their life going in a straight line. A particular incident when they were kids, say they were abused or whatever happened, and we go back to that time, on that time-line, until they were whatever age it was. So say they're seven years old, and then I get them off the time-line. The minute they're off the time-line they are dissociated, the minute that they are on their time-line, standing – so there's movement here – the minute that they're standing on the time-line they're in the experience. They're seven years old again. The minute they are off, they're however old they happen to be.

Then I ask them what resources that they needed at the time, in order for them to get through that experience. I ask them what experiences the other people involved – their mother, their father – say it's with their father: what resources did he need in order to be different? Then we go back, and we go forward into their life – say the father hit them or whatever, at seven. Okay, what resources did he need? So we go forward into their life. So the father needed patience. We go forward – get on the time-line – go forward into their life, a time when they were patient. Beam that patience to your father, imagine your father receiving that patience. They're in there, imagining they're patient, beaming that patience to the father; father receives that patience.

Then the client will step in and be their father, and imagine their father different this time. And beam that patience across to the little kid when they were seven. Then be the kid receiving that patience. Notice how different they are, then. Then any other qualities that the kid will need. We go and get those. Say the kid needed courage: go to get courage from part of their life, beam that courage across to the little kid, and then imagine the kid having that courage. Then with all the resources that the kid has, and the new belief that it's created – say, for example, if I just backtrack a second, the first time when someone goes back, they formed beliefs. Usually we do this because there are unwanted beliefs, 'I'm not good enough', or whatever, and it's come from a time when their father hit them or whatever it was. So then with the kid who received all the resources from everywhere, we look at what new belief is formed. 'I'm great, I'm safe.' With that we walk forward in their life to that, with this feeling of safety. Yes, does that help?

But it can't be that easy ...

There are so many other things I do where I'm not just using NLP, but I am using a mix of therapies. My experience and intuition, for example. One of the core things is to make sure the male and female side of somebody get on and are balanced because inside is a direct reflection of their relationships outside. So whatever the male side of them is like, if it's a woman their male partner will be like that and that is the sort of man they will attract. So to make sure there is healthy communication inside will assist their relationship outside. So I may ask questions such as: 'What does your male side think of your female side? What doese she think of him? How does he want to be? How does she want to be? How does she want him to be? How does he want her to be? What does he think of that? and so on.

How do you do that?

Just speaking. We put the conscious mind to one side and ask the unconscious mind to come forward. It's almost like it's a shift of consciousness. I speak to their female side, or I speak to their male side. I say: 'Just imagine now that you're female, what do you think of him? First answer please.' So there are so many different ways. Then I also work with the concept of 'parts'. If I talk of the mind being made up of a sum of parts, and these parts sometimes get stuck at certain ages of development and may still be experiencing anger or resentment or frustration or loneliness from that particular incident that happened at that age when the issue was unresolved. Then my work is to contact that part that is stuck and to update its information, and go back to clear the issue in order to assist the part in becoming more resourceful and having more resourceful beliefs. And only then is it healthy to grow the part up to the person's present chronological age. The obvious outcome is to have all our 'parts' merge and to retain the child spirit of being present, curious and playful. Then there's the 'Aligned Self' process, where we're aligning the senses in a particular situation of difficulty with somebody else; where we find that we're not centred. Now if the mind understands the senses, then being centred would mean being centred in your senses, surely? The word 'centred' means centred in your senses, because the mind understands the senses.

So somebody in a situation with somebody else is in the middle of a row – and you remember you must have been in certain situations where you've had arguments with somebody and you felt off-centre. Usually their eyes are out of their sockets, when we look back, they're not hearing properly what the other person's saying, and feeling – not only their feelings but the other person's. And their internal voice is coming from some place apart from their throat, for example. So another thing that I may do is realign their senses so that they can become fully grounded and fully conscious, and in themselves. Often it means getting their eyes back in their sockets at that particular time, their internal voice in their throat, hearing through both ears, and giving back the feelings – anyone else's – and just keeping their own. Whatever they may be. It doesn't matter whether it's anger or joy, so long as it is fully and purely their own. Then there is often a sense of being much more grounded. Seeing, hearing, feeling much more, and being more in themselves.

So that's another thing that I may do. You see it's very difficult to pinpoint all that I do, because it's so many different things. Sometimes there's movement in it, sometimes it's sitting. A lot of it has to do with intuition. It isn't just from the NLP background. Somebody can do a practitioner training, a Master practitioner training, and go and practise NLP, but it does not mean they will be clear themselves if they haven't done enough change work themselves. It is vital that the person who is practising NLP has done so much work that whatever issues their clients come in with – whatever issues my clients come in with I've got to be clearer, that is the number one thing. That I am clear about these issues, otherwise I have no right to be a personal development coach. I must be clear about those issues.

It's not just from NLP, because it's good to have a mixture of things. I'm not saying NLP is the be-all and end-all, because I've done a lot of other therapies. And it's from all those therapies that I use my work, not just NLP. Someone says 'Is that an NLP process?' I'll say 'I don't know what it is, but it works.' It's a mixture of things.

Why is NLP so strongly associated with hypnotherapy?

Because of Milton Erikson. A lot of the language that we use is hypnotic language. Milton Eriksonian hypnosis – use of language – and how use of language can assist someone in becoming much more resourceful. We do use hypnotic language in order to enhance the change work. And at the same time we can use language solely for change.

Can you give me an example?

Well, for example, I may use certain things. Someone comes with an issue, and I can say from very early on in the session, 'the problem that you *used to have* ...' or 'When you *used to do this*', using language where it puts the problem in the past. We haven't even done anything yet. But I've put it in the past, and then you can tell if it works, because at the end of the session, often the person will use the past tense when talking of the issue they used to have.

What makes a good therapist do you think? What are the necessary skills?

Intuition is a big thing. Coming from a place of *love*, caring for that person, and really wanting them to make changes. And obviously having the skills to do it. The answer is always if the person comes back. If they come back we know we're doing the right thing. You know it's working. I'll tell you what it is as well – how we can tell if we're doing a good job, as well as the difference between psychotherapy and NLP, maybe. When I see my clients in the street, whether they've done a seminar or whether they worked individually with me, when I see them in the streets, which I do – obviously at times in London – their faces light up. If they'd come to me with issues and all I had done, as maybe some psychotherapists do, is talk all the time about their problems, it would have anchored. Every time they see me they think of their problems. Because they're used to it. So if I saw them in the street and I was dealing with just their problems the whole time, and constantly focusing on their problems, I'd say: 'Hi, how are you doing?' and they'd probably say: 'Oh, not that good really. Well I've still got this ....' However, because of the work that I do and how it is shifted, where we look at what they want, whenever I see somebody in the street, their face lights up. I've been anchored to positive experiences, positive feelings. That is important.

What kind of agreement do you make with clients first time around?

No promises, nothing. They come to me, we do something, they leave happy and ask for another appointment. If someone I think doesn't need to come to me any more, I tell them. They usually know as well. And its at the most six to ten sessions later.

That must make it hard to keep on getting new clients?

All I know is that I'm true to myself, and true to them. The universe will do whatever the universe does in return for that. The aim for NLP is that people become masters of themselves, and don't need me. I'm just a guide for that moment in time. Some people may come back a year later; come and do a seminar if they've done individual sessions, or do individual sessions if they've done a seminar.

Do you do any hypnosis?

A little bit, yes.

In what circumstances?

I use it during the processes, just to enhance whatever it is that we're doing. We're hypnotised every day; it's just a way, a use of language to enhance the resourcefulness of the client. A way of contacting the unconscious or subconscious mind. Getting the conscious mind out of the way, and that's it. It's just a use of language that allows us to go that little bit deeper. We're hypnotised every single day. We stare up (a hypnotic technique) at a film screen, at the TV screen; we look up at the advertising billboards. We hypnotise each other unconsciously all the time. We have a conversation and you're hypnotised by me. Or you talk, and I'm hypnotised by what you're saying. Hypnosis is happening the whole time. We're in and out of it continuously.

How do you do this with people?

You want blood, don't you!

Britain is not exactly – say, compared to the States – a therapeutic society is it?

Yes, much slower to change. It has in the past been much more difficult for an English person to get to the seminar than somebody who's foreign I would say. Although the English are becoming more aware of their need to make changes. There is a fear of contacting feelings, and there is a lot of being cut-off from the neck downwards. Separate thing, the head and the body, which is amazing considering the body is so much more of us than the head, that we spend so much time on the head. I think the sort of people that I attract as well are people who want to get connected, because I'm also a dancer, and a performer, and am very in contact with my body. I attract a wide variety of people in business, arts, therapies, teaching.

Can you talk about the seminars you run?

The seminars that I deal with again are different, it's a different thing. Let me just explain to you what we do.

I teach a weekend introductory seminar, whereby people come to learn basic NLP skills for themselves. On the first day we deal with use of language, use of body language, communication skills, the connection between how the eyes move and the mind. An advanced form of goal setting called 'Outcomes', where we imprint what we want into our senses. So that's the first day, and then the second day, once we've got all those basic skills, we start to deal with how to break habits and unwanted behaviours. How to get yourself into a resourceful state, how to motivate yourself, how to look at your past from a new perspective. All of these things are basic skills that somebody can go away with and use. They've already shifted over the weekend, they know what to do. The results are incredible, just from those very simple, basic NLP skills. The people on the seminar are learning new information, they're expanding their conscious minds and have more resources to assist them through life.

What do you think is optimum mental health?

Someone who is true to themselves, who is true to other people as well, because they're who they really are, and can be who they really are with people from all different walks of life. That means giving to themselves, giving to others. I'll tell you what, it's coming from a place of loving people, and that probably sounds really esoteric or ungrounded, but to be able to communicate. If love is to be able to communicate well with themselves and with others, then that is healthy and that *is* grounded. To be able to communicate, and be true.

How do we know who we are?

Oh, well, you can only know who *you* are, and I can only know who *I* am.

What does that mean really?

Well, you know if you're being true to yourself. Maybe sometimes you don't, or you do know, and that's why you may go to a therapist, because you don't feel like yourself. I'll tell you what, many people have said to me: 'I get lonely, I feel lonely.' A number of people have said this to me recently. However many people are around them they still feel lonely. It's because they probably haven't contacted who they really are, haven't allowed that 'them' to express themselves. And that 'them' is the child spirit, is the self that is true to themselves. If they feel angry they can be angry. If they feel happy, joyful, whatever – be it, just be it. And be truthful.

Where do your clients' problems come from? What are the origins of their disquiet?

It's a direct result – the world they live in from pre-birth, birth to post-birth.

Can you elaborate?

Well, we're a result of everything that's happened to us. Family, teachers, friends, kids at school, all our experiences. However, saying that, people can deal with things in different ways. It depends on how we look at our experience as learning and feed back or doing something different or an excuse to be a victim. Some people may say it's genetic as well. Some people may say it's astrology – planets. I've no answers for that but I do know that we are a result of what happens in our lives and the people around us.

Do you work within a code of ethics?

Yes. With a client you mean. Yes I do really. Because the most important thing is that I am there to serve *them*. There's something called ecology in NLP, where we check with them and all the 'parts' of them if it's okay to make these changes. That is a very big thing in NLP – is this okay to do this? If it's not okay, we need to find out perhaps what part is objecting to them, and what the reason may be, and deal with that. If it's not ecological then we cannot proceed until it is.

Can you elaborate?

Is it okay to make this change? It's one of the first questions. Or if you could have this change, would you take it?

Do you take into account how the partner of one of your clients might feel?

No, because once they've shifted, their spouses will shift. That person shifts who's in the room with me; their relationships will shift. Once they've shifted, the usual patterns of communication that have gone on will shift. Because one of them isn't playing any more. They're doing something different. So the person with the most flexibility rules the system.

You're very confident at what you do. Why is that so?

The effects of the work I've done, and also who I am. I know what I do works – I've seen it many times.

Do you worry about 'therapeutic burn-out'?

No, because I'm also an actress, and so I am filming and performing regularly, and dance is a major hobby as well. So I don't really get burn-out, because I do other things. That's what's so great, NLP allows you to bring into your life whatever you do. To train in NLP is to bring it into your life, the amount of uses that it comes to in being a performer and every profession are quite incredible.

Can you see how some people might see NLP as a quasi-religion?

Well, there's no religion.

Well, very American, very self-improvement – like est.

Totally different from *est* – *est* is a five-day seminar that you do. NLP is ongoing skills to use through life all the time. Is there anything wrong in something being American? The Americans have produced amazing things, they're totally progressive and a lot of us love going over to the States, because they have things there that we don't have, and you can learn things that we don't teach.

Have you had clients who have talked about 'false memory syndrome' – that ideas have been planted ...

Yes, right. I've had people come to me like that; a few who have had that from other therapists and have said, 'My old therapist said I must have been sexually abused.' NLP doesn't do that, it always comes from the client. All I do is ask questions.

How would you know the client was right?

Usually because they say: 'I didn't think this until I went to ...' And then they come to me and we eradicate that. To be honest, let's say they were sexually abused, and let's say that it didn't come from someone else, it came from them. We can clear up that – obviously there are issues around it – and the thing is really to get people into the present and the future. 'Oh, it's ...', is often an excuse for people, 'Oh this happened, this happened, so I'm like this.' It is an excuse, it is a crutch – and that's not being master, that's being victim. It's like listening to a doctor who says your back's never going to be better.

Would you like our society to be more of a therapeutic one?

Yes. I remember at drama school, because I went to Central, and one of the directors once said: 'I think all the actors need therapy, they don't need drama school', which I agreed with, although both is ideal. If we looked deeper inside ourselves. Men and women are different, as well, and if we looked a bit deeper, or asked questions, we'd communicate much better, have better relations, be more giving and happier.

Your future?

Connecting the arts more with NLP. I'm researching that right now.

CHAPTER 12

Psychotherapy and Race/Ethnicity

Lennox Thomas

Lennox Thomas is Clinical Director of the inter-cultural therapy centre, NAFSIYAT, London.

Can you tell me how you came to work in therapy, be a therapist?

I started my career in child care, even before that I began voluntary work with young children in a play scheme. I went on to work at a psychiatric hospital as a volunteer, and between A Levels and not knowing what else to do, I decided to take up an appointment in child care in London. I left my home town in the Midlands and worked with young people who were considered to be disturbed and their parents. This brought me closer to an interest in what had been written about children. I think the first writers were people like Winnicott, and Professor Elias from Leicester University – sort of investigating children's behaviour.

I became more and more interested, and eventually I trained as a social worker, and began my own personal analysis. When I began my own personal analysis in the early 1970s it hadn't occurred to me that maybe I would be working as a therapist ten years later, but that's how I came.

When you say your own personal analysis ...

I went to a psychoanalyst.

How would you describe the tradition you work in?

The tradition I come from would be considered to be psychoanalytical. And I think it began right from my professional training, it was actually about sorting problems, understanding people's problems and helping them to solve it. There are very different approaches to therapy – therapy as growth, therapy as self-actualisation, the way that I approached it was therapy to make people better. To help stop them being mentally ill or disturbed with their children and families.

I think there could be a big dysfunction between the ideas and what I do, because I think that the whole area of intercultural therapy – working with ethnicity, race and psychotherapy – is quite an unknown area. So to some extent we've had to draw on as many people that we could possibly find who made some connections from orthodox psychoanalysis or psychotherapy. But thinking about people like Klein, Anna Freud, Bowlby and Winnicott, possibly the closest – Jafar Kareem who was the founder of this place – are the people that I think are drawn on in terms of my fundamental understanding of psychotherapy and psychoanalysis.

Psychoanalysis seems extrememly 'white', if you know what I mean ...

Yes, considering that he was himself a Jew, who was being persecuted by German Nazis, it's actually quite fascinating that he began no discourse about that – and in fact many of the people who followed him didn't either. But I think that they had their own pressures. I think that during and after the War, even before perhaps, people who were different tried their damnedest not to be seen as different, because of the obvious fears of being singled out. I think also, in terms of their own psychology, people wanted to belong – pretend that there was nothing that distinguished them from the other people that they lived with communally.

But I think that things changed. I think it started in the '80s, and there were lots of public concerns about black people, and people from ethnic minorities and their mental health. There were lots of public concerns about young people and family life, and children ending up in children's institutions. This culminated in concern about how black people accessed the psychotherapeutic services. I think that it brought to people's thinking that maybe there is something about the psychology of minorities that has to be thought about, and I think that is where we started from. Jafar Kareem, the founder, began from working in Haringey. He worked in Haringey with Greek-Cypriot and Turkish-Cypriot young people, who were in generational problems with their parents. He found that the traditional services – the child guidance services – really were quite racist in terms of offering them no means of understanding themselves, and the parody was that there is the professional taking sides with the children who were becoming westernised, and said to the parents: 'Well, now you're in England, you've got to behave like the English.' This was no answer. He felt that he had to try and find some way of understanding people's cultural experiences, their transition experiences, and helping them to value things that are essentially theirs, in order to understand their pathology, or what's going wrong with them.

Can you tell me about your organisation ...

Right. To say what we're about. Well the only opportunity we want is more money, more funding, from the government, if possible. [Laughs] Yes, the organisation started in 1982, and it began quite modestly with one person who was trained as a psychoanalytic psychotherapist.

He was a psychology student. He'd just graduated in Calcutta, around the time of the partitioning of India in 1947. And he'd been arrested by the British, because he was protesting – part of all the young people running in the street. His best friend and fellow student was killed in the street by the British Army, and his parents just wanted to get him out of the country and get him away from the trouble as soon as he graduated. They sent him to London to do a postgraduate course in Psychology at London University. Of course he couldn't settle. So what he did was, he went to where the War was. He went to Austria to work in a resettlement camp with people who, at the end of Second World War, were displaced persons. He worked there from the late 1940s, early 1950s, until he went to Israel with some of the people who'd been sent to Israel. He worked also in Israel in community psychiatry with Gerald Kaplan who was very interested in community-based psychiatry. Eventually he came back to this country in the early '60s, did his psychoanalytic training with the BAP, and then worked and settled. He kept becoming restless, because I think he'd lived this kind of exciting life, working as a therapist or as a welfare worker, with such an interesting and diverse group of people. I suppose working in north London just didn't seem that interesting. [Laughs]

He created his own excitement. He created his own controversy with his colleagues, saying: 'What are you talking about? What's all this about? Why should they behave as though they have no previous existence, no life, no culture, nothing that's theirs?' Until he found this untenable. He couldn't work with his colleagues any more. There was a group of psychiatrists and GPs who were friends of his – sort of encouraged him to start this small project working with people from a variety of backgrounds. And it was fun for him. He decided to second mortgage his home to start the project. But then the local Health Authority, I think Islington Council – one of the first organisations – said, 'Well if you're going to see people from our borough, we'll give you this small grant.' Then the Committee Health Trust gave a small grant, and the Centre has been open for business.

The Department of Health gave us a research grant to look at the efficacy of intercultural therapy, particularly working with people at the sharp end of mental distress, like people who'd been discharged from hospital; people with psychiatric disorders. It continued to be quite useful. People made quick recoveries, and the majority of them had actually got back on their feet, and got back into the job market or whatever, and it was quite encouraging. There's a book written about it, which you've probably seen, called *Intercultural Therapy*, Blackwell Scientific Books 1992. There have been research reports written before that.

So the place has grown really. At the beginning it started off with one person, Jafar, who was able to speak many of the Indian languages – Punjabi, Urdu, Hindi, Bengali, Hebrew, a bit of Yiddish [laughs] – myself, and one Greek-Cypriot social worker who subsequently trained as a Child Psychotherapist. And it moved from there really. Roland Littlewood has always been quite interested as a consultant and a supervisor of the research, along with Dr Souranghu Acharyya who is also a psychiatrist. It moved on from there to encouraging more people. We have quite a lot of people who were very interested, who then went on to do psychotherapy trainings, and they've come back and supported us in some way or another by giving time free or supervising people. The place is actually run with a paid staff group of nine, and some work one day, some work an afternoon, some work two days, because they have their other work. They couldn't possibly live on the salaries if we were to employ them full-time. And there's a group of trainees, people training as psychotherapists or counsellors who give their time freely – they give three hours free for supervision in return.

Can you talk about the people you see ...

A third of the people refer themselves, and that third tend to be those who are depressed rather than people who have major psychiatric problems, although that doesn't exclude them. A third are sent by in-patient services like psychiatrists, psychiatric nurses in hospital wards. And the other third are people who are sent by social workers and general practitioners. But that's how it basically works out. I've got a feeling that the self-referrals are growing, but I think that is in line with everything else – people are more aware of therapy and counselling, and would be more likely to refer themselves.

The kind of ethnic groups that refer themselves: the refugee communities are growing largely. The Turkish, Kurdish, Horn of Africa, Somali, Eritreian, Ethiopian groups are growing considerably. And as a result of that we responded by setting up a refugee project that will work with young refugees – school to college age, 12- to 21-year-old groups.

People from the Indian subcontinent, people who are largely Punjabi-speaking, and Gujerati-speaking are possibly the largest single referral group; the Indian subcontinent, more than India. Then there are Caribbean people, and people from West Africa. Some refugee people from Africa – like Angola, Zaire, Mozambique – people who have been former refugees. And South Americans refer themselves.

Are many suspicious of psychiatry?

Well, maybe the people who actually refer themselves or get referred here are people who wouldn't have such a block about western traditional medicine or psychiatry. The group who are suspicious, or have a kind of a dual relationship with counselling or psychotherapy are the West African and Caribbean group who, on the one hand – some people will say: 'Well it might be useful', and on the other hand will say: 'Well the reason why I'm like this is because someone's actually put a spell on me, you know, it's *obeah*.' So the people can actually come along with that duality of thinking at times. So it would be Caribbean/West African people who'd come along with that kind of thinking. This thinking also exists in people from the Indian subcontinent, but not to the same degree.

I think people will see us as – even if we're not going to be able to have the great power to remove what is impeding their life or causing them problems – but we'd still be a sympathetic ear anyway. And that's a very interesting metaphor, that if we're not seen as useful, then we might be just friendly and kindly. [Laughs]

How do you incorporate the fact that Britain is a racist society into your work?

Well, it actually begins with the assessment, because I think it has to start right from the beginning. I think that if someone – as you say – actually experiences a sense of not belonging, not being wanted, having a rough time in their day-to-day life, having shit put through their letterbox, or seeing the swastika painted on the edge of the block where they live – how do you live with that 'niggers out'. But people have at some level been able to shelve it, because you can't have emotional responses to it every time, so you shelve it, you sort of stockpile it, and either you explode or you have ways of talking to people who are sympathetic about it – in your family or in your friendship groups – or you just totally ignore it. In the assessment, people are asked whether or not they feel discriminated against or whether or not there are things about how they live, or the way that they live, that are actually damaging to them.

Women will be asked that as well – about being a woman. About the experience of being a woman. Because an acknowledgement is made about the reality of racism and sexism. Those forces in people's lives have to be acknowledged, because in a way it's a bit of a sham if you're saying: 'Well, we'll only deal with this bit of your hurt. We'll only deal with this bit of your disturbance or your concern, but we'll totally ignore the rest', which is that if you're a female you can't get out after nine o'clock at night, or if you're a black person you can't walk down Brick Lane feeling safe about it sometimes. It's one of those things that is rarely dealt with, and some people actually face these issues daily.

Often, people will say: 'Well, you know, I manage, I cope, you know. It's all right, I manage, I cope.' And we have to say: 'But, you know, maybe there's more that you want to say about that, because we all manage and we cope, but sometimes it costs us something just to manage and cope.' So it will be a flagging up. People will later come back and recount an experience. Sometimes people will say: 'Oh no, fine, it's all right, what I really want to talk about is the fact that I hear these voices', or 'my wife's planning to leave me', or whatever, but then after some time, people might come back and say: 'And it doesn't help either, that the edge of the block where I live there are swastikas painted, and three doors down there's this white kid who constantly comes and does so-and-so to my flat.' So they will actually look at it as part and parcel of the accumulation of stress. But not as the central focus. I think that something fascinating happens to people, particularly the ones who are born here, or are raised here from very young. That they actually find a way of dealing with it, I mean goodness knows how it happens. I must have found a way of dealing with it, but I don't know the mechanism – that's what I'm really interested in – how it is that you actually do survive in the light of what appears to be massive racism. You have to make it not massive in order to survive, don't you?

What range of people do you see?

It's a very broad range actually. Someone who could have just walked out of the local hospital and the psychiatrist said: 'This person needs some supportive psychotherapy in order to survive in the community.' It could be someone who has had a very severe psychotic episode. The very interesting pieces of work that we've done are with people who've just had their first breakdown. Working with them is usually very rewarding. Because it's quite interesting that the episode – it takes a long time before they have another episode. And I think it's possible actually to work with people, to help them, to strengthen their experiences, to help them get more rooted in reality, to prevent them from having more psychotic episodes. Anyway, so we get people at that end.

Most people who have psychotic breakdowns, it's usually a self-disorder, isn't it. Self in relation to the other or the external world. And I think that the particular way that we work is about helping people to identify themselves, particularly as black people, as women, as people being discriminated against. It's a very individual and personalised experience. It also is not just within the context of their family or inside their own head, but in the context of the world around them. I think that is quite helpful. I think it's quite useful in terms of reorientating people about their life experiences. I don't know, but I've got one of the hunches that maybe that's one of the things that's helpful. Though one of the things that Jafar Kareem found was that black people who have psychotic disorders, and come into an organisation like this which has a large number of black people, attending to their care – that it is quite a helpful, curative experience for them. It is an experience that they probably wouldn't get anywhere else. Maybe that is the kernel of the efficacy. I think it goes beyond that though; I think it's the mode of the therapy as well. It's the kind of – the axis on which you work. It's not just looking at internal experiences, but looking at family and outside world experiences, and the context in which people live as black people, as black men or black women or whatever, and actually looking at all the stereotypes that surround them. People actually feel that they live stereotypes, because they've been very easily appropriated by society at large.

The range of problems ...

People that have got psychotic problems, probably those are the people that I think that we like to work with, because we don't think that other people work very well with them. People who present with couples relationships – we get a lot of mixed couples, mixed relationships. And oddly feeling that they wouldn't get a reasonable hearing elsewhere. Very interestingly, the white partner is the one who generally initiates the contact, saying that 'I'm white, my wife's black. I don't think that going to the local Marriage Guidance Council, they'd understand anything about how we live. They wouldn't understand anything about how our children have acquired their identity. So is it possible for us to see one of your counsellors who do marital work?' Very interesting.

We also work with a lot of children. A lot of children and young people who've got borderline delinquency problems, identity problems. Black kids who say 'I'm white'. In fact the classical case is a young child that I'm seeing, aged nine, saying that his parents aren't his parents, and that he's really white, and that he doesn't belong to them – quite seriously believing it.

A lot of young Asian men and women presenting for the ordinary things of growing up and leaving home. For particular things about fearing arranged marriages not so much, but some feeling that their lives have been curtailed, the anxiety of being curtailed or whatever. A lot of young Asian people now who are caught in that trap of themselves being very western, and their parents being very something else, being very eastern. Which is something that Caribbean children had experienced 20 years ago, which is this great difference in the world view of parents and the world view of children. I think that was very worrying for the Caribbean community, and it's now a big worry for Asian teenagers and their parents.

Quite a few people are presenting themselves with problems in work. People actually identify themselves as not performing well, feeling restricted at work, feeling that they can't get the best out, that they're not achieving their potential. And it's usually a neurotic condition. But some of it's linked with their identity, with who they think they are, and who other people think they are.

You've obviously worked with white patients ...

... really, I shouldn't know anything about black people at all. I trained to work with white patients, the training patients that I had when I was doing my training as a psychotherapist were white; the supervisors supervised me working with white patients – not that they had any great reference to the fact that I was black and they were white. The patients themselves spent a lot of time denying it. I did have one supervisor who was very interested in the racial difference.

How important is it to the clients to have a black therapist?

I'm not sure how important it is, because not all the therapists here are black or Asian. There are white English people here; white Mediterranean people here, there's a whole range of people. I don't think it's that important.

I think it's important given that there isn't any of this service available elsewhere. I think that if other organisations were able to provide a service that is sensitive to people's race or ethnicity then it wouldn't be that important. After all, white people are always going to be in the majority of providing psychiatric services to people generally, and black people in particular. It would be a nonsense to say that black people could only work well with black people. I worked very well with a white analyst, half of the time, and with a black analyst the other half of the time. But it's something about – what I think the magic is – that black people who come here will say: 'Well at least I feel as though I don't have to worry so much about being discriminated against, or feel that I'm being viewed as a stereotype. I think that I might be looked at as a real person.' That is what I think people will actually say.

And anyone can learn that ...

Anyone can learn, absolutely.

Is the mental health system improving for black people?

The heavy end of the mental health system I don't think changes much. I don't think it changes much at all. But I do think that people who are training as counsellors, probably more as counsellors than as psychotherapists, they have much more access to these sorts of ideas for some reason. I think that the psychotherapists, psychoanalysts, psychiatrists and the psychiatric system – it's going to be a long time before that changes. And I don't know what the difference is. Maybe it's because counselling actually advocates meeting the client as another person. It's not really tooled up with professionalism and science and tricks, so it actually makes the counsellor much more sensitive, or want to be aware about how they operate with the other person. I think the other psycho-services are probably much more reluctant, because they rely very heavily on their tricks.

What happens when someone comes to you?

You'll have to keep prompting me, because I shall just go off. [Laughs] The agency works on a short-term, twelve-session basis – assessment plus twelve basis – so that's the main part of the work. But there are some people who don't fit into that. So the people who are going to be long term, we tend to distribute among staff – not everybody has a long-term therapy. Most people get an experience of working with both long- and short-term clients. Interestingly most people who come and get a short-term contract are quite happy with it. People have come with a problem and they want help to find solutions. To that extent I think that we're quite interventionist, because the assessment in particular is very interventionist.

If I go through it, there is a standard yellow form, general health questionnaire, that is gone through, looking at all sorts of things about people's past experiences, where they live, who are their kin, who do they feel most comfortable with, who do they think they would be able to best work with as a therapist. And they're allowed to think about it – man, woman, black, white, Indian, Chinese, Japanese, whatever. And people will say – not that they will necessarily get that therapist, but it's actually a good assessment tool, because you can ask more questions about it. About gender issues, about race issues. Making acknowledgements about it, that life is obviously difficult for women, or black people for example, and maybe there have been experiences that you've had where they might have felt discriminated.

Similarly with abuse, the assessment might also name this. This naming makes it easier for the client to talk about this in the therapy if it was their experience. So the assessment is very interventionist, and it allows the therapist to be less of a blank screen. The person doing the assessment will try to meet the person much more, and that's one of the reasons why we think that we can ask more questions. When the client gets their course of twelve sessions, it's likely that they'll be seeing somebody else. So the client can then retreat and choose how they want to approach the things that have been flagged up in the assessment, or the things that have been bubbling in their mind after the assessment. It is quite useful to have a very active assessment, because it stirs people up to think about things, and feel things before therapy begins.

The model you work with ...

Well it's not very different from other brief psychotherapy models. Everybody seems to have ended up around 12 or 14 as the brief model, particularly those working in a public psychotherapy/counselling service. One of the reasons why we do 12 is that we wouldn't be able to cope with the demand if it was unlimited, we'd be inundated with requests. Some people come back, some say: 'Can I be referred somewhere else?', and some people say: 'That was fine, that was quite useful for me. I realise that I'm not going mad, that I'm actually reviewing experiences from my past, that I've been quite depressed, but I know that this is quite all right to do, all right to feel.' So people actually respond in different ways to it.

So someone comes to your door ...

Over the next 12 weeks they will come in, they will sit down mostly, and talk about their experiences, and boy!, they'd have a lot to talk about. Because usually they will have written to us to say why they want to come here. So there's a lot for people to talk about. There's a lot of thinking has gone on before they've actually arrived for the first session. What happens – *therapy*. Talking, listening, some interpretation, some questions, pretty much the usual stuff. The mode of it is very much the same.

Can you put more flesh on that ...

Well I find that people will usually talk about their lives. People – in the first couple of sessions – will talk about their social history. Which gives a kind of a context of their present experience. I'll have to try to focus down on a particular case, think about how it actually has gone. People will talk about their experiences, and before they think about coming to therapy, they are reviewing their lives anyway. They're reviewing their experiences. Sometimes their whole lives, and sometimes a particular part of it – the troublesome part of it – they'll be reviewing it. It'll be going over and over and over in their minds.

Then, what happens is – just like in any other therapy – what people focus on, the problematic areas, they start to tease it out. Why did you think about committing suicide? Did you feel that you had to? Were there any voices? Who did you feel you would be satisfying by destroying yourself? It's actually asking all the usual questions that you would about people's behaviour. Asking questions about what – if – just thinking about this particular woman who attempted suicide. If there was anybody that you could go to to talk to about this experience, in your family or friendship circle, who might that person be? What might they have said? So it is actually being very active. Instead of allowing people to have things rattling around in their head. We pull them out and have them discussed. And not just waiting for the free association techniques to take place. Some of it will be associative – people will come and talk. But then we will take some and say: 'Right, I'm going to ask you something about this. What do you think?' And getting the person to comment as if they were the therapist. Or: 'If Auntie Marge was the sort of person who would be sympathetic to your feelings of wanting to commit suicide, what would Auntie Marge have said?' So it's bringing in some outside influences and being attentive to their social connectedness. Systemic techniques are quite useful with clients who present as very isolated.

Do you keep records?

Yes, we do keep records. We have to keep a record. What we have to keep – the assessment, we will keep the person's referral letter, the assessment will be written up and kept because the assessment is done and discussed in the clinical meeting, when we're trying to find the most suitable therapist. Some very brief notes will be kept about each session; not everybody will keep notes, there isn't a hard rule about that. But there has to be a summary and evaluation of the whole process of the 12 sessions. And that's really looked at against the assessment and the letter, to see how things have gone. Because every one's reviewed. But the clients who actually use the service have feedback forms that they complete. They complete a feedback form after six weeks, which is sent to me. It's not seen by the therapist. One is also completed at 12 weeks, at the end of sessions.

Are people usually nice?

No, sometimes people say ... look, I'll show you some challenging opinions, like – if I've got any fresh ones here, otherwise I'll have to go into
the file. [Searches]
    This is very interesting.
    Okay, the first question is: 'Do you feel that your therapy is address-
ing your problem? If no, where and how does it fail?' and someone's
actually said 'Yes', it's actually meeting their problems.
    'Do you feel the therapy's helping you, if no, why is this?' and the
person said 'Yes, it's helping.'
    'Is the therapy what you expected?' 'Yes' 'If no, in what way should
it be different?' They haven't actually commented.
    'Would you recommend it to a friend with similar difficulties?' 'Yes'
'If no, for what reason?'
    'Are you finding the therapy difficult?' 'Yes' 'If yes, in what way?'
'Because I feel that many of my problems will not be solved in a short
time.'
    'Do you feel able to discuss issues openly with your therapist?' 'Yes'
'If no, in what area will the difficulties arise?'
    'What are the good points about your therapy?' 'The therapist
wants to understand my problems, and to try and help me as much
as he can.'
    'What are the bad points?' 'It needs to be more time to diagnose
my ... this point ... spoken English ... not terribly clear.'
    Well this person has ticked 'yes' to everything, saying it's fine, except
at the bottom. It says 'I have problems/difficulty in transport, and I've
got problems with motivation due to apathy.'
    'What are the good points about the therapy?' 'Opportunities to
open up on my problems and help to analyse my situation. Longer time
might be necessary to counteract many years of depression.'
    So those two have been about time.

*Some people say that so-called 'talking therapy' is best with articulate
people ...*

Well it's bollocks, isn't it? It's a class rationalisation about poor people.

But it's true nonetheless that the working class tend to get more ECT, etc ...

Well absolutely, it's happened for years, and it still happens. But it's
nonsense, because working-class people, and black people – even people
who don't have English as a first language are able to use skilfully their
second language to try to get some understanding of their situation. I
feel that it is a class issue, and it also involves race and language. The
argument doesn't necessarily follow that if someone isn't intelligent –
well intelligence hasn't got anything to do with it – but that if people

aren't skilled with language (middle-class language) that they wouldn't be able to deal with therapy, which is a middle-class thing. Therapy doesn't have to be a middle-class thing. We have made some impact on that idea by providing access, and radio counselling programmes have helped with this also.

If you actually train a working-class person to be a therapist, then presumably that person can speak to other working-class people using the same language and idioms, and they'd be perfectly understood.

Psychotherapy isn't a form of fixed language. You don't talk about transference, and projective identification with people. You talk to them about their experiences in a language that they'd be able to understand you in. Those technical words are not part of the discourse: that's for your own assessment, that's for your own understanding. Language is just not an issue, it shouldn't be an issue at all. So much so, that in fact we've had an art therapist here who specialised in working with young people with learning difficulties. And it's been very, very successful. She has found that a lot of the young people with learning difficulties have been able to come regularly, and have found it useful and challenging – not because of the linguistic component of it, but because of the expression. They've painted, they've talked about situations, they've tried to represent it, and they've tried to describe it in their own words, in their own time. Lots of people have challenged that notion about the linguistic component of psychotherapy. Valerie Sinason from the Tavistock Clinic has been working with people with learning difficulties for many years in therapy, and finding a lot of success.

Is it racism among mental health professionals that makes them behave the way they do to black people?

[Laughs] I think it's racism and class bias. I think it's a rationalisation, because people should know that it is possible to work with black and other minority people therapeutically, not depending on language as the only tool. For years people have been working with young children in therapy.

How are blacks usually disadvantaged in the mental health system?

Well they're far less likely to be given the talking therapies, and much more likely to be given medication, *modicate* and long-term depot injections, without talk. It is possible to get both of them going side by side, but they're often not referred to the therapists, counsellors or community psychiatric nurses for talk therapy.

Group therapy is also a rare commodity, and sometimes even if they are referred to group therapy they're disadvantaged if they're in the minority, or if the group is run by white people who don't have an understanding of the dynamic issues of being a single white/black person in a mainly black/white group. There are a lot of things that are weighted against them and black patients have found the obstacles in the choices affords them no choice at all.

Some black and other people have been very concerned about the over-representation of black people in mental hospitals – between six and twelve times more than white British people. Irish people were over-represented as well. This happens in a way that provokes thinking because they're not over-represented in their countries of origin. It makes you wonder what it is about living in England and all its attendant problems that are driving black people mad.

What do you think ...

Well I think it's a whole range of things. It isn't just ordinary naked racism, it's something about a system. It's something that working-class people are going to share as well. It's being part of the group that we are not going to pay any attention to which black people become part of by being here. It's a whole range of concerns, and we can't just simply say that it's in psychiatry that black people are disadvantaged. You have to look for it in housing, in education, in the employment market, the criminal justice system: it's everywhere. But I think that the mental health service has become the net where it's all collected eventually.

Can we talk about the differences in family life in different ethnic groups ...

Sure. Yes, there's lots of difference. I do think that Caribbean/African/ Asian families are actually viewed in a very different way. The family is viewed as a safe harbour. When it's safe, when it's a good family, it's a protective detoxifying haven from the outside world. I don't know that white families operate in exactly the same way. The black family is a buffer between the kind of harm – physical harm – that the individual can experience in the outside world, and the psychological harm that the children experience in the outside world. It becomes a place where racism can be detoxified, can be talked about, can be made reasonably safe. It actually has a very different function. One of the things, when you're talking about family life, I think of cornflake and soap adverts. These lovely TV families sit around, doing the TV family business, all perfectly normal; it seems so innocent and so nice. I don't think that the experience of black people has that innocence, and I don't think that Jewish people who lived in the East End in the '40s, '50s had similar lives. Their families also performed a function. It was the one place where you felt that you ought to be safe, because you could face so many dangers outside of the home, but relax and use each other for support.

So when there are problems in such families, it requires a professional who has a particular understanding of what this family is about and how it works. What is the family function? They won't be explicit. If you actually say to an Asian family: 'What's so different about your family from the white family living next-door?' They'll say: 'Well, not much really. We've got children about the same age. We both go out to work.' But it's something that happens, and people don't actually notice that it's happening. That they're actually bringing their children up to feel safe, understood, to give them an opportunity to detoxify the daily accumulation of racism, and a reasonably positive sense of identity does not seem to count for much. I'm really surprised that more black kids don't grow up more messed up than they do. It surprises me and it's testimony to the families that raise them.

What I'm saying is that I actually think that black families, Asian families, Caribbean families, and African families actually do a bloody good job. I think that the comparison is looking at the children who are brought up in institutions where they don't get this. They don't have family there to socialise them into how life really is and how prepared they need to be to face it. White institutions socialise them into false white lives. Many young people brought up in institutions come out feeling that a great disservice has been done to them. They realise that things aren't quite like they thought they were. They'd been led to believe that white people are nice, because the people in the care institution were nice, and good, and kind to them, by and large. They then find that the reality is not quite like that, and white people, just like everybody else, are different. The real deficit is the experiences with black people who they fear or feel uneasy with.

Among white people there is this kind of pull to tell black people that white people are okay really. It's actually in their interest to do that. Children in institutions don't get told about the pitfalls. They don't know about the problems that they will inevitably face.

Can we talk about the economics of therapy?

Yes we're in an unusual practice because on the face of it people take it free. Some people contribute, and some people do pay a fee, a very reduced fee. If someone is in employment, then we say: 'Well, how much do you think you can contribute towards your therapy?', and they'll say: '£5', '£3' – fine. But I do think that paying something out of your own pocket gives the user some right or esteem when using it. I've actually worked in several settings where people pay for their therapy, and I don't know whether or not they made more of it, I don't know whether or not they used it more, but I certainly know they claimed it as theirs. They can complain, they can be difficult about it. They actually have a different kind of attachment, not always, but I think there is something about it, I wouldn't be hard and fast, but 'paying means better, and non-paying means not good' – I don't think that necessarily follows. But I do think that if people are able to own it, purchase it, then I think they feel more right to it.

Are more black people training?

Yes. There are a lot more Asian, Caribbean, African and Turkish people wanting to train in psychotherapy. A lot of them are training because they feel that they didn't get that service offered to them. That's not why I trained, interestingly enough. It was a different time, a very different time. And it was to do with my own discoveries and as a recipient of analysis. Not because I strategically thought, 'Well not many black people are being offered psychotherapy, so I must train as a psychotherapist and be the one person who offers it to them.' No, that had never crossed my mind.

Is child abuse as prevalent in the families you see as in white families?

Same. There are times when we have referral letters, and they're all saying: 'I've been sexually abused as a child, was abused physically ... '; so many that it's very depressing.

A stereotype is that it doesn't happen in these 'close-knit' families ...

Nonsense, it happens everywhere. That abuse doesn't happen in close-knit families? These nice places. Nice people don't do terrible things to their children. They do. It seems even more terrible. Because what is supposed to be a safe haven from the outside world, becomes a place that's frightening and terrifying for black children.

A child psychotherapist once said to me, that one of the reasons that black children prefer to have white foster carers and white case-workers is because they'd been abused by their families – fascinating. So I then said to her: 'So when white children are abused by their white parents, do they want to choose black foster parents and black case-workers and therapists?' And she said: 'Well, it's not the same, is it?' [Laughs] But there's something about the bogey about black people as well. There is something about – the bogey that black people abuse their children. Especially if they're Muslim and speak another language. There's also the stereotype about black men and sex, they're seen as animals basically. It has affected white people's psyche. You tell me of a white person who's never heard of the stereotype of the black man, and about black women, how well they do in bed.

The Naomi Campbell advert – you remember the supermodel Vauxhall campaign? All the other supermodels were the lah-di-dah fey, white girls with blonde hair, and they were decorative. Then Naomi Campbell came out with the whip and the leather. It says something about black sexuality, doesn't it? A message is certainly being conveyed about who or what blacks are.

Eating disorders ... rife?

Yes, it's quite serious. It's bulimia; it's overeating and sicking. But, yes, a lot of people, a lot of young women present with eating disorders, men as well. But women in particular.

Are there other therapeutic approaches you feel uncomfortable about?

No, not at all. I don't worry too much about other people's therapies. As long as they don't try to crush people. As long as they give acknowledgement to other people's realities. I think that we need a range of different therapies. Not everybody's going to want the same thing. I think that there's a place for Gestalt, there's a place for group, there's a place for re-birthing, there's a place for primal screaming. There are times when I've wanted those places too. I've not gone to them, I've gone to groups. During the '60s and '70s I did the groups [laughs]. My analyst thought it was a good thing actually. Thankfully I had an analyst who wasn't acting like God, and I said: 'I'm doing a marathon group this weekend', and she said: 'Oh, all right, I'll see you on Monday.'

How do you measure success? What, for you, is optimal mental health?

I suppose the two things are related, aren't they? That people can feel contented. That people can feel that they can get on with their lives, and that it's possible to stay alive. That's how I would feel happy about someone finishing a therapy.

I can remember seeing a young man, one of the first people that I saw at NAFSIYAT, who I saw for a year. And I saw him twice a week sometimes, and three times a week at other times. He finished therapy. He was a young British-born Caribbean man who had been very badly abused by his mother. She'd particularly singled him out of the three children as the one who most resembled the father who had walked out. She really singled him out for particular abuse, really terrible abuse. This kid just didn't feel that he could continue to live. He felt that his mother wished him dead, and he couldn't live with the thought of having a mother who was still alive, who wished him dead even though he had no contact with her. He left therapy feeling that he was okay, that he wasn't ugly, he wasn't stupid as he was given to believe, that he wasn't thick – he learned to read at the age of 18, incidentally, having been brought up in care institutions. He felt that the only people that loved him were the white carers in the children's institution. But he felt that he could survive. He'd be able to survive. He could leave therapy and he would survive. I don't think he left happy. He wasn't happy when he left, but he felt that he'd manage. Thankfully he has. This is several years later, thankfully he has managed. But I don't think that happiness is something that I can offer. I can't offer happiness, wish I could. I wish I could find some way of making him smile, making him happy, providing him with a relationship that he'd feel comfortable in, but those things he didn't get. The desire to kill himself, the belief that he was ugly, and thick and stupid, and black and ugly, which are the things that he'd been poisoned with at home by his mother, he left not believing in those things, and that it's all right for him to live. He pursued his career. He's a very clever young man who really should get a lot of recognition. But I suppose someone who doesn't think much of themselves and doesn't think that they're lovable, would have to sell himself.

What do you tell people ... promise them, when they come to you?

Well, we can be there to help them, by listening to their difficulties, and helping them to make connections in their lives. Of course that's only applicable with some people. Some people come for different things. Some people come because they've just come out of hospital; we probably have something much more basic to say, which is that we'll help them to make sense of the experience of their hospitalisation, to make sense of what it is that might have led them to go into hospital in the first place – which we can do. Whether or not that translates into helping people not to go into hospital again is another matter. But we think that it does, especially if it's early in the cycle of going in and out of hospital.

What is most important – the technique or the relationship?

I think that the most important thing is the relationship. That we have to be able to make people feel at ease. It's not going to work if someone doesn't feel comfortable with you and they're not able to say. If they're not feeling comfortable, they're not saying – forget it. You haven't got therapy. You've got someone who's very uncomfortable. Forget brief therapy, forget long-term therapy. If the client cannot feel comfortable, being in the therapy with the therapist is not therapeutic. Start again with somebody else: don't blame anybody, but just start again.

You've got to be able to feel that you can say something to your therapist that will not frighten them so that they're not going to shriek in horror and withdraw in horror. So the trainees are taught to be receptive, to be able to listen, and always to be attentive to someone's comfort in the consulting room. Technically there are lots of things that I want to cram into the trainees' heads about psychopathology. Having a good understanding of psychiatric conditions, for example. Because I think that that's what hovers. One has to have that at the back of one's mind. With some basic things about child development and that one is able to use Winnicott and Klein, etc.

Melanie Klein's understanding and observation of young children, and the experience of young children, is brilliant. Spot on. It's not ethnically coded; I don't think it necessarily needs to be. There are some things that have to be different because of – we have to bear in mind how people raise their children differently – in Asia, Africa, or the Caribbean, very different. But apart from that, apart from looking at those differences, our understanding of very early mental development is very important for people to learn as trainees. Learning the skill of analysing the transference, about what happens between you and the patient/client and about the meaning it has, and what phase it's in with that person's own real life experiences.

Can that happen in such a few sessions?

Yes, it can, and it does. But of course, the transference does not become the focus of great debate. That's one of the differences, that you understand where you are in the transference with the patient because of the way that they're behaving, but you don't spend a lot of time talking to them about it. That you have at the back of your mind, trying to find the strategy of actually making use of this information in terms of that person's own development and perhaps about what's going to happen next. So you're making a connection with them and their real life without saying: 'What's going on here is between me and you.' You do the next thing. You go on to: 'What use do I want to put this to? – this information about that person's relationship to me in the transference. What's the next thing I do with it?' – instead of actually discussing it with them at great length for many sessions, with their denials and their feelings about it. But what do I next do? I go to the next thing which is – if, for example, it's about a parent transference, and there's something going on in that person's real life about their relationship with their partner, their wife or their husband, or their employer, then you think: 'Well, if this is happening with me, in what way might it be affecting other relationships? Let me think about what that person said about their relationship with their wife, or their employer, or whatever.' And you might be able to use it there. You might be able to use that as some kind of notion of what's going on, but not for discussion between you and the patient at great length.

Have you been unable to work with some clients?

Well, I haven't rejected anybody because I don't feel that I can work with them, but I'm trying to think of someone who's actually been here and I haven't been able to – I can't, no.

How do you finish treatment ...

People know when – they know that it's twelve. I've just finished twelve with two people. For one of them – he's a young man who's just got out of hospital, he's only 19, first admission. I intend to continue. We will follow up in a few weeks. I think he needs a break to re-evaluate, he needs to live a little before we start back. The other person is someone who's experienced a depression – a refugee who experienced severe depression – five years after being in this country, and being relatively safe (delayed reaction) like the ride across Lake Constance thing. He's got here and he's alive, and God knows how. He learnt about the dangers that he was in and collapsed in a heap. He's all right and he should not need any more therapy for the time being.

What are your views about ethical codes?

Crikey, I wonder if our ethical code actually says anything about race or difference? Do you know, I haven't thought about it. Shall I just quickly look? [Pause]
     The beginning of the code of ethics actually points out that there are other policies, an equal opportunities and an anti-racism policy, that is displayed in the waiting room. And that this code of ethics has to be viewed in relation to those other two policies.

> In order for the patient, or the patient's guardian to make informed choices about therapy at this centre, the nature of therapy and inter-cultural therapy has to be explained. This will be done at the assessment. Patients in brief therapy will have an opportunity to comment on the progress of this treatment by completing the six-week and the twelve-week feedback form.

That's the only thing that's said about that.

Presumably you discuss a lot, the specific work you do with people who already are disadvantaged ...

In our place? Oh, absolutely. We spend a lot of time talking about it. You know the meeting where we discuss the assessment – that is a very important arena to reflect on the assessor – the person who did the assessment and the client – and to look at what has actually gone on. For a whole range of reasons – for gender reasons, for race reasons, cultural reasons – to see whether or not that person is the best person to work with the client, or if there is somebody else that really ought to be selected. It is very important that people don't get bruised a second time, in a place which they might have considered to be a safe place, because it professes to pay attention to people's culture, and a sensitivity to their experiences of race or gender issues. Just like the black family, as I was saying – we have to be particularly concerned about not abusing our users. Abuse is what they get outside, and this is supposed to be a healing place, a place where healing and understanding can take place.
     Because we are probably the last resort, people have been to the district general hospital out-patients, they've been somewhere else, and *somewhere else*, and probably they've only just found out – like you – about this place, after they've done lots of other things. And we shouldn't be a place that will further abuse them.

What new problems are you seeing these days?

The new thing that's coming into the work is the issue of racial identity in young African-descended, Asian and mixed parentage children, and how the psychological mechanisms that are used by these young children to make themselves safe, harm them. What do they do to survive when they don't see themselves reflected positively in society at large, but probably see themselves negatively reflected? What happens to those young children to actually make them survive as viable people, with some value? So what is it that happens? How do they protect themselves from it? That is one of the things that we are very interested in at the moment.

I was going to mention 'politics and psychotherapy'. Is it something you think about, or have done?

Well, yes, I have. I've thought that there's something about psychotherapy orthodoxy, everybody wants to be considered to be a respectable, viable, top-of-the-pile therapist. I think that the use of the word 'politics' is actually an insult. If you say to a therapist at a case conference: 'that is political', it's like saying to them 'you're crap, you're not a technician, you're not a therapist, you're not working analytically', and for somebody like Andrew Samuels – have you come across Andrew Samuels? Andrew Samuels is probably one of the only psychotherapists who'll actually stand firm and say: 'Yes, politics is a very important component of my work, and should be an important component of everybody else's work.' It's only just beginning to come back, and very few people are interested in the political issues of difference, the small 'p' differences in psychotherapy.

Even people like the Women's Therapy Centre have had a struggle with this, and they've been going for a long time as an organisation. I actually don't know to what extent they are hard about the political component any more, or whether or not they're more interested in pushing the orthodoxy. I think people want to belong, they want to belong in the community of psychotherapists. The community of psychotherapists – those at the top, the more orthodox people – are actually saying that if you want to belong then you've got to be neutral, you've got to pretend that you're a person, you've got to pretend that you're a man, you've got to pretend that you're white and you're wealthy, and you don't have to see differences, you don't see those differences at all. Which I think is counter-therapeutic and stupid.

How can we on the one hand talk about the importance of the transference and the different components of it – like contemporary transference, not historical transference, but live, how I feel about the man who's sitting in that chair and he's my therapist. How can you actually get an inroad into that if you don't think about politics, or personal politics? The groups that people come from. You can't really do a proper job therapeutically if you ignore it. How can you as an academic, middle-class, now academic person – I'm doing *you* now [laughs] – how can you actually not recognise that maybe a poor, black, single woman managing on her own with a family – how can you explain her anger towards you? Or her feelings about you, her resentment towards you? You're only protecting yourself by saying: 'There's no difference really'; you're protecting yourself and you're damaging that person's opportunity. They should have the opportunity. You should have it in your mind that this person will notice that difference. Even if you are going to be myopic about it, the other person will certainly notice you're different. They'll notice your home, they'll notice the street you live in. They'll notice the way that you speak – you can't hide from it. [Laughs]

CHAPTER 13

Psychoanalysis

Adam Phillips

Adam Phillips is the author of a number of books including
Winnicott and the acclaimed *On Kissing, Tickling and Being Bored.*
A psychotherapist, he works both in the NHS and in private
practice.

Can you tell me how you got into this kind of work?

When I was about 17, one of the things I wanted to be was a wise man, for
some reason, and I read Jung's *Memories, Dreams, and Reflections.* I was
interested in those days in what I thought of as the depths. And I read
Jung's autobiography, and I thought: 'This is it. This is a really exciting life
about the depths.' My heroes in those days were writers really, rock stars,
and sportsmen, but this introduced me to the idea of a psychoanalyst. I'd
never met one. So I thought: 'That's obviously what I want to be.'
    I very quickly lost interest in Jung, because from Jung I started to
read Freud, and Freud was the person that really interested me. The
other experience I had that was very powerful, was that I read Winnicott's *Playing and Reality* when it came out. And I read this book, and I
thought 'This is it.' Now I don't know what I thought it was about, I
can't imagine what I thought it was about, but I really thought this was
a great book – and I was about 17 or 18 when it came out. So there
was a combination of things. My primary interest was in literature,
which I was reading at university. I didn't want to be an academic
because reading was a private pleasure and passion for me. And I also
had an idea that if I was to be an academic I'd be using texts as a way
of having conversations with people about their lives. Plus Freud really
made a lot of sense to me, and I thought he was a great writer.
    So I then conceived this idea. I would become a psychoanalyst – what-
ever that was. Before I took finals at university I wrote to the Institute of
Psychoanalysis which somebody had told me about. And they wrote me
back a really very nice letter, saying words to the effect of, 'You really are
rather young to be doing this, but if you're still interested after about the
age of thirty, then do get in touch with us.' Then my girlfriend at the time
discovered that there were child analytic trainings. So I thought 'I'll try
those.' So I wrote, I looked at the prospectuses, and I really didn't like the
sound of the Tavistock Clinic, or the Anna Freud Centre. But I did like

the sound of what was then called the Institute of Child Psychology. What I liked about it was that it was at least nominally eclectic. So I applied there before I took the finals, got in, then because I was so young, I was about 21, they suggested that I spent a year growing up. And I went to York and started a PhD, which I did for a year, on the American poet Randall Jarrell and the effect of Freud on descriptions of childhood in modern poetry. Then I came to London and trained.

What do you do currently?

I spend half my week at what was the Department of Child and Family Psychiatry, at Charing Cross Hospital. It's now the Wolverton Gardens Child and Family Consultation Centre, because it's become a Trust. My job there is about – half of it is seeing children for individual therapy, aged as it were, two to sixteen – seeing families for a kind of psychodynamic family therapy, although I'm not a trained family therapist, I've worked with family therapists. And the other half is spent supervising people who are seeing children individually. Then the other half of the week I spend at home seeing adults and adolescents privately, and writing.

How would you describe the tradition you come from?

I think it's middle group Freudian, that's to say the tradition of people that in a way starts with Ferenczi – starts with Freud, then goes on to Farenczi – then there's a hiatus which is Balint in a way. But then the group of people that I found, and still find, in a way inspiring were Winnicott, Marion Milner, Masud Khan, and Rycroft to a lesser extent. But the kinds of things that these people were talking about seemed to me to be very interesting, absorbing, close to my heart.

How would you begin to describe what you actually do?

Well, at its most minimal, I do two things. I listen as attentively as I can, but without *trying* to listen to what people say to me, and I notice what this evokes in me. I collaboratively produce redescriptions of what's going on with the people that I'm working with. Of course the truth about this is that there couldn't be a generalisation, because there's a sense in which I work differently with each person. I've also learnt a lot from family therapy. At least three important things from family therapy. One is the significance of transgenerational histories. The other is the significance and the meaning of scapegoating in families. And the third thing is to do with the significance of double-binds. All those ideas are integral to what I do. That combines itself with a more or less Winnicottian developmental model. Giving an account of this is misleading, because it suggests I've got conscious voluntary access to this repertoire of theories. Actually all I know is that I read the psychoanalytic books that I love and like. (I mostly don't read psychoanalysis.) I work with colleagues. I find myself saying certain things to certain people. I'm aware of the power of certain kinds of models, that's to say Winnicott's ideas of holding, Bion's ideas of reverie, Lacanian ideas of returning the signifier, simply meaning picking up words that people say and putting them back to them and wondering where they go with those words, how they fit into their lives.

So it's very much of a miscellany, and I follow my inclination. I don't have a conscious sense of a programme, but I have some sense that I know what I'm doing, which doesn't mean that I always know what I'm doing, or that that's necessarily true that I know what I'm doing, but it feels like that sufficiently often.

I'm curious about what people are able to feel and think and say in each other's presence, and the way in which people can say, sit in a room together and kill each other's pleasure, in each other's company. How that happens.

So one of the things I think I'm trying to do is to make it possible for whatever is said or believed to be entertained, as in looked at from different perspectives. To be seen to lose its absolute quality. So one of the things I think one's doing is analysing people's will to believe, people's need for convictions, what people are using their beliefs and convictions to do. But also, of course, I'm doing what I think of as ordinary orthodox psychoanalytic things. That is to say, I analyse defences. I show people the ways in which they go about not knowing and feeling things. I look at and try and describe the repressed repertoire of thoughts and feelings, and versions of the self that might be around.

I try and link up people's stories about themselves, with the kind of stories in the family, both transgenerationally and immediate family of origin. I also look at what people use these stories to do. I suppose what I'm interested in is people's curiosity and people's capacity to be absorbed in things and people. I mean you could call it people's capacity to love. But I think it might be more interesting to say that I'm interested in the ways people stop themselves being curious, or stop themselves finding the things that matter to them most.

I'm also interested in showing them, I think, the paradoxical nature of their acts. And by acts I mean also words. That is to say virtually nothing is unequivocally bad or good, and it seems to me one of the drawbacks of Kleinian theory, for example, is that it's pre-empted this issue, it's as though it's already decided. There are certain parts of the personality that are bad called the 'death instinct', and the question then is: 'How do you have the best kind of relationship with this part of yourself?' I would want to be showing people in a sense the complexity of their acts. That they're doing an awful lot of things at once, and saying an awful lot of things at once.

The other thing I think I'd be wanting to do is to show people how interesting their lives are. Because when people come for therapy, it's as though they've been compelled through suffering to be interested in their lives. It's almost like they've been reminded that their lives matter to them, or that their lives at this moment matter to them in a way; they have to think about their lives. I would want to show people how easy it is to lose interest in your life, and that actually your life is very interesting. I would also want to kind of run together a psychoanalytic and an existential approach. By that I mean – to put this very crudely – if somebody comes to me and tells me that their parents or their childhood has ruined their life, I want to analyse their anxiety about making choices, their fear of freedom. If somebody comes and says to me 'I can do anything I want', I want to talk to them about their parents.

Are there particular types of clients who come to you?

I think it's inevitable when you write books that you create a group, an imaginary group. That is to say, certain people will feel an affinity for whatever reason with what you write, and therefore who they imagine you are. I'm not sure there are *kinds* of people actually, but I think that people come with a transference to me that is often along the lines of – of course it's very specifically individual, but if I could generalise it would be something like – a sense that I'm interested in psychoanalysis as one story among many. Which means that I'm very interested in psychoanalysis, but I don't think it's the supreme fiction. That at any given moment Wordsworth might be as useful to us in this room as Freud might be.

I don't tend to get hard-core scientists. I don't tend to get people who are on the verge of converting to Kleinianism, Freudianism, whatever. But I think the differences between the people I see are probably broader than the similarities.

How many come to see you for 'educational', or self-developmental reasons, and how many are in distress?

Well, there's obviously an overlap between those two things you've mentioned. That's to say somebody who'd come consciously with an educational wish that quickly collapses into something else, and vice versa. But no, people who come to see me are suffering from something. Of course I take problems seriously, but I think of them as part of a larger, unconscious picture. And people come with a large array of preoccupations and problems. In the hospital work I see what I suppose people in my kind of work would think of as an ordinary range of childhood growing-up problems – bedwetting, sleep disorders, ordinary bits and pieces of naughtiness and delinquency, all that kind of 'what it is to grow up in a family' stuff. Obviously there is an extreme end. I've seen a lot of adolescents who've tried to commit suicide, for example. In private practice again, it's a very broad range. Because I don't think diagnostic categories are interesting, they don't seem to me to add anything to the conversation that I want to have, I can't really type the people that I see. But they're certainly not coming for a seminar, and if they are, then that's what I analyse.

What happens in a session ... the length of time ...

Again I have to preface this by saying it's impossible to generalise, but broadly speaking people come for 45 minutes, but I don't end mid-sentence, there's quite a lot of flexibility here. The amount of conversation that goes on is very variable. There are periods when I am silent, but it's much more of a conversation, than is – at least the accounts that we get of classical analysis. There's a very good story about Winnicott who when he went for his training analysis with Strachey, he went five times a week, and after six months Strachey hadn't said anything. So Winnicott got up from the couch and said: 'Look, I've been coming here for six months, you haven't said anything.' And Strachey said 'But you haven't either.'
     I don't go in for those kinds of things. I have a conversation with people, which of course involves silences, pauses, etc. I value the psychoanalytic ethos of erring on the side of saying less. I always answer questions, but I also sometimes say as I do with children: 'Guess first, and then I'll tell you.' I do think it is a reciprocal venture. By that I mean, of course there's a big difference in the fact that somebody's in need of help, and somebody at least nominally isn't. But I think we can't help but both be involved, and I don't therefore assume that everything is transference, or that everything is projection. I assume, that is to say, that the person who is normally called the patient is as perceptive about me as I can be about them. That what we're involved in here is a process of endlessly inventing, and reinventing, and redescribing each other.

Do you set out contractual agreements ...

Yes, I was going to say. I set out basic things like how much I charge, arrangements about holidays and so on. People have the choice of lying on the couch, or sitting face-to-face, although most of my work is face-to-face. I also explain psychoanalysis as I go along. That's to say, at the beginning I say: 'If there's anything that they feel mystified by, or they find themselves agreeing to because they assume I must be right, that they must feel free to say.' Obviously I make the primary point, which is: 'You're free to say whatever comes into your mind, but nobody's ever been able to do that. Still, it's a useful picture of what might be possible.' But I explain psychoanalytic theory as I go along, and I assume, of course, that the patient has as elaborate a theory as I do.

Which bits of theory ...

Oh, well, transference, dream work, primary process, the defences, and the central significance of sexuality. Those for me are my preferred favourite stories about what's interesting about living a life.

What do you tell them about what you can or can't do?

Well what I say is that the only way they can find out what this is like, is by doing it. So I often say: 'Come to three sessions, see what you think. And I won't reject you, but obviously you're free to reject me.' I don't make promises, as in I never say, 'I can cure you of this.' I never say even 'This will work.' I always say, 'There is no way of knowing this. All I can agree to do is to help you to understand something in my own way. And you'll have to see whether and how this works for you.'

How long do they tend to stay for?

It's very variable. Some people stay for several years. Some people come and it's as though they just need to make what feels like one important link. So they might come for a few months, for a few weeks. I see a lot of people on demand – that is to say, instead of them coming regularly every week, they come when they want to. And I keep patches of time for that. I'm wary of long-term treatments. For me psychoanalysis is somewhere you go via in order to get back into the world. The risk, I think, of psychoanalysis, is that the patient might end up feeling this is the most interesting conversation going, whereas from my point of view this conversation is interesting in the service of relinking you with the world where you can have sex with people. Where there are all sorts of adventures to be had. So I'm certainly wary of what people refer to as 'intensive treatment' or 'real psychoanalysis' or 'long-term treatments'. For me a long-term treatment – of course some people need it, I don't want to simply discount this – but broadly speaking, for me a long-term treatment is a failed treatment.

Sexuality seems to have been forgotten in much of current psychodynamic writing ...

It's really amazing that sexuality has disappeared from the picture. People are interested in things like truth or authenticity. It really is as if people believe thinking is better than stroking. That seems to me absolutely astonishing in many ways. Well for me, Freud's theory about sexual development – the simple fact that, I suppose it's a quasi-biological fact, that we begin in very intimate, very sensuous emotional contact with another person. That we are essentially bodily selves – organisms. That we desire each other. That we have very strong affections, longings, bodily feelings for each other.

Freud's point about the ego being first and foremost a bodily ego, this seems to me a point about sexuality. That sexuality is the medium of contact. Freud's idea about the diphasic nature of sexuality – the sense in which there's infancy in which there are these passions; then there's a kind of latency period, which I don't think there is really, but certainly in adolescence there's a reworking of these Oedipal, sexual, incestuous motifs, feelings, thoughts, drives. One of the important things about Freud for me is that he talks about a part of the self that really is out of control, in a sense. That it's the part of ourselves that makes a mockery of our ideas about ourselves. And it seems to me the primary point is that we desire each other, that we're creatures of desire, and that desire is always in excess of the object's capacity to satisfy us. That's to say there's something unappeasable about it.

There's also something unmanageable about it in a certain sense, and there's something intrinsically conflictual about it. And I think a lot of post-Freudian psychoanalytic theory is, as Freud predicted, a defence against sexuality. For me a life devoted to reparation is a wasted life. This again is where I think Winnicott has a very interesting covertly sexual theory. Winnicott's ideas about the ruthless use of an object and so on, have clear sexual affinities – that we need to be able to be both subjects and objects to each other. We need to be able to be used, and to use.

Sexuality is what makes us all lose our composure. There's no embarrassment when you're talking about reparation, or gratitude. Talk about sex, everybody gets a bit agitated, for perfectly understandable and good reasons. And by the same token, this is where the action is.

How does this actually work out in psychotherapeutic practice? Say someone with low self-esteem ...

Well again we have to make this up – there's a fictional person and it would be different with every person. I would want to understand a whole range of things. First of all at its simplest, what the history of that feeling is. How it comes about. If we start right at the beginning. What does the psychobabble phrase 'self-esteem' mean to this person? Once we've got over that – and we could spend years getting over that – I'd be interested in the history of this story he has evolved about himself. I would think of this as fundamentally – unless I had reasons to think it wasn't – I would think of this as Oedipal conflict somewhere. And I would also talk about the anxieties about feeling attractive or feeling confident. The sense in which it might be safe, for example, to feel unattractive. So I suppose I would be analysing, on the one hand, trying to understand or describe the catastrophes associated with having – what we'll call for the sake of this conversation – high self-esteem. And the function of this belief about himself in his total psychic economy. I think – what I would again think of as a fundamental kind of human anxiety – which is something to do with excitement. The terrors of excitement. The terrors and the pleasures of excitement.

Are there some people you feel you can't work with, and if so when do you turn them away?

Yes. I do it as immediately as I can. I go very strongly on first impressions. I'm not sure there are any other kinds of impressions. But there are certainly people – as in ordinary life – there are some people with whom one can talk, and some people with whom it feels very difficult.

Sometimes you think the difficulty is part of the interest, as in you feel like, even though you can't have a conversation, there's a conversation waiting to be had here. Sometimes you get the feeling, of course you could be wrong about this, there is no conversation here.

Sometimes that's sufficiently interesting not to be an obstacle. Sometimes you think it's an obstacle. I don't know what my internal criteria are, because they're mostly unconscious I think. But again, Winnicott has this story about how somebody said to him: 'What's the definition of mental health, or how do you know you can help somebody?' and he said: 'If somebody comes along and they bore you, they're really in trouble, don't take them. But if you're moved or you're interested – there's something there.'

Now clearly, it's a preposterous story, but as an emblem or a parable of something it works for me. If I feel moved by this person in some basic sense, or they make me curious – and I don't have to spend long with someone to be interested.

Is it the skills that are important in the work or the relationship per se?

I think it's dodgy this, because clearly it's a denial to say that there's no technique involved. But I think there's a good argument for wanting to distance oneself from a technological view of this. That this is akin to a surgical operation. So you're more or less skilled at doing the surgery, it doesn't feel to me that it's like that. I think it is to do with old-fashioned words like 'character', 'disposition', 'one's humour' (in the old-fashioned sense of the word). I'm very curious about other people and their lives, and how they have their thoughts and find their place in the world. I don't find it difficult to like people. I'm also interested in listening. Let's say I like listening. It must be some kind of erotic pleasure. I'm also just very interested in the effect people have on each other; what it is to sit in a room with somebody and find you have certain feelings and thoughts, and they do too, and how this comes about. I also think that I'm good at making links, and putting disparate pieces together. And also with kids. We have a good time. I don't believe in therapy as an ordeal, or truth as an ordeal, I really don't. I think there's plenty of ordeal around already. So that I think certainly, the kids know – and adults know in a different way (that I like to be amused). That there are laughs to be had here – we're in it for the laughs as well as everything else. Which doesn't mean that we're going to stand on our heads to entertain each other. But it doesn't mean that we can't do that. I don't think tragedy's more truthful than comedy. I also don't believe that there are depths, I think there are words and feelings.

But it's so much a one-sided view this, because of course, you'd have to get the account of all my patients. Then you'd have an interesting composite picture. Because of course, one of the things that's going on is the mismatch between all these ideas I might have about myself, and their sense of who I am. And that's where the therapy goes on. It's between those misrecognitions. Undoubtedly some people would find me deadly earnest, rather boring. And different things at different times.

Transference, Dependency. Do these processes rely on the fact of lengthy therapeutic relationships?

Yes, well I think this is all omniscient. That's to say I think no-one can know beforehand the process of a relationship, or what is going to happen. There are of course people who need to believe that they know the future. So they might, for example, have internal maps about developmental processes, or they might have a very powerful internalised map about what is supposed to happen in an analysis. For me that is the antithesis of what an analysis is. An analysis is a sequence in which the two parties do not know what is going to happen, by definition. Transference is the most ordinary thing in the world. Transference, it seems to me, is just – and countertransference – simply we invent people on the basis of past relationships. They both disabuse and confirm these fantasies we have about them. And that's called having a relationship. You're right that transference overlaps with the idea of dependence. That we're dependent on each other to make sense of ourselves, however provisionally. That we're forever inventing each other. The problem is when the invention gets stuck. It's when somebody thinks: 'Oh yes, I know who he is', or 'I know what he's like', or 'I'm the kind of person who ...' Now for me that's akin to a symptom.

Do you worry much about such processes?

You can't help but worry. By worry I mean think. Think in a way that's sometimes painful. But I think once it begins, people begin to get under each other's skins, they start thinking about each other. And there's a sense in which that's one of the things I do. I think about the people I see. Sometimes that entails my worrying about them. But we're certainly involved. It's not a nine-to-five job.

Are you interested in any combination of techniques, or integration of approaches?

Yes, but I'm certainly not interested in integration. I think it's very difficult now not to think in terms of repertoires rather than convictions. In terms of theories. Everybody is more than aware of the insufficiency of their theories. I don't see why this is such a problem really. It seems to me obvious that we believe all sorts of different things at different times. The idea that we've got to stand up and be counted in a certain sense, I think is partly to do with the capitalist economy in which there has to be a commodity to sell, and we have to place ourselves. I like what *you* call sloppy eclecticism. I mean that I like the sense that we are a miscellany rather than any kind of machine. That our preferences are quite fluid at different times. That we don't have to affiliate, and that there are good ways of being both intelligent and kind, that aren't based on fanatical convictions, or hard and fast theoretical allegiances.

Other approaches ...

... You see part of the mystification of analysis is you really can't know what goes on in an analysis. So somebody might come to me and describe their analysis, and it might fit in to my prejudices about a certain kind of analysis, but the truth is I really don't know what went on in that analysis. I've seen a lot of 'casualties' of orthodox Freudian analysis, and orthodox Kleinian analysis. And by that I simply mean that rightly or wrongly, these people have all felt either misrecognised and/or damaged or traumatised by the treatment they had. I don't think that necessarily means the treatment was intrinsically traumatising, but nevertheless it was experienced as such.

For me, the kinds of analysis that don't appeal to me are the kinds of analysis in which the trauma of the child with the inaccessible parent is simply recreated. I'm really not interested in being immensely authoritative, silent, deep, thoughtful, all that sort of oracular stuff. I think analysis should be in the best, most exciting sense, ordinary. Much more akin to an ordinary conversation than it is to some esoteric rite. I think that people take flight into positions of internal superiority out of fear. It seems to me obvious why people need to believe, or need to be orthodox whatever that is, and it could be for exactly the same reasons that people need to be eclectic. Let's say people have different ways of orientating themselves. I'm just wary of the people who are really worried by the fact that there are millions of therapies around, for example. I think this is a very good thing.

And I think that people should be accountable. Let's say, for example, if somebody goes and takes their child to see a child psychotherapist, I really think they should interview the therapist about what the therapist believes a child is. Because I think some parents would be really very surprised about what some psychotherapists think a child is. In other words, you need to feel free to get a sense of what the story is you're walking into here. Anybody who goes to see an analyst or a child psychotherapist is walking into a very elaborate set of stories about what a person is, what development is, what a child is, etc. And I think that, insofar as it's possible, people should be free to find out what the guidelines are here.

Despite being interested in other approaches do you yourself feel bounded by the psychoanalytic tradition?

Yes, I think, more or less. Bounded by the analytic tradition and diverse literary traditions. When I come across Gestalt therapists or whatever, like all other kinds of therapists I liked some of them and didn't like others, lots of these therapies seem to be very interesting. But I think it's inevitable that one lives in a very circumscribed professional world – partly by choice and partly by accident. I think Reich, for example, is very, very interesting. I think it's very bizarre that Reich seems to have fallen off the end of psychoanalysis. I can see why for a lot of people, psychoanalysis is too – the wrong word – cerebral. Some people simply don't find talking works for them, and then they should do something else. It's a very specific kind of therapy, psychoanalytic therapy, and it suits some people and doesn't suit others.

Are you restricted, do you think, by the narrow range of people you see?

Oh no, not at all. Well I'm not sure I can explain it. I can tell you the story of it. Most of my professional life has been spent seeing people from very different cultural, educational backgrounds from my own. I don't have a preference for people who are articulate. I've also found that an awful lot of people from very different class backgrounds can use psychotherapy. I've got no doubt about that in my experience. I think there's a risk in seeing people from very similar backgrounds, that there is an easy collusion available. And that the denial of difference becomes a problem.

One of the things that I liked about the Health Service as I knew it, was that child psychotherapy was available to anybody. The problem with private practice obviously is that it isn't. For me psychoanalysis should be available for everybody. It should not be an upper-middle-class enclave. I think for anybody, the most articulate and the least articulate, it is about learning to talk. For everybody, learning to talk is incredibly difficult. However articulate you are, talking is incredibly difficult at some level. And that's what is being addressed. It's finding words for what resists words.

The efficacy of psychoanalysis ...

I think it's a question of whose criteria one wants to be bound by. By certain criteria psychoanalysis obviously doesn't work. Those are not my criteria. I think people should look at psychoanalysis from as many perspectives as they can come up with, and evaluate it from as many perspectives as they can come up with. And for some people, this will then prove that psychoanalysis is redundant, and then they're the people who shouldn't participate. Because it seems to me that psychoanalysis really is for the people who like it. It's not something that psycho-analysts should be going about converting people to, or trying to per-suade people that it works. It seems to me pointless. Nor should they, unless they want it to be, try to make it scientific, or try to join the science group. They may want to, in which case that's how they should pursue it. I think there are all sorts of different criteria. The risk is that psychoanalysis becomes very conformist, as in it simply complies with and pampers the dominant scientific criteria of efficacy.

So what can it do? How does it work, when it does?

I think we don't know the answer to that question, and I think we couldn't know the answer to that question.

There's a real difficulty here, and I don't think the enigma of this should be elided. How does it? And I think the answer is – we really don't know. What seems to be the case is that we change ourselves by redescribing ourselves. That we began in a conversation which was actually a non-verbal conversation, that evolved into verbal conversations with our parents, our siblings, our families and so on. So in some fundamental sense we construct ourselves, and can only have histories in language. So it seems to me uncontentious that language makes a difference, or language is the difference. Not that other animals don't have a version of language, but they don't have our version of language.

How talking works is very unclear. Yet it seems to me that it is clear that simply through this exchange of words people can feel an amazing diversity of things with amazing degrees of intensity. So these absolutely intangible things called words, that are just in the air here, seem to reach into us in very extraordinary ways and are very powerfully evocative. And it may be – as in music – it may be tones as much as contents and meanings. But there's something about this intangible exchange that is powerful.

The other thing that I think psychoanalysis is very good about is the way in which change is both unpredictable and also deferred. That is to say it is entirely conceivable that somebody could come and see me for a year and feel that nothing had changed, although of course, it would be interesting that they'd kept coming, but they could keep coming just because they believe I'm right. That it must be good because it's psychotherapy. But it might have no tangible effect. Yet in three years time, or five years time, or 20 years time, they might begin to note the effects of it, or to feel it having made a difference. In other words, we metabolise words at different rates, and with different rhythms. My experience is that redescription is very, very powerful. If you say something to me, and I say something back to you slightly different, something takes. Something becomes food for thought, amenable to a diversity of perspectives, it opens up. You come with a conviction about yourself to me, and we start looking at this and moving it around and recontextualising it, and you begin to tell yourself different stories about yourself.

Who decides whether the patient is 'improving' or otherwise?

I think that only the patient is in a position to decide what an improvement is. Of course, I've got an idea about what a good life is,

and how people should live, but so have they. So my primary crite-
rion I think is their sense of how things are going. Whether it feels –
for whatever reason, and they may not be able to articulate it – that
this conversation's worth having. This is competing with a lot of
things. You could spend your time and your money doing a million
other things – why come and speak to me? And that's the question I
think, that's always got to be in the middle of the picture. That
people have a sense that they can more or less articulate, that this is
making a difference. They also have a sense of when they come to
the end of it. Of when actually they want to spend their time and
money doing something else. Which is not to say that it doesn't come
with some regret or confusion, but nevertheless, a point comes at
which people feel – I've done this now.

Before the words, conversations, isn't a liking of the therapist important ...

Yes, and I think that this is something that psychoanalysis needs to
demystify for people. Because I think when people go and see therapists, the first question is: 'Do I want to talk to this person?' which
reduces itself at some level to: 'Do I like this person? Is there something about this person's presence that gives me an appetite to talk
to them?' And I really do think people should take their impressions
seriously. The problem of course is that they're very much in need, or
they're desperate, or they're suffering very badly from something, and
people can feel that their impressions are invalidated by that state.

But people get stuck with cold, un-giving therapists ...

Yes, and I think that's covert sadism. I think it's very fundamentally about
being kind to people, but kind as in the seventeenth-century sense of the
term – we're all in the same boat here in some fundamental sense. And I
really do think people should be very suspicious of all the deliberately
unfriendly, deliberately withholding therapists. Which is not to say that
there aren't periods when that kind of behaviour is useful, but I think
there's an awful lot of inner superiority at work in this stuff, and I think
there's a lot of cruelty.

Freud talked of the central importance of 'love' and 'work' ...

I don't know if I go in for that kind of stuff. Certainly I can't imagine a
good life where people didn't have the capacity to love people and
things. I think the work bit is a slightly dodgier one. It obviously depends a bit how this is translated, but by work I would mean people are
able to find things that they really are passionately interested in or
curious about, and then finding the ways to pursue those curiosities. If
that's work then, I want it. Of course people have to find or have the
wherewithal to make their living. There's a real economic base here.

That is also too easily ignored, I think. Psychoanalytic theory has always been terminally naive about issues of class and money.

Are you tactile at all with your patients?

Yes, I'm freer to be affectionate with kids than I am with adults. I think that what psychoanalysis is good for is showing people what they use sexuality to do. In the psychoanalytic situation I would want to articulate, put into words, the impulse to touch, which isn't to say that one wouldn't feel affection. And I don't feel at all phobic about shaking people's hands, or any of that stuff at all, but I do think this is the place where we think about our sensuality, and that we articulate something about it. I think for children it is bemusing and bizarre, and I think they're right, to enter into a relationship with adults where there is no touch.

Now obviously child sexual abuse has terrorised people about all this, but I think there is – as it were – an ordinary currency of affection, that is what I would want to think of as a nourishing environment for a child.

I can remember when I was training. I was seeing a little girl of six, and she was bouncing up and down on the couch in the room, and she fell off the couch, and I cuddled her. I took this to my supervisor, and my supervisor said to me: 'I wonder why you did that?' I don't think that's an interesting question.

Some therapists talk of the 'real work' going on between the sessions. They often give 'homework' ...

Well, I don't give people homework. I think it's impossible to know what the most significant bits of the therapy are. I think clearly an awful lot of therapy is unconscious work.

Can you elaborate ...

Well let me give you the mystifying answer to that first, which is things are going on that we don't know about. That's to say we're metabolising what we've said in the session in ways that we don't know about. It's being cooked. I think it's true that a lot of interesting work goes on between sessions. Just as a lot of interesting work goes on between meals. I think we don't know what it is, but we try and track it. But I think there are great advantages to seeing people once or twice a week. And partly, and I think this was part of Lacan's rationale, which obviously is partly garbage and partly interesting – that if you have a shortened session it's like you stimulate mental work in the patient.

Are you interested in work like Laing's in the connecting of the micro with the wider world?

I don't know about that, but I'm certainly interested in doing it. I admire Laing a lot for those reasons, and I admire the way in which he wanted to broaden the system, as in really produce an interesting, complicated context in which a life evolves. I don't feel brainy enough to make a lot of those links. I don't have the capacity, whatever it is, to connect too many of those realms, but I would like to be able to. And so I think somebody like Castoriadis for example, is a very, very good example of somebody who is linking realms. Because a life shrunk to its familial context or its individual internal world context is not a life. A life's an extremely complicated thing embedded in a whole range of overlapping contexts, of which, clearly, one of the most important must be an economic, or a political economic.

Some people say if the patient pays for the session they're more committed to it ...

I certainly don't believe that if you charge them they're more committed. I don't know how anybody can know that. How's commitment going to be calibrated? I think people are committed when they find a conversation that really interests them. Money is clearly very important – *it's a deal*, and that shouldn't be mystified although I think that it's very difficult to speak of it in a non-mystifying way. I have a basic fee. Obviously in this economic climate people can go from being really quite wealthy, to being quite poor quite quickly. And I charge people the whole spectrum from virtually nothing, to full fee. I certainly would not stop a treatment because somebody couldn't afford it. And I would always tailor the fees to what they could afford, and I don't mean afford as in ascetically afford, as in you sacrifice everything to come into therapy. By afford, I mean that I want to charge people an amount such that they are able to go out for meals, go to the cinema, have a good time. I don't believe in this as the necessary centre of your life. Or as some noble aesthetic ideal.

I can give you an example, although it's a slightly specific example. I see quite a lot of adolescents. When they make the move from being paid for by their parents to paying themselves, which is obviously symbolically very significant, they have hardly any money. So I either charge them very, very little, or for example, in the past people have done things like make tapes for me at the end of every month because I like music. So they paid me with a tape of their favourite music.

I didn't go into this to get rich, and I want to earn my living, and I want to live in the way that I want to live. Within those parameters I want to make it as available as possible.

Can we talk about the UKCP, and registration ... Will it kill innovation?

Well it might have a paradoxical advantage, which is that it'll kill the profession. That's to say it will shrink to a body of orthodox, consensual, accepted ideas. And that in itself will create a counterculture. I think there's a real dilemma here because on the one hand, the idea of institutionalising psychoanalysis is a contradiction in terms – you can't institutionalise the unconscious. On the other hand, how do you choose people to do trainings? There is an inevitable sense in which institutions take people who are as nice as themselves. And that there's some kind of liberal mystification when training institutions are taking rebels. It's like a piece of glib liberalism, because we know that the institution and its rebels do each other's bidding. There's nothing more compliant than being a rebel.

I think it's rather a good idea, that there should be a diversity of trainings that have really quite specific parameters and ideals, and aims, and objectives. And that people take it or leave it. The risk is you have overarching bodies that decide what an analyst is. Because clearly – how do you know if you are an analyst? If you go to Sigmund Freud and he supervises your case, and he says: 'Yes you've done this, this is very good', does that mean you're an analyst? Who's in a position to say? Nobody is. This is a really interesting dilemma. It isn't solved by simply, as a kind of performative utterance, somebody saying: 'I am the Institute of Psychoanalysis, I will confer authenticity upon people.' It's a parody of analysis. Because one of the interesting things that psychoanalysis puts up for grabs is the question of legitimation – how does somebody know if they're an analyst? And the answer is – somebody else tells you. But who's told them? Who decides on the criteria?

Are you involved ...

Yes, I can't help but be. I'm involved as in I'm a member of it, and I'm a member of it by virtue of being a member of the Association of Child Psychotherapists, and the Guild of Psychotherapists. Now in order to get a job in the Health Service as a child psychotherapist, I have to be a member of the Association of Child Psychotherapists. I've no objection to being a member of that Association, but that's the logistics of it.

How do you monitor your own performance in the sessions?

Again, there couldn't be absolute criteria here. I think the criteria are mostly tacit or unconscious, and therefore potentially mystified. It's not a mystery to me when I'm having a good conversation, and by that I mean, we forget ourselves and it's clear that somebody's talking about something that really matters to them here. Also I think it's often clear, even though it creates a lot of anxiety when a relationship has ended. I think relationships have a shelf life. Nobody knows what it is, but Ron Greenwood said: 'My philosophy of football is very simple. You've either got the ball or you haven't.' Well I think it's true of relationships too. But the consequences of this are very traumatic, obviously, and people

can spend, as it were, a whole relationship not facing the fact or negotiating the fact that the relationship's ended.

I think one of the things it's useful to be attentive to in analysis is when
it has run its course. People really should be doing something else.

Ron Greenwood – England or West Ham? [Laughs]

West Ham!

*Your conversations with your patients can, presumably, be based on all sorts
of things, including empathic understanding ...*

Oh, I think the language of empathy and understanding people is a
mystification. I think that we don't know what it's like to be somebody
else, we have imaginings about these things. People don't understand
each other, because how would you know if you had? What people do is
they go on inventing and reinventing, describing and redescribing. I
ascribe something to you about you, and you give it back to me, and
you tell me what you think of it, and it goes on. But it's not as though
you are like a triangle, and therefore something that I could understand.
I think you're something quite different, which is a person. People are
not subject to being understood. There is an experience which we tend
to describe, which is called feeling understood. I think feeling understood probably means something like feeling somebody has some imaginative grasp, is on one's side, all those kinds of things. But I think it's a
piece of psychobabble.

*I'm interested in existentialism as I guess you are ... however, the uncon-
scious for you is so important ...*

But I also think it's equally important to imagine a life without an
unconscious. And I think you need to be able to entertain contradictory
ideas here. That's why I think it's really useful to have Sartre and
Freud. Freud saying effectively: 'There is an unconscious that is in a
sense determining one's life.' Sartre saying: 'This is bad faith, we'll do
anything to avoid the fact that we're making choices into an unknown
future.' I think we need both views. I really do. I think that as Sartre
said, the idea of the unconscious could be the worst piece of bad faith
that we modern people have taken on. I don't think that's entirely true.
But it can be used like that.

I continue to find it hard to see you in the analytic tradition ...

I don't think I've described myself in the analytic tradition, except when
you've asked where I place myself in the analytic tradition. I am a child
psychotherapist – that's what I trained as. My affinities are much more for
a whole range of writers than they are for specific psychoanalysts. I think

you're right, you see: I don't think one needs to locate oneself, except insofar as one is selling something, one is a commodity. And also in the sense of giving people a sense as far as one's able, of the kinds of ideas one believes in, the kind of internal guidelines that are at work here. I don't think psychoanalysis is important. I don't think the future of psychoanalysis matters. What matters is people finding a language to talk about what is important to them. Now for me Freud has produced a language that's really very good for that. There are plenty of languages, but for me that's a very important one. So I don't feel the need to affiliate myself, but I also don't feel the need to disaffiliate myself, as in simply to say: 'Well Freud's just one among many.' Freud's very important to me because he's given me a language to think about the things that matter to me. Other people have too, but his has been very important.

CHAPTER 14

Psychosynthesis

Naona Beecher-Moore

Naona Beecher-Moore practises psychosynthesis in London.

How did you become a therapist?

Well I have a very long and complicated history. I was one of those unique human beings who was a child star in America. I went on the stage when I was 18 months old, and I was – from the time I was 18 months old until I was seven – I was known as the 'southern baby', and I tap danced and sang. The things that people did in the late '20s, early '30s. Once I 'retired', I went ahead and lived as a normal southern girl, including going through university, getting married and having a family.

So there have been three areas that have gone through my life. One is the theatre, the other is psychology, and the third's religion. And so I've been both a singer, and a dancer, and an actress, and a producer, and I've worked with the Actors' Studio in New York as a producer. I started a theatre in New York with my first husband, Sidney Lanier, called the American Place Theater, which is still in existence. This was a theatre for people from other disciplines – writers, poets and so forth – to write for the theatre. So that went all the way through. I suppose when I was about 25, when my first child, I must have been about 30, when my first child was five years old, he started singing and it scared me to death. Because it made me – I was immediately panicked that he was going to – in some way he'd have to use his talent. I wasn't even aware of what the fear was, but it was so vibrant, that I thought 'I'd better get myself to somebody to discuss this.' So I went into Freudian analysis which was all that was available then, and I did Freudian analysis, and then I did Jungian analysis, and a didactic analysis. I came to this country to work with Anna Freud, to become a child analyst, but at that point I was a single parent with small children, and it became very clear that I couldn't do that and work with disturbed children. So I put it into the future, and said that at some point I would do this.

So I went ahead and did many other things, and then retrained when I was in my early fifties. And the reason I chose Psychosynthesis was because I had in early 1970 gone to Esalen, and I had trained as an encounter leader, I had trained with Fritz Perls and Gestalt, I had trained with

Janov and the Primal Scream. I was one of those groupies, I used to go to
the States and just take every training going, and then come back to
England and not use it. Because I felt using it was almost an ego trip. The
encounter work particularly. That's judgemental, but I take full responsibility for it ... [Laughs]

So I put off doing it, and then somebody rang up and said – friends
of mine from the States – rang up and said: 'Oh we've found this guru
in Italy. You've got to come with us.' And I said 'No', I was up to here
with any sort of thing, didn't want to go. Finally I agreed to go for the
ice cream, because I like ice cream, and it was Roberto Assagioli and
we worked with him for six weeks, and because of this, and this is even
more strange, he had me doing free drawing during a time I was working with him. And I became a designer for ten years with no training at
all, except my free drawings which I enjoyed very much.

But then my partner had a nervous breakdown, and I came to another one of those times when you have to decide, and I thought: 'Well
now's the time to go back in and train.' I went to the Psychoanalytic
Institute here in London, and was ready to retrain – go ahead with my
Jungian work. But then it was a choice between Jung or Freud, or
Klein, and I suddenly couldn't cope with any of those choices. Then a
friend said to me 'Have you ever heard of psychosynthesis?' and it was
as though a bolt from the blue had come down. Because it made so
much sense to me. Because psychosynthesis is a way of working which
incorporates all the classic traditions, but also allows an enormous space
for other things. It's known as the psychology with the soul, because it
also includes the higher self.

So I trained in my early fifties, so I not only work as a trainer, now
I train other people but I also have a one-to-one practice. Long but
precise story.

How would you describe psychosynthesis?

Well, for me as a therapist, and for me as a person as well, psychosynthesis is a mode of working which allows the freedom to incorporate any number of other disciplines. So it means for me, looking at
most other disciplines in psychology, they depend very much on the
Judaic–Christian tradition. Whereas in psychosynthesis we can incorporate with Hindu, with Muslim, with Buddhist, with any tradition in
terms of religion. The basis of it is that it includes the higher self,
which we look at as a touch of divinity. When I look at you as a
client I see you as a divine human being who knows more about your
journey than I'll ever know. My job as a therapist is not in any way
to question that, but to mirror for you what I see you doing in your
life patterns, so that you can choose whether to change or to stay the
way you are.

So it relieves me from having to help you. I can't help you. The only
way I can work with you is to be as clear a mirror as I can. And in

doing that I use everything that I know how to use that might be useful for you. For me, mental health consists entirely of being able to act rather than react.

So part of my work, in fact the most important part of my work, is to help you look at patterns that have started in your life, whether or not you wish to keep them. Whether they are any longer useful.

Additional concepts?

Yes – two; the most important first of all, as I say, is looking at the divinity in each human being and their potential. The second is based very much on a book that Assagioli wrote called *The Act of Will*. It's being able to use, learning to cultivate, the will. We are mostly brought up with the Victorian concept of the will as something that we have to force our way through. Whereas Assagioli's belief system is that the will is letting go of old tapes, and beginning to choose again. And how to cultivate this gift really. He looks at the will as something that comes – that is a transpersonal quality – that's very much like love, which is to be cultivated.

What kind of clients do you work with?

I work with a range of people. I work with children, generally children who are specially gifted in some way. My youngest client at the moment is six, my oldest client is 83. And I work with a range in between. People come to me in crisis generally, needing to stabilise in some way. The crisis can be an eating disorder – with the six-year-old, it's that he's extremely gifted and finds it difficult to cope with finding out exactly where he is in relation to other people. So my work with him is to help him know that he's fine the way he is but he also has to live like everyone else. And it's really witnessing to him as a child and his abilities. With the 83-year-old it's just the opposite. It's helping her learn that she no longer has to get up at 7.30 every morning and pursue the kind of life that she has pursued. That it's time for her to recognise her life wisdom and begin to *be* rather than *do*.

With the ones in between, I work with a lot of businessmen. The work with them varies between mid-life crisis – 'I've done everything I can, now what do I have left?' – to finding ways to overcome fear of death, to deal with a sense of frustration, often in business. As I say, eating disorders with women are the most common I suppose.

I've now discovered that as a therapist as I move in my life, I reclaim certain parts of my own past. I'm more able to work with people that are involved with that – I'm working now with more and more actors, and that work is really around being able to separate their acting roles and their real self. Being able to reclaim who they are when they're not working. I'm working with two or three writers, and that's around the loneliness of the artist, and the sense of frustration and exposure and nakedness that comes with producing work, and then having it reviewed and sometimes understood, and other times not understood.

I'm also working and continue to work with a group of extremely bright people who were a product of the university years, who went through the whole drugs, drink, and the ones who survived now are having to reconcile their lives with what's left – often a sense of bleakness now that they're no longer on that perpetual high. And learning to reclaim some sense of joy.

Do you turn people away?

Yes. I don't like to turn anyone away, but one of the things that I have learned, is that – somebody said that your mind can lie, but your gut can't – there are people that when I meet and talk to them I realise that I'm not the person for them to work with. I would consider it arrogance on my part to feel I can work with everybody. So I have a list of people in various parts of Great Britain, and London in particular, that I can recommend people to. I always say if they're not happy please get back to me, because I think that it's a very brave thing to do in the beginning to come to a therapist. So I don't wish to in any way discourage that, but I also know that quite honestly there are people that I'm not right for.

Do you talk contractually with people when they first come to see you?

There are two things. I have a sheet of paper which I give people, which I'd be glad to give you, which explains the basic things around therapy. By and large, I'm just present with them and listening to what they expect. I tell them pretty much what I've told you: that my job is not to help them or to make them any better, but to help them see what they're doing. And the choice is theirs. The frustration is often when you work with someone and you see them approaching a point in their lives where they *can* choose, and seeing them choose not to choose.

But I have to let go of that, because the only time I get caught is when I have an attachment to a result with a client. I can't allow myself that indulgence, because it's not me, my skills can be useful but it's not me that does the healing.

What happens when someone comes to see you?

All right. If you come to me for instance with a presenting problem that is a fairly simple one, then I always make a contract to see you for six sessions. At the end of six sessions we review. My contract is always to work with you as long as you want to work, or feel the necessity to work. But I also want you to have an escape clause, shall we say, after six weeks. So that if it's not working that – and this comes from my own experience of having spent five years daily on a couch, and not being able to have any escape clause at all, not that I regret that time but that's not what I do.

So I would see you for six sessions, and then again for another six sessions to see where you were in relationship to whatever the problem was. If you found this work helpful, if you felt complete. I have worked with people for as little as six sessions; I have worked with people for two or three months. It really depends very much on what the problem is. I've also worked with people for five years.

By and large I use a variety of techniques. I use active listening – just being available to listen, to paraphrase, to mirror, so that the person hears what they're saying. That's the simplest thing that I use. I use guided imagery.

Could you explain ...

Active listening is listening and repeating. For instance, if you say to me: 'And then my husband proceeded to blow up', I'd say: 'I hear you say your husband blew up, could you say more about how you experienced that. How did he blow up? What did he do?'

Mirroring is very much the same way, but in repeating, beginning to help, it's almost as though you act as a television screen, but verbally.

Now in imagery, there are various ways of using imagery. If, for instance, someone's working and then says: 'And then whenever my son says this, I get this terrible feeling in the pit of my stomach', I will sometimes say: 'Will you just close your eyes for a minute, and let an image come of what that feeling is in the pit of your stomach', and they might envision an octopus. 'Can you talk to the octopus, and ask the octopus what it needs. What is it, is the octopus frightened, what's going on with the octopus? Just begin to talk to the octopus.' That's one way of using imagery.

Another way of using imagery – if, for instance, someone is frightened of doing a new job. They'd come into me and say 'I'm about to start a new job tomorrow, I feel enormous fear around this', we'd look at the fear and then I might say: 'Close your eyes and let's just take a small journey.' I'd have them imagine they're on a seashore, and I'd do that by saying: 'Can you hear the waves, can you see the waves? Are there any birds there, can you feel the sand under your feet, can you smell the sea?' So you'd use the five senses. Then I might say: 'And now you see someone coming towards you, can you get a clear picture of what they look like? This is someone who cares a great deal about you, who understands you very much and who has a gift to give you, that will help you with your job tomorrow. So don't censor when the gift's given to you, just be aware of receiving it and ask this person any questions you want to ask them. Talk to them about what the gift may mean if you don't understand it.' After the gift's received you have them continue to walk on the beach, do the whole sense memory thing again, and then come back. And then report to you what they've experienced. That's another way of getting a person to get in touch with what it is they need to have the energy or the strength to face the next day.

Another way of using the imagery is to say all right, you get an image, and the image is the octopus. All right, I have some paper here and some pens. Draw that image and see how you feel as you draw it, look at it, and see what it means to you. So I keep paper there all the time, and felt tip pens. So I use drawing, I use imagery. I use just listening, being present with people. I use toys quite a lot. And as you'll see over there, I have a sand tray. I use sand play work from time to time, when people are stuck and really don't know what's happening and they can't really express what's going on for them. Then I take them over and let them play with the sand tray. The way I use it is very simple. I just let them do the sand play and then tell me the story of what's going on in the sand tray.

Could you expand?

The sand play therapy consists of having a sand box, and I guess it's about two feet by one foot wide, two feet long. This is a confined space which feels safe because it *is* confined in structure. Then on the shelves I have about two or three hundred objects of all sorts, ranging from animals, to trees, to houses, to churches, to angels, to witches, to motorcycles, to pirates, you name it. Everything I can find that's small, I collect them all over the world, and people give them to me as well. Then I have natural objects like stones and little bits of bark, and shells and things.

So the point is to have the person go and see the thing that appeals to them most. And to put it in the sand tray. When they feel that they have finished with the sand tray, they have everything in it they like, then I say: 'Is there anything you'd like to change? Is that the way you like it?' Sometimes people will change things around, sometimes they won't. Then I'll say: 'Now tell me the story, you start off "once upon a time"', and then they tell a story of what the sand tray has said. Then when they finish I'll say: 'Now are you happy with it this way or is there anything you need to change?' Again often they will change things and then the story will shift and change.

The whole purpose of imagery and sand play work, and being a mirror for people, is to help make explicit what's implicit. For so many of us, we know we've got a problem, but we can't seem to get it out. So any way I can find, including stuffed animals – as you see the couch is filled with them – sometimes they'll have animals talk to one another, or they'll talk to the animals.

One of the primary bases of work in psychosynthesis too, is subpersonality work. It's very easy to understand if any of you have ever had an internal argument. One part of you saying: 'I think I'll have a chocolate', and the other part saying: 'You know that's silly, you don't want a chocolate', 'Yes, I do', 'No I don't'. That's a trite example, but there are heavier ones. There are parts of our personality that are in conflict and so when I work more long-term with people, I'll often do sub-personality work. Because the argument becomes intense, and they get really stuck, and the bad news is that they're stuck, and the good news is that they begin to hear two different voices. I sit in the third seat and can help them begin to look at those two voices. So that's another technique that I use.

But I suppose on the bottom line my real sense is that I don't do anything differently than priests, rabbis, doctors, family, wise people have done for generations. It's just that I have perhaps more techniques to use, but for me the healing is *just being present*. I will always believe that when I train people, and I supervise people, I say: 'If you have to figure out what to do with a client, get up and leave the room. Think about it outside and come back again, because at least they'll know you've gone. Then we won't continue this terrible pattern that parents have of saying "yes, yes, of course you know I'm listening" when they're not.'

For me, the real healing is being present with another person, and being truly there for them. This is what the training is, this is what takes three years to learn, is really to be able to focus and let go of your own ego, your own self – except as an instrument – in order to be present.

Transference ...

It is inevitable, but the depth of it is dependent upon the psychological awareness of the client. And it's a very important part of the healing process, I think. Because if your therapist isn't your friend, who is? If the therapist can't be on your side, who can? So I suppose when you said, 'Are there people I can't work with?' there are people that I would not have a good countertransference toward; I would not really like. I might respect them, and think they were fine, but there's not that sense of communication that's important.

The depth of transference depends very much on the length of time that you work with someone I think, and I laughingly say that when a client thinks you're marvellous, that's not transference that's reality. When they think you're awful, that's transference .... [Laughs] But I know there is both those things. And there is a graph where the client will just think you're marvellous for a while, and then as they begin to reframe and reclaim themselves, they'll begin to see your feet of clay.

What kind of people make good therapists?

I really do think therapy is an art form. Whether you're an analyst, whether you're a psychiatrist, whether you're a psychotherapist or counsellor, I think there are certain people who have a gift for being present with other people. It's known as charisma, it's known as stage presence, it's known in various other forms as other things, but I think that there is a certain quality, that is an innate quality, that you can't teach someone. You can train people to know the techniques, to be good counsellors, but a very fine therapist I think is like a violinist, it's an art form.

For me the most important quality as I've said before is just being present. This is why I think it's incumbent on a therapist to keep up their own therapy, to have supervision when they need it to continue to grow and learn, and also never to get into tunnel vision. I think it's important to go to the theatre, to read novels, to be in touch with the art world, to keep up with scientific things, to understand medicine, to be able to send your clients – if you need to – to a doctor to understand what's going on physically for them. Just to have a well-rounded life and not to get caught up in just being a therapist. But the basic gift is just presence, is to be totally present with someone.

What kinds of qualities does the 'innate healer' have?

One of the things is curiosity. They are honestly, honestly curious about people. That they're innate detectives. They want to know what's going on. How this person's doing this, why they're doing it, when they're doing it. I sometimes think it's like a picture puzzle, with missing pieces, and it is the excitement and joy of finding that bit of information that goes in here. With that curiosity and with that quality of detection comes an ability to let go of themselves – and I don't mean the higher self, I mean their own ego – and be truly present with someone. I think it's the same quality scientists have, or artists for that matter, who want to experiment with colour or sound or, as you, with film, or with anything. That sense of excitement.

Does it help if the therapist has 'suffered' themselves?

Well I don't know anyone who's had a life without distress, and I very much believe in the wounded healer. I think that we heal our own wounds often. The phrase that always comes to mind is: 'Never criticise a man unless you've walked a mile in his moccasins', which my grandmother told me when I very young. 'Never judge a man unless you've walked a mile in his moccasins.' Now I may not have walked in the identical moccasins, but I will often have walked on a path that's similar, so that therefore my empathic response to someone is important, and my life experience is important in that way. I don't have to have been abused to understand abuse, because abuse has an enormous variety of flavours.

But I do have to be able to be in touch with my own pain and with my own sense of woundedness, in order to empathise with someone else's wounds. Does that answer your question?

Do most of your clients go through similar 'stages' when working with you?

I think it depends again upon the client. I have had clients that I have worked with over a long period of time: one that comes to mind is a woman who was totally isolated, really had never had any relationships, she had been a server all of her life. She looked after other people, but she'd never had any real relationship. We went through a long period of treatment where she really went through the whole transference, all the transferential stages. Went from deep regression into a very early stage of babyhood almost, to dismissing me as a teenager. That was a very interesting, and clinically interesting, piece of work. And was definable as such.

There are other pieces of work that I can't see, until it's over, exactly what the transition periods have been. I've just been working with someone who was in what I would define as deep spiritual crisis. Because of a group of love experiences that happened all at once. He is now through it and sees what was necessary for him to integrate around that. That was a definable line.

Others are not so easy because they take two steps forward and one step back. Particularly working with eating disorders and working with children (by children I mean young people) who have ME – things like that which are very long term. It requires enormous patience on everyone's part, because it's not something that can be categorised.

How eclectic are you?

I'm very eclectic. Assagioli was a Freudian analyst and he was a friend of Jung's and they worked together for some time, so it's very difficult for me to tell you when I use what. No it isn't difficult, it's easier. Let's see if I can just take a minute. [Pause] One of the things that I learned from Jung is that I'm an intuitive and there are times when I do know that I have to stop and let it come to me, rather than answer right away. [Pause] One of the psychiatrists who I work with sometimes when I need to have a client under medication, sometimes feels that the work that we do can be very dangerous in his terms, because he feels that imagery is so effective, and that if it were used in the wrong way or by the wrong people that it would be very destructive. You could say the same thing about classical analysis. I happen to know someone who's been in analysis for 22 years, and goes daily to someone called, I think, Dr Kafka. That's enough to make you a little bit nervous. [Laughs] So you could say that that's a misuse.

The thing that psychosynthesis does allow is – Dr Assagioli said: 'Do it my way and you'll fail.' You need to have a tool bag as filled with as many things as you can get, and to be as well trained as you can be, and to continue to grow and learn in order to help, to stay with people and mirror clearly. I suppose that's what I really believe. I believe that no, it's not necessary for everyone to have to be five days on a couch. It's not necessary for everyone to go three days a week. It *is* necessary for some people. And thank goodness those things are available. But it – for people in life crises to stabilise – can sometimes mean having someone say: 'You're right, you're right, you're absolutely right, and now how do you choose to do this? Or how does it serve you to continue to be a victim, continue to be cast about by circumstance? What are you getting from this?'

Can you explain the 'synthesis' aspect ...

We do what we call 'top-down, bottom-up' work. On a psychosynthesis map which is shaped like an egg, the top third is super conscious, or the higher consciousness; the middle strip is called the middle consciousness, and there's a circle within that called the field of consciousness, and that's where we all live, in the field of consciousness; the bottom third of the egg is the lower unconscious. In psychosynthesis theory, we believe that the higher self is both inside and outside the egg. So it's connected with the eternal collective unconscious. In that self is what we may be, who we may be, our whole sense of potential. And what's happening is that our sense of self is trying to get into our field of consciousness to help us be what we could be. So it's as though that's sending down qualities to help us, like love, or will, or power, serenity, whatever's necessary.

But it can't go straight into the field of consciousness without touching off things in the lower unconscious. Now in most fields of work in psychology, people spend a lot of time digging in the lower unconscious and not integrating it, in my experience. Takes a long time for integration. On our map we believe that you never touch off something in the bottom that doesn't reflect in the top. So that you are working from both areas. The whole point is to integrate it into the field of consciousness.

So the work can be – when it comes in the field of consciousness – it can sometimes, you'll find two sub-personalities that will immediately clash, that can't be integrated. But then you begin to work through that, or sometimes there's too much energy coming through from the transpersonal, which we'll call a spiritual crisis, and people will exhibit all sorts of mental disorder. Because they find it so much to deal with. They sometimes have visions, they sometimes have precognition, they sometimes have sleeplessness, enormous amounts of energy. Then it will start to touch off things in their childhood, and their lower unconscious, lots of forgotten or remembered patterns. The point is to hold them until they can begin to integrate into the field of consciousness. And that's – how long is a piece of string? Sometimes it's a long process, sometimes it takes two weeks.

So Assagioli was ahead of Maslow?

Very much so. It's a sort of a frustration in a sense, because a lot of the new books that I read, like Thomas Moore's *The Care of the Soul*, and *The Care of the Soul in a Relationship*, and a lot of other books. Stanislav Grof, all sorts of people, have used a lot of the theories of psychosynthesis without giving credit to it. This would not have worried Assagioli for a minute, because he very carefully at the end of every book said: 'More research should be done on this. The egg itself has no solid lines, they're all open lines everywhere, so that things can come in and out, and flow in and out.'

You probably heard, Jung said: 'Thank God, I'm Jung and not a Jungian', because of the concretisation. And Assagioli was very insistent that this should not happen. Which is both the strength of psychosynthesis and also its weakness, because it doesn't have a great field of literature, and it's not something that is that easy to define, any more than I'm defining. Simply because there's so much work to be done, and the shifting and changing as new insights come in.

Presumably the cognitive-behavioural approach isn't that useful for you?

Sometimes. Sometimes its very useful. They can be, some of the things in that, just as in neurolinguistic programming. It depends – again each individual is so individual that the more gifts you have the more things you have available to help them.

Do you 'touch' patients?

Again, depending upon the client. I never would touch a patient/client without asking their permission. But I certainly have, and I will often hug clients at the end of the session, because that's who I am. I'm a southern American originally, and I'm a toucher. [Laughs] And all my clients know it. I warn them ahead of time. And there are people I would never touch, the clients that I work with whose boundaries have to be very carefully taken into consideration, particularly working around someone who's been badly abused in any way. I am very careful, very conscious about that.

I do use a lot of Gestalt techniques. When people need to express anger they can beat away on a thing or two. I also encourage them at home to beat on mattresses, or 'weed' is the best thing I encourage them to do. Weeding gardens is terrific. Working with teenagers, who need to express that sort of anger.

With businessmen I have them go off and play any sort of racket game, like squash, and encourage the anger to come out physically. We don't use body techniques per se, we do body training with our trainees – and I have with some clients who have had to regress and then move forward, I have held and rocked people. But when I train people I always say that it's very important that you are aware of doing it for the client's good and not yours. So that I'm very careful about physical contact, if I feel that it's only for me and not for them.

Do you think you're particularly good with certain kinds of clients?

I used to work a lot with anorexics and bulimics, when I first started. Now I have people I supervise, that I send them to. At the moment I think that I'm only working with two anorexics. The work is very heavy, very tiring, can be soul-destroying in some ways. It can be very painful, and the having to let go of attachment to yourself is a constant thing you need to do. So I don't work so much with anorexics any more.

Again I suppose it's my own process, as both in age and in experience, that now I suppose I do more work – I suppose I describe myself as 'walking with people' now more; sometimes I'm ahead of them, sometimes I'm next to them, occasionally they're ahead of me. I sort of walk more with people on their journeys now than I did before. I suppose I work with more men than women now. And work more with older people. No that's not true, because I've worked a lot with younger people too. As I reclaim or claim my own body, mind, feeling, experience, and my age and life experience, the people who come to me and whom I see are commensurate with that I suppose in some way.

I'm very careful about my qualifications, and so I'm an accredited BAC counsellor and I'm also a member of the UKCP. I'm also a member of various other organisations, professional organisations. Because I think it's important to honour those things. I possibly turn away, I say with deep humility and almost embarrassment, I turn away five to seven people a week. All my clients are word of mouth. As I said to my husband this morning – I'm almost afraid to go and speak anywhere because every time I do I have more people wanting to come and see me. My books are full. Having said that, there's always someone who's going to get through to me, and if they do then I know I need to see them.

So my husband says: 'You should see three people a day, and leave one lucky draw.' But I'm afraid I don't stick to that, I see four to six people a day. I try and stick to four, but sometimes I see more. And I now have started a network for children, particularly, so that I supervise a group of young therapists who see children, so that I don't have to turn children away.

[Pause] ... The Freudian 50 minutes?

No, I started off using an hour-and-a-half. I use an hour, sometimes and hour and 15 minutes, sometimes it's a little bit less. But it's almost always an hour.

How have you come to know that your work is effective?

I think immediately of one young woman who came to me, who was one of a family who had never been able to form a lasting relationship with someone. And her deep regret and sadness. She wished to be in a relationship, and looking as I say at the model I've been talking about, I suppose we worked for about three months and at that time she said that she felt much more secure about what some of the contributing patterns were, and so she was ready to stop – knowing that she could come back any time she wanted to. The next thing I heard she had found a man and is now married quite happily.

Now I love happy endings, she's since rung me and she's said: 'Will you see this person, will you see that person, will you see another person?' They're probably not going to be the same happy endings, but that's a very simple life story that to me is gratifying. I know that the work we did is work that she would never have been able to do on her own, simply because it was a lot around her family patterning.

One of the best pieces of work I ever did was helping a solitary person. Agreed to take two cats, and also we went through and talked about behavioural therapy. We got Delia Smith's *Cooking for One* and *Cooking for Two*, and we discussed buying wine glasses and how to buy sherry and how to entertain, and what rules to say when people came to stay, and things of that sort. This was at the end of a prolonged therapy. That to me was very touching work. She is now able to cope very well in life situations.

I had one young woman who was an architect, who was very unhappy, and she started doing free drawing, that's another thing I sometimes use. She is now an artist and no longer an architect, and has done quite well as a fine artist. Her life's switched around, because she chose to come out of a discipline that she'd only done to please her parents, into something that was freer for her.

And failures?

Absolutely. One person that I worked with and was able to take her out of a situation when she had been very caught in a solitary pattern, and she began to go out, she began to be able to go and sit and have coffee in places, she began to have friends, and then she got very frightened and went straight back into the old pattern again. That disappointed and upset me, and made me feel very sad. But then that was her choice.

That's what I mean about needing to let go of an attachment to result. Because she could see what needed to be done, and what the step was to do it, and just chose not to, went straight back into the old pattern of 'It's not the fear of the unknown, it's the fear of letting go of the known.' So she preferred to stay with the known, even though it was a dead end.

So mental health is all about autonomy?

Choice, it's around choice.

And mentally unhealthy people ...

React. Continue to react. Work from a place of no choice, and – we all work from a place of no choice still, because none of us is perfect, and we can't have choice without awareness. And to me that's what therapy is all about, it's becoming more and more aware of who I am, why I behave the way I do, when I behave the way I do, how I do it, and then choosing whether or not that's what I wish to do.

Are you aware of how the changes in your clients might affect their partners?

It's my belief, and I say this to my clients, 'Yes, as you change it's going to have ramifications to all those around you. And if you can stay in touch with the fact that by shifting and changing you're giving them the opportunity to shift and change. But during the period that you're changing it's not going to be a comfortable time for them. Because when the rocks in your head fit the holes in theirs, and then you move, they don't like it. Whether it's your husband, or your children, whoever it is. But if you can hold on to the fact that this is also giving them the opportunity ...'

In my own personal experience when I started retraining, it was very difficult for my husband who was a pragmatist and a sportsman and a businessman. He just didn't like this at all, and we went through some rather rocky times where he was not at all happy with me. I had to hold on to the concept that that was the truth, and the joke is that he used to tell people that I was training to be a physiotherapist. A great friend of his was the naturalist Peter Scott, and Peter came one day and Beecher said to him: 'Nan's training to be a physiotherapist', and Peter said 'Well I have this pain in my neck', and Beecher said: 'She only works with heads.' ... [Laughs]

Shortly after that, at a party, someone came up to me and said 'If you do what your husband says you do, I think I need to come and see you', and I said: 'Oh, what did he tell you?' and he said: 'No you tell me what you do', and I replied 'No way. You tell me what he said', and he said: 'Well he told me that you work with people in life crises to help them stabilise.' So somehow – I never told him that – but this is where he had grown. He still doesn't know exactly what I do.

Someone told me he thought therapy was essentially a moral pursuit ...

I honour what he says. I suppose that in holding each person as a divine human being, I hold both the sun and shadow in you. So I can't make a moral judgement, because sometimes the shadow is stronger than the sun.

How does the 'transpersonal' manifest itself in your work?

When I work with someone I look to see what it is that's trying to come through to them from their transpersonal. What quality is trying now to manifest itself in their life. It can be trust, it can be power, it can be love, it can be any number of things. And how they're blocking it. For instance, I was working with someone this morning who's beginning to get in touch with his own sense of power. He's had a deep attachment to being a young boy. Whatever age he is. And in doing that it served him because, as long as you're a child, you don't have to be an adult. Suddenly a crunch came in his life where he had to start taking responsibility for being an adult, and it meant being in touch with his own power, and doing the work we've done he now suddenly hears that for the first time. Now to me that's transpersonal. To me that's something that is – it's been like watching someone fight against it for weeks, and finding 38 ways not to do it. But finally, face-to-face with it, saying: 'Yes, well this I need to do. I need to grasp this', and the shift and change in him as a person is even physical. To me that's the transpersonal at work. It's making the implicit explicit again.

What must a trainee therapist believe in, if they claim to believe in the transpersonal?

They must believe that a person is more than their body, feelings and mind. If you believe that a person is only a primate, and all he consists of is the body, feelings and mind, you rule out the transpersonal. Jung, of course, was heading toward it very much so, and very much in his own belief system. And among some Jungians it is accepted, but among others it is not. Kleinians and Freudians and many of the behaviourists don't believe that man is any more than that.
  To me that's leaving out a great and a very important part of a person.

Can we talk about the ethical issues?

I'm very aware of a code of ethics. In psychosynthesis we both train and accept the BAC code of ethics as well as the UKCP code of ethics. And they're pretty much the same. I adjudicate sometimes with ethical groups, when – I feel so strongly and so – I suppose this is where my prejudice, where my judgement comes in. I really find it very difficult to be understanding or forgiving of people who betray the code of ethics. The whole sense of respect for your client is terribly important, terribly important.

Might registration affect creativity?

I do understand creativity, and often in my own work I use, as I say, toys and play therapy, and I have people listening to humorous tapes, and I recommend books, and I do all sorts of bibliotherapy in terms of having read everything from Gerald Durrell to Plato, but there is a point where the respect for a human being is terribly important. And again, I think that if the therapist does anything for his own benefit rather than for the client's, that that is abuse. It can be abuse. And of course we all make mistakes, we all make unwise choices on occasion, but there's a difference between that and the ethical code.

Do therapists 'burn out'?

I'm very judgemental about burn-out. I think therapists who burn out are irresponsible. I think that's silly. This is why I say you can't have tunnel vision around this. One of the most important lessons I learned was when I stop, I read murder mysteries and junk novels, and watch mindless television, and go to see stupid films, because I get psychic indigestion if I don't. That famous Jonathan Miller quote from *Beyond the Fringe*, 'I don't go to the theatre to see rape, incest and murder, I get enough of it at home.' You can't work and be totally present with someone, even four hours a day, and then not be tired. There's just no way.

One of the ways that I rest, is that I do different things. I train abroad quite a lot – I train in Sweden and in Holland; that for me is a rest. Because I love airports, you can sit and dream, or stare into space. No phones, nobody does anything, and I love staying in a hotel all by myself. That's a rest, and also I do groupwork when I go there. So I'm working with different energies. I try once a week to go to the osteopathic clinic for children. On Tuesday afternoons I work with an osteopath called Stuart Korth, who teaches other young osteopaths. They use me primarily to work with autistic children. Just changing, doing different things is – but I also, when I'm not training on weekends, I go to the country with my husband. I have a husband and four children, and eight grandchildren, and they'll keep you sane.

Your view of 'false memory syndrome'?

I have a view of it and my view is Freudian. Freud said: 'There are no lies', and that no matter what your client tells you, that is their truth. And I stick to that, I believe that to be true. I've had clients tell me things that were absolutely unbelievable, and I knew to be untrue, but that is their truth and it's not for me to judge. It's my job to help them integrate and begin to see what's behind it.

Now in terms of false memory specifically, I very much disagree with having anybody go to a parent, because they're not talking to the real parent anyway. They're talking – when you're working with someone who has been abused – yes, the abuse did happen or didn't happen, but they're talking to the inner parent. That's who they need to straighten it out with. So I would never ever recommend that anyone go to their parent and accuse them of anything.

Do you think the British are especially coy about therapy?

I'm southern American, and therefore I've always felt at home in Great Britain, because in the south of America, you say one thing and mean another. You have what I call a Japanese tea ceremony way of life. But I remember when Esalen first came to England in the '60s, they came over with the predisposition and with the whole prejudice saying: 'Oh the British are so uptight, they won't understand.' I said, 'Be careful, because if you go into that,' I said, 'who's going to deal with all these major-d's?' – they had all these major-domos outside, because the men on the Inn on the Park didn't know what this crazy group were going to do. I said: 'Who's going to deal with them?' Nobody'd thought of that, so I dealt with them. You'd say to these sergeant majors: 'Lie down on the floor now, we're going to do a little deep breathing' everybody would lie down on the floor. I said: 'If you go in there and tell everybody to take off all their clothes, they will, they'll shock you to death, because the British are very open once they trust you.'

The Americans are band-aiders, and I can say that as an American. They like quick fixes, they like quick highs, they do not like to go down and really have to deal with things. The British do. And I find that it's important to have a cynic, it's important to keep your cynic always with you, in this work as well as everything else. Because a cynic is also your discrimination. It's the part who helps you find the charlatans. The one who helps you say: 'That's not right for me.' I think it's terribly important.

Should school children be taught 'emotional literacy'?

Yes, and I'll tell you something that's happening which is fascinating. In London now there's something called 'A Place to Be'. There's a very fascinating young woman who started this, called Camila Batmanghelidgh, and they go into schools and they have a room in a school that's called 'A Place to Be', and they're bringing counsellors in from all sorts of disciplines to work with children. They find the disturbed children in the school, and send them once a week to work with these counsellors. What they're doing is slowly establishing emotional literacy through that, and I think it's terrific. I'm supervising some of the young counsellors who are doing this, and it's a way of introducing something that is not threatening in a school. It doesn't have to be in the curricula but can be part of what we do to introduce this. I think it's very important.

What are your thoughts about fees?

I have a sliding scale, and the reason I have a sliding scale of fees is because I do not feel that therapy should be class-oriented. So I take ten per cent of my clients for very low fees. By very low fees I mean one to three pounds. Because I never want to be in a situation where I'm only dealing with the rich and the elite. I think that's obscene quite frankly. I understand why people do it, because if you're spending £40,000 getting an education or getting your training, you've somehow got to earn it back.

I also believe, and Masson says that in his book, that there are people who really believe very strongly in what they're doing, and that they're very honest and straightforward, and I don't wish to prejudge them either because I know that there are very many analysts who are very fine people. I don't want it to be a white, Anglo-Saxon, upper/middle-class thing. At the Trust where I work – Psychosynthesis and Education Trust – we have trainees in their last year of training, and they work for clients for low fees. They go out into doctors' practices, they go to various schools, they go to the Royal College of Art, they also take individual clients. They're very well trained, but we have about 25 to 50 every year who are doing low-cost counselling. I, as their trainer, encourage them once they go into practice to continue that, to take ten per cent of their clients as low cost. I feel very strongly about that.

Do you always enjoy what you do?

Always, so far, yes. It's the one thing – I've had a long checkered history and many careers, and it's the one thing I know that I can use all of me in. And I find that extremely gratifying. It's also something that I get better in as I get older. It's something that I feel I'm not going to have to retire, nor do I want to retire. And I think that it's something that you just get better at if you really love it.

CHAPTER 15

Bioenergetics

John Andrew Miller

John Andrew Miller has been leading Bioenergetic workshops since 1982. Co-founder of the Bioenergetic Partnership, London, he also sees individual clients.

How did you get into this business?

Well I'd been living and working in an environment in which there was already a lot of psychotherapy. One of my standard jokes is that the first adult book that I remember as a child is Freud's *Interpretation of Dreams*. I had therapy as a child which was, not just a life-saver, a *sanity* saver. By the time I was in high school, I was seen as the high school playground psychotherapist. When I got to university, I was offered a standard psychology course: chance to do a degree driving mice crazy. I opted for history, thinking that it would get me quite a ways away from psychotherapy. Only to discover when I started lecturing – partially because I was not much older than my students, and partially because I had all this knowledge – that students were gravitating to me to talk about their personal history. My colleagues, and particularly my Head of Department, were noticing this, encouraging it. And I thought that if I was going to be in this position, then I certainly had to be sure that I was knowledgeable about what I was doing.

So I went back into therapy as an adult, and then I had the chance to do some training. I also saw a big gap in the market. There was no place for someone like myself, who was not medically qualified and did not have a degree in psychology, to learn academically about psychotherapy. I floated the idea of a London-based Master of Arts in psychotherapy, which was accepted by Antioch University, Yellow Springs, Ohio USA. I got that degree off the ground and under way, and ran it for six years, during which time the university technically went bankrupt, and we didn't get paid. I was offered another teaching post, teaching counselling skills, and then the pressure of the job was so great, that I was advised by my GP to leave Antioch.

I didn't know what I would do, but clients appeared. From there on, I have mostly been finding ways of combining therapy and academic work on the one hand, and furthering my training on the other.

Can you talk about how your approach differs from Lowen?

Well Lowen is going through a difficult patch. It's rumoured that Freud managed to contradict himself completely in the 23 volumes, and then Bion did it better yet, being able to do it within the covers of one book. And Lowen is also in his old age going full circle.

I think the major difference if we approach the question that way, is that Lowen would believe that he is capable of diagnosing a person from the body, and that the relationship between the therapist and the client isn't very important. I would see that how the relationship is developing between the two of us is important, and if I listen carefully, I'm then able to build on the words that the client uses that are in fact body words, to get a more accurate insight and diagnosis of what is happening in that person, both psychologically and physically. While Lowen was very skilled at what he does, I've seen other people try to ape Lowen, who say: 'ah, see that, or this, or what have you', and the poor client is either dumbfounded or absolutely in awe and feels they have no skill. Whereas I'm much more interested in seeing and building on the skills that the client has, and trying to – almost from the very first session – look at ways in which I'm helping the client to discover the resources which are there already, and empower the client.

Someone I saw today kept using a phrase about not knowing where she stood, or being in a situation in which she felt she didn't have a leg to stand on. Although at first she denied that there might be any connection in the problem she was trying to outline, and how she embodied herself in the world, she kept coming back to leg metaphors, and to talking about how awkward she felt standing up. Let us suppose she comes back for another session, or 'x' number of sessions. It's a fair chance that a lot of the work will be around what she remembers when she did learn to walk, but more importantly what sort of key times was it hard either literally to stand up, or metaphorically to stand up. We will use exercises which will help to strengthen her legs, and try to monitor what changes there might be as she starts to feel more powerful, and feels that she can create a place for herself. She should soon feel she is able to stand up for herself, or put her foot down, or take a stand.

Bioenergetics is unique with its emphasis on the body ...

Yes, although Gestalt would come a close second. And that's not surprising since Reich, the originator of this sort of therapy, had Perls, the originator of Gestalt, in analysis with him in Berlin – I think in 1929. That might be another way of answering your earlier question, that I would be paying attention to how a person habitually uses his or her body. Helping the person to explore what those movements might be expressing, which some people would say is a very Gestalt way of working, instead of merely putting a person through a series of exercises which Lowen has described. So we're back to you moving *your* foot and perhaps exaggerating that, amplifying that, exploring what that might be saying. Are you trying to orchestrate the conversation? Are you finding this boring, and marking time? There could be many different meanings. For me to come in and say to you: 'This is what the meaning is', I don't think helps. But as we explore it, often earlier or at least more emotional material will surface.

To get back to your question: Bioenergetics posits a certain primacy of the body which has earned it its reputation. Lowen and others state 'You are your body.' A well known book is entitled *The Body Reveals*. Bioenergetics is, I think, unique in looking for a correlation between the problem the person brings to work on in therapy and the holding pattern that person exhibits. The therapy certainly believes you can diagnose precisely a person's history and psychological problems by accurate reading of the person's body. Bioenergetic Analysis may also be unique in its mixture of techniques developed both within Bioenergetics and taken from other therapies to promote expression and resolution within a therapy session.

But as I indicated with Gestalt, many other therapies besides Bioenergetics have a body orientation: Transactional Analysis says 'think sphincter' while psychodrama actually mobilises the body. Psychoanalysis gave us the developmental sequence of oral–anal–genital which Lowen has expanded. Like Gestalt, elements of these other therapies have become part of Bioenergetics, frequently reflecting the interest and/or the previous training of the Bioenergetic practitioner.

How precisely do you make the body–mind connection? I mean where is the memory exactly?

I think there are two questions in that. How do I make the connection? and where is the memory held?

We are taught that trauma is held in the musculature of the body. Usually, the contraction is a bodily defence against unacceptable feelings. Sometimes those feelings are forbidden, eroticised feelings; sometimes those feelings are a way of erasing, blocking out memories of humiliating or guilt-ridden or damaging, unacceptable feelings. Frequently, by tightening and forgetting, the client is keeping a memory and a feeling about it quite separate. But while I may have a good idea of what ails the person in front of me, I can never be sure until I explore with my client the process that person might be going through. So again to use you, as you are tightening [back here] are you doing that out of awareness – not being conscious of it in your mind – what happens when it comes into your awareness, when you start to loosen it and move it? But if you follow that through, amplify that, what do you come up with?

Now, a theorist has very much influenced me, one of Lowen's early colleagues, Stanley Kellerman, who keeps saying: 'Well we have a mind to think. And frequently the imagery or the words make sense of what's happening – will have to go through the mind – in order to be understood internally, let alone by somebody else.' I would hope to model using my mind to understand and make sense of a connection between a bodily feeling and a developmental dilemma, hypothesising what the dialogue or the connection might be, and again working for an integration or a reintegration of things that might be separate.

What's the current state of Bioenergetics? I know you're interested in combining it with object-relations ...

Bioenergetics seems to be dividing into different parts, as it becomes more mature. There are people certainly in Europe, and some people along the West coast of America who are very much combining object-relations theory with Bioenergetics, and looking at how a person tightens where there is a failure, or when there has been a failure in the relationship with the primary caretaker. And that by using that knowledge diagnostically, and using knowledge of how you then might work to unstretch, to loosen, it's possible to work very actively, very quickly with a lot of insight – even a lot of excitement.

Lowen himself, now 85, 86, has gone back into his very early (1950s–1960s) way of working which seems to be almost 'hit, kick, and scream and you'll be all right'. This approach worked well at the time because most people coming to him came after a long psychoanalysis, they *understood* everything, they were just aware that they were not happy enough with their lives and something was missing, so he could concentrate on the physical opening because these people had all the mental capabilities of making sense of what came up. Recently Lowen has insisted that mainstream Bioenergetics and mainstream Bioenergetics practitioners follow his movement of back-to-basics.

So you could say that I'm out of the mainstream, because I don't follow that. But I know that I have a number of people both here and in America who are very fascinated by the connection with object-relations. And I certainly think eventually it will not be about how Bioenergetics becomes a very rarefied, purified therapy, but how it makes links with other therapies.

It's not just about trauma, is it?

Well. There's almost no definition of good mental health in Lowen's works, and that is one of the criticisms both within Bioenergetics and from outside Bioenergetics. The one definition that Lowen talks about is 'an easy flow of energy between head, heart, and genitals'. And if you read Lowen's books, basically he is talking about early events – *Betrayal of The Body* is about the schizoid character structure, *Fear Of Life* about the Oedipal character structure, *Narcissism* about the different narcissistic forms of character structure. But almost as if everything is set in place by the age of five or age six.

Now, life goes on after that, and I have done very exciting work looking at the shock states which can happen at any age, but cause a bodily reaction. Thus a sensitive use of Bioenergetics can help a person come out of the shock state. And I think it's possible to work with someone on a very current problem like a marital problem, without necessarily having to make reference to early experience. But the emphasis is, I think, in Bioenergetics, almost too much on trauma, and although the promise is great sexual fulfilment, not a tremendous amount of emphasis is on joy.

You talk about building on people's resources. So do clients do work – homework – between sessions?

I think it is unreal to expect that the therapy can only happen in the therapy session. The people don't have a life outside of therapy? About homework. I tell all my clients to go and take up swimming, because I do a lot of swimming, but as people get more into their bodies, they take up running, or they start doing martial arts and I see very significant changes happen, and I believe that integration – what happens outside the session, inside the session – is very important. I don't think these people feel they're sadistically/masochistically driven to exercise, but as they become more in touch with their body, they're more intent and more content to move their body, breathe more deeply, feel themselves physically and mentally.

A different way of answering your question is that of course people come with different levels of distress, and different levels of intelligence, and different levels of ego strength, and that any good practitioner with any persuasion finds a way of meeting the client where the client is. Jung was a classic example, being one of the foremost Freudians of his time, saying that the first thing he had to decide was whether he gave the person a Freudian analysis or a Jungian analysis. I would go further and say that what's appropriate at one time in a therapy may well cease to be appropriate later, as the person develops. So I would try to meet my client from where the client is, or I would talk about building on the resources which is one of the ways in which I guess I'm trying to get a sense of where the client is – a person who's had a fair amount of therapy, or comes in with a lot of self-knowledge, would be a very different person to work with than someone who may be equally as intelligent and knowledgeable, but may have come in after a quite catastrophic family loss, and can't really draw on those tools.

Are there, generally speaking, people who are more susceptible to Bioenergetics than others?

Well, I've thought a lot about that. I have both personal experience and knowledge of Bioenergetics working very effectively with people who otherwise are supposed to be incapable of psychotherapy, either because they are so mentally ill or inarticulate, or what have you, or obsessive. And

I can think of other times where I've tried very hard to work with some-one, and I haven't found a way of effecting any change. It's not a question I've been able really to answer in the last four weeks since you first asked it. I know if I have a strong reaction to the person, unless I feel I can live with that and try to unpack it, I might refer them elsewhere. I had one client who I'm convinced should have worked with a woman therapist, but she insisted upon working with me. But that's more along what the issues were, than whether that person should have worked in Bioenergetics or not. Perhaps I am saying something about how I work. By nature I'm quite cautious, so that I will very gently bring in a body manifestation, I can feel quite content just to use my body knowledge with someone who's frightened of too much coming up too soon.

Does Bioenergetics – like some other therapies – suggest that you do not work with some people?

I think I am saying that, as I do not work exclusively Bioenergetically, I might be using other skills with a person who would be ill-advised to embark on Bioenergetics. Also, Bioenergetics in what context? I find clients with abuse issues take to Bioenergetic exercise work better in a group than in individual sessions; in those individual sessions, we can explore verbally the material revealed in the group. Psychotic people need very deft handling, so they ground themselves in their own body and start to have a sense of having and controlling their own body. Because I think it's difficult on both sides to decide just on the first meeting whether this is a good enough way to work. I usually suggest that we work together up until the next major holiday – summer, or Christmas, Easter – and as we approach that time, review what's happening and what's working, and what isn't working. And I'm pleased to say most people do stay. But I've had one or two who have left, and I think that was right and wise. There are people who really don't want an insight approach, there are people who are very frightened of what they'll discover, and – that's not to say it's impossible to work with them, but I would rather work *with* my clients than against. And somebody who is very happy to get medication, and a more cognitive, more – I can't remember his name, whoever it was who said 'Every day in every way, I'm getting better and better' [Lennon & McCartney] – more self-hypnosis, positive approach. If that's going to work for them – fine.

How much is your work dependent on knowledge of the body?

It's a difficult tension. I think most of us don't feel we know enough anatomy and physiology. But I think that the positive side of that is that most of us have done a lot of reading in anatomy and physiology. Most of us, certainly in the group that I knew, went out and did life-drawing classes. I'm constantly reading books and articles about how the body works, and how there might be a psychosomatic correlation.

And the training is getting better. Because again there's a historical background, that most people originally training to be Bioenergetic therapists did it as a second training, usually after medical training. So that it was assumed that they knew about all these things, whereas increasingly as there are non-medical practitioners, people don't come in with that knowledge. In Europe the emphasis is much more on the psychodynamic relational aspects, and how the client might be telling you things that talk about his relationship with you, even if using body terms, so the anatomy and physiology aspects may be less important. When you say to me you know all sorts of things about the spine, I'm also aware of all the things I don't know, and need to know. Training is a lifelong experience. Each person comes in and challenges you to learn more. Each session provides a constant tension between the physical aspects and the verbal aspects, the somatic aspects and the psychodynamic aspects.

What happens when someone comes to see you?

At the first interview, I ask them to talk about themselves, and then try to make some connection between what they're telling me and what I notice in their body. Particularly if there's time, I will try to do some simple bodywork, both so that they have some idea what they're getting into, and I get a sense of how we're working. So that I might suggest they lie down and work on their breathing, and then see how they react if there is touch. Because it's much easier to work Bioenergetically if there is physical contact, and not everyone feels easy enough about that. I'll try to find out if there's any medical history. And another way in which I might be different, is that I actually ask them if they've come with any questions about me, or about how I might work. Sometimes those are uncomfortable questions, but I think it's quite important to allow that to come out, because it's an almost untainted time. I'm sure there'll be transferential issues behind the issues, but there isn't yet the strong psychodynamics between us.

Assuming the person comes back, and is in some sort of crisis, they're likely to come in and start talking about that crisis. Should they get a divorce? Are they homosexual? What to do about a dyslexic child? Most people come in with a problem on their mind, and that to my mind needs attending to before any of the more basic reconstructive work can take place. Sometimes people come because they are just very depressed or very low, or they know they have ME and they don't know what might be behind that psychologically. Then often I'll be very – if you want – traditional, try to get as much family history, as much medical history as I can. Sometimes we use drawings or time-lines to see if they're repeating patterns.

Now in classical Bioenergetics, as I understand it, you wouldn't pay any attention to that. You might have them to start out, doing some standing grounding exercises, or hitting the bed with a tennis racket, and occasionally that's right for some people to start with.

Then I think the art of Bioenergetics is figuring out what point to start bringing in a physical expression of what's going on behind – often that's because some part of them isn't moving, or conversely some part of them is being repeated. A person who just sits there and is drawing their forefinger down the side of their eye, is talking about some sort of sadness, or some expression that needs to come out through the eyes. And it's possible then to build on that. Frequently, for example, the depression's about the loss of someone. So talking about the distance between the two of us – what feelings of loss they might have between sessions, and then trying to not so much act out, but act in what it's like going out the door, or what it's like when we're on different sides of the room. Again that helps to get into deeper feelings, and often more rapidly. I think sometimes it's at that point that people choose to stop, not that there have been very many, but the reality dawns that there's something just quite colossal that has to be faced, and they're unwilling to face it, or I'm not skilled enough in finding a way that seems safe to face it. Termination, however, happens rarely.

The usual problem of Bioenergetics is that people are overwhelmed by feelings. It isn't that not enough is coming up, it's that too much is coming up. And that's the other part of the art, because of course what to me may seem very small, and not overwhelming at all, may seem far too much for other people.

Are things coming up because of the breathing work?

Well, the general loosening of the body. But having said that, people loosen in a variety of ways, and for a variety of reasons. The fact that somebody else is there attending to them may be as much at work as anything else, because I know all the classical Bioenergetic standing, hitting, breathing can also cause the client to tighten, not loosen. That's where I think other forms of therapy are also effective, particularly psychoanalysis. If a person feels really held by the analyst, they can start to loosen, they don't have to hold themselves together. In France in particular, the psychoanalysts are doing marvellous things in terms of correlating body manifestations with body presentation, or the psycho-analytic concepts. Lowen wouldn't buy that, but it's true.

You ask what happens when we move on. I try to notice changes in people's bodies. Are they losing weight, are they looking less haggard, is their hair/skin colour more vibrant? At some point I will either hear or I will ask: 'Are people saying anything to you about how you're looking different?' And I'll hear: 'Oh, yeah. My boss said today how much more assertive I am', or 'I saw a friend for the first time in a month and he said "my you're walking tall".' Trying to see whether from the environment there are mirrors back talking about how a person's becoming more vibrant in their body. Now some of that helps me to know if I'm on track. Clearly some of that re-inforces the person in the therapy – that it is also happening, it's not made up. The real therapy doesn't happen just in here, it's happening outside.

I think as we work on, a few things happen. One of which is that the basic problem might become more focused and more defined, and another might be that the person stops needing to talk about one topic, and will temporarily feel very stuck. Often, the stuckness seems to mean the client is moving into a newer, often deeper area. During that period it might be that we do much more bodywork, much less talking work. Or sometimes it's at that point that people will go and start having regular massage or Alexander technique, or take up a new sport.

I have my pet theories. Most of us have about three important layers to work through. And sometimes you do that with one therapist, and sometimes you might do it with a number of different therapists over a number of different years. I used to think that Bioenergetics was a very quick therapy, but either because I've changed, or I know more, or I'm more skilled, now people are tending to stay longer, and tending to want to work through different levels with me.

It's hard to say how people end. One person just stopped because of a study commitment abroad, but also seemed ready. He went from looking like a prepubescent person, to looking like a man; he started to stand up to his father, and point out the unhealthy dynamics in the family. Yet I think he would happily continue in therapy with me if still in this country.

Sometimes the therapy brings about a divorce, and that brings about financial problems, or emotional problems, and people stop. Generally the endings tend to be when people feel they're well enough to be their own therapist. That would seem to have nothing to do with Bioenergetics. You could be in that place in any therapy.

Some therapists encourage patients to linger on ...

Sure. And some Bioenergetic therapists would say that a person could not leave until they have a perfect orgasm. I would always like to think people leave because their sex-life is better, but it seems to me there's much more to life than just that. I'm happy when someone leaves because they've got a new job, and feel they have the skills to manage that job – it's a challenge, it's not a crisis. Or they've had a few times of coping well with problems with their adolescent son, and they feel that next time they will be able to do it on their own. Often people *do* report that their relationships are better, or more likely they report that their relationships are more alive. When the fighting was going on, the fighting seemed really dreadful, but when things are good, they feel really good. I ask that people take at least a month, and usually longer, to finish up. I also invite people to come back or drop a line or what have you. I know some therapists feel that when it's finished, it's over; never come back. But I've actually had some people come back and do really excellent work having spent a year, two years on their own, piecing together – continuing to be their own therapist – piecing together things about themselves, and discovering some important piece of the puzzle which they needed or wanted to come back and work on.

Now also it would seem to me not very specifically Bioenergetic, except that Lowen originally worked in a very odd way – sometimes seeing a client twice in one day, and then not seeing them for a month. The reality for me is that sometimes it's important for a person to come back or drop a line, and I too am human; I enjoy hearing that someone is getting on well, or that a problem which seemed so insurmountable has been overcome.

Presumably you don't look forward to hearing from all your ex-clients?

Sometimes people go, and you know you'll never hear from them, or you think: 'I don't want to hear from them.' But I think the art of therapy is in the countertransference, and my best people, the best work I think has often been with people who I haven't liked – you know we all like some things and not like some others – and I have had to try to unpack what it is that I don't like, believing I reflect what other people in this client's life also don't like.

Is there a danger in noticing too much the transferential aspects, and ignoring their problems?

I think it doesn't work that way, Bob. I think that a person says something, and I'm aware of either a mental or (often) a physical reaction, and then it's my job to try to make sense of that and find a way to bring it back into the session. So that one person goes out and another comes in, and I immediately have a headache, I need to know what that's about. Then I might listen and hear that of course, this is what the husband's always complaining about, and having a sense that something happens almost at a somatic level which is also happening here.

Maybe the answer to your question is to say that transferential aspects often do link up with, or help to understand, the presenting problem(s). My partner uses the example of a piece of fruit: for her, problems are like the skin of an orange, which you have to peel away to get at the pithy bits, the more difficult, fragile, but rewarding bits.

I think it does help if you like your clients, and generally speaking I do like my clients. But more important is to be attentive to what's going on, and to allow a whole gamut of feelings, and to work on the feelings – if I feel really positive about a client and I'm looking forward to seeing that person, there is information there which may be as important to unpack as with a client I can't really face. But because I'm contracted to face, I face. And that first client might be very seductive, may be playing some number on me that he or she plays on other people in their lives. It's a good distancing technique to be all sort of surface and lovely, and warm, and beautiful, and not let any of your inside out, because it's too dangerous.

But transference does not 'have to happen' in Bioenergetics ...

Certainly that was the 'old-time' approach, and it was even implied at the last international Bioenergetics conference, that transference does not occur in this sort of therapy. I see it differently. I think transferential things do take place – countertransferential things may take place – the difference in Bioenergetics is the expectation and the knowledge that it will also happen on a body level, and how to use it. Then also how to use body understanding, bodily exercises to explore it.

Can you talk a little about the cathartic aspects to Bioenergetics? Are such aspects still central?

Of course a place still exists for the very expressive work in Bioenergetics. I am not sure all expression leads to catharsis, and I think catharsis without understanding means at best temporary relief. But yes, catharsis through expression can be a goal. As you can see, this is a steel tennis racket here and two large cushions. As I said earlier, when Lowen started he had mostly people who had been through successful psychoanalysis, and who felt that there was something quite important missing in their lives. So these were fairly rigid, fairly well defended people who had been in analysis presumably, certainly historically it was likely, with mostly refugees from Nazi Germany who had congregated in New York. Who had had to find their own coping mechanisms to set up in the midst of the Depression and in the midst of the War, at a time when America itself, in the post-war era, was very rigid and very defended. So that these people got an analysis which helped them to become very rigid and very defended. Some psychoanalytic texts would say that a person who is well defended is a healthy person. So much of the early Bioenergetic work was about loosening these defences and working on this rigidity.

And the 'hit, kick, and scream' era of Bioenergetics which is well known, well publicised through the movie *WR: Mysteries of the Orgasm*, that highlighted the cathartic end of the spectrum. But 30 years later, different people are coming forward, with different problems coming out of a different culture, and we're back to asking what is the art of therapy? It's about matching what is right for the person at the time, so that sometimes it might be the same exercise but for different reasons – the person who was here before you was talking a lot about being hard-hearted, and being unable to have a loving relationship – and *you* come in with that curvature, with that, I would say almost, collapse in you. For both of you some work on the ball, a large gymnastic ball behind my chair, would help you to open this area. But I imagine that the histories which would come out would be different. The person

might follow you – might have great difficulties in standing up for him-
or herself. This person might be better served by a whole different
range of exercise to get in touch with the legs and the power in the
legs. Frequently after a period of time, people themselves have some
idea of how they need to work and what they need to work on. And
instead of being very Lowenian and saying 'Do this', I'll try to elicit
from the person the way they feel they need to work, and then we're
back and forth: 'Well if we change this, what happens?' I like that
creative aspect of working with someone.

*If someone has nothing to report do you, the therapist, take charge of the
session?*

This I think is one of the greatest difficulties about Bioenergetic training, which is that it has been very much the 'expert knows' approach,
which we talked about earlier. It's hard to match that with a much
more analytic, 'allowing to emerge' approach. Will I take charge?
Maybe. [Laughs] It's really hard to say. Some of it will depend on what
I know of the client. What has happened in the last session/sessions.
What I'm unlikely to do is take charge and run through a series of
exercises just because that's what I think is right, but I might more talk
about, and try to unpack why there might be silence, or not talking, or
what might we do. But control is always a big question. Because no-one
wants to be out of control, and no-one wants to be over-controlled.

Are some clients reluctant to be touched, and is that necessarily problematic?

The first part of that question is easy to answer – 'Yes'. The second
is more difficult. I certainly have been challenged by working with
touch-phobic people. I developed all sorts of new techniques, because
I've had to develop them, in which they do the hands-on work. But
as a result, I think – in teaching and in running groups – I've become
much better. I think touch is such a basic means of human communication. Something is lost in not touching. Had some of these touch-
phobic people stayed a long period of time, perhaps we'd have got
more into why they couldn't be touched; what might have been an
underlying wish to be touched, from the fear of being touched in a
certain place, or a certain way.
   Clients also get touched in many other ways, through the voice,
through the eyes, through the quality that the therapist's body models,
being relaxed or tense. We put a lot of emphasis on eye contact and
allowing expression through the eyes.
   You go from where the client is. And certainly where I part company
with Lowen is that for me it's important that I feel I'm respecting the
other person, the other person's bodily integrity. It's also important to
me that they feel they are respected, so if a client says 'No touch', then
I do not touch.

You talked about people's overpowering feelings. Presumably a Bioenergetic therapist really has to know how to handle such things ...

I agree that you do have to know. I monitor a client's breathing in case of hyperventilation, which usually denotes panic and can often lead to panic. A few clients have shown a tendency to hurt themselves doing hitting or kicking work, so I need to watch for that. A common problem for beginning therapists is knowing how to do a small amount of Bioenergetic work in a session, not a lot. For the dilemma centres on stimulating enough but not too much – both therapist and client want enough to happen in a session so as to advance understanding, deepen feeling, and have that 'yeast' that will continue to ferment between sessions. Two things help me here: supervision and an idea of safety. I think that it's alas almost impossible to know everything that you need to know, and for me that's why I get a lot of supervision. I learnt from my training analyst that you always respond to a telephone call if asked to ring back, you always let the client know that you are there. That provides safety for people who've discovered a lot about themselves, and perhaps too fast and furious. In the day-group we run, the group has been creating the safety. I can think of one situation where members of the group stayed with a person for a long time after the Saturday group was over, and that eventually one person actually delivered her home, and then in the intervening weeks before the next meeting, different people rang up and made sure she was okay – certainly the period from the group until she got to her own therapist.

I think that's – I don't mean it to sound dismissive – but I think that's about as much as you can do. The common fault in Bioenergetics – beginning Bioenergetics practitioners – and where it has got its reputation is that it has been fanning the flames and urging people to go on and on, and do more and more. Originally I thought there was a lot to that. But in my old age I do actually think that checking out with people what's happening, and whether they feel they could or should go deeper, or sometimes just set in place, hopefully I think this is where we need to stop for the while. It's very important. And it's particularly important in an individual session where judging the amount of time left, and how much more can come up versus how much more has to be tapped out is important. I have been accused of looking at my clock about every 30 seconds. I think it is a gross exaggeration, but it is true that if a person is deeply into a process, I have to allow enough time for him/her to come out, so the session ends on time. And that part of the sense of safety comes over a period of time, of knowing that that's possible. Again it may seem that there's little to do, but we have a waiting room, a place for people to take coffee or tea. And I will often say to them: 'You need to spend some time quietly before you go off, you cannot just end the session here, even though we have ended, and go off in your car, or on to the Tube.'

Can we talk about the economics and time of therapy ...

If I had my perfect world, I would see each client two or three times a week for an hour-and-a-half session. Not many people can manage that financially or timewise, and some people do come for a standard 50-minute 'hour'. The economics of it are difficult in the sense that I know that I'm going to want to earn a good-enough living, so that I'm not worried about money and I am able to have some enjoyment of my own life. On the other hand, pricing oneself so high that only a certain strata of people can come isn't very good. Although usually if someone comes and is unable to pay a lot of money, I will put a lot of effort in trying to find someone who is just starting out, or might be attached to a clinic. How much work do I do in a week? I try to balance my work-load. Over the last few years I've been working with Metanoia as their academic co-ordinator, piloting three of their training diplomas to accreditation as Masters of Science degrees. I'm involved as postgraduate co-ordinator of the Association for Group and Individual Psychotherapy. I hope this other work provides some balance. And I swim almost every day, and usually walk as much of the way here as I can afford timewise. I certainly try to monitor the amount of hours that I work a week. I put it that way, because if a person is in crisis, it's often impossible to say: 'No, I won't see you because I'm going over my hours.' And during the recession, it's been tempting to work a slightly greater number of hours, because people might have to leave. Therapists are very bad at taking care of themselves, because they're so busy taking care of other people, and I sometimes wonder about that with myself.

Do you keep records?

Yes. I always take notes of the first session. I usually will go through a period of taking some notes on each client and rather the way Joyce McDougal does, if I'm stuck with a client, I'll start taking notes about them. I myself have not been very happy with note-taking, for usually I go back over the notes, and either they don't relate as much as I would like to the session, or the client has moved on and the next time the notes don't seem to be terribly related. Plus it's very difficult to work with a person both physically and verbally, and get it all down in note form.

Registration, the UKCP ... will it stop innovation?

Well there are different ways of answering that, as always. There are other organisations such as Chiron – a centre for Bioenergy – which do have a body approach. More significantly the only reason that the British Institute for Bioenergetic Analysis, or under its current name, the British Institute for Analytical Body Psychotherapy, did not become a member of the UKCP was that it didn't have enough members – you had to have 30 members, and they were short of that number. But otherwise, the Committee was very happy to have Bioenergetics become part of it.

... innovation ...

I think that's a worry. There are a couple of parallels. There was a time when in order to become a doctor you didn't have to go to medical school and in order to drive you just bought a car. I think none of us would now go to a doctor who hadn't been through medical school, and got medical training. Clearly there's no guarantee that the doctor would be good, but nonetheless we do all look for some sort of quality assurance. And I think most of us think that it's a good idea that people are tested and licensed to run cars. The question is whether the UKCP will stifle creativity, and that I don't know. I don't think it will *necessarily* do that; I think it's more likely to make it more difficult to set up new training programmes. But there are arguably too many training programmes anyway. New approaches of working with people could be incorporated through existing training programmes, and existing training organisations. That's not to say that they will. Some would say it is unlikely, but it is possible!

From the other side, I have been involved where some therapists were demonstrably being unprofessional about how they practised, and that's not a happy situation either.

Is it a precondition for a therapist to have been 'hurt' themselves?

I think originally for sure, because there was such a stigma attached to being a therapist, and being in therapy. These days I would imagine there are people who come into the field just out of interest, and yet most people have had some insult to their integrity, so that you would be hard put to find a person who doesn't have something to work on. I think Jung's idea of the wounded healer is still quite valid. I'm inclined to think that certainly the people I have as supervisees who are practitioners or training to be practitioners, certainly have ample stuff, ample hurt, to work on.

You appear very confident about what you do ...

Well. Confident up to a point. This person I mentioned earlier who moved out of the country used a really lovely analogy: it was like I had taught him to ride a bicycle with the side wheels on. He imagined – and I think he's quite right – that there's quite a lot more for him to work on, and probably he will go back into therapy in the country he's going to. And this time it'll be like learning to ride a bicycle without the side wheels. I know that people can teach themselves to ride a bicycle, or teach themselves to swim or what have you. But I also know that often somebody else being there providing the side wheels, helps.

I think complacency and dogma provide the greatest obstacles in psychotherapy, and I certainly review my work, both by reading and by supervision and talking about it with my partner, and trying to be undogmatic. I'm certainly happy when things go well for my clients, and I'd like to think I have a part in that. I'm also aware that our lives are so complex it's unlikely to be one single person, one single factor. What concerns me in terms of the 'outcome studies' is not so much how the person feels immediately after leaving therapy, but how they are in about four or five years time. I suppose that's one reason why when I do hear from a client who left long ago, I am pleased because it's one of the few bits of feedback that I have.

What qualities are necessary for a therapist to possess?

This gets back to your earlier question about 'are therapists made by their environment to look at themselves, so they then become therapists to help other people?' I think you do have to have a lot of curiosity and imagination about other people and it probably helps if you like people. I think by extension you need a lot of curiosity about yourself. I imagine there's quite a mixture of healthy and pathological narcissism, and hopefully the balance changes. An ability to work on your own. An ability to work, often without any results for a long period of time. That might be another reason why I try to get some idea from clients what their other people are telling them, different things about themselves. Lastly, another quality: something about being able to get very deeply emotionally involved, while being able still to think, and then to be able to cut off.

Controlled emotional involvement?

Yes. And something about being able to apply what you do for other people to yourself. Which I think is where a lot of people come apart.

Can you elaborate?

Well. When I find myself in committee meetings weekend after week-end, and telling my clients about how they have to create some time for themselves to read or be with their children, or play with their dog, I'm aware of the dichotomy. And there's the paradox, that if you're good in the field, you're then in a position where it's often impossible or very difficult to say 'No'. You're telling people all the time to create bounda-ries, but it's very hard to maintain your own boundaries.

Is 'therapy' increasingly more acceptable – so much so that it's an 'educa-tional' venture for some?

[Laughs] I think in answer to the first part, 'Yes', there's a perceptible acceptance of therapy, and there clearly has also been a perceptible criticism of therapy. I think people are more aware that not every therapy and every therapist works. But that already says something about more familiarity. And possibly some disillusionment about therapy as not a panacea. It is often hard work. Therapy is still not always accepted: just a day or two ago, some new person was saying how she wanted to come, but she'd have to be very careful because in the London business world, if anyone knows you're in therapy, you're a marked woman.

Are people getting healthier and coming more for education, or getting less healthy? That's a more difficult one to answer, because I think people have higher expectations. People then imagine things have happened. I've a colleague who went on and on about how she wasn't breast fed, and how this was the cause of all her problems. Turned out she was the only child in her family who *was*, and the whole drama of not being breast fed was in her mind, based on her being the eldest and seeing what happened with the others.

I have many colleagues more senior to me, who say people are more ill. What seems to me to make more sense is that we live in a more mechanical world. There clearly are people who have never experienced life without the television, or, now, without a computer. And of course human relations do not just happen at the press of a button. And, as I said, there's something about people having greater expectations, but feeling also greater loss. Now does that make them more ill? I don't know. I would like to think parenting has become better. And what we do know is, over the century that psychotherapy has been in existence, that different ages, different presenting problems, are in the forefront. People have greater awareness of what is possible, and I think more questioning of false societal values. Certainly what has changed, is that people feel more able to explore things that otherwise would have been dismissed as just impossible, like sexual abuse – by a vicar, or by a mother, or what have you – and that while some people certainly dream it up or put two and two together and get five, there are times, when dealing with this area, that these things did actually happen. Or there is enough of a reality that it's impacting on how a person relates today. Are they more ill because there's more awareness, or life is so much more complex? We could say they're saner because they're able to bring it in and talk about it.

CHAPTER 16

Groupwork

Anne Geraghty

Anne Geraghty has worked both as a clinical and educational psychologist, and has run workshops worldwide. Currently she practises from the Amap Organisation, London, which she co-founded.

Can you talk a little about how you became a therapist?

Well I've had two different strands of my life that came together really. One was doing a psychology degree and then research for a PhD in developmental psychology. Later I worked in child guidance with Family Therapy, and play therapy as an educational psychologist. I was very young and inexperienced in working with children, and I found it hard to deal with the extent of their suffering, and powerless. It was very painful. So then I decided I needed to work with adults, because that's where the source of the problem seemed to be. I did an MSc in clinical psychology and I worked within the psychiatric departments of psychiatric hospitals.

Meanwhile the other strand was my 'spiritual-political' consciousness, which started with looking at the suffering of the world, and assuming that it was because of capitalism and the oppression of the working class, and people's alienation from the fruits of their labour. Later this then moved into a feminist perspective – the 'personal is political' – which involved my developing ways in which we could use therapy and the processes of therapy to examine the internalisation of our patriarchal oppression. That it wasn't sufficient just to change the external material, it was necessary that we looked at our internal conditioning, etc. That then took me on a journey which involved my exploring all the latest developments in therapy (this was in the early '70s), so it was looking at the things that were coming from Esalen and America. And in those days somebody would come over and run a group in the latest technique, and then the next week we'd run a group in it. It was very free-flowing, experimental – looking back I'd probably be horrified – but at the time it was very creative, playing with our political understandings as well. That linked in with, more and more, the work that I was doing within psychiatry. It became more and more difficult for me to marry the two. At that point I then left the NHS and started to set up private ways of working with people that was outside that kind of psychiatric system.

So I'm just describing the two strands that then came together. Well actually, no, they didn't come together then, but they've come together since. So I had both sides of me. What happened was that I then began to try and introduce some of the humanistic psychology techniques into psychiatric units in hospitals. But of course it was difficult – the limitations, the fear of the institutions, the whole conceptualisation of people's unhappiness as an illness made this marriage that I was trying to bring about impossible. Meanwhile I was going deeper and deeper into my own exploration about what it was to be a woman in this culture, because I was very feminist at that time – and also what it meant to be a human being in a culture such as this, which did severely limit our capacity for creativity, pleasure, joy. So what did that mean for me personally as well in my relationships? At the time, it was learning how our personal relationships had a political dimension. That they weren't separate from the institutions of society, they were actually an intrinsic part. What happens in the family is a mirror of what happens in society, and that is the primary learning that we go through – it often happens first in the family. This is very deep and painful stuff to start finding out about. This was the early '70s, mid-'70s by now probably. What happened to me was a growing recognition that this revolution which I'd so blithely talked about in 1968 actually meant a revolution of the self, in terms of my conception of self and who I am. In other words who and what I am is vastly different from what I think I am. And that meant deeper and deeper explorations into this.

Can you elaborate on the 'self' ...

The self, *me*. For example as I grew up, my understanding of who I am evolved out of my responses to what was happening around me. I learned – that everyone's unique. I then learned to hide, kill off, bury certain parts of me because they were not meant to be – especially being brought up as a traditional Catholic – and other parts of me were encouraged. I would therefore put a lot of energy into developing those parts. Then I became identified with the selves that had been permitted to live. In other words, my survival techniques had involved my killing off certain parts of me, or at least burying them, denying them. And then I became identified with those parts that are allowed, and I think and believe that this is who I am.

So the discovery of the full truth of who I am is a long and sometimes painful process. All therapists will say that. It involves not just looking at what happened in my family, but what happens in society. School, the institutions and the structures that create what we think of as reality.

So at this point I experimented with LSD and other psychotropic drugs, hopefully to penetrate the very nature of reality itself, or what I thought was reality, because again the reality of who I was was revealing itself to be much greater and more complex than I had imagined. That eventually took me to the East because the eastern traditions have

a different way of examining the self, which begins from the point that
what we experience as reality is false. They begin in a way from the
other end of the spectrum and then journey that way into a recognition
of the self as the self that is eternal, that is beyond form, that exists
outside time, that is your original face, that is your true nature, that is
the source of your being, it is the god within, and that this self is
independent of the society, the family, the attachments, the desires, the
to-ing and fro-ing of daily life.

   I started trying to find that, having started from thinking I am this, and
finding out that the this is actually much, much more than I thought it
was. I went to India and explored meditation and the discovery of the self
using meditation – and, as you know, I went to the Rajneesh Ashram, in
Pune, this was in the mid-'70s. Here there was a synthesis of the eastern
techniques of meditation and the Western processes of self-exploration,
psychotherapy. And the other thing that was tapped into there was the
power of the *group*.

   So you had three things going on there, and it was a very, very
intense, powerful, creative and energetically alive place to be. It used
meditation, techniques of psychotherapy, and the power of the group
energy. The whole is more than the sum of the parts – you get a group
of people together, something gets created that's more than the sum of
the individuals. Jesus said something: 'When two or more are gathered
together – there I am.' And as I understood it, the 'I' of that 'I am' is
something of which we are all part, yet which is greater than us. In
Pune this was then projected on to Bhagwan [Shree Rajneesh]. And we
needed a figure, probably to generate it. I think you often do initially.
Though now we need to get away from this projection and claim it for
ourselves.

How would you describe what you do these days?

Well I think that one of the primary themes is empowerment of the
individual. That's a reflection of several different things, and it's reflected
in the different things that we do. I am now the director of the Amap
Organisation, which is a group of 14 therapists who work in different ways
involving the body, heart, mind and soul. We are also attempting to work
together as a group in ways that recognise both our separate unique
individuality *and* our interdependance and the power of the group. We
organise workshops, courses and trainings in counselling, bodywork,
group dynamics, etc. The trainings involve understanding, experiential
exploration, practical learning, which are ways in which people are then
empowered to communicate more effectively, create their own lives,
develop a profession. It also gives them the chance to start to trust themselves, listen to their own truth, feel their own uniqueness. And that's one
of the things that I think is very important for me, and the whole place:
that people can come here – anyone – and feel welcome. It isn't just for a
particular sub-group, and that every single person's individual uniqueness

is respected. Virginia Satir did research into family dynamics, and she observed that one of the most frequently found dynamics in what she called 'dysfunctional families' was that the uniqueness of the children wasn't recognised.

So this is a very key thing, because as soon as you're willing to recognise that each person is unique, then you can no longer claim any authority over them, you no longer know what's right for them. You can listen to them and you can offer your experience, but ultimately their uniqueness gives them their own sacred space – that it's theirs and theirs alone – and that they alone ultimately have the authority on their lives. And that within them will be the only place that they can find their truth.

One is recognising people's uniqueness, which is empowering, and the other is that what *is*, is greater than what we might want, or think, or hope, or whatever else. That whatever is happening will show us what's needed, and that there's no need to be different. If you have a goal for therapy, for example, to get more in touch with your feelings, to get more loving, to be more open, to be more assertive, to get less hostile or whatever – if you set up such a goal, then those parts of us that don't fit into that goal either get killed, or denied, or hurt, or pushed away in some way. So that actually you are interfering with the truth of yourself, and your clients and limiting what can be expressed, or be lived. You are also often repeating in a different form the repressive conditioning of your childhood, the legacy of which brings us to therapy in the first place.

So instead of having a goal which has a particular form to it, the goal must be to find out about who you are, just to encourage this unique piece of life to reveal itself and be lived in its fullness. And there's a mystery in this and an aliveness that's greater than anything that my hopes and fears might tell me I need. I feel that this is extremely important. I think it's one of the big mistakes that I certainly have made, and that a lot of therapists make, which is that therapy is some kind of mechanistic tool to fix us into the way in which we should be, rather than a process of self-discovery which has an unknown aspect to it. An open-minded enquiry involves a kind of surrender to the truth of what I am. I definitely went into therapy thinking: 'I need to be different, there's something wrong with me, there's something damaged. I've got to put it right. And what is wrong with me is this ...' And as I went on through my therapeutic process, what I thought was wrong with me kept changing, but there was always something wrong with me that I had to work on, to fix, until eventually I realised that I was *me*, and I would always be me, and I was going to be me however much I might wish it were different. I was going to be me until the day I died, however much I might wish to be different, better, more whole, wiser, etc.

This level of surrender to the truth of who I am, paradoxically enabled a process to happen which was what I was looking for by trying to be different. An ease and relaxation arrived.

What ideas lie behind your work?

Well the ideas that inform Amap are in one way a reflection of my own journey which has taken me through so many different processes, that my own understanding has evolved by digesting different things from different places. So we are a very eclectic mix of the humanistic tradition, psychodrama and the work of Moreno, person-centred Rogerian counselling, Reichian bodywork, and approaches such as Gestalt, voice dialogue, inner-child work, primal, encounter, art therapy. In our trainings, for example, we actually cover a very broad framework, and the onus is on the individual to digest all these different theories, these different processes, and find out what resonates for them as having a meaning and a truth. So that when they're working with their clients, they are aligned within it. So we don't say: 'This is the way to do it', although actually I myself teach the Rogerian client-centred part of the counselling training, because I feel that's very, very deep stuff. Although I think it's often misunderstood. It's about being with what is and letting that show you the next step. So it's a very deep process. It's what I was talking about earlier.

However, we also have someone who teaches the psychodynamic work and looks at the whole psychodynamic school of thought. Again, as I see it, everything in life seems to have two sides, and there are limitations to some processes, theories, practices, and there are creative aspects to it. If you make both those sides available, different individuals will respond to what suits them.

You see individuals too, don't you?

Yes. On a one-to-one basis, everyone who comes has an initial consultation, and that at the moment is with me, because I've got the overall view of everybody and what they do, and I've got a good feel of that. So I sit with them for an hour and find out whatever they're willing to share in that one session, about what's happening now, what may have happened in the past, what they're looking for, what they need, and also what will be the kind of language that they will communicate in, and what kind of processes will help them best. That may be bodywork, Gestalt work, primal work. It may be one or two sessions, it may be ongoing psychotherapy, it may be a mixture of bodywork/counselling, it may be voice and movement work, it may be one of the groups we do – for example, a women's support group – it may be any one of these things. Sometimes it may take more than one session to find out – but usually one's enough – what they need. Then we draw up a programme of sessions or groups that meets what they're looking for.

Again, I listen to the individual, I'm not imposing a particular framework on to them. I'm listening to them – what is it that *they* need? – and I'm asking them to see if they can articulate to me what it is that they need. What it is that – it's somewhere in them and they will know it – what it is that's going to help them. For example, financially, some people can't afford very much, so that's part of the picture too. We have scholarships on the courses and we have sliding scales with fees. So it's again very responsive to the unique needs of that particular individual.

Can you talk more about your one-to-one work?

Well, the way in which I work very much involves all the different things that I've accumulated as I've gone through my journey. I will listen to what is happening, and as we sit there together two things are happening: one is the relationship that develops, which is the vessel in which the healing, and the growth, and the realisations are going to arise. So one thing is the nature of this relationship, and the other is the processes that help us, and particularly the client, to meet the truth. Because once you meet the truth of yourself, then the next step that you either need or want will quite naturally, organically be here. So that's the two and to that end I might use anything. I might use Gestalt, or voice dialogue, we might sit in silence. I'm going to share some of the truth of me. I might say: 'I'm feeling there's something here. I don't know what it is; I'm feeling a bit uncomfortable, are you feeling that?' So there's an honesty in the communication.

You interpret ...

Yes. This has to be done carefully, because if I'm going to start bringing in my own intuitions and feelings, then it has to be done very carefully, otherwise I might just be indulging myself or totally projecting on to them. Because what this approach says is basically you have two human beings here. Some of what will be happening will be a mirror of a childhood pattern, with a parent figure and a child, and the vulnerabilities of the person will be mirroring the vulnerability, and helplessness, and pain they had as a child, and their various protection systems. Some of what is happening is two human beings as equals, struggling together to see if we can reach understanding and manage to communicate. And some of what is happening is two people who don't know what's going on, and are completely helpless in the face of something far greater than either of them, part of a mystery of which we know nothing.

So even in this one relationship there are many aspects to it. And of course there's the hidden aspect which is the inner child in me, and the projections of parent on to the client. So there are many dimensions. In a way, what I'm saying is that the river of what's happening will flow through all of these. If I'm committed to attempting to become conscious of all of these, then I'm going to use a variety of techniques. Some of which wouldn't be appropriate in other situations with that same person.

For example, if we're exploring an aspect of the person that is very vulnerable, feels afraid and abandoned, I may in that exploration be very warm, holding and supportive. But there may be another exploration where they need a lot of impersonal distance so that they can come freely through their own process alone, and I'm going to be a much more detached and impersonal presence, a witness. So of course this puts a lot of onus on the therapist to act with great professional integrity, and really be committed to their own self-exploration, and to develop the ability to be aware of their own truth, in that moment as well.

So it's a lot of responsibility for the therapist. When Freud was first creating psychoanalysis, they were all on each other's couches, bringing out this stuff, the first time ever in human culture so it was extremely intense to say: 'I hate my father.' Up until that point you never said that – it wasn't allowed, it didn't exist. Well it did, but it was hidden. Out it comes and it's so energetically powerful. They were all on each other's couches, and were psychoanalysing each other – boundaries, contracts didn't exist. It was a hot-house; powerful, incredible, revolutionary – it was really pushing back the boundaries of human consciousness. They didn't have all the built-in safety systems that we now have. A lot of them have evolved to stop what is very often an abuse of power. Because a therapist has tremendous power. So a lot of systems have evolved to protect the client from that abuse of power. And it is needed.

What I am suggesting is that instead of creating a particular technique which protects the client, the sincerity and commitment of the therapist can be the protection. But like any process which has a tremendous power to heal, there's also going to be a tremendous potential for harm.

Transference, countertransference ...

I think they do occur, and I think they occurred in Freud's day very intensely. But I think at that time the repressed conflicts from childhood, and the fears and hostilities that had to be – in order to be civilised – denied, are now more readily available as part of our normal cultural exchange. So that in our sexual relationships we share our feelings of shame, and fear, and hostility. In our art we express that darker side. I think we've got too attached to it now as a culture. In our culture now, that expression of the instinctual chaos has got channels, it's out in the open. Therefore the intensity of the transference is very, very much less now in therapy. Where it happens the most intensely is in our sexual relationships. And that is where the transference now is, and that's why sexual relationships now have such a potential to heal and wound. Because that's where we bond and the instinctual urges emerge, and more powerfully, because you're naked skin to naked skin, holding, you're making love, you're touching, so that what gets woken up are those primal energies that had to be sacrificed to enter society. The transference that happens in a therapeutic relationship is now a pale shadow of what happened in Freud's day, and as a result I think the nature of the therapeutic relationship, one-to-one, has also shifted to include – yes to acknowledge that there are the aspects of transference happening, and countertransference – but that there are also other dimensions happening. Two people both of whom have suffered and are struggling. Two people with existential anxiety. Two equals. So I think that has to be acknowledged as well.

Yours is a humanistic, almost transpersonal approach. Could you talk a little about that?

I'd have to go back a bit. Someone who's had a great influence on me was Moreno. He was around in Vienna at the time they were all intensely discovering psychoanalysis, though he abandoned the couch and worked anywhere. He was not coming from a medical model at all, because he wasn't a doctor. He approached it as an artist saying the therapist had to be a friend, not a doctor.

What he taught was that the source of human unhappiness is that we have lost touch with our creativity, and our spontaneity, and that to remedy the pain, and the human misery that gets called in the more medical models an illness or a disease and therefore needing a cure – he was saying to ease this unhappiness we have to tap back into parts of us that we've lost touch with as a culture and as individuals. He said that modern human beings fear our spontaneity like primitive humans feared fire. That we had to reconnect with that fire. He said the therapist is a friend, not someone who has some kind of authority, not a midwife to the unconscious in the way Freud meant, but a friend. A friend who has certain techniques that can help trigger new alivenesses or new possibilities. So that's why he invented psychodrama.

Moreno's influence has been hidden, because in the heart of his work was also a critique of society. When you're working within a medical model which relies on – concepts of the normal and the diseased – then you have to make assumptions that what is society's accepted model of behaviour is the goal of therapy. So that has a limitation, it cannot become a critique of the way in which we organise society, and so obviously Moreno, who did, didn't spread so widely, and it wasn't so pervasive in its impact as the more psychoanalytic traditions have been. Though in my opinion his ideas are far more profound.

Fritz Perls started reclaiming some of Moreno's ideas, and reaching into the wisdom of the East and the humanistic psychologies of the '60s synthesised this, and Reich, and probably some of Maslow at the time, Carl Rogers, Fritz Perls, and Moreno. It was part of that whole '60s wave of consciousness. There was a whole generation who didn't go to war, so the power and intensity of youth, and the passion for the future, instead of going into the battlefields and getting scythed down, it went into all sorts of things. And even more significant, the liberation of the power of women from the depths of the collective patriarchial unconscious where it had been imprisoned for centuries.

So that tradition has, in my opinion, kept itself alive and is still alive now, because it has continued to enrich itself with the development of ideas in the arts, in literature, eastern ideas. I would say that some of the humanistic traditions have now solidified, but then it was a new river, which was recognising that we did not just exist as an individual that needed to be fixed in order to live the normal life. That we had the potential within us which is far, far greater than we've been taught or allowed to even imagine, and that this possibility is a possibility for me as an individual, and it's a possibility for society and community.

That's a different model completely; to look at the journey of self discovery as growth rather than as a journey to get back into normality.

How does the 'transpersonal' fuse into this?

Well again, it has several aspects. For me personally it happened in different ways. I think it happened for a lot of my generation in different ways too. We took psychedelic drugs which opened the doors of perception, revealing levels of reality that were not the space/time solidity that we had got used to conceiving of as reality. Plus there was a huge – maybe it wasn't so huge, but it seemed huge to me because I was a part of it – wave of us going to the East to reclaim some of the traditions and the wisdoms of the East that had got lost in our western materialism. In that, too, there were recognitions that our individual self is itself a construction of reality which is limited: that I exist as a separate individual, all of which is within me, and I also exist as a part of something much greater. And that one aspect involves claiming all that I am, developing my authority – which in the East might be 'I am', or 'I am that', or 'I am God' – and then the other aspect is to realise I'm part of something much greater, and that in my relationship to the greater, again in the eastern wisdom, I surrender to this. That there is a oneness with everything which involves a level of surrender of the self.

So reclaiming that wisdom of the East and integrating it with the understanding of the West is a vital part of transpersonal psychology. The East evolved those understandings partly because life was so tough, and it was so hard that a level of surrender was a survival mechanism. If I'm just a slave to my own needs for survival, or I'm enslaved to some system that keeps me in this caste or whatever, then to enable me to live a life that has some kind of serenity in it I'm going to learn the art of surrender, aren't I? So while the East was evolving the mystery of what it means to be surrendered to something greater than yourself, the West was developing the equally vital wisdom of the importance of the individual. That I am *me*, I am not just a daughter to this person, or a member of this class, or part of this community, and I am not just defined by my relationships. I am me, and I am an authority of my own life – and the *American Constitution*, has it enshrined this in law? The freedom of the individual. That freedom and power of the individual was being evolved in the West. And equally important, because that's freedom. I don't just want to surrender to something greater than me that basically leaves me disempowered with no authority, but neither do I want to be just an individualistic self that therefore is just out to get what I want with no reference to the whole.

So the two polarities need to be married. And the transpersonal therapies have been an attempt to marry the recognition that we are individuals with our own unique authority, and the recognition that we are part of something greater into which we surrender. But a lot of the transpersonal therapies have – probably in order to reclaim these wisdoms beyond the individual that there is something greater than any one of us – lost sight of the power and significance of the unique individual. It's a marriage – like all marriages, it's got tensions and conflicts. That's what I think the transpersonal is.

You particularly enjoy groupwork don't you?

Well I like group work a lot. In fact most of my work now is in groups. I do do individual work, but my primary focus is groups. What do I think the pros and cons are? I'm obviously going to say the pros first, because I think groups are brilliant.

I was just talking about the synthesis of these two wisdoms, that in a way are opposite. That we are a unique individual, we have everything within, and yet we are also part of a whole which is greater than us, that we have to let go into. In a group, this dynamic is stimulated and challenged in a way that in individual work it is not. Because when a group of people get together, you have the individuals but you also have the group entity.

A common language evolves; there's understanding; there's a level of trust that grows; there's a love that arrives, hopefully (I'm talking about my ideal picture here) and the level of sincerity with which people have communicated and listened to each other, in time does seem to create a pool or a body of wisdom which, after a time, the group can then tap back into. There often comes a changeover point, and I find this often in groups. I start off as the group facilitator – very together, very available, very clear of my own fears and hopes, there to support and nourish the group. I'm checking things out, holding them in terms of being professional or clear in my communications, energetically holding the group and as time goes on, the processes involved create a sufficient body of understanding, which then begins to hold the group. At that point there's a subtle changeover, and I can enter as me, as a me which also has hopes and fears and confusions. Then another level of honesty arrives. And the wisdom of the group starts to teach us. So for example, something may happen and we may as a group say: 'Well what is this about? Let's ask the group', and different individuals will offer their wisdom, and it will be greater than any single individual, including me. I love that bit, because then there's a much deeper truth. Because then not only do you have the processes of the therapy or whatever's happening, of which I'm the

facilitator, you also have embodied in that process a recognition that we're
all equal, we're all human beings. Plus I learn new things about myself too.
   It's a very difficult thing that if you're running a group, and I know
this so well, because I've fallen into this trap myself often – especially if
I'm running a training – at the beginning I look like: 'Ah, this is a bit
like how you're supposed to be, articulate, clever, together, smiling,
basically sorted.' Now that needs often to be there at the beginning, so
people feel safe, they feel they're going to be held. I'm a bit of a
mother figure, they feel like, 'ah this is someone they can learn from,
she knows what she's about – you can see she's sorted.' As time goes on
I love the process of dissembling that, because there is a part of me
where I'm together and I'm professional, but there are definitely other
very different parts too!
   It's a profoundly healing process for people to realise that this game
that we're in of becoming human and learning how to love and be
honest with each other is not the game of trying to be perfect, or
getting it together, it's a game of being who we are. So that as I
disassemble the near-perfect image, that I'm very good at doing an
Oscar-winning performance of, at the beginning – it's wonderful for me
too. Because I know the danger of getting identified with that image,
because I've done it. And I had to suffer a lot to come back to earth!

Are there always key processes that take place in groupwork?

I think so. I'm just going to have to free associate here, because I've
never thought of it quite like that. One of the key processes is the
relationship that the group facilitator has with their own process. If I as
a group facilitator am willing to continue sincerely to discover the truth
of myself, that is the best way of holding a group energetically. Because
it also means it is safe, the journey of self-discovery is safe.
   We have to talk about the danger of groups as well because the
person who's running the group is in a position of great power, which
therefore can potentially be abused. And the power with which they're
playing is the power of the group. A good group leader will be able to
do that. There is an energetic group force which has tremendous power
for healing, and a tremendous power to abuse. We originally experience
it in the family. We often in therapy look at what happens between us
and our mother, or us and our father, or a client and those individuals,
but actually it's even more key what happened in terms of the relationship between the parents. It's the atmosphere. Just as important, if not
more so, is what happened between a family.
   So often the woundings that we experienced in that first group are
mirrored very often in the ways in which we relate to future groups. So it
has tremendous power to hurt, and the power of the group leader is great.
In fact Moreno called the energy that is generated when people get together – he had a lovely word for it – 'transcendental-interconnectedness'.
He also said that if God were to return to earth, he'd come back, (I'll

forgive him for not using she) – he'd come back as a group, because the energetic truth that arrives, which is greater than the individual, is quite wonderful when it happens. But that can be used or abused.

So one of the primary things that needs to happen, is that the group leader is willing to continue to re-examine themselves, because abuse of power is part of human life. So you're bound to abuse your power, there's no way round it, it's just part of life. The only thing you can guarantee is that you're willing not to be invested in a position of power. That's all you can do. There are times when I've hurt somebody in a group. Three weeks later, because I've hurt them and I'm in a position of power and it's taken them three weeks to come back to me, they say 'I didn't like that', then at that point I have to be willing to look at what I did, and not just stay invested in my position. If I in that process discover, yes, I did hurt them, because of some fear of my own, then that has to be followed by my redemption of it if you like, by feeling really sorry that I've hurt them. And it can't be manufactured. This has to be genuine.

So the relationship that the group leader has with their own process is the single most powerful dynamic in a group. If my relationship with my own process is one of fear then that will enter the group. It will not allow a free-flowing movement between the unconscious material and what can be said and talked about. If I've got a relationship with my own process of willingness to meet it, that will be mirrored in the group in a healthy climate, or healthy culture of honest communication. That's the single most key thing really.

So that one of the things that has to happen is that the group leader has to embody the same truth that the group is attempting to reach, which is the spirit of free enquiry and honesty. That's the single thing that has to happen. That's even before the group begins. And it's not that the group leader's not going to make mistakes, abuse their power, because they will. We're talking about the nature of being a human being, aren't we?

What's the best length of time for a group to run?

Well in my experience if a group knows that it's going to last for three weeks, ten weeks, a year, two years there is a dynamic which seems to come into operation that quite naturally takes care of that. I've run groups of three weeks, and I've run groups of two years. I've run groups of four years actually, but that was a particular kind of group. They're all different, but I don't think it has to be of a particular kind. I've found that groups of two years are really, for me, my favourite. I don't know why, I think for me what happens in two years is you begin and you can take your time to create a level of trust and safety that then allows people to start to share on a deeper level. Which then allows them to begin to challenge – after a while – each other's defence mechanisms. Then when they find that safe, they then begin to challenge *my* defence processes.

And then when they find that safe, there's a level of playful freedom that emerges, which then means that I as a human being can enter. I like that bit, because I can enter as me. Then we find – there's a level at which the group – what do you want to call it, the transcendental interconnectiveness or God in the form of this group, whatever you want to call it – this energy of which we are all part starts to feed back to us. People then start to get a different level of truth about themselves, which is not a simple, analytical one – a much deeper truth arrives, which is often not as confrontative as people might imagine – the confrontation usually happens earlier. It's a much deeper, healing, level of acceptance of who they are, who we all are. At this point you're not doing therapy in any easily defined form at all. What's happening then is the group are *being* together, and in that it's my favourite bit. Then you've got the time to end. That's always sad. The death of the group. The loss and goodbyes. Although what has happened lives for ever in our hearts – love in this particular form ends.

What kind of range of people do you see?

Because we've got a team of therapists, for example there's one therapist who's absolutely brilliant with people who've never done anything to do with therapy or growth or consciousness or anything. They come to her and it's as if she's very good with breaking down these complex processes into 'baby food'. She's able to communicate in a way that completely makes sense to them; it's often very concrete, it doesn't lapse into growth jargon, it's just a gift. Now I don't have that because I know how easy it is for me to lapse into jargon which they may not understand, and I've done it before I realise it, and hopefully I don't do it too much or I apologise when I do. But it's a gift and she has that gift.

Somebody else has another gift, which is when people are starting to feel their energy for the first time. In other words, they're beginning to realise that what they are thinking about themselves in life is just a small fraction of what is actually happening. What's happening is their bodies are feeling things and they are having instincts and inclinations which they don't usually let themselves feel. She is excellent with working with people who are beginning that process.

They've all got a particular talent, and it's interesting that the talent or gift that people have is usually the other face of some way in which they've been wounded. My personal childhood core wounding if you like, was to do with my religious upbringing, in which there was no place for me to live as me. God was everywhere, and he was male, and omnipotent, could see everything – there was no place for me, not the me that I am. I had not only to behave and feel in 'good' ways, I had to *be* 'good'. Yet the me that I am is a mixture of all sorts of things, and there was no place for all of these.

I am now excellent at creating places in both the Centre and the groups, where people can arrive as them, and if you noticed how I described it, they eventually arrive with a level of self-acceptance, and then I arrive. So my gift is the creative side of my wound, and that happens with a lot of therapists. But because many therapies are often more rigid or fixed in their ideas about what therapy is, it's very hard for the uniqueness of the therapists to be acknowledged. There is an old tradition in this country of healers, and that's in a way what we're talking about, because there are people with gifts in certain areas.

Getting back to my question ...

I will see everyone for an initial consultation which is to work out what they need – a group, sessions, whatever.

I want Amap to be somewhere, and we as a collective want it to be somewhere that anyone can walk into and feel welcome. We may not be able directly to meet what they need, but we have a whole list of contacts and people that range from doctors, to psychiatrists, to spiritual healers – and we want anybody who comes in there to be met as a human being, as a fellow member of this planet, and to receive something. Even if it's: 'We don't feel we've got what you need, but go here.' This is a personal passion of mine really. Otherwise you end up in a very dangerous 'us' and 'them' situation, and I've been in that too you see. There isn't an 'us' and 'them', there's all of us.

Could we talk about ethical issues? Also economic issues ...

Well, yes. It is part of the philosophical background to Amap if you like, or the ethos of the place, that we as human beings are on this planet together, and when the Apollo spacecraft took a picture of earth, that was in a way the external manifestation of our realisation as a species that we've all got one home, and we're in the same family. And that includes the animals as well. That leads to the recognition that we are all interconnected, that we need each other, that we're in this together, and that we are faced with a crisis of political, economic, ecological, spiritual dimensions, and that collectively we've got ourselves into this situation, and it's going to take a collective effort to get out. It's no longer enough just to say 'It's up to the individual.' We have to learn how to work with each other, live with each other, help each other out. It's no longer enough just to free the individual, reach the top of the mountain of enlightenment, and all is within me and I am free. That's not enough.

You've got to go back down the mountain, down into the valleys again, as a human being, reaching out to each other and saying: 'Look, let's help each other out, we've got to get this together.' Again the communitarianism reflects this, the new ideas within the political scene which transcend left and right, as was. I'm an old lefty of course, so I've got leanings that way, but still the recognition that the rights of the individual, which is vital, has also to be married to the responsibility of the community, means that, in terms of the work that we do, we have to recognise that we need each other. That therefore, as a group of therapists, we help each other out. We cross-refer. The needs of the clients mean that I'm not just going to think, 'Oh I need x clients to pay my mortgage' – that's horrible. I am committed to – what does that client need? That client may need this person. I'm not enough or I'm not the right one.

So that's one part of it. The second part of it is the financial part of it. That it's not the amount of money we have that's key, it's our relationship with money, that's the important thing. If I'm obsessed with accumulating money, I'm going to hurt myself and the people around me. Now I'm not against money, and I'm not against rich people either. I just feel that our relationship with money as a society has got really damaged. That means that when clients arrive one of the wounds that they bring with them often, is their relationship with wealth and money. It's not good to demand – it's how I feel – that they reach a certain level of financial freedom/solvency before we treat them, because then I'm not living up to what I said earlier, which is that I would like everyone to get something of what they need.

We have scholarships for all the courses which people apply for, if they want, if they can't pay anything they can get a scholarship. And okay, they have to be limited in their number because we're a business too. We have a sliding scale so that when people come for sessions, one of the things that gets clear in the initial consultation, which is easy for me to do because I'm not entering into a therapeutic relationship with this person, is how much they can pay. So therefore I am freer to find out what kind of financial situation they're in, and again we can then meet it.

Some therapists are willing to do it for very little, and some aren't. I respect that, because again I don't want to impose on everybody. I think that the way in which we relate to money as a society is one of the collective wounds that needs addressing. All sorts of things need addressing, collectively; it's no longer just the individual wounds that need healing, it's the collective wounds that need healing too.

When I was a student in 1968 and in IMG, I was there because the suffering of people presented itself to me in a collective form, and I'm still somewhere responding to that. My own need to be part of the community and my recognition that the individuals we see are wounded not just within themselves personally, but as members of a wounded community, is central to my work.

Some therapists are non-tactile, others touch a lot ...

Well I think there's a time and a place for both, because sometimes someone will need to feel their distress with no interference whatsoever, and just to be with it and meet it alone, and with the dignity and totality of that meeting. Sometimes they will need to be sat next to with tissues, and even be held in your arms so that they cry all over you, and you get their mascara on your best sweater and it doesn't matter. Again the needs of the client are what dictate what happens, rather than a particular system.

So my responsiveness will sometimes be very, very silent and respect-ful, feeling my own equivalent helplessness. Sometimes when people are feeling their level of helplessness they do need to feel it alone. Sometimes they really have to have that human connection which allows them to let go into you as the therapist, and really feel your body as a safe place for them to be able to let go into.

Would you like our society to be more conscious of therapy?

Well I would. I'm bound to say that because for me personally, and for the work I do, I've found that these processes and ways of examining my life and my relationships have helped me to be more alive and to have more love in my life, more honesty, more fun, and so I'm obvi-ously going to think that this is a good thing, because it's been a good thing for me. But on another level, I don't think that therapy is the only way to do it: it's *my* way. I think there are other ways of reaching into people's need for love, or reaching into people's hidden creativity and helping release it. That might be art – we don't take care of the arts in this culture. I think what happens in schools is so painful. It is the domination of the mind over the body very often. It is a way to keep children off the streets, sometimes, little more. Instead of children being respected as the future, they are seen as irritating sources of need and trouble, and that's terrible. So to me one of the biggest things of all would be schools. That's where I started out, working with children as an educational psychologist, and the pain of what was happening was too great for me actually to work with it then. In schools there are so many possibilities that could happen that respect the child's natural, instinctual intelligence.

So that's another thing. I think also the way in which, probably just the architecture – I don't know – the organisation of traffic, there aren't places where children can play very easily. There's all sorts of ways in which our community's health is being hurt.

Do you think there is any sensible way of monitoring therapists?

My position is extreme. I don't even know whether it should go in the book, but I'll say it. I actually think there are as many – in fact Carl Rogers says this and he was a very respected member of the establish-ment. He basically, and I agree with him, said: 'There are as many charlatans who are accredited, as there are who aren't.' And the prob-lem with accreditation is that the very accreditation process itself has in it an inherent problem which is, the only way in which you can monitor somebody's expertise but also professional integrity, has to be in terms of observable behaviour. And observable behaviour can be defined as these trainings, or this much experience, or this articulated philosophy. But what it can't do is examine what I think is the key, which is this person's willingness to be hurt by their client. This person's willingness to be vulnerable. In other words, to not just be identified with a certain position in relation to their clients, but someone who's willing to be hurt by their client at some level. If I'm going to ask my client to be vulnerable then am I willing to be equally vulnerable? I'm not talking about revealing my life – that's just an imposition – but am I willing to meet within myself the same level of truth that I'm asking from them? How the hell can you measure that?

Similarly in groups. If the major, single, most significant factor which minimises hurt in a group is the relationship the group leader has with their own process, how can you monitor this? And I rather like the old British tradition which basically allows healers a lot of freedom. Some-where – I'm not saying this is perfect either – it removes one level of abuse which is the abuse of the institutionalisation of who can be a therapist and who cannot. Because who holds that power? What do they do with that power? Who decides this? We're bringing in the government. Of course I don't trust those systems.

Yes, it is true that people go to therapy and re-experience the same abusive relationships they're trying to get away from. But that happens, with very accredited, totally establishment figures. In my opinion, some of the worst abuse happens in those situations.

Have you thought much about so-called therapist 'burn-out'?

I have, actually. Well what we've done ourselves, we belong to a thing called the Independent Therapists' Network, as a body, as a group. We are linked in with another group. And so we help each other monitor, so we have an outside view – we are in groups of three actually – so it's a little modular system. So it's self-monitoring but you do need an outside input periodically to look at the workings of the Centre. Because I might think I'm doing a great job, but we might all be in, not a *folie à deux*, but a *folie à quinze* or something. So we need that, and vice versa. It keeps alive our process as a group, and helps monitor things that obviously we may not have noticed.

Similarly, for each individual therapist we have our own supervision group, but we also have supervisors. I have three different supervisors I go to for different teaching, because I can't keep up always, I like to have somebody who helps me stay in touch with the latest thing. So you need that supervision; ongoing, external input.

If I find I'm spacing out, something's going on which may not neces-sarily be burn-out. Something may be going on that I need to look at. First, I may have a hidden resentment towards this person. Second, they may remind me of somebody I know that I don't like. Third, I may be feeling bored but unable actually to deal with the issues of my boredom, so I space out. Who knows – I may be so preoccupied with my own life that I am unable to put that aside, to be with this person. So first of all if you're spacing out, you have to examine what it is. I mean some people go to sleep; I've had people come to me and say that they went to psychotherapists who fell asleep, and something's going on here that is not just burn-out. It's like, 'do I really want to do this job?' This job of being a therapist is painful, it hurts, you have to keep looking at yourself, you have to be willing to be hurt by your client if need be, you have to be willing to feel their hurt – it's painful. It's a commitment, it's not easy.

So why do you do it?

I don't know. Why do I do it? I don't know. I've tried to get away from it three times. Three times in my life I've reached a point where I've thought 'therapy is dangerous'. The last time I thought therapy to be essentially an abuse of power. There was something that happened in the nature of the therapist/client relationship that of its essential nature was abusive. And there was no getting away from it, in two ways.

First, the authority and the power relationship reflected the authority and power relationship in society: teacher and parents, priests, whatever, and that was just a repeat of that power abuse that children have. Second, it was an abuse of power, because therapy was being used a bit like a mechanic might fiddle with a car engine. It was an abuse of the self. Instead of meeting and living myself as I am, this was a subtle attempt to fix me, and so I left.

I went to teach maths to children who were having trouble. What happened eventually was that I was teaching these kids maths, and they all learnt their maths, and so people wanted to find out 'how come they're learning their maths?' And I didn't know. They watched me teach. And what was happening (which I didn't know about) was that I was taking care of them. If they didn't understand something I would say: 'Whoops, sorry, I haven't explained it right', because I know maths. I went to university originally to study maths and I know maths can be broken down. If you can't understand maths it's because it's not been broken down sufficiently into small units. So that if they got it wrong it was because I hadn't explained it properly. So immediately they felt better. So the nature of the relationship that I was developing with the kids was enabling them to become sufficiently self-empowered and trusting themselves to start to think 'I could do this'; it was nothing to do with the maths. It gradually brought home to me that there was a way in which I could be with people that was not abusive in the way that I thought it was and which could help them. And so I responded to the inner call yet again, to try and ease people's suffering.

CHAPTER 17

Personal Construct Psychology

Fay Fransella

Fay Fransella helped to introduce the work of George Kelly and personal contruct psychology in the UK with her book *Inquiring Man*, co-authored with Don Bannister. She lives in Cornwall.

How did you become a therapist?

Well I suppose by using PCP [Personal Construct Psychology]. As I said, I've had no training at all and I don't think I am a psychotherapist – I do psychotherapy. I think it's very difficult to like PCP and work in the clinical setting and not become interested in helping people change.

How would you describe what you do?

I suppose the simple way is to say: 'You're a person, you come because you've got a problem. My job is to try and understand the problem from *your* perspective.' To do that there are many skills a PCP therapist needs. One is to know Kelly's theory about how people may go about the business of making sense of the world, and to know about his – what he called 'diagnostic constructs', which I can explain if necessary. So I have that.

So when I – as I have to do – put my own value system out of the window when you're sitting there, I only listen to you as far as is humanly possible through your constructs. I know of no other therapy that says that. I have no knowledge at all of where you might go, how you might be helped. Only by listening to you, and doing my best to get into your shoes, and look at the world through your eyes, can I then step back afterwards and say: 'Now, what does all that feel like? He does seem to have difficulty in pinning things down – loose construing?' In other words I then start to apply some of the ideas in Kelly's theory that might account for part of your problem.

We might have three or four session where I'm doing nothing more than trying to get an understanding with – if you like in non-lay terms – the types of personal constructs you're using, the types of experiments you're conducting that make you have the problem that you have. Because all behaviour is an experiment which is another vital idea. So you don't look at the person's behaviour as a reaction to something, or something to be interpreted. It's an experiment that person is conducting to check out some of their own construing. So you ask yourself: 'What experiment is that person conducting in their terms?' Another question you ask yourself is: 'What's the person not doing, by doing what they are doing?' Because bi-polarity is also a vital thing.

So, there am I, sitting there, having got rid of all my own values. That's quite a difficult thing to learn – when we teach psychotherapy it seems to be quite a difficult thing to learn. Once you can do it, it's no problem. Then we just listen, and then at some point you have to say: 'Right, I think this is why the person is stuck.' The person is stuck, they can't generate new experiments and so on. So the whole therapy's about helping the person get unstuck. And move forward.

For the uninitiated could you talk about Kelly's theories?

Well it's a theory and a philosophy. It may or may not be important for you, but his first degree was in Physics and Mathematics. And his theory in some ways is a theory of physics translated into psychology. That is quantum mechanics-type physics, in that, yes, there is no truth. All we have are approximations to it in our interpretations of what might be. There is still a reality in Kelly's terms, but my truth's not better than your truth. So his model of the person is 'man the scientist', and the philosophy is 'there are always alternative ways of looking at any events; no-one needs to paint himself into a corner, or be a victim of his biography, or hers, but we can be a victim if we construe it that way.'

The theory is set out like an engineer's blueprint – what is it about? It's about construing and construing systems. If you take the fundamental postulate, where it's all encapsulated really, it's about a person's processes. It's about an ongoing person, we never – we can't stop any human being, or living matter for that matter. A person's processes are psychologically – not biochemically, not neurologically, but psychologically channelised, *channelised*, which has some sort of directive feel about it by the ways in which we *anticipate* events. So we've got a notion that the psychology is anticipatory, because the construing is our interpretation of the here and now. And the only way we can see whether we're right or not is to behave. So that's another unique feature, basically, which is quite hidden. That the experiment is our behaviour. So we never know whether we're right or not until we behave. But by then we've moved on. What are these constructs? They are ways in which through the years we have seen how some things are similar to each other and different from others. Tables and chairs and human beings and whatever. But at the end of the day, I meet you and I have to construe you in some way – the contact is in itself construed. I may be wrong, but I've got to set up something, and then I test it out, by behaving. Teaching is a good example. I always give that as an example. I say: 'I look at your faces, I may have got it totally wrong.

You may all be reading newspapers and have gone to sleep. Then I have to decide if it's your fault, or my fault' and things stem from that.

But it's quite an ongoing notion, and all the corollaries are about the constructs; bi-polarity is vitally important. Constructs aren't little dots, dotted around in our heads; they're organised into a system. And I say: 'Why should it be in my head?' I don't know, but I feel my constructs are fit. Then emotions of course, come into it, when our construing isn't working properly. And of course, Kelly did the thing that upsets people, he redefined things like anxiety and fear and threat and so on. Because he was very grandiose, he did try and create a theory of the total person. No-one else has ever tried to do that. A lot of people have buckled things on as they have gone along, but he set out to create a theory of the whole person.

I think he wrote two theories. There was the skeleton, which are the corollaries and so on, and then there was a whole theory of experience. And I just don't see why/how people can't understand it. If – take the notion of threat – when you perceive something as true, which is going to cause you radically to change your core construing. That hurts. I've found the description of Kelly that I was getting for my book, the negative ones, I found them quite threatening. Made me quite uncomfortable, because if they were true and I couldn't find an adequate explanation, I'd have to change my construing of him, and I have a lot hooked on to him.

The whole of psychosomatics – indeed the whole of psychology – talks about the interaction between mind and body. All he was saying was: 'Why do we need to keep them separate?' Construing is as much by your guts – you meet someone and you don't like them – 'I don't know why I don't like them, I just took an instant dislike', that's the non-verbal world. And I find it very difficult to explain these. If someone comes, let's say with acute anxiety. You think about what did Kelly suggest might be a way of looking at anxiety – 'confronted by events you can't construe' – so you try and find out what is the world this person's living in that's facing them with events they can't construe. Quite often it's something as central as the self.

Kelly was very anti-deterministic wasn't he?

Kelly says you're not determined by anything, except yourself. We've created ourselves, nobody else has. No-one's made us be the people we are. Of course we have a culture, an environment, but within that two people could grow up totally differently.

Are childhood events important?

Yes. They're important if the person thinks they're important. There's no way you know – at some point we *have* to go back to childhood. If the person is saying: 'Well of course it's because this happened in my childhood', you might go there. But you don't *have* to go there, you do deal with the person in the here and now. You're still dealing with the here and now when they're talking about their childhood, in that sense. You're not trapped by your past: you may have outgrown it, you may have in Kelly's terms, updated it all, and it happened – okay.

What might happen when someone comes to see you?

My pause is because you are eclectic as far as methods are concerned, but you have a very abstract theory which guides you. If a person, as quite often happens, a man daren't express emotion because it would tear him apart, you might just pick up this cushion, and say: 'Okay, that's your wife, or mother or whatever, talk to them.' That would be a method to help them reconstrue, but by and large to answer your question properly – I can only say how *I* go about it.

I believe people who come for the first time are very anxious. I start from that premise. They're not quite sure what all this is about, whether they've made a terrible mistake. So I give them a little talk, and once we've talked about them a bit I say: 'Well, this is how I see things, this is my view. I don't have any answers. You have the answers, my job is to help you find those answers. And it'll be hard work. You'll have homework to do, and we'll be designing these things together. I won't be telling you what to do at all, but I will be working with you, and it'll be a partnership', these sorts of things.

Because if people want to be told what to do, as a lot of people do, 'Come on what's my problem?' 'I'm not going to tell you what your problem is because I don't know.' And they'd say 'Well that seems interesting.' I usually say: 'Well go away and think about it.' If they say: 'No, okay, I'm prepared to give it a go', my first job is to get as much information from them as I can. And this is where I think grids come in, not that they're essential by any manner of means, but it's a structured way of getting constructs from an individual.

Can you talk about 'grids'?

To start with I might do it the standard way, which is to say: 'Well you've talked about your father and your mother, and your wife and your sister. I'm going to write those on cards. I'm going to ask you to talk about these people, in more detail – anyone else important in your life?' 'Oh yes there's Auntie Mary.' Okay so we might have eight cards, and then the standard way, modified according to the individual, is to say: 'Okay, let's look at your father and your mother, and you. Any important way in which two of those people are alike? Makes them different from the other?' Again words can change. 'Oh yes, two are bad-tempered ... ' so you're being in almost conversational mode, getting the person to tell you how they construe important individuals in their life. Then you might decide to do laddering next. Are you into laddering?

Please explain ...

Name three important people in your life, let me help you do a ladder for *you*.

Alex, Jess and Michéle ...

Can you immediately think of any important way in personality terms, characteristics that two of them share, make them different from the third?

Yes.

What would that be?

Let's think ... [Laughs] ... two have generous natures, the other is a little more mean.

In general, is mean the opposite of generous nature?

I guess so.

Okay, now if I were to ladder that, and that's already quite an abstract construct, I'd be saying 'Which would you prefer to be?' I can guess ... [Laughs] ... You'd prefer to be generous, but the person must then say what they'd prefer. So the similar question is 'Why? Why do you prefer to be a generous sort of person, rather than mean? What are the advantages for you?' I'm asking now. No-one's hearing it but you.

It makes me feel a better moral being.

Whereas if you were mean?

Well that's morally undesirable.

I don't think I can say why do you want to be a better moral being, it seems to be a fairly abstract construct. In my terms you've gone from there and zoomed up to there. But laddering in my opinion is one of the most powerful tools at the command of a PCP person. If it's used properly, and it's not always used properly. Because I don't think it's something you can learn from a book. Some people on our courses, on our three-year courses, take a long, long time to do it.

  Okay, so those are other constructs. So we've got generous, mean, we've got bad-tempered, good-tempered. We might have ten, with their opposites. And if we're doing a grid, I would simply lay out the eight cards of people, and I'd have a grid made with horizontal lines and vertical lines with the intersects, and one construct on each line. And I would explain that I was going to ask the person to think of this generous/mean as a seven-point scale. So we'd think of father – giving a 1 would be totally generous, 7 totally mean, or does he come somewhere in the middle? Or his father on generous is a 3, and so we'd just go through rating each person on each construct. Then we have a grid format which will then be analysed in a variety of ways. What it does, is sometimes to show you patterns, relationships that haven't come up in conversation. Of particular interest, I always think, is where the self comes, that's how the person construes themselves in relation to those others, and where the ideal self comes. If the ideal is miles away, the question is 'Why?', and I'll always feed it back, saying: 'This is the pattern, does it make sense?'

. One example which I've used quite a lot, with another sort of grid, is this man, who I actually video-taped in the 32 sessions, and he had a lifelong problem with vomiting, when he got upset from the age of eleven or something. He'd had five years or so of psychoanalysis. He said he had improved a bit but still had the problem, and he'd read *Inquiring Man* and it seemed to be the sort of thing he wanted. He was a very interesting man. One of the things that came out of the grid was that he had a very successful father who was in the film business, and he was a producer or director. Success was a major thing to this man. He had the opposite to success, which was not yet successful. But in any case we did this grid, and I was fascinated, I got carried away with my own delight in the grid. Because success was full of meaning and everything marvellous, the opposite pole not yet successful, the only thing sat there was *me*, the self. So I brought this – totally not suspending my own construing – and said: 'Look isn't that lovely?' or words to that effect. And the silence told me, and I thought: 'My god what have I done to this man?' It seemed like an hour, but it probably wasn't all that long. He said: 'Yes, that is how I feel. I don't know how to get from there to there.' Grids can be quite powerful.

If a grid reveals that a man sees his wife in very similar terms as he does his mother, how do you change that?

I suppose it depends how he sees them. It's often the case, I think, isn't it, that the person is searching for someone who is like mum. But of course you can't marry mother because that's wicked, and so they become hostile in Kelly's terms, they keep making their relationships fail. Setting things up and making them fall. For some people, I think you can actually discuss that.

But I am struck by the power of the cognitive. With a person like that I don't think they need to experience things, I don't believe they need to punch pillows, or maybe eventually they do if that's what they want to do to mum. But to start with people are happier talking. Then later they might need to go back to childhood or think about that and so on.

How long might you see people for?

Well I advocate having contracts with people depending on the problem. If it's stuttering, which is a world I know about, if it's stuttering then I know it's going to be a long thing, and I'll say six months. Then we will discuss it between us how far we think we've got. But otherwise ten sessions for me is a lot. I may say 'Well, let's give it six, commit yourself to six.' I ask for a commitment, and then we talk about where we've got to – 'Would you like to work on having another six or whatever?' But if a student goes on for more than 20 sessions, I want to know why. Twenty is a long time, but if you can see a pattern emerging that's fine. But 20 is short-term for a lot of people.

Do you take on anyone as a client?

Anyone, that's right. Basically that's what it should be. The limitation is the therapists themselves. I just do not believe that there is a human being who can get on with all other human beings. I just don't believe it. I know that I have difficulty with people – very tight construers – I'm very happy with schizophrenic people whose construing is loose; have no problems. With the young man I was talking about on the tapes, which I've sometimes shown to students – sometimes he'd have a three of four minute silence, I didn't mind that at all. They can't stand it, the students. So some ordinary therapists are like that too.

I can't stand the opposite, the paranoid sort of person – drives me crazy.

Give me an example of the 'tight-construer' ...

The paranoid person. The person who believes everything is all set and just so, and good and bad, and right and wrong. And – having said that – people who stutter are very often very tight construers. But that is for their survival, it's not because they actually are – oh God, I nearly said the awful thing 'not that they're really like that' – it is there for a purpose. There are some people for whom it is life, that is the way things are. 'And I don't know what you can do for me ...', and I feel like saying: 'I don't know what I can do', but there are other therapists who do very well with that sort of person.

What qualities do you think therapists need?

Kelly listed them, of course, he listed everything. He said they must be very creative – he said that the therapist is the validator of the client's construing, that is the therapist isn't a person in their own right. If they're to be helpful to the client, they've got to live in the client's world, and react in a way that's helpful to the client up to a point. But to help, they need to be able to be creative, to think of ways which might help that client reconstrue. That's often setting up experiments and so on for them to carry out in the week in between. So good creativity is high on the list.

Can you elaborate? An example ...

Well the one that comes to mind is the one that I enjoyed very much. It was a very attractive girl, young woman, who felt she was overweight, and by laddering we found out that she did think that if she were a normal weight she would be so attractive that men would want to rape her, she would be so attractive. So I thought: 'Well that's what the books say – people say, but I've never actually heard anyone say that before.' I knew she had a very attractive sister, so I asked her whether her sister had been raped. 'No, no.' 'How did your sister avoid it then?' 'I don't know.' So I thought, I decided that this was a myth – my diagnosis – and you have to act on your diagnosis. It was a myth which had to be invalidated. Let's see whether she really believes it. So I said: 'Now, you're in the South of France, and just sitting there under an umbrella. You've got a bikini on and you're absolutely as you think you should be. And of course a lot of men around. Can you imagine that?' 'Yes.' 'Tell me what's happening.' And of course the men were looking at her, and I say: 'Well what are you doing when they look at you?' She said: 'Well I looked at one', and I said: 'What sort of look?' So I soon found out that she was giving the 'come hither' look, you see. Imagination. She said: 'Well how else could you be?' Then I said: 'Well during the week, why don't you watch as many pretty girls as you can in that sort of setting, in a bar or something. How do they deal with the glances of men?' She never sort of got that. So it was something that arose naturally during the session which might have and did help her.

Do you always give people 'homework'?

I try to because I do think that most of the work goes on between sessions rather than in sessions – it's only one hour a week. The whole of life goes on out there. I think it gives some purpose. A person gets a feel that they own the therapy more, that they know they're doing something.

The therapy lends itself to that kind of work ...

That's right. Once they get the notion, and I've tried to teach them indirectly the theory, the notion that behaviour's not fixed, not automatic, you can change it.

Transference ...

Oh yes, yes. Three of Kelly's unpublished papers are on transference and interpretation. He said: 'Of course you can't deny it.' He said there were two sorts – I forget exactly, because they're not notions I use

FAY FRANSELLA

much. But one is, there is a negative sort of transference when the person really does throw at you all the parental-type things. You've got to break that, you can't allow that to happen, unless the person is so vulnerable that they have to have that support to start with. But otherwise you use it, and I use that word advisedly, you do use it to the client's advantage. That's part of the relationship after all.

Is PCP all about techniques, or about the relationship too?

Oh, the relationship's got to be a trusting one, oh yes. On both sides. And it's got to be an involving one; the whole notion of the person/scientist of the therapy room is the laboratory, where the person feels free to conduct experiments they see they can't conduct in the outside world. So yes, it's the trust. There's something in the relationship that stops dependency happening. Because you're always saying: 'It's you, it's not me, it's you, you're the independent one, you are creating, recreating'. You're not saying that out loud, but that's what you're implying. 'I'm nothing really, I'm just a foil.' I think that probably does stop too much dependency happening.

One thing we haven't mentioned is where the unconscious and that sort of thing comes in. As you know it doesn't. It doesn't in the Freudian sense, in that there's no dynamism attached to it. But there are non-verbal constructs. Pre-verbal construing is an enormous part of the theory: that is, constructs that have been developed in childhood, with no verbal labels on them. If they're carried over into adult life, they can cause problems. Now you say: 'How do they do that?' Well, I've only got one example fixed in my mind. I don't think it happened to me but I'm beginning to wonder. In any case, this little Annie has got three uncles, and two of them are clean-shaven and one of them has got a beard. They all love her very much, but are very distressed to note that she runs to the clean-shaven ones, and draws back from the one with the beard. Can't understand it, as they all love her. But in any case, little girls probably know that beards are nasty on the face – she's got a construct. Now in Freudian terms that would have the energy attached to it, the feelings would stay – not in PCP terms, it's a construct. It's only used when the circumstances are appropriate. So it's not used until she grows up, and at 17 goes to university, meets a young man, everything's fine and, guess what? He suddenly decides to grow a beard. The construct comes out now. She doesn't remember, the relationship gets all fraught. So the notion of the pre-verbal construct is a very powerful one in PCP. A lot of therapy work is about trying to get a verbal label attached to that. But the dynamism is missing.

You don't have to trawl back into early memories ...

You don't have to trawl back, that's right.

What is that attraction of PCP to particular people, do you think?

Well I think it attracts anybody. It goes along with your own construing, makes sense in your own construing terms, a behavioural-type person out there wouldn't see any sense in it. Most of our students are not psychologists, on our courses, they are practitioners; they're in the hard end of the business, like nurses and social workers and teachers. And have to do things.

Do you think many people are actually practising PCP by default?

No, I don't. I think it's far more difficult than that. I think there is something very important about – the one about not going back to childhood – those sorts of rules. The therapist *literally* believing they have no answers, literally believing they have no answers. The one about suspending your own values, they really mustn't come in – very difficult to learn. I'm sure there are other things too. Things about loose construing and schizophrenia for instance. You have to be on your guard, recognise loose construing for what it is. If this person is pushed too hard, where do they end up?

Who decides when the 'treatment' is over?

When the client starts to say something like 'Well I really only come for you', or you find there's nothing to talk about. You keep having to create things, and so you bring it up and you say: 'It's funny isn't it, we seem to have run out of things to talk about.' 'Yes, yes, well I was thinking about that, but I had my appointment today, and so I thought I couldn't let you down.' The client is on the move again.

Presumably you believe that it is an approach that gives clients some skills to take into the world?

Yes, that's very interesting. That's very definitely so. They learn about their own construing, they learn to stand back and say: 'Well why am I doing that?' – doesn't stop you doing it at the time, but you can do something later. I've just done a chapter for – there's an Open University series, where they take one client and they get six different therapists – well I've done one, and it happened to be an Indian psychiatrist as a client. I haven't had the stuff back, but one of the things I asked the client to do was to write a self-characterisation, which we haven't mentioned, but a very simple little tool, asking the person to write a character sketch of themselves in the third person. In the feedback of the session, when the author of the book goes back to the client and asks what the client felt about doing these things, in it he said: 'That self-characterisation,' he said, 'I'm going to use that myself, now, from time to time. Very useful.' So yes there are many tools and I think a person can become their own therapist.
　　One of the advantages of the grids and self-characterisation might be

that they save so much time. Within two or three sessions you've probably got as much information as it would take another type of therapy ten sessions to get – I may be underestimating it – but you do get information very, very quickly, and very important information sometimes.

How are spouses affected by their partners undergoing therapy?

Again, going back to people who stutter, that's a major thing. They've been married in the context of their speech. I make it a point always to spend quite a lot of time, saying: 'Well how is your wife liking the changes, and what's happening?' I used to think of having the wife along, then I thought 'No, no', the client must learn to put himself in his wife's shoes – because it's nearly always men – and get that relationship going. That's usually okay, but not always.

Couples work doesn't appeal ...

Personally, no.

Groups?

Groupwork is fine, but getting a group together is quite difficult, we've never succeeded at the Centre.

Can we talk about the UKCP?

I shan't say anything if you publish it ... [Laughs] ...

Can we talk in the abstract? It might rid us of charlatans, but stultify creativity ...

Exactly, I think it's as simple as that. If I had to go one way or the other, I'd be against registration. But it's coming and I do think it's stultifying, I do think there will be very few new therapies created – maybe that's a good thing, I don't know. But how can a new therapy be created, if you think about it? When you've got such a great organisation like that.

I think people on the whole are stronger than we give them credit for. That is, okay, there are charlatans in every business, in medicine – they keep getting struck off the books – of course there are charlatans. But psychologically, I do think people are stronger than we give them credit for sometimes. I'm sure I could be tougher with clients. But whenever I've made a mistake, or been aware I've made a mistake the client has managed to cope. Mind you, I've recognised the mistake and so I've done my best to make sure the client is okay.

Have you created your own personal ethical standards?

Yes. I'll behave as me as a person. My normal thing. I'm not a hugger of people. Some people are. I think you've got to be natural with a client, and then you can operate different sorts of roles. If they want to hug, then fine, but I wouldn't initiate one. I think that, basically, I do what seems most likely to help my client, using personal construct theory, and do not do things to satisfy my own curiosity. Apart from that we have the PCP Centre's and UKCP's codes of ethics.

Is the issue of money – therapists' fees – problematic for you at all?

Well I've worked all my life in the public sector, so I've never really had that problem until I started – no, that's wrong, I did at University Medical School, had private clients – but being brought up in the medical world, they all have private clients themselves. It seemed all right. But certainly at the Centre, a lot of our students had great difficulty, and maybe I was doing a Kelly when I think about it. I said they must deal with their own charges with the client. They must collect the cheque from the client themselves. Because otherwise they were going to shelter behind some secretary and I think that the money transaction is important to learn about and not to be afraid of; silly to be afraid of it. The person's buying a service, they've chosen to come that way.

How do you self-monitor, in your work?

An essential feature of personal construct theory is the notion of 'reflexivity'. That is, the theory as much accounts for the therapist's behaviour, reactions and so forth, as it does for the client's. You are therefore constantly asking yourself why you did that or did not do something else. Also, when things are not going as well as you think they should be going, you seek the answer in yourself and not in the client. Self-monitoring is thus an integral and vital part of the personal construct psychotherapist's activity.

Are you in favour of introducing 'emotional literacy' to school children?

We did some work for the further education unit – it was Kent Education Authority at the time of all the strikes – and they were trying to push through a new method of teaching which was PCP-type methods of caring for the individual, listening and so on. And getting that sort of relationship going. It failed, of course. But some of the teachers – I'm not sure if this is answering your question – some of the teachers became very fascinated by PCP, and we held a series of workshops for the teachers. How could they come to understand their pupils better?

Now I'm quite sure that those teachers if they really bought PCP would start to inculcate the same sort of notions in the pupils. It would become reciprocal in that sense.

What do you see as optimum mental health?

Kelly's model. The only model really that you have is that the person is able to continue to go out and conduct new experiments and to seek to enlarge life, and make things more predictable, and deal with problems by trying to understand them rather than becoming hostile. So it was in those sorts of terms. There was no peak experience, there was no ultimate goal. I've always thought the humanist goal as I understood it, maybe it's changed – get rid of all your hang-ups, be yourself – you become dehumanised. Ultimately if you had all your hang-ups smoothed out, what's left? The hang-ups are what make you the person you are. Okay, if they cause you distress or others distress, then by all means. But if you're prepared to put up with it, and others are prepared to put up with it, and of course it's you, why should you get rid of it?

CHAPTER 18

Transpersonal Psychology

Ian Gordon-Brown

Ian Gordon-Brown is the joint founder of the Centre for
Transpersonal Psychology, London. He has written widely
on Transpersonal Psychology and other issues.

Can we talk about your background, and how you got into this line of work ...

There's very little that doesn't pertain. Like a Catholic mother and an
Anglican father set me up with guilt. My father was in the regular army,
but got out in the 1920s and lost what little money he and my mother had
in the crash of '29. This turned him in an alternative direction, to mystical
thinkers like R.W. Trine, and eventually he turned up on the door of Alice
Bailey's teachings. When I reached my teens, my father was naturally keen
to introduce me to these teachings, and once I took a look at her books I
knew I had *arrived home*. They were my spiritual home.

Of course initially, I was overly devotee, but that went in time
and I began to explore more widely into Oriental philosophy, Hindu
teachings, Buddhism and so forth. I came across Theosophy and
Anthroposophy. Later I met up with thinkers like Auribindo and the
Agni Yoga Society. Alongside all this I was at a school called Bryanston which in those days (the 1930s) was a really very progressive
place. We had a parson who spent many years in India, but was also
a Christian mystic. So I contacted the Christian tradition. Bryanston
was a school that was very interested in creative thinking in relation
to politics, sociology, education, and the Arts. I went there in 1938
at the age of 13. At that time there was an explosion of interest in
preparing for post-war reconstruction.

So another stream that developed in me was social conscience,
which in those days of course was radical and socialist. World affairs
fascinated me. At one stage a friend and I started something we called
the Pioneer Youth Movement. Its aim was to set up discussion groups
on current affairs, not only in our school, but in schools and youth
clubs throughout the land! I think it lasted two years. I was good at
most games so life was busy.

Then I went into the Forces and was saved from being killed by the
fact that air crew training was much delayed because casualties weren't as
great as had been expected. I went to Cambridge on an RAF short course

and did the first year of a degree course in parallel with basic RAF training. Eventually I switched to the army and ended up as an officer in charge of a personnel selection team processing new recruits – I was just 21 at the time.

I had read Economics when I first went to Cambridge, but the personnel selection experience moved me towards psychology which is what I read when I went back there in 1947. I'd always been interested in psychology and was reading Jung in my teens. But Cambridge psychology was academic and behaviourist in the extreme and I did it for two years. Then – although I didn't know what to do – I thought I would teach. I had to do three weeks probationary teaching practice before my course. One sample lesson was enough! I decided it was the last thing I wanted to do. So I shopped around, bumped into a friend just back from America who pointed me towards the National Institute for Industrial Psychology who took me on. My life has been full of significant chance meetings. At the Institute (NIIP) I got my postgraduate training and experience, was involved in personnel selection, assessment, vocational guidance and the early days of human relations training for managers and supervisors. I was there five years.

I was making something of a name for myself as a speaker, and then, does the 'Saturn return' mean anything to you? – well Saturn takes 28 to 29 years to go round the sun, so a Saturn return is when Saturn is back where it was when you were born. And on my Saturn return – and astrologers will attribute various meanings to it – but what happened to me was that again, due to a combination of circumstances, I 'jumped over the wall' and joined the headquarters of the Alice Bailey movement (The Lucis Trust) in this country, at that time out in Tunbridge Wells. By then I had married and had a couple of children, so there was a fair old financial sacrifice for all concerned. But it was compensated for by the fact that we were able to buy some land and build an American ranch-style house. My wife was Canadian. I settled down for 15 years as a headquarters worker and after five years the headquarters moved to London. I took charge of a couple of branches of the Work including World Goodwill because Alice Bailey not only wrote books and founded a Meditation Training School, but developed service activities as an outer expression of the inner work. On behalf of the Trust I got involved in a scheme to establish an international, non-governmental organisation centre in London. Never came off, but we got as far as negotiating with the Crown for the Cambridge Terrace site on Regents Park. So I was involved on the one hand in the rather special and specialised world of the esoteric, meditation, full moon meetings, and spiritual counselling. And on the other with practical activities in the field of United Nations work, human rights, and public education.

Gradually I became dissatisfied, not with the philosophy but with ways in which the Lucis Trust work was being applied. So like a good pioneer I sought to change the situation, was full of creative suggestions, and must have been an impossible colleague, because in 1969 I got the sack. About which I am quite open, because it is perfectly clear to me in retrospect that for at least five years I had been colluding to get the sack, because I couldn't actually walk out myself.

The eventual timing of leaving was the right moment. But it's difficult to get a job when you've been 15 years in an esoteric group. [Laughs] But I bumped into an old Chinaman, name of John Ward Davo. I say an old Chinaman – he was English but I am sure his last incarnation had been in China. He ran an organisation called the Industrial Co-Partnership Association, and had given it the Yin/Yang symbol as its logo. The organisation promoted profit-sharing and a bit of tame joint consultation. And I walked through his door two days after his Board had agreed he should start looking for a successor. He took one look at me – we had met before over this International NGO Centre Scheme – and said: 'I see you as my successor. It'll take me a little while to get you in, but ...' So I got in six months later, and spent the six months after that wondering how the hell I was going to stand it for the three years before I would succeed him. He was a lovely man, but didn't know what needed to be done to change his organisation.

Anyway, life/destiny had something in hand for both of us. He and his wife were killed in a car crash in France six months after I had joined. So I took over. My feeling is that he was ready to go and while I may not have been all that was required of a director I knew exactly what business the organisation should be in, which was Industrial Participation and trends to make work more democratic insofar as the companies that were funding us would allow. So an old friend of mine, David Wallace Bell, who had been running a programme for settling refugees in the Middle East, joined as deputy director. We got a new chairman, Nigel Vinson, who became Lord Vinson and chairman of the Development Commission. And we turned the organisation round, including a change of name to the Industrial Participation Association just in time to be active in the Industrial Democracy debate of the '70s, when Britain joined the Common Market. We were the only organisation to present jointly agreed Management/ Union recommendations to the Bullock Committee on Industrial Democracy.

In the meantime, after being sacked, I had thought: 'Now what do I want to do with my life? This is a critical moment – I'm 44.' Incidentally the psychology of NIIP, and all the rest of it fitted me beautifully for the industrial world. But I did not want to do that for ever. It felt like a temporary assignment. I decided that what I really wanted to do was to take part in the preparatory work for the *coming schools of initiation*. Believing that in the next century which is now very close, we would begin to see the establishment of spiritual training schools – spiritual disciplines – which would make our present understanding of the psyche somewhat primitive. What was needed was a lot of ploughing over of the land of human consciousness, mulching and composting, putting the sheep and cows to pasture so that it would be enriched. The

world of the human psyche needed to be enriched. I'd known Sir
George Trevelyan (a leading figure in the consciousness raising movement) for quite a long time, because I'd periodically gone to lecture at
Attingham Park, his Adult Education Centre. So I went to see whether
I could get a job with George. This was in '69 before the industrial job
came up. However, what he could pay me wouldn't have kept my children in food, let alone me. Nevertheless I knew that that was what I
would like somehow to do.

In 1971 I met Barbara Somers, who's my work partner, life-partner,
who jointly owns this house with me. We obviously had the same areas
of interest, and she joined a small group that I was involved in. Then I
had an out-of-the-body experience. I was away with a couple of people
whom I knew, and I came back into my body in the fairly clear way
that one does when it's a really important experience, hearing myself
say: 'Well at least I have a degree in Psychology.' And adding as I
entered my body, 'and what do I not have?' and having a feeling that
something very important, at least by my standards, had happened. It
was as if a green light had been given. So I thought: 'Well what I don't
have is clinical experience. Never been in analysis. I have assessed, and
interviewed, and counselled until I'm blue in the face, but I've never
been clinically trained or been on the receiving end.'

I started to look around, and had a short spell in analysis, but it wasn't
satisfactory. I did a full Jungian analysis later. So I decided that I would
see whether I could fix up somehow to work with Roberto Assagioli, the
founder of Psychosynthesis, because I'd known him for many years, because he was an intimate friend and colleague of the Baileys. I'd first seen
him on the platform in 1947, flanked on the one side by Foster Bailey and
on the other side by Alice Bailey. So I went out to Italy and he said: 'Well
it will be too difficult to work. Why don't you go out to California and get
yourself some psychosynthesis training?' And so I did, and very good it
was. I went there for a couple of months and the idea was that I should
come back to this country and help to re-establish psychosynthesis. *Syn-
chronistically* on the same training, there was Roger Evans (founder with
Joan Evans of the Institute of Psychosynthesis in the UK) and Tony Cork.
The Americans, I think, obviously preferred Roger to me, because I was
getting on – I was in my forties – Roger was in his late twenties. I had the
disadvantage of being tarred with the brush of esotericism. Now they were
all tarred with it of course, but they said: 'You can do anything you want
under the psychosynthesis heading. But if you do, you must cease your
public connection with the esoteric world.' I said: 'What? You must be
joking?' They said: 'Yes, it's absolutely essential.' And of course there had
always been this wall of silence around Roberto's esoteric work, very
necessary to protect it in the early days. I said 'It's no longer relevant in
the conditions of the UK', and basically what they said was: 'We have John
Birch down the road, and we had this other guy not so long ago –
McCarthy – and we daren't run the risk.' It was the psychosynthesis
people who suggested that I/we function under the transpersonal label.

Which was in fact a very good suggestion. Barbara Somers, with whom I was now in a very close relationship – and we were planning in some way or other to work together – her roots were Jungian, and Tibetan Buddhism and Zen, and not psychosynthesis. Not against psychosynthesis, but her heart was in the Jungian stream. Not as necessarily represented by some present-day Jungians, but as the spirit of Jung might have developed it.

So under the transpersonal label it was.

Transpersonal meaning what, precisely?

Well first of all, an umbrella term. The formal movement – Transpersonal Psychology – was founded in 1969 with the establishing of the *Journal of Transpersonal Psychology*. But before that you had Assagioli, you had Jung, you had Maslow – well Maslow was, I suppose, the front figure publically in the founding of transpersonal psychology – but there were also people like Victor Frankl. A whole range of psychologies. And you see, this is something that's been concerning us at the moment. Because people are uncertain as to what transpersonal psychology is. They try to make defini-tions, and one person's definition doesn't fit another's. Wilbur's got his line, and we've got ours, which is not against Wilbur but different in a number of respects. In 1975 Charles Tart produced a book called *Transpersonal Psychologies*, and I think we should be talking about transpersonal psychologies not transpersonal psychology. If you do that, you can have an umbrella perspective. Perspective would be the word. I think we may change our name to transpersonal psychologies rather than transpersonal psychology. Then you see, a whole range of other things come in – for example, all the Oriental psychologies which form a very important part of our perspective.

So, definitions ... 'human potential', the way that psychology links up with spirituality ...

Well yes, both of those are useful definitions – they're not ones I would quarrel with. What we need is an 'and/and' perspective. Not 'either/or'. For example, I would say that the central tenet of transpersonal psy-chology is belief in the existence of Self (capital 'S'), an 'x' factor, it is the Soul or *Atman*, by any name in many traditions. We're not a blank sheet when we're born. We come from somewhere and we go to some-where, whether you believe in reincarnation or not. The Self is on a journey, and there's two journeys going on. One is the journey of the personal centre – the personal ego seeking the Self and initially project-ing the Self on all manner of things outside, from art to Bhagwan, to communism, to John Major, whatever. But there's also the journey of the Soul seeking the person. As the individual gets to the point where it can be actually useful to the Self, the Soul, then the Soul begins to exert its drawing power, and shakes you up and maybe gives you a crisis and a peak experience or two, so that you are drawn towards the

Self, and at a certain stage the dominant feature or factor is increasingly the Self, the Soul. Then you begin to get lives which are destined
in a small way, or a bigger way – the lives of great souls who obviously
come in with some message, contribution, teaching or whatever to give
to humanity – and others who if they manage to go far enough in life,
may be given a small task to see how they do. [Laughs] A lot of that I
think comes around the stage of the Baptism experience, and the subsequent confrontation with the Devil in the desert. And a lot of people
are at the stage where they are being given a venture, a project, something to do, to see how they get on. We learn to work by working, and
failure helps the learning process just as much as success!

What do you do in your sessions? With individual clients ...

What do I do? I suppose I would see my task as helping them to
become themselves. Who they most truly, essentially are. This means
that with some people you take one sort of approach, and with others a
quite different one. So far as I'm concerned, I'm at the stage where I
can pick and choose my clients, because I'm sufficiently well-known to
have more people wanting to see me than I can possibly cope with.

I'm now 70, and so although I want to continue working, I don't
want to have quite the burden of the past. I think I'm probably best
fitted to help people by 'walking' alongside them at certain stages of the
spiritual journey. If somebody's not drawn towards the spiritual journey,
or has got personal problems and that's all there is to it, they're probably better going to somebody else, because although I think I can
probably help I would prefer to spend my time with somebody who is
closer to the bits and pieces of the journey that I've done. With some
people I know exactly where they are, because I've been there and
maybe still am. And then I can help, and what I do is to get them to
listen to their inner voice/voices. It's a process of turning a dialogue like
the one that we're having into an inner dialogue that the person has
with themselves.

So, for example, we may discover that there's a five-year-old hurt
child within, and if that happens one of the things that I would be
concerned to do is to help that five-year-old child actually to speak.
Because for the most part, the adult within has been putting it down, or
when something goes wrong punishing it and blaming it. So the child
within is nervous about the adult in whom it lives, and moves, and has
its being. I find myself saying to the adult: 'Listen, don't speak *for* the
child. Listen to what the child's trying to say, and let *it* speak for itself',
and you can hear if you're somewhat experienced, when the adult is
speaking for the child. You meet mother along the road with little
Tommy, and you say: 'Hello Tommy, how are you?' and mother says:
'Oh, Tommy's fine, thank you.' Well that [laughs], that's not the point,
it's Tommy who has to answer – needs to answer. So you get to the
point hopefully where your client can actually begin to establish or to

recognise when he or she is speaking with his/her voice, and when they're allowing some other voice to speak. This can lead to a triangular dialogue – between you as therapist, your client, and one of your client's inner figures and it can be most creative. *And of course some of the other voices, or one of the other voices will be the Self.*

There are various ways of doing this. It can be like you listen and you hear what they're saying. I work a lot with energy and symbolism. So if somebody's not feeling terribly good, you might say: 'Well where do you have that feeling? Has it a location?' They might say: 'It's in the front of my body.' So I say: 'Well, just stay with the feeling', and I might at some stage say: 'Can you get an image for that?' They might say 'Yes, it's like a marsh, *or* it's a bit hard like a rock', or whatever. Then you would find yourself developing a triangular dialogue with the marsh or the rock. Has the marsh or the rock anything to say? What would the rock like to have happen to it? What was the marsh before it became a marsh? And so on. The process of dialogue when you've got an image.

I work with the chakra system also, and the parts of the body that are energised either painfully, or creatively – symptoms as symbols of something that's going on. You have a pain in the neck, and you get an image for the pain in your neck. Suddenly the person sees their boss. A pain in the neck is often due to a battle between the thinking and feeling functions. Case of somebody who was subject to migraine headaches, and one day came in with a cracker. I asked her just to get in touch with the headache and feel it. Which she did, because she'd done a bit of this imagery work. I said: 'Could you find out where the headache would like to go, where the energy of the headache would like to go?' And she went into herself and she said: 'Well it wants to go into my stomach.' I said: 'See if you can let the headache energy go into your stomach. Just relax and let it go.' So in a moment or so, she started to weep. I said: 'What's happened?', and she said: 'The energy wanted to go into my stomach and it's there' (that was when she started weeping). And I said: 'How's the head?' 'Oh,' she said, 'the headache's gone.' So she wept on for a while, and then she wiped her eyes and blew her nose, and said in effect, 'Look I must stop this silly nonsense, and come back to working with you.' Which she did. After a minute or so I said: 'How's the head?' She said 'The headache is back.' A simple and common example of a feeling problem being dealt with by being taken into the head. Of course this is just step one. The problem is not solved. Now the client needs to discover an alternative and more creative way of handling her emotional tension.

That's a terribly simple example of the way in which energy is very often locked in the wrong place. Like referred pain. You feel the pain *here,* but the real trouble is *there.* You get the same sort of thing in the energy world of the psyche. A lot of people think that the heart centre is in the front of the body, that's where everybody normally feels it. Well the jewel in the heart lotus is in the spine, at the back between the shoulders. You can give people exercises to see how they experience it in that position by doing a visualisation exercise to open the heart centre, or the heart, using for example, an exercise visualising the blossoming of a rose or a lotus. Once they have their image in position and open you can ask them to imagine the lotus or the rose moving back and then moving forward. A majority of people find the back position stronger and safe and the front position more sensitive and vulnerable. So you can give people experiences of this. I should add that we are not just concerned with an image or a visualisation. The quality of the energy and its feeling and its place within the total psyche is of central importance.

A lot of people these days are at a point where the crown chakra is beginning to open. They don't realise this and get worried about feelings and tension and discomfort that are often associated with the process, like pressure on the head, or a feeling like a metal band around the head, for example. And because I have worked with people and have my own experiences of the crown chakra I would say, depending on what's happening, 'Look, just see where the energy wants to go.' Now note what I'm saying. I'm not telling the client to send the energy where *I* think it should go. That's the wrong kind of guidance. The client's psyche should be encouraged to become the guide. Our task as therapists is to facilitate the will of the Self, and help the person to recognise the part of the Self that's around, and to meet its needs. Because very often the needs it has are positive and beneficial and useful to the organism. Coming back to the crown chakra, if the person doesn't know what to do, then I might say: 'See if you can imagine that there's a lotus in the head, and have it open out like a flower. See what happens if you do that', or 'what happens if you create an image of the tightly held energy flowing out.' It's quite extraordinary how powerful this sort of thing can be, and how fast it works. There is an esoteric statement that energy follows thought, and the eye (visualisation) directs the energy.

In your sessions, what happens ...

I always work from a transpersonal perspective, and use a wide range of techniques and approaches, depending on client need and how I am feeling! Imaging, visualisation, Gestalt, working with chakras, dreams, long guided daydream, various forms of bodywork, working with transference and countertransference. And of course talking. I will often spend say 15 minutes in an imaging mode, and then the client and I will discuss what came up. At some point I will ask for a life history in writing – a CV if you prefer, often no longer than a page of A4, to give me some of the essential facts of a client's life. But I like to start straight in and rather dislike first sessions which are just given to the case history and going through the formal motions.

But you work with the body too ... [using left hand as he talked]

Look I note that you're using your left hand, moving it around. Can you just stay with the left hand and move it. Do it. Now. Yes, you were talking to me and you were using your hand, can you just say something that you were saying and use your hand? Now, I've made you self-conscious of course. [Laughs] But I'll say: 'Find out what it feels like to move your hand like that. What does the hand say?' I might say: 'Look, could you take the right hand out from where it is, and put the left hand down for a moment, and see what it's like trying to use the right hand to speak with me?'

It's difficult.

What is difficult? You mean it's easier to speak with the left? Do you see what I mean?
   Now I could make some judgements about that, but all I asked you to do was to attend to the hand. Now if there was something happening in a session that struck me as in some way of a symbolic significance like repetitive gestures, I might pitch in like that. And there's all sorts of notions about the right side of the body and the left side of the body. The left brain controlling the right side of the body and the right brain controlling the left side of the body. I take them very seriously, but try to observe the golden rule that the important thing is what it (symbol, image, gesture, feeling) means to the client.

Do you work with the breath?

If I notice something going on with their breathing, I will ask them to attend to their breathing. I don't on the whole go in for, as it were, asking them to do belly breathing and to exaggerate. Why don't I do that? It's too simple and I don't necessarily believe in it. But I will pick up anything that seems relevant in relation to the body or to the body and the psyche. You see, now you've got your hands together [laughs], and that's a fairly typical integrated type of symbol, or is it prayer? I don't know.

How do you mean ...

Well I have found very frequently that when people bring their hands together there is a sense in which they're bringing something in life together. So from my experience, that's based on my experience. I can say that to you here and now because we need to do shorthand style. But with a client I wouldn't make a judgement about that. I'd say: 'What's going on now? You've got your hands together. Will you just stay with that?' I would let them discover what it meant for themselves. So far as you're concerned ...

Do you begin with contractual talk?

We will have discussed the contractual basics before the first session. My sessions last normally an hour to an hour-and-a-quarter. I have a standard fee and a scale for people who can't afford the standard fee. I say that I'm in charge of the time-keeping, and if you go over time that's my responsibility and I don't add to the fee. I'm not a particularly good time-keeper, so sometimes sessions go longer than that. I believe that the 50-minute hour is theoretically sound if you're seeing somebody three or more times a week. I think that it makes very little sense if you're seeing somebody once a week, or less frequently. If you're seeing people three times a week and you break it in the middle of something, they can pick it up next time. But if you're seeing them once a fortnight, it's much more difficult. So I refuse on theoretical grounds, and I emphasise that because I think the theory is inadequate, to be too rigid on time.

Now I accept that there are disciplines of time that are a requirement that clients need to learn, that a therapist needs to practise in order for their own mental health and so on. But I do not believe in rigid rules. The psyche is not like that.

How do your clients decide it's time to finish their therapy with you?

It depends on the client. You could well get the sense that the time is coming when you should be finishing, and the question is then – does the client feel able to raise it? And if they don't, I may say: 'How are you feeling? I sometimes wonder whether you may not be thinking that perhaps we've done what needs to be done for the moment, and that you'd actually like to have a break.' So we would talk about it. I had a man once who'd come to work on his masculine, and at a particular stage – he was actually lying on the floor down there – and he'd got in touch with an angry figure, and I said: 'What is the angry figure thinking at the moment, or saying? What does the angry figure want to say?' And he was a bit embarrassed. I said: 'Come on.' He said: 'Well the angry figure is saying – you should stop therapy.' I said: 'Well, let's hear a bit more from the angry figure', so the angry figure spoke a little bit more about it, and I said: 'Well that sounds as if we ought to listen to the angry figure.' So we came back, and I said: 'What's your feeling about what the angry figure was saying?', and he said: 'Well yes, I think probably it's right.' Stopping much earlier than we had agreed. So I said: 'Well look, you can always come back if you want to, but let's make this the last session.' [Laughs] He'd actually got what he wanted to – to develop his masculine side – here was his masculine side saying something. His masculine side needed to be listened to. I didn't need to treat him as if I was a therapist who knew what was the best thing – here was the masculine saying 'I think we should stop therapy', so I would say 'Yes, yes.' We can always start again.

Can we discuss transference ...

The transferential aspects are always there. But what we do in our work, and I speak for colleagues like Barbara and others, is that the transference of the client is usually on to the persona, or whatever bit it may be of the therapist. You need to recognise that, and then the next stage is to recognise the Ian Gordon-Brown inside you as client, and that's a stage in the transference which is often ignored. The therapist works with the transference out there. Basically what you're working with is – why do you project that particular thing on to me? So you work to get a recognition of what's going on within, and the transference/countertransference within the psyche of your client, and it seems to me that that's where the transference needs to move. There is a dictum that there is an intra-psychic counterpart of every interaction between client and the outside world, betweeen therapist and the outside world. Our view as transpersonal psychotherapists is that this intra-psychic dimension needs early recognition, which is of course a stage in the process of withdrawing projection.

Techniques or the relationship per se. Which is the most important?

I think a technique that is used as a technique out of the relationship context is a gimmick, and therefore not desirable. I think that essentially the first relationship is the human relationship; and then the next bit of the relationship is the counsellor–client relationship, or the therapist or the analyst relationship. However, you see, I'm talking out of the perspective of clients who sometimes have very serious problems, but who have a degree of insight. You may well have a client who is really very fragile, where it's quite legitimate for them to be looking at and wanting a mother figure or a father figure. And where if you try to push that to become an inner reality too early, it will be experienced by the inner child as rejection. So it may be necessary at first to, as it were, accept the projection of the child within, and work with it. Be the good father, or the good mother, or the good whatever is wanted. From that point help the adult in the client to parent the child within that is seeking from me what they never got either from mother or father, or the person with whom they live and move, and have their being. So the process then is to get the child to the point where the child says: 'I'd like to become a bit freer, and I feel I can.' Now that can take a long time.

I had a client who had a perfectly appalling background, from both mother and father. In fact, so bad that she went a long way away and didn't come back until she felt a duty to come back, because they were both getting old and one of them was dying. So she did come back, and that brought all the things to the surface, including this desperately hurt four- to five-year-old kid. When we got to the point where I had identified the child, and the adult client had identified the child, then my sessions would be littered with questions like – how did little 'x' feel about that? So I was actually counselling or giving therapy to the two of them. Whenever I greeted them I would greet both of them. I would say 'goodbye' to both of them. Quite literally.

So what was happening through that process was that the child was becoming recognised, the child was beginning to feel valued, the child was given a place, the child was able to make some sort of decisions like – when we go out of here I'd like an ice cream – or whatever it might be, very simple stuff at times, to the point where the child was free. Now maybe the child should then grow up or not, I don't know. That's up to the child to decide or at least to discuss with the adult. There's nothing wrong in having a five-year-old child, if it's healthy and enjoys itself. So that kind of approach is one that I have discovered to be very effective.

I was reading Grof's book on spiritual emergencies ...

Well I think there's a sense in which all spiritual crises can be spiritual emergencies and will have that dimension. It depends whether the individual is willing to consider that as something that's real or whether it's just a fantasy so far as they're concerned.

Optimum spiritual health is becoming who you are and following what is your path, and the path may be the path of the politician, or the artist, or the person who makes money and uses it well. I don't limit my definition of the spiritual. I think the transpersonal doesn't and shouldn't. I think you go beyond that to the notion of archetypes – not in the Jungian sense – but the different archetypes of the Self. I see myself essentially as a priest/healer, teacher of consciousness, along the line of the second ray of Bailey. The love–wisdom line.

But I've got a ruler in me, and in the earlier years the question of who was primary and who was secondary was very important. I liked the world of politics, I enjoyed being in charge, in fact I used to say I always joined a small organisation so that I could start near the top. [Laughs] But as life went on it became clear that the ruler in me was a secondary figure, and that the primary figure was the consciousness teacher priest/healer. So the King has to serve the High Priest, not the other way round.

Then I had a scientific mind. I felt quite at home in some ways at Cambridge. I disagreed with the philosophy, but the analytic, experimental approach was one which I enjoyed. It was a prison house eventually and I needed to start to recast my mind, give it a new sort of energy, make it – in the Jungian jargon – switch it from a thinking sensation mind, to an intuitive thinking mind. So, if you start to limit the notion of spirituality, I think you shut things out. You don't make it any easier for the person to find out who they are. So many people will regard the power archetype as bad. I don't think it's bad. One of its functions is to set people free.

So people are often in the wrong place at the wrong time ...

Or they punish themselves, because a part of them says 'what you ought to do is to like it', whereas in actual fact what you ought to do is to recognise that you don't like it.

Why are we the way we are, do you think?

Ah. Why do you ask me? I think you'd have to ask God that one. [Laughs] Why are we? Well let me give you *an* answer from my own journey. In the early years, I didn't know what path I should be following, I knew that I was interested in a range of things, I didn't know how I should be following it, I didn't know whether I should marry the woman that I had proposed to – in fact I felt as I was doing it that I was doing the wrong thing – all of this. Very normal. Later on, I began to feel that, looking back I could begin to see that there was a pattern. I couldn't see it looking forward, but looking back I could see that there was a pattern. There was even a pattern in my work in the second spell in the industrial field.

I'll put it to you this way. There's a personnel department up there, and every now and then they send out a message saying: 'Look we've got a job coming up, nobody in our team to fill it, can we have anybody on assignment for a few years?' Now I think that my job in the transpersonal was not quite ready to happen in '69. In '71 when I had the out-of-the-body experience, it was ready to be kicked off, but it still took me five years before I was fully over in the transpersonal world. There was a long time when I was doing both jobs in parallel. But I could see that the experience that I got in this secondment to the Industrial Participation Association was actually of great value. I got an insight into and learnt some things which actually were necessary about the collective, about the organisations, and about the kind of people that functioned in them. I can honestly say that I think that the manufacturing industry is the salt of the earth.

So I can say in my life that looking back, it makes sense, it was almost as if I was born to do something like what I am doing, and with a bit of luck and a bit of help I've got there. Some people however, they have another sort of lesson. There are people who can decide at the drop of a hat that they're going off to Latin America for a couple of years. I wonder how they do it and where the money comes from, but they do. What's their lesson? I've come to the conclusion that the lesson these people need is to discover something about the value of their choices, not just to go off on a whim. Not lose the spontaneity, however. But somehow or other, understand something about the meaning of it.

But I think most of us come in with particular lessons to learn, with particular qualities to develop, sometimes particular jobs to do. Most of us are a bit like the curate's egg – where it's good in parts – we're not all even at the same stage of development. We may be quite underdeveloped in one aspect of our nature, and quite far advanced in another, so there's a balancing-up job to be done for most of us. Jung talks about the bi-polar structure of the psyche, and how in the first half of life mostly we live out of one side of our nature, and that in the second half of life we need to balance up. *Becoming whole,* among other things means working through all parts of our nature. I think that there's no doubt that there's a huge

range in the evolutionary journey between, say, Christ, Buddha or
Krishna, or the equivalent people along the political line, or whatever, who
are great souls compared with average humanity. And average humanity
today is pretty advanced by some criteria of the past, but actually quite
limited in consciousness, and more unconscious than conscious. There's
an awful lot of people at the moment, I think, going through a process of
the second birth. Like the birth of the Soul, of the Self. *The awakening.*
The process before that is often very destructive and people find themselves in mental hospitals. The process after it needs a certain amount of
digestion, because in terms of the journey of the Soul – it is a major step.

I like to take the life of Christ as a paradigm of the developmental
process: there's first of all the birth initiation – and it wasn't until Jesus
was 12 that he said to his parents: 'Wist ye not that I must be about my
father's business.' Like he, at that stage, just on adolescence – in other
words just about to become a very young adult – needed to find out what
his life was about. Today a lot of people are doing that. They suddenly
awaken to the fact that there must be some path that they should follow.
Some people find the path very quickly. Other people spend the whole of
their life, following one guru after another. Always looking for them, never
quite finding. Well that's obviously something in the one who searches,
but that's a very important stage. I call it the stage of shopping around –
and that's exactly what people are doing. You don't learn discrimination
by being told that that's the journey you should take. I have a son, who
when he was 25 decided that he should become a doctor. I could have told
him that when he was 14. He didn't listen to me. [Laughs]

Once you find your path, the normal stages will include the stage
of the devotee – you're devoted to it; accepting the disciplines, and
eventually moving to the point where you discipline yourself. But
you're still tied to the particular path that you're on, and to break
that tie most of us have to go through some disillusionment process.
So we break it by being disillusioned, and we realise that the teacher
wasn't all that they were cracked up to be, like they had feet of clay,
but of course they did from the beginning. Then you get to the point
where you're ready for the Baptism. And the Baptism is the point
where the personal self and the transpersonal Self come into a new
relationship. The transpersonal Self begins to take conscious charge.
So I think that the life of Christ is an amazingly accurate paradigm
for the growth process. For example, why do we meet the Devil in
the desert after Baptism? [Pause]

This is a very interesting question. I think the thing is this. At the
Baptism, because the Self begins to have a new relationship to the personality, we actually have power. We become powerful. A bit too much to say
that we can get what we want, but it's a new situation, and so our motive
has to be tested. The tests of the Devil in the desert are all tests of power.
Some people slip through [laughs], and then you get people who get
carried away, inflated, fanatical, your Hitlers and your Bhagwans – very
gifted souls, but not yet perfect – I hesitate to say, they trick the Devil,

but they're quite different from the behaviour and the performance of people who are pre-Baptismal.

How pre-determined are we? So to speak ...

Well I think a lot depends – this is where I come back to Saturn and Jupiter. Saturn – you have a life where the lesson is to learn to live within, as it were, the structure and framework that have been provided. And Jupiter – where you're left very, very much freer, and you need to learn the lesson of how to be free, and how to be responsible, and how maybe to limit yourself. Most of us can be found along the spectrum somewhere between those two extremes. I reckon that my life was on the structured end – I won't say I didn't have any choices, but when I look back on the choices I took I often think I couldn't take any other choices than the ones I did.

It's difficult, isn't it? I think that we've been talking very much within the context of an individual's life, and an individual's choice, but we're all of us born into a particular time-cycle and the collective situation. There are times when what's going on at the collective level overrides the individual whose life is relatively insignificant. One of the things that I've often puzzled about is – take something like that plane disaster up in Scotland – Lockerbie. Now you see, some people didn't catch that plane. They felt they should not travel, or by some accident, or some quirk of fate, they missed the plane and are alive today. Other people caught the plane. Now you find constant examples of people who didn't catch the plane or whatever is the equivalent. A train disaster in the 1950s. I had a cousin on that train. On an impulse just before the train crashed, he got out of his seat and went into the corridor. Everybody else in his carriage was killed. Now how does one read that? The other end of it is, how does one read all those who got killed? I don't know. It's easier to find a reason for the person who escaped.

CHAPTER 19

Rebirthing

Margot Messenger

Margot Messenger is a psychotherapist with a private practice in London. She employs numerous techniques, especially rebirthing.

I was just going to say what I would like – and you can join me if you like – I'm just going to breathe and centre myself a little bit before I talk with you ... [Pause] ...

Can you tell me how you got into this line of work?

Teaching was my meal ticket for many years. I trained to be a drama teacher at the Central School of Speech and Drama originally. Went a circuitous route through educational television, and went to the position of deputy headship. Wasn't happy doing it. Began to look for help with the stress, didn't feel I was getting job satisfaction, and so on, and found an acupuncturist. Decided 'Right this is it, there's another way of working, I'm going to be an acupuncturist.' I resigned my deputy headship before I even had a place at acupuncture college, and got the place at the acupuncture college and found part-time work, teaching in youth work, which together were paying more than my deputy headship paid and left me space to study acupuncture for two years.

Towards the end of the second year, I was involved in a car accident on my way to the college for the lecture. Just the same weekend in this block of flats here, my neighbour had invited me to a party and I had met a woman there who was a rebirther, Meg Haucke, and I liked her. We talked briefly. I was very keen – I was just about to go to Leamington for another weekend's training – I was going around taking as many acupuncture pulses as I possibly could, to fill out my homework. That weekend I had the accident, I was literally knocked off the road to the college, by a ten-ton truck loaded with scaffolding, going into the side of the taxi that I was in with a friend. Fortunately no great damage was done, I was knocked unconscious, lots of fears and stuff. It changed my feeling about going to Leamington for that training. I found it really difficult to continue going up to Leamington. And the first time I went up I stood on that corner, and just had a good think, and thought: 'Right, what is all this about? What is going on?'

I continued for that year, passed my exams very well, and was due to go to the clinical year the following year which would have involved me going up every weekend instead of one weekend in a month. And I sat in my kitchen looking around at my home, thinking about what that would entail, and thinking: 'What *am* I doing? This feels like climbing up Everest or something, and can I keep all this going?' Well while I was thinking about all that, my downstairs neighbour said: 'You remember Meg that you met at my party, and she said that she was going to start a group for women to go and have a support group around rebirthing? She's going to do it tomorrow night. Do you want to come and have a rebirth?' And so I said, 'How much is it?' It was a fiver, so I thought 'Fine, I'm willing to throw a fiver, she seemed a nice enough woman. I'll go and experience it.' And so I went with my neighbour.

When I was waiting for her downstairs I noticed one of my ex-partner's poems was on her fridge, because he'd been her neighbour too. And it probably started a train of thoughts and feelings which, as soon as I laid down to do this breathing, encouraged by this woman, all this stuff started to come up, and she encouraged me to keep breathing, and keep breathing, and keep breathing. Something shifted around my perception of that whole situation, which was – previously I had seen it as being a terrible failure on my part, and I suddenly saw that I had been the one to perceive that the whole thing was not working, I'd cut through something, let it go. The only person I hadn't let go – freed – was myself, and that felt like a lot of baggage to put down within the space of an evening's session, just through breathing. And I was very intrigued by the whole process. That started the whole thing for me.

Bearing in mind that you do other things, other than rebirthing, how do you begin to describe what you do?

I guess I share the tools that have worked for me in as far as I've been interested that they've worked and tried to find out what they are and how to use them. They have come to me, they have helped me. So if somebody else would like to try them and see if they work for them then I'm very willing to offer them, and support them while they try them.

Rebirthing is becoming consciously aware of your breathing, and how, by becoming consciously aware of your breathing and connecting your breathing, you can stay with something and stay in the moment and be really there with it and focusing on it, until possibly you will find a way of accommodating what it is that has come up, which is positive for you. A way of accepting something and taking from that, and the courage to move on. And the other side with the breathing is actually taking responsibility for what you're thinking, what you're feeling, and what you do. So if you can take responsibility for it, and be with it, and breathe, then amazing things do seem to happen.

Can you tell me about the history of rebirthing?

Well this breath yoga has been around for thousands of years. There's nothing new about it. But a man called Leonard Orr in the '70s, he actually started doing this kind of breathing first in a sauna, then in warm baths that he had. And he found that if he breathed in this way then things would come to the surface, maybe things that he had blocked, because when something difficult is going on, one of the first things to be affected is our breathing.

So what happens is that you reverse the process, and by connecting the breathing, you connect – perhaps you go to a point where you haven't been able to connect, and you're given another chance to connect your breathing as these feelings, and maybe pictures, come up for you. He worked with that in his bath, and my understanding is that he was an American guy who hadn't had an easy upbringing and had a lot of pain, and he chose actually to breathe his way through all this stuff.

Initially people thought you had to do it, it was all about the water, so all this hot-tubbing and everything, and they didn't quite understand how it was going to be for anybody, and some people like Leonard Orr are very courageous around all this sort of stuff, and they'll stay with it. I think some other people really got freaked out around it, and I think rebirthing got a very bad name, and deservedly so in my opinion. Because it was messing around with something in perhaps an unsafe way – I think it *was* unsafe – initially.

And then eventually they got to the thing that, okay, it wasn't the hot water, although that certainly added a dimension and it is a dimension still in rebirthing, it was the breathing that was the real thing. That you could do it – dry rebirthing – with somebody who understood, to encourage somebody to keep breathing no matter what, encouraging them that they're actually in the now; right now they are safe and they can actually experience these things, feel these things and move through them and be empowered.

I think there's some confusion in some people's minds simply with the name of the process – rebirthing. Does the title actually mean anything?

Yes, it's interesting because it was discussed at the AGM just a couple of weekends ago. And every so often there's like a lot of confusion around this name, and shall we change it, and so on.

Well, our first breath is taken at birth, and if we're going to connect with our experiences then it's about *all* our experiences right from the beginning. So I see that as being quite an important thing, that is signalled in the name rebirthing, and also it's a transformational process, in a sense of actually going through a period of major change and being transformed, reborn.

So actually I like the term rebirthing. In my experience, it took me a very long time before I went through what I experienced as my birth trauma. I went through a whole bunch of other stuff which wasn't at all about birth. It took me years of working with the process before I got there. For other people it's not like that, it comes up fairly quickly, it comes when it's relevant to come, I think.

What happens when someone comes to see you? Do you have contracts, do you have informal agreements, do you set goals ...

The contact is usually made, as you made contact with me, on the phone. I do not publicise my address anywhere, not in *Breathe* [Journal of Rebirthing] – anywhere, so the first contact is on the phone.

Could you just tell me why that is, do you just want some privacy?

Yes, I work from home, and so if somebody's interested in working with me, doing individual sessions – my method is to suggest that they come and see me and meet me, and we have a cup of tea together. And they bring their questions, and I bring mine to that interview. So that's where we start. There's no commitment on either side, there's no charge for that, and for me it's about my commitment of my time, because actually, there are some people that I wouldn't consider it appropriate to work with rebirthing. So my questioning is very much about that and I also like to have the time in a very informal way just to get somebody's energy generally, and for them to have an opportunity to get mine. Do they feel comfortable? Because if we haven't got a level of trust at that basic human level then nothing's going to go on between us.

So that is the first thing. At that interview I am very careful to show them the code of ethics and practice and to say that I am very glad that we have that – the British Rebirth Society – because that is the safe boundaries which make it safe for us to work together. I show them my qualifications, I prefer to have pictures on my walls, so I don't put those round ... [Laughs] ... But I think it very relevant that they should see those. And I give them the pamphlet from the British Rebirth Society to read.

I give them my business card, I give them something called 'The Five Biggies', by Leonard Orr, which are things that very often come up when you work with a rebirthing process, are predictably: *the birth trauma*; *parental disapproval syndrome* – which is like – the whole concept of that as I understand it is that we are all wonderful beings of radiant light, *truly*, and we're not recognised as such, and so we have a lot of repressed stuff and that is visited – in the biblical terms – on generations, so that can come up, how they have taken on limitations from parents' attitudes; *the specific negatives* – things that you acquire in your life like 'I'm no good with money', or 'relationships don't work for me', or whatever it is, negative patterns; *the death urge* – like 'I've had enough of this, I'd just like to call it quits right now', and that you have these two things going all the time, and in as far as one is stronger than the other, we stay alive. And rebirthing would say that – and I'd go along with that, because it empowers me, not because I can prove it –

that it's not a great meat-cleaver coming down from the sky. All the time I feel positively committed to being here, being alive in my body, then there's no reason why I shouldn't actually be healthy and functioning and doing that – so that's empowering; *other lifetimes* – now I keep an open mind about other lifetimes, could be like some dream story that you tell yourself, some kind of waking dream. What people make of it is entirely up to them, but, including myself, sometimes people have had experiences of seemingly a different character, a different place, different clothes and all those kinds of things. And the story has been relevant to my *now*.

And so, that's just like, 'Well here you are', so it's a little bit of a test like, 'Are you ready for any of this to come up?' Because not everybody would actually want to touch it with a bargepole. And it's as well to know that, then. Some people are very excited and intrigued by it.

So then we talk and a big question for me is: 'We live in a very stressed society, it's around us all the time. What do you know about your coping mechanisms?' And I share mine, because as a rebirther it's about practising honesty, and I tell them that rebirthers are rather different in this way. I'm not somebody who's going to sit here, behind some impassive wall, but I don't take over someone else's session, I would hope. But nonetheless if there's something going on with me I will share it. And so it also alerts them to the fact that I'm a person too. I share my coping mechanisms and also I am aware of them, and notice and try and do something about it.

So they tell me theirs, and I also negotiate that a lot of these patterns have been here for a very long time, and I don't particularly think it's helpful to think in terms that you are going to shift it … [clicks fingers] … like that, bingo! And that sometimes it is a question of complementary practices, working with the thoughts and with the breathing, and it's like finding a balance with all of that and being supported, and so I suggest – you know gestation is nine months, I give one session as a gift as a form of tithing, because I really do believe that this process works on all levels, and that's a way of acknowledging that, and so I negotiate for ten sessions with them, to give them support. If somebody tells me that they are into taking dope regularly or something like that, or are heavily into alcohol, I may think that this is not appropriate, and I probably *would* think that this is not an appropriate thing.

I give them my questionnaire, and the questionnaire goes further and will ask about medical background, psychological background and so on. And there again, it's very much being open. I'm not going to take on something, if somebody has a medical problem or a psychological problem, then they need to be seen by somebody else, and I would hope that I would suggest that. So it's screening. Quite a vigorous screening. And so if they are still interested after all of that then we discuss terms, and maybe you want to know that as well?

Well I was going to ask you later about that, about the economics of therapy …

Well shall I put it in now, or do you want to save it until later?

If you want to. Some people think if people pay it really makes them committed to the work. Others say it's a pity you can't give poor people the stuff.

Yes and I agree with that, that's why I'm very happy that I was part of a working party to draw up a list of competencies – you might want to take that away with you – for rebirthing, which means that rebirthers can now register with the Institute for Complementary Medicine. The Institute for Complementary Medicine is pressing for things like rebirthing to be offered through GPs on the National Health Service. And that I'm really committed to. At the moment that doesn't exist, so it's very much about me having a balance; I feel I commit myself very thoroughly and I give a lot of energy if I give my commitment to working with somebody. And it isn't about me mirroring victim stuff to somebody else. Because if I feel I have to take on the problems of the world and sort them out I'm not going to be any good to anybody. I would like a fair exchange, I keep my costs as low as I can, I don't want to price myself out of a reasonable bracket, I offer a sliding scale. I'm also open to other forms of exchange which some people offer me in terms of if they have something that I could benefit from – that I want as well – then I'm willing to negotiate along those lines with them.

So basically I offer rebirthing now in two contexts. I offer what I call straight rebirthing, which is an initiation, support around learning the breath techniques, plus affirmation work, plus some business about looking at dreams and so on which I see as all part of what's going on mentally for somebody, in two-hour sessions. And for that I charge £40 for a two-hour session in the way that I told you. Then you can have what I call, borrowing from Stephen Brooks, integral therapy, which is like the whole of me and all the tools that I've acquired. I offer that in three-hour sessions. So that might be a bit of voice dialogue and then the rebirthing. It might be a *Jin Shin Do* acupressure session for some blockage that I've observed somewhere in the body. What else do I do? Those two things definitely, I can't remember what I do ... [laughs]... oh hypnotherapy, that's another big one. There might be something that can be helped through hypnotherapy. So I will include that. So that is a regular three-hour session, and I charge £50 for that. And if you have the two-hour one you can still have any of the other stuff, and you can opt in for an extra hour, but then I'll charge you £15, so that will be £55. And I do that very much, when I change my prices or whatever, that is very much a business of my actually meditating upon it, and feeling what feels right and feels good within my body. It comes from that central space in me.

So then, okay we get to the first session. So the person turns up to the first session, and if I haven't taught them at the original interview I teach them 20 connected breaths (which is the way we started) to centre ourselves and actually observe what's going on with the breathing, what's happening in the body, how the person is feeling, all that. Sometimes we get very dramatic reactions just from that. Then we set up a thing: 'Okay, what changes do you want from the session?', and then it's a question of questioning, quite precisely. 'What changes do you want? Why do you think you haven't done it like that before? How will you notice that those changes are happening?' Basic things really. 'Do you want the changes in every context? What could go wrong? What do you get out of having it the way it is?' Really pushing. And we have that, and particularly about how will you notice change I think is a very important question. Because people can so easily on a bad day think, 'Oh nothing works, it's all rubbish', and in fact if they look, there have been changes going on. So it's very important, I encourage them to set the benchmarks for their own change. And we review that, certainly by session five, we'll review it – that's halfway through, to see what's happening.

So it's quite systematic, in the way I work. That usually takes the best part of an hour to do that for the first session. And then it's 'Okay, so now would you like to work with the breathing?' Personally I don't attempt to force the breathing at all. It's like noticing what's happening and mirroring it back to the person, the whole time. 'Are you aware that you, actually your breathing is very shallow at the moment?' I'm also aware that – because my hypnotherapy training made me aware of this – people do go into a trance state. Breathing takes them into a trance state. And so, if you've got the rapport, it is possible to use that. You can use suggestibility, but I use that very carefully. I don't do very much. Leonard Orr says: 'The less you do the better rebirther you are.' So it's very much just being with the client, and I go into some kind – I breathe too at the same time. And I go into some intuitive kind of space, hopefully. I do, I work from a different space at that time. And so when they're doing the breathing, it's very much – there's a mnemonic BRAID – so that 'B' is the breathing, connecting the breathing, consciously connecting the breathing so that there isn't a gap. And then actually noticing – it's very interesting – you can notice where somebody's energy is. Some people are very [up here]. Well it might be an idea for balancing them, to bring their breathing lower down. Somebody who is getting very spacey, it might be a good idea to bring their breathing up. Or they're going unconscious, so you bring their breathing up, not spacey but if they're going unconscious you can bring their breathing right up. There is also a thing in rebirthing which I'm aware of, is that it links in with embryology, and the development of the lungs. Our very early lungs, they grow from the top, so our very earliest stuff is often held up here, and so I'm aware of that and so it could be some armouring around here, which encourages a person to breathe there – so we notice that breathing affects the whole body, every cell of the body. 'How aware are you of the breath travelling in your body, and where are you aware that maybe it's tense and blocked, and on the outbreath you can consciously relax those spots.' So it's encouraging them actually to use this – usually when we breathe very fully, we're immediately expending it into some kind of activity. But here you're still, mostly, it's not that you have to be, but you can actually be in stillness and focus on the way your energy is travelling through your body on the breath. And that for me as an acupuncturist was a very interesting thing, because I could actually be aware of energy travelling in my body in the way that I had been trained to be aware of it.

Could you just explain for the reader how they do it? Do they sit, do they lie? What exactly do you do, do you make them take deep breaths, shallow breaths ...

Initially I would suggest lying down. And some people – there was one guy who said to me: 'You're going to have to be very passionate with me', he speaks English as his second language 'because I go to sleep.' And lo and behold, I went off to go to the toilet before coming down, and he was asleep ... [Laughs] ... He'd take a couple of breaths and he was asleep. So obviously lying down was not appropriate for him. So I had him sitting up. In the end I had him standing. You can have people standing, you can walk, there isn't one way. It's like how can you be conscious with your breathing? But very often you can, you can have a nice alignment of your spine, you can really relax, draw your knees up if you feel better that way, that's to do with the position. And then, yes, be aware of the dynamics of the breath. Of the full breath. You can breathe faster, more slowly, and really explore those dynamics, and what happens when you do it. So it's about not being stuck in one particular pattern. Because this is what they're coming for, they're coming for change. And insofar as their breathing mirrors what they're doing, then changes can be suggested.

So yes, I don't personally subscribe to a particular way of breathing. Even really poor breathing, going unconscious or whatever, well that's what you need to mirror back to the client, because that's where they are, and it – for me, for them to breathe for me – I didn't take on his responsibility, you know, 'you have to be very passionate'. I supported him in actually seeing that he could become responsible for breathing consciously or not. So now I have a deal with him – that he tells me – if he wants to go to sleep because he feels suddenly overwhelmed with tiredness, he can sleep for ten minutes. But don't let's pretend that that's rebirthing breathing, 'cos it isn't. 'All right go to sleep, have your sleep for ten minutes. I'll wake you up in ten minutes and we'll have another go.'

Subsequent sessions, do you repeat more of the same?

Yes, and it's always different. Yes it's about people becoming aware of their breathing, and how they are with it, and sometimes you have what rebirthers call a 'breath release', where suddenly the breath seems to be flowing and more powerful and everything, and you can be with that – suddenly aware of how most of us underbreathe the whole time, and how good it can feel when we breathe fully.

And sometimes chemical changes occur in the body, which are painful, to the balance of carbon dioxide and oxygen, which rebirthers need to be aware of because then people get this muscle spasm called 'tetany', which is painful, very uncomfortable, and it's about the balance not being right. Trying to run before you can walk, really. And you can carry on through that or you can think: 'Okay, well I don't have to do that any more.' I went through agony with tetany in my legs initially. And sometimes I can feel it coming up and I think: 'Okay, ease off on the exhale, I don't have to go through that number.' I don't necessarily believe that all good changes come through suffering these days. Some people really feel like something's happening.

Is the idea ultimately to give them a tool, that they can take away?

Yes, absolutely, and so more and more towards the end of the sessions it's about encouraging them, asking them whether they – initially it will be: 'Do you do 20 connected breaths sometimes? Do you use it in times when perhaps things are coming up that you find quite stressful? Do you notice your breathing?' And then it will be: 'Well, do you ever lie down and have a breathe?' And: 'Can I do it on my own?'

What kind of dramatic things may occur in rebirthing which is advantageous for the client? The concept of birth trauma intrigues me. Is that an important thing?

Yes, birth trauma is important insofar as although we're not verbal, we can nonetheless have concepts at that time. And so if we're going round with some kind of concept from birth, which is: 'Okay, so it was a difficult birth, and the obstetrics team hurt the baby, when the baby came out', and then the person can go round with – well, I can't prove this – but if patterns come up in that person's life of 'I've been hurt again', it's like: 'Okay, so maybe that's coming from some kind of concept around birth.' And it's like: 'Okay, that's as it was then, and if I go round thinking people are going to hurt me, then it's amazing you can get that, because you're actually setting yourself up for it. So are you going to be responsible for actually opening to another kind of thought, and breathing into that?'

How does that link with the rebirthing process? Do you relive it?

Yes, in a different kind of way. When it came up for me, and I'd rather speak about myself than anyone else's process really, it was like I was aware of a terrific amount of anger. I was aware that – my mother wasn't in a space to receive me, she had a lot of trauma going on. My father had died in the War, and it seemed there was a bit in me that says 'People aren't ready for me. Perhaps it would be better to forget the whole idea. I'm quite happy to just stay here and just forget all this idea about living.' And I was really angry with the obstetrics team that pulled me out with forceps. Fury.

So does this come up because someone is talking to you, or is it something that intuitively comes through the breathing?

Intuitively comes through the breathing. Just through my feelings, and a lot of it is feelings. Sometimes they can be pictures or whatever, but a lot of it is just a sense of just going with these feelings when they come up.

What kind of things do the clients come for? The range. What do you think rebirthing is particularly good for?

It's quite a range. There's a lot of course which comes under the self-development bracket. And particularly I think within the climate as things are at the moment, our emotional selves have a very tough time of it. So I think rebirthing is particularly good because it is – I just felt able to be vulnerable in rebirthing, to find that it was something that I could lie down on the mattress underneath a blanket. For me that worked, because I surrendered to that in a way that some other therapies – I'm like 'Oh I don't know if I want to do this.' And I'm in my head. In this I go back to my baby state. My vulnerable baby state, and I'm willing to be with myself as a very vulnerable, very intuitive, very aware being, and picking up things that at other times I just don't pick up maybe in the same way. People who are having rebirthing – if I put music on at the end, at just a very, very low level, all their senses are much more keenly attuned. And so that is another big by-product – certainly I have a number of people who work artistically. A lot of musicians I've had, dancers ... it can be very creative.

Other than self-developers, what kind of problems do people come with?

Gosh, it's quite a range really.

Do some come because they want to be in some sense healed?

I don't know if they want to be healed, because I'm very clear about where that comes from and whose responsibility that is. I can't fix somebody. I'll support somebody while they look at what's going on for them, and perhaps with support they can look at some pain, some ways in which they handle things, perhaps be willing to take that on board, and change something. It's up to them. So I am very wary about being seen in that light, and I'm very quick to dispel any of that. Because – this is what I love about rebirthing – it's about taking responsibility. And in as far as I allow

myself to be set up as the one who's going to do it, that's not encouraging
someone else to be responsible.

You were earlier saying that people live too much in their head ...

Well I don't want to say 'Live too much in their head'; I didn't mean to
be critical about it. I think it's just a fact, that if you're trying to put
something into words, then you're calling on that, whereas I think these
energies, they sit in our bodies. And rebirthing is about breathing into
your body, and feeling your physical feelings – and it's amazing how
something that starts off as maybe – I had a woman just the day before
yesterday, it must have been, having a tightness coming [up here] and
just being with it and relaxing on the exhale and breathing into this
tight area, and then an enormous, she wouldn't know what it was, just
enormous grief and tears and sighs, and just to release that in a safe
space. You don't have to know what it is, there's a lovely saying, I
probably got it from one of my trainers: 'If you're throwing out the
garbage you don't have to read the labels on the packets.' And this is
where rebirthing is different. It's not about analysing all that stuff. So
you feel this grief inside, well if you're carrying that around in you, it's
okay to express it, to be, or if it's anger, to shout.

*When you're with a client, how much is just verbal, or do you massage
them, touch them? How much of it is tactile?*

Here is very much a thing about asking the client how they feel about
that. Some clients love it, and some clients would feel very nervous about
that. So it's working that out, and indeed there is a certain amount – it
feels good sometimes to stroke somebody's head, sometimes even to lie
next to them, really rebirthing-fashion. A real closeness. If somebody
turns over on their side, I normally support their back, because during the
birth process there's a lot of that being squeezed, and to support somebody's back can be a very effective thing.
    It's a lot about intuition and it's a lot about trust and honesty
between the client – they can say 'No, leave me alone', or whatever.
And building that kind of rapport.

*What do you think optimum health is? Or do you just want them to be
happy with themselves?*

Much more the last thing I think. Because my own sense is that in as
far as we experience *dis*-ease, it's because of something that's going for
us which sometimes is part of the whole process, that aiming to be well
and fit and .... all the time is maybe denying something. Sometimes the
only way our – I think the body is a great teacher and this is why I love
working with rebirthing and the connection with the breath and the
body – because the body teaches us and actually doesn't lie to us. You

can conceal lots of things, but the body just says 'Hang on a minute, maybe you can be the big man and think you can get up at the crack of dawn and go on until midnight, and so on, but actually I know otherwise. I'm going to show you a vulnerability about yourself', and whoomf! you're laid flat. Fine, it's probably better that than if it didn't happen. There's listening to those signals.

Are there any clients in your own experience, who've failed to benefit from the process?

Yes. I've had my ones that I haven't been so happy with. And then it's time for me to look and think 'What did I do wrong there?' I once did a check – which is why I screen people quite carefully now, about what they know about their coping mechanisms – because I once went through and did a check on the people who worked with me, who committed initially for ten sessions and didn't make it through ten sessions. And it was just amazing, it was an incredibly high percentage, 80 or 90 per cent came down to one single word which was 'marijuana'. I was taking people who were into recreational drugs, and they wanted it, and there was a lot of them who were very open to that whole thing, and yet in the *now*, in the reality of their lives, they didn't stick. So that's one reason for that.

So that was one bunch of flops, if you like. Then there have been people who, for one reason or another, I have felt that we could establish rapport but the rapport has broken. And sometimes it's been perhaps because of something that was going on for me, something I didn't make clear. There was one person that went a long way I felt, and then there was a time when she couldn't come, and she let me know with just about an hour or so's notice. And I hadn't clarified my procedures around that. I was a bit pissed off, and I forget, I can't remember clearly, but I said something that she took exception to about that, and she didn't feel that she could trust me anymore. So I'm very careful now. I say: 'I require 24 hours notice.' That broke our rapport.

Someone else, I think, had some kind of issue about – I don't know – they didn't trust me, we had some trust issue going. It was like, 'Why do you always sit in that chair?' 'Well you can sit in this chair if you want' ... [Laughs] ...

Someone else, actually just on Tuesday, someone that I'd put a lot of effort into – but I feel again sometimes I can trip myself up and get over-responsible. Someone who wanted to do it and then their wife had an issue with how much it was costing, and so because I have a thing that says I don't work just for money, I actually gave him a reduced rate for it all, and I think maybe I took on too much responsibility. And his feeling is he didn't get as much out of it as he wanted to get out of it, and I'm thinking: 'Yes it's very interesting. I really pulled the stops out for you around money and all the rest of it. Maybe I just took on your stuff, and this is why it didn't work.' So that's what I'm filing away at the back for me, and thinking: 'Ah, another time I can be a bit clearer about that.' Because it's a developmental process for me too.

Do you keep ongoing week-by-week records of your clients?

I do. I'm probably unusual in that. Well [this] is my pad, and as you see it's got a sheet of carbon, so I give my clients the top copy and I keep the carbon. And it reminds me of the work that we have done, what we've worked through, what's come up, and if I'm finding – if I'm wondering how that process is going – I can go through my notes and look and think: 'Now I wonder what I could do to support them more?' I keep notes on the breathing. Very careful notes on the breathing – how it is. I keep notes on how they are with their affirmation work and all the work on the thoughts, the issues they come with.

Can you explain the affirmation part of it, because that's the central part of rebirthing, isn't it?

It is yes. There are different ways of working with affirmations. There's a book on rebirthing called *Rebirthing – The Science of Enjoying All of Your Life*, by Jim Leonard and Phil Laut. And the way I work is pretty much in accord with what's there, because you can go round saying: 'I'm happy and everybody loves me, and prosperity flows my way.' You can say that until you're blue in the face, and if you don't deal with your negative side that says 'Everybody loves you – what about so and so?' then I don't think that's going to shift anything at all. It's just going into total denial of where you are right now. So the way I suggest clients work with affirmations, is with what's called a response column. And I suggest that they work with it, not only in the first, second, and third persons, because 'Okay, there's the thoughts that I have about me, there're thoughts that I have received from other quite powerful people, a lot of them in the past – parents, teachers all the rest of it, religious leaders – that I've got going on for me, and there's also how I perceive people might perceive me, third person.'

So working with affirmations is about doing it in blocks of ten, again. Three first, three second, three third and then going back to the first. And with a tenth response, which is: 'This or something better now manifests for me, Margot, in totally innocent and harmonious ways for the highest good of all concerned.' I can't affirm something that perhaps involves somebody else, I can only affirm for myself and my own change, and that catchphrase is about being in harmony, and so on. And I think that's very important on the spiritual dimension of all of this.

And it's about: 'Okay, so life is easy for me, Margot.' Right, okay, (maybe I'm into some kind of struggle or other). So I write 'life is easy for me Margot'. 'How many evenings have I had off this week?' So maybe I'll write that down, that's my response. And so on, 'yes, life is easy for me,

Margot. Bit of a struggle around getting all these repairs done in my home.' I begin to become specific and that can focus my energy, and I can then get out of my negative responses – it's like catching negative thoughts. Okay, celebrate. If you're clear that you've got a negative thought – celebrate. Because that's the first step. If you accept that negative thought, then that's the first step to turning it around, going deeper, looking at further negative thoughts and turning them around.

So it's a whole process like unpeeling an onion.

So when does the affirmation work occur?

There are certain things that people may present to you as ways they feel about themselves. If you get that coming from a client – wonderful, you've got something. Sometimes there are things that can stimulate it, like: 'I've got a bunch of thoughts for them to grade and see what brings up stuff for them.' Sometimes it comes up through the body. I think the work of Louise Hay has been very supportive for me in this, because I'm a body therapist, and I see rebirthing as body therapy. Like the fact that someone has something coming up in the throat. So, 'Okay, what are throats about? Throats are about our channel of expression.' So maybe this person isn't actually opening themselves to their self-expression in some way. So you can actually feed in affirmations – if I get really clear about it, I'll actually say something to a person as they're breathing. And they – maybe that thought will be helpful, if not they can say: 'Do you mind? Will you shut up while I'm doing this?' ... [Laughs] ...

Can you just explain to me again, because I don't think I've understood it, the role of the affirmation in rebirthing. It's like encouraging people in positive thinking – is that what it is?

Well, it's about taking responsibility for your thoughts, for your feelings, and for your actions. So affirmations – if you're going to take responsibilities for your thoughts, if you have a negative thought, 'Ah, it's all a load of rubbish', or whatever, then energy follows thought. So if that is your thought – 'It's an unsafe world and they're all out to get me', that's what you're projecting. So if you find that people don't actually want to be your friend, or get close to you or something, then take responsibility that you're saying, 'I don't trust you, stay off'. And, okay, are you happy to continue like that or would you like actually to change that set of circumstances and see that, maybe you can take responsibility, and 'I trust myself and others', is perhaps an affirmation that you'd be willing to work with.

And how does it dovetail into the breathing?

Because as you work with the affirmations you integrate them with the breathing, and you breathe in as you write the affirmations. And if you have a thought given to you as you're breathing, then you can breathe that thought in and say it inside your head, and see what happens. Integrate it.

What do you think, speaking for yourself, are the necessary skills to be a rebirther?

I think one very necessary thing is actually to practise what you preach. Actually to work with this process in an ongoing way yourself, and be committed to doing that. Because I'm only as good as I'm honest with myself, and use these tools in my own journey. I think it is necessary to be okay around a whole range of emotions, and feel safe when people are expressing emotion and celebrate that as a way of being. And to be very interested in breathing, and people. It's a weird thing to be interested in. Some people say: 'Breathing, how boring!' ... [Laughs] ...

Do you see rebirthing as part of the transpersonal arm of therapeutic work? Some people are happy to see people as the sum of their minds and bodies, merely ...

Sum of their minds and bodies, you've thrown me a bit. There is something for me that is beyond the mind and the body, certainly. And, yes, for me it's working towards the transpersonal through the personal and the interpersonal. In rebirthing, it can be a very personal experience. There's the interpersonal thing of building up the trust and the rapport – it's all like a mirror of what's going on, and if you can be happy and content, and in the now with yourself and all that's going on, and you can do that in the presence of another being, let alone in a group session with several other beings, I think this is a wonderful way forward. And then you can be in that for other people that you may come across. That's how I see the transpersonal working, really, in moving out in ever-developing circles.

When you said earlier that some people say 'How can you be interested in breathing, it's so boring', bearing that in mind and knowing that the reader isn't actually here, having a session, how would you put into words how breathing can have a profound effect on you? It's a hard thing to describe isn't it?

I don't know, because I haven't really answered that specific question before. I think again it's one of those things that putting into words *is* hard. And if someone will just perhaps even do 20 consciously connected breaths, they can have an experience that gives them 'wow'.

I think that the key is that you're helping them breathe in ways that they've forgotten ...

Exactly.

Can you tell me about the ethical issues of rebirthers?

One of the most common ones, I suppose, is that whole business about the relationship. If somebody is dealing with their emotional stuff and they see you as a safe person to be with, and if you have your emotional stuff going on, then you'd better declare it. And sometimes it gets quite embarrassing to be a rebirther, because you need to be very straight with this stuff. There are a couple of men that I've worked with that I've needed to declare that I find them very attractive, and it's been okay because we've been able to work. There was one person that also found me very attractive, and it was time for us to be very clear about that, that we were *not* going to be in a therapeutic relationship any longer, we wished it to be something else. So quickly, like a hot potato, I gave him to somebody else to work with.

So that's an ethical issue, and one I think is very important, and that's why I'm really glad that the British Rebirth Society have drawn that [code] up.

Another one that's at the top of our list is actually that rebirthers work for something other than monetary gain. And I think – and many people come and think – 'Just sit next to people while they're having a breathe. Money for jam, isn't it? I think I'll have some of that.' And it's very wonderful actually to see how that can quickly get weeded out. I think it's very essential, and because rebirthing is going into this very vulnerable, intuitive space that you go into, people pick it up, and that goes. That is why with me around money, I need to know that I'm coming from my real truth with that. That I really feel that I'm worth this amount.

I had a big issue when I went for ten sessions with a male rebirther, having done my initial ten sessions – because it's suggested that you work with a man or a woman. Did my initial ten sessions with a man – and he charged twice as much as I charged as a rebirther. And the first session was about clearing that he wasn't twice as good as me. He had a big issue around money, which I'm more content to let flow.

So when you say that the ethical statement says that you have to make it clear that you're doing this for more than money, what is the other thing that you're doing it for?

Tremendous job satisfaction. Just wonderful to hear about the changes that people make in their lives, and to be privileged to be a part of that. Wonderful, it's one of the most rewarding, certainly the most rewarding thing that I've come across.

What kind of self-monitoring do you engage in?

As I said, I do keep rigorous notes, so I can go back and look and see what's happening there. I am a trainer/practitioner, so I have people in training with me, and that means that we can get together, and I take that space as well, and so I have colleagues with whom I can discuss what's going on. And I have my own sessions. I have a hot-tub session that I do once a month, and I go there, and that is my supervision as much as anything.

Can you describe that, for people who don't know what it is?

What a hot-tub session is? Okay. It is about recreating as near as we possibly can an actual birth situation for yourself, where you're in water at womb temperature which is very hot actually – about 104 degrees Fahrenheit. I actually usually cheat on that, it's usually about 100 at my hot-tubs, because I find that a bit more effective. And using a – if you want, you don't have to – but one way is to totally immerse yourself in that water, with a snorkel to breathe from. So there you are, attached by a tube to your oxygen supply, in water at womb temperature. And amazing things happen, around – okay, you can say it's about sensory deprivation, I'm sure that is a part of it. You've been *sharing* with people beforehand, an awful lot of loving support, compassionate support is there. You know that you've got goodwill coming towards you, compassion and all the rest of it. And there you are, and if you choose – you don't have to – to be without clothing, so again that's about really being open to your vulnerability. And staying in the *now* with – what happens when you do that? Noticing your body, noticing your feelings, expressing, not going into catharting, that's something going on and on and on. But if you have something come up and it would feel good to release it, then release it.

And so you do this once a month?

I do that once a month.

How long do you stay in the water for? Does it vary?

It varies, yes. A good support person will say: 'Are you sure that you're complete?' – and completion is when you feel you could go on for ever.

Have you many thoughts about other therapists? Are there things that you're not particularly keen on?

Obviously, it's very interesting isn't it that some people stay with things that you wonder why on earth they ever did. Obviously there must be something that they got from it. But I did have one client who said to me something about that they had been *ten years* with a psychotherapist. And this person had actually said: 'There are some people who are just so wounded that they just need holding for the rest of their lives, thank you very much.'

Now where the independence is in that, I don't know. So I don't think that's particularly empowering, but maybe there are, maybe that's a different way of working. It's not a way I would feel happy about working.

Can you just go back to the hot-tub thing a minute, is that just for experienced rebirthers? You wouldn't do it with your clients?

Oh no, no, no, I would. That is for people who have had ten, or nearly ten, dry rebirthing sessions, who have an experience of themselves breathing through issues as they come up and being able to handle it. And then, it's more advanced. It's about keeping clear in order to work with other people for me. Because if I've got stuff going on, I need to deal with it, and the hot-tub is a wonderful place for me to go and deal with it in a supported atmosphere. The dry rebirth sessions – there are now three of us supporting those group sessions, so if one of us comes with a load of stuff, we'll have a rebirth. Two of us will work and one can have a rebirth. So we very often take that space as well.

CHAPTER 20

Psychotherapy for Women

Sally Berry

Sally Berry is currently Clinical Director of the Women's Therapy Centre, London. She is also a psychotherapist in private practice.

Could you tell me a little about your background?

Do you mean personally or with this therapist thing?

Essentially, how you got into therapy.

Well actually I came into it through teaching. I taught what in the States was called special education, and I came to this country to do that kind of teaching. I was working on an American military base as a special needs teacher, and I got involved and interested in working with the families of the children. Because I began to see that the kind of issues that were coming into my classroom, were coming from situations in the family setting. It began to make understandable the children's behaviour and their experiences and even their educational development. So I got interested in working within a clinical setting on the base, and that connection put me in touch with an organisation that was just beginning here, which is called the Arbours Association. So I made a decision to stop teaching and decided I wanted to pursue another way of thinking about working with people. Because I had found that the element I most liked about the teaching was the relationships. So I lived for a time in a community and then I was involved in a crisis centre that the Arbours Association set up in the early '70s, lived there for several years, and did a training through the Arbours Association. I'm actually still involved with them.

I came into therapy through that direction, through the Arbours community crisis centre. The early '70s was a specific time where there was a community-based belief in psychotherapy, and the desire to help people was extremely strong. The living situation was the way in which change was seen as possible. If you believed that you felt you needed to be involved in that process, you actually needed to live within it. And I think that that probably forms very much my belief about therapy still. Because I think it makes a massive difference if you actually have a very close experience of what distress does, both for the individual who lives with distress, and the family network. I think it puts it in the context, and I suppose that kind of structure really does still reverberate, in my understanding of people's inner world and their experiences.

How would you describe the tradition you work in?

Well I suppose it has a strong psychoanalytic base. I think from that it's moved. Certainly I think that at the Women's Therapy Centre (WTC) we feel we offer psychoanalytic psychotherapy. But we understand that in a particular kind of way. Each therapist has always chosen how they worked within the context of the WTC. Locating the work to give maximum access to the women we prioritise.

So that they're actually in a physical place, how the access was given, the language used, all of that situation has always been something we keep trying to refer back to. So that if you actually are interested in having a community situation where there is an availability, you have to consider how you present yourself and how accessible people find you. Because of the number of women that we have phoning us, they have difficulty in getting through.

So it's not the usual Freudian '50 minutes'?

No, no, not at all. I think that in some way the Women's Therapy Centre in the beginning set up by Susie and Luise asked a question which is – was it a relevant need? Was there really a need for the Women's Therapy Centre, and would it work? They set it up in the April of '76, and I joined in the autumn of that year. I think that what has to me been extraordinary, because I've been involved in some way all of this time, has been that that original question, the answer of it has continued. That women have from the very beginning phoned, asked for, wanted and come in massive numbers. Certainly we've never been able even to begin to touch the kind of number of contacts that we've had. There's been a difference, the number of women who are phoning who don't have financial resources is much greater now.

We've always had a strong element of providing access to a therapeutic experience without a financial situation stopping that. That understanding in this kind of setting might be very different from what an individual therapist might say in their private practice setting. Individual low fee in the private sector might be £10 to £15, at this point in time, but if you're talking about someone on benefit, who must pay for transport and/or child care, that's completely impossible by and large for a whole group of the population. So I think we've always attempted to make a low fee mean an accessible point. It might start at a minimal contribution or no contribution at all, except the energy and the commitment to the relationship. I don't think it's ever been based on the idea that you had to pay for the situation to work. Although I think we have the very strong idea that if a woman can make a contribution, that does help us to be able to continue to offer the service, and offer it in the broadest possible range to other women.

In the past there was this notion that psychoanalysis was only for the so-called 'articulate' ...

Well I think that depends on what it is you think psychotherapy is about. And what the relationship actually offers. I feel it certainly can be accessible in an easier way if someone already has the verbal skills, and also has some emotional articulance. But those can be taught. Access can be created to therapy, and the way that's done is by having the belief that someone is interested and committed in struggling with whatever issues brought them forward. If you are prepared to help them learn what the language is (because I think it *is* a particular language), and certainly some aspects of it are quite useful to build into the relationship as part of a repertoire. I think the woman has to be prepared to talk about her feelings. You also have to take immediately into consideration the difference that coming from a different setting does mean, in relationship to what it is to share intimate information with basically a stranger. How that sense of trust and belief in the process gets built, how the actual therapeutic relationship gets established and nurtured, so that that process is going to be possible.

What happens when someone comes to see you?

I think that in some ways that can only be answered on an individual basis. I don't think I work, or anyone here works, the same with everyone. They clearly have structure, and there is a level of difference within the Centre – everyone doesn't work in exactly the same way. As far as the range of problems is concerned, we have anything that you could imagine, that would prompt someone to come for therapy. One of the reasons why the Centre both was set up and has continued is that it had a particular idea to offer therapy for women by women, and that was seen as a way of trying to establish a sense of safety. It has to be also looked at in the terms of 20 years ago. At that point I don't think the whole idea of women's psychology, or that there were particular issues that might be much more relevant for women, or that there might be ways in which women might be able to make a connection with another woman that could be more helpful, was common. All those ways of thinking have now become much more part of the language, for example, issues around eating problems. The whole concept of eating problems – even the word bulimia, anorexia was just beginning to be touched on. A lot of those terms, in fact a lot of that way of thinking has been affected by the kind of work and the commitment to that level of work that's happened here. That the idea was actually to see women, and then to look with them through a frame that included women's lives, and to think about women's psychology in a concentrated way. To examine the given, not to take everything through the theoretical frames that already existed, to struggle with that, to see if we might differ with certain attitudes and ideas, to examine how that difference might actually make the connection with women more possible.

A woman comes into a particular setting we try to create, and we try to make it as friendly as possible. The rooms themselves have curtains in, we try to create an atmosphere where the chairs are comfortable, where there is as much welcoming as possible, and women can come into our tiny waiting room. It is possible to go next door and make yourself a cup of tea or a cup of coffee while you wait.

So that there is a sense in which there is an attempt not to make it foreboding and forbidden. That it is a process of trying to create an emotional access as well. I think in some way that there is always that struggle once the woman walks into the room itself. That we try to look at why she's come in. What kind of issues have brought her into this situation, and also try to understand what she might have felt, that this situation may create some kind of sense of safety. I think that that's probably much less the issue now than it was in the beginning, because I think psychotherapy as a word, and as a process is in much broader usage. Because I think that we really are finding women, many women, who don't necessarily know what it is but know that they're interested in some kind of help, coming into the Centre wanting to try to understand what kind of difference psychotherapy can make in their lives. I think they're almost always coming because there are issues in their lives that are causing them some kind of distress or pain. And they want to try to understand that.

The issue of women analysts and women patients ...

I don't think it's such an issue now, although I think 20 years ago it was seen as quite radical. I think that it was also seen as excluding, I think that the idea has never been, even though it's very clear that we offer a service to women by women, and in that sense, by putting those words in it, I think what we were trying to do is not say we weren't offering anything to men but we don't directly see men. But our belief is that we're offering a service for women that has an impact on relationships and therefore through that it can also affect other people's lives, and we felt that that would be our way of attempting to think about the whole structure and the whole necessity. And that it did seem necessary actually to have a situation where women could feel that that's the situation that they could be assured of.

Do you think it is problematic for a male therapist to treat a woman?

I don't think it has to be problematic, but I do think that by and large the kind of way of thinking that the analytic structure may have organised may not necessarily include a gender consciousness. And may not ask soundly and deeply about those issues. And may not have explored. Now that doesn't mean that I don't think any man working has had that struggle or those thoughts, or could be supportive or helpful or therapeutically rich in the experience that was available. Nor do I believe every woman has done that piece of work.

But I do think that in some way if you try to consider it and if you try to create an environment where thinking about women in that kind of way and also I think seeing it as a resource. Because I do think that one of the things that happened early on when we had a large workshop programme was that allowing women to connect with other women in a particular kind of way was a very powerful experience for everyone involved. The women in the groups and also the workshop leaders and the convenors. We now have a smaller workshop programme for women, and I think that the power of being in a situation – I wouldn't in any way say that it's not problematic because I don't think that women immediately only feel supportive in relationships to other women. Of course they have issues with women – but I think the power of actually being in a situation where they can see some of their own experiences reflected in other women has an impact that is quite extraordinary.

We've run, for the past three or four years, groups for incest survivors, and I think that kind of connectiveness – and we're running them in two separate ways, a three-month group and a six-month group – the power of this kind of setting, with women coming together having shared at least that experience, and also seeing in a group setting the kind of impact and the pain it's caused in different kinds of ways, and different women's lives, is the possibility of actually doing something through that setting, that I don't think that you can do in a one-to-one setting.

What happens when someone comes to see you?

I feel that I have to answer more generally, and then I'll answer more specifically. Because at the moment here, because of my position, I don't actually see individual clients. I have for many years, but I don't at the moment. I have a private practice. I also supervise the individual therapy. I feel slightly concerned in the sense that I know that I'm speaking for a group of people and that I do know there is a broad range of individual difference in that. That's always been nurtured and held.

We do use a time structure here, we do use a 50-minute session. And I think that that's as much a logistic issue as I believe it is in any kind of therapeutic structure. I don't feel that 50 minutes is sacrosanct, I think it's, logistically is a time frame where you can actually take someone in and do a piece of intense work, and take them out and then somehow have a breath, and then continue to do that work. I have never read anything that convinced me of the perfection of that amount of time, nor would I necessarily think that that's the only structure that one can use. In a setting where there's such an intense pressure on space, it's very difficult; people can't work in any way they want to do in terms of time, because the rooms are booked in particular kinds of ways and you have to be aware of other people.

Certainly I think people have perhaps changed that structure: if they felt it made sense for someone who was travelling a long distance, they might have had a different kind of time, but by and large that's the frame we use for individual work. But I think as far as trying to create access, I think we went through a period of time at the Centre, where we examined time to create a much broader cross-cultural experience at the Centre. One of the things that we found when we tried to focus our work on creating access – we did a project on creating access for black women to therapy – that we did feel that we learned a lot about how you actually had to approach a woman in a therapeutic setting, if you wanted her to be able to make the engagement necessary to do the piece of work. That did mean very much trying to create the language between the two of you, and some kind of sense of safety. So I suppose that that's what I feel by and large needs to happen initially, because if the relationship doesn't get established, if the woman doesn't feel safe, I can't see how any kind of – whatever one's theoretical belief is – you can't do anything if you don't have a relationship. I think it's through the relationship that the work takes place.

I think that theory facilitates that and helps you make sense of it, and helps you try to create your own understanding of what the woman is telling you. But if you don't help her begin to unfold her story then I don't believe that process will happen.

So someone comes to see you ...

Well I think the first question is whether what we have available for her makes sense for her. I think that the initial session, the consultation, is about that exploration. Because we do work in a variety of ways, in the sense that we have different kinds of contracts that are offered. We have some short-term work, we have a group of sessions that we do where a group of women are offered nine individual sessions, with the idea of moving into one a year group after that. So it will depend on what is available at the Centre and the issues the woman brings. Because there is assessment; is it possible for the woman to fit – is it possible for the woman to make use of and to find help with what we have available? So that we attempt to do an assessment looking at what she needs and balancing it with what we know we have available. That is a tension that exists for all the therapists, whenever we're doing assessments, I think. Because in an ideal world you would see a woman, and ask yourself what really makes sense for this woman? Is it an open-ended therapy situation on an individual basis, or an open-ended group? Does she need a piece of work here and then this? There will be a whole range of possible responses to that. I think we attempt to think that, but we also attempt to think that in terms of the reality of what we actually have available. So that reality certainly does come into it.

Because we have a small number of open-ended sessions on an individual basis, and the flow through of that clearly is not great. So the chances of being offered open-ended therapy is not as great. Then we offer different kinds of contracts, so the contract also has to meet the needs of the woman. Obviously if she's coming in an extremely disturbed and distressed state, where we feel that a brief piece of work would not make sense, then we would try to offer her something longer term. If we don't have that then we try, we might try, to deal with her in some other kind of way. I think one of the things that we have done is that we've increased the number of open-ended groups that we have, as a way of creating access to women so that the structure about how long they can come into therapy isn't only defined by the structure of what we have available.

And the theoretical tradition behind the groups?

Well I think they certainly have a very strong analytic base. I think they also have a particular attitude about a women-only situation. Because I do think the group has changed by the fact that it's led by the therapist who's a woman and there are only women in the group. So I think that that changes the dynamic. Then I think it also depends on what the group is, because some of the groups focus on particular issues. We have themes in some of our groups that still have an analytic base, but we have compulsive eating groups and groups for bulimic women that last one year and that's the focus in that. The reason that we try to time-limit those groups is that we don't want to focus only on that issue in that woman's life, but try to look at that issue in quite an intense way, and then perhaps broaden it out into another situation. The woman might go on to something else, having perhaps looked very closely in the company of other women about those particular issues. I wouldn't want to say that in a theme-centred group, that's the only thing that gets dealt with, because it clearly isn't, it's quite broad based. But at least that's the cover that all the women have come into it through – cover's the wrong word, but the idea that they've had, and the same thing with the incest survivors groups where that is a point of connection around the particular issue, not that we assume in that brief period of time there's going to be a resolution of the impact of that kind of trauma.

It certainly can be the beginning of the piece of that therapeutic work. I suppose that that covers the shorter-term work that we do, we understand that it's a piece in a process rather, and we understand it as complete in itself, but not complete meaning the whole therapeutic process. Because I think you can't offer someone a brief piece of work without sometimes touching on what might happen if you had a longer piece of work to offer them. So I think if you hold a very strong frame around that thinking – how can this enable something to happen for that woman in that period of time? – then you can see that she can work in that situation. I think it does take a strong hold to be working with women in time frames. I think that to me is the greatest difference about doing this kind of work in the kind of privileged situation in private practice, where you actually can and do offer people an open-ended setting.

Is there a sense that 'the group' is the second-best option?

I think there's a lot of struggle not to have those feelings here. I think that there is also a real attempt to try to struggle with the question about how you make a presentation for someone who comes for an assessment, that can show them that a group can be a therapeutically rich experience for them, not what's available. Analytic groups form a major part of the therapy provision, as we are offering about 20 groups. There is that tension of trying to approach it in that kind of way. That there are reasons why a group might work extremely well for someone, not because we can't offer you the individual. Which may be the reality, but may not be the only issue. I think in some ways psychologically, it's a struggle that the Centre has to make as well. I think that women ask for different things. Some women simply want some kind of help, and usually what they want help for is to stop whatever it is that's causing them pain. They know it's a therapy centre, but that's not really what they're looking for, they're looking for something to make something different for them in their lives. Because I don't think our experience is that, by and large, our client group is a group that's coming to explore their feelings. There may be some women who come for that reason, but it's not that kind of situation, it's because the intensity of their lives is such that they feel something needs to happen within it. And they're looking for that kind of experience to change.

How do you fuse your political consciousness – especially over the issue of gender – with your analytic perspective?

I think it's actually an error on my part not to have said that when I was talking about the frame. Because I do think that from the very beginning one of the major tenets if you will, was that a woman lived in the real world, that she was coming from a setting, and an experience and a real world experience. That that was the way in which her inner world was understood. Through that as well, rather than that her internal experience was the only thing that was focused on, and I think that that's an experience that has intensified for us over the years, in the sense that as the economic situation has really become more and more dire, the level of real world and real life experiences, horrific life experiences about housing, about domestic violence, about incest, about sexual abuse, all of those real world experiences are coming through the door with the woman. Contributing to and are factors in her inner experience. And I think that that's an absolutely crucial aspect of what we believe, which is that all of these things are contributing. In some sense one would be concerned if the woman wasn't having some distress, given that level of pain that she's brought into the situation; that you would be more concerned about someone's mental health if they weren't experiencing some pain because of almost unspeakable experiences, and clusters of experiences that happen in their lives. So I think that that piece has to be present in whatever kind of theoretical understanding you're attempting to construct. I think it's also why there is such a strong commitment for us to be able to offer therapy to women who can't afford to pay for it, or who would feel it very difficult to find a therapeutic experience in any other setting.

I think there is a cluster of women that we feel that we can provide something for in a particular kind of way. I think we have tried to look at women who might have had long-term psychiatric experiences where they might not be seen as being able to make use therapeutically of experiences. Where in fact that assumption has been made as an idea rather than as a personal decision about an individual woman. Because I don't think that you can assume that because someone might have been in and out of hospital for a number of years. It may have been they actually have not ever had a personal connection with someone who explored for them how all of this began, what kind of factors in their life *really* are contributing to it, what kind of emotional factors are heightening that experience. So that if you can provide the space to let that unfold, it does begin to make sense, and patterns do emerge, and the possibility of understanding that and therefore making it intelligible, and through that making the possibility of change exist. I think it's really very much trying to do it that way round.

Do you try and help women solve their 'practical problems'?

I think there are tensions about those issues. I don't think that by and large we move into a social support situation. I think we do hold a line in that, but that doesn't mean that in the therapeutic relationship you may not support the woman to move on those issues herself, or to direct her toward help that may allow her to make that movement. So that the difference is which way round you understand you do it. I don't think that we can take on board doing it for her, but I think we can take on board helping her to be in the position where she can do it, or where she can make a connection to someone who may be able to help her do it. I think that one of the things that's of concern at this point is that the actual reality of the kind of resource that exists outside is narrowing. So that where, five years ago, there was someone in an appalling housing situation, or where there was domestic violence, the clarity of where you might direct her or help her make connections into a real situation that might begin to affect her real circumstances,

seemed easier. You have to struggle much harder. I think also one of
the difficulties is that you have to be in relatively good mental health to
be able to negotiate the system. And I think that that's a tension that
we find all the time. Because if you're in massive distress, if your whole
world is collapsing internally and externally, the capacity to get help to
stop that is actually very, very, hard. You have to be able to negotiate
forms and different agencies, and it doesn't mean that you can't do it,
but how to get help sufficiently to get to that point I think is a great
difficulty.

To be an effective therapist must you yourself suffer?

I do think that you have to be very interested in why things happen
within yourself. I don't think in some way it's just chance that some
people are drawn to the profession of psychotherapy, or even particular
aspects of psychotherapy. I think there are interests that connect within
oneself with that, and that may be through a very painful process. You
may have come to therapy because of issues in your life that you're
trying to make intelligible. But I think you have to be interested in the
process and in believing in the capacity to change. I do think that that
happens for people in quite different ways. But I think that that has to
be an element in it. And I also think that there has to be a desire to
engage in that kind of relationship, and to be able to find the possibility
of listening to someone with sufficient inner boundaries, that you're not
overwhelmed by it. Because certainly if you worked in a setting like
this, and you have however many clients, between five and ten, it's a
situation where you have a group of eight women, and those women are
actually exposing massive distressing experiences, where your capacity
to deal with them is based on your not being overwhelmed by that, but
not being unmoved by that. So that you have to have a position where
you are affected by it, but you don't go under from it. Because I think
that having strong boundaries as a therapist is an absolutely crucial
element. I suppose I believe absolutely that that comes from having
done work on yourself. Having explored that through your own therapy
or analysis, having good training that creates a strong and clear theoretical base that you dip back into, but also the capacity to allow your
client to tell you something about their world that you can bear to
listen to, and then take back rather than your having to tell them how
they have to relate it. Because I believe that someone actually has to
unfold their story to you, rather than you telling them which direction
to go to. In some ways you always do anyway, because therapeutically
you respond however much you attempt not to; you do respond to
certain aspects and pick up certain threads and not others. As you
must, because in a time-limited situation you have to think: 'This one
makes sense, I'm going to pull on this one, this one I'm going to leave.'
And you do that all the time. But I think in the process itself you have
to be very clear about how much you can and cannot do, and also what

kind of help you need, because I think supervision is a key factor, and certainly we have a strong commitment to that on a weekly basis. Where there is someone else who can help you deal with what gets stirred, or help you make intelligible through a different kind of theoretical understanding, or struggling about it, what's going on, and I think if those things don't happen then it is very, very difficult to keep doing the work.

Can we talk about the 'societal causation' of women's problems?

I suppose that if you put women in a particular context at this particular time, there are massive pressures on them, and I think in some way our understanding of eating problems is based in the society itself. The pressure society puts on women and women's bodies, and their relationship to their bodies. Because I think it's very difficult for a woman not to have *some* kind of issue about her body. I'm not suggesting that men don't, because I believe they do, I just think that those issues and those difficulties are actually different, but they certainly exist at the same time. But I think that the kind of pressure that happens through the media and through advertisements, and through clothing, all sorts of ways that women are continually told who they should be, how they should look, all of that, and also what is desirable, and how they can understand that desirableness in themselves, is so very powerful, that that in fact is something that we are all partaking of. It doesn't mean only a group of women who are defining themselves as having issues around an eating problem. I do think that the majority of women have some kind of issue about their weight, in one way or the other, in their lives. I think maybe all people do, all men as well, but I wouldn't say that just simply because I don't have that experience, and so that I haven't thought about it in that kind of way. But I do know that I have in the past had discussions with other therapists who don't necessarily work in the same kind of way, or who don't think about eating problems in the same way, and I can remember talking to someone who said that they'd never seen a woman in their practice who had an eating problem. I suppose what I felt was exactly the opposite. I'm not sure I've ever seen a woman who didn't have, rather than a problem, an issue around eating, and around her body size and her image of herself, and the way in which she felt she presented herself in the world.

So I think that my assumption is that *all* women are looking at ways of defining themselves, and also in struggling with that definition, so that they don't feel that someone else makes it for them. That they somehow retrieve it for themselves and can own it, and therefore feel a kind of empowerment, the feeling that you do have some kind of control over how you relate to your body, what food you put in it, how that affects you, how you see yourself. So in that sense that's quite a crucial element of how you think about it, because I think it's going to be a struggle for any woman. And that if you in some way do that, if you have that as an idea, then you do assume that there's going to be a dynamic in the therapeutic relationship that reflects and relates to that. It may well not be the major issue: in some way once you allow that to be there, you see it, and to me that's one of the things I feel has changed. That if you begin to explore the possibility and allow something to be there, you begin to uncover it. I think that that's absolutely clear around the whole situation about sexual abuse in its very broad definition, and whether what is happening is that we're uncovering masses of abuse and whether this is something that actually had been touched on a long time ago in psychoanalysis and then was let go of because of the massive problems that that implied. Which is certainly something I think. They probably came very close to understanding something, and there were many social and emotional and perhaps political reasons that made this a very difficult position to hold, and given the beginning, the newness of psychoanalysis at that point, got pulled away from. But I think that it's extremely clear to me that there are issues around the effects of one's family of origin, and whatever kind of situations that you encounter in that, and whatever the word abuse might mean coming through that thread. Because I think there are masses of abusive experiences that children have.

What do you particularly value about the analytic perspective?

Well, certainly I think that one of the contributions is about unconscious experiences, but I do think it's extremely important to put any kind of reading or theoretical views that you are partaking of into the context of which they were constructed. Because I think Freud reverberates a particular time, and comes from a particular experience and situation. As all sorts of people who've written do. I think you put them in that context and you use them through that, rather than using what they're constructing as fact. Because I don't understand theory as fact. I understand that it is something that's quite malleable, and that it does change and it does move. I don't think we yet know enough about the mind and how it works, and unconscious processing which is a construction, and childhood experiences – while it's difficult for me in some way to get so concerned about something as contentious as false memory. It's because I don't understand memory as being true. I don't understand it as being false, but I understand it as being a construction. I think that memory is about a compilation, that when people have memories from their childhood, they may well have a memory that may have happened over a long period of time that is experienced as happening at one time. I think that that event itself, or that way of thinking is quite important in trying to put together what's been brought to you as a picture of experience. But what you can do is absolutely pay attention to the continuing reverberations. I think you can tell when someone has had horrific experiences, even if what they're telling you is not the actual reality of what that experience was. Even if people can say: 'Well this didn't happen, or that didn't happen', it doesn't mean – I also can't see any reason for someone to construct only something horrifying. What the need for that is. If there hasn't been pain and distress in that situation why is it necessary to find a way to communicate about it?

Ethical issues. Is there much research on male therapists and women clients – where there's been problems?

I think there have been different articles coming out. If what you're asking me is – is it possible for there to be something where the boundaries of therapy are not appropriately held? I do think that that occurs, and I don't think it's based in some way on the training of the therapist. I feel that in my experience it has happened all across the spectrum. I think the question is how that gets dealt with. I suppose that when I was speaking before about the issues of boundaries for therapists, I feel that one has to be rigorous in that particular area above all else. It is possible to understand how a situation could become incredibly intense and emotional. But I think that what is unacceptable is to feel the therapist ever forgets that they're the therapist in the setting, and therefore with someone who's actually in a more vulnerable state, who is dependent on them in particular ways, and who has reason to believe that they will absolutely hold the structure of that relationship in the terms in which they'd understood it. So that I feel that if that is held, then what is happening can be contained and made sense of and used. If it's not held I think it's broken. And I think in that sense, it's irretrievable.

It's very hard. I think that's why therapists need to have done a lot of thinking themselves and to be very clear, and also to feel supported and to be connected to other people. Because, by and large, if you're working on an individual basis with someone, you are there the two of you, and what happens in that room belongs in some sense to the two of you. And I think you have to find a way to keep a balance about that situation, to keep the reality that you have to be connected to the person's real world, as well as their inner world. If you forget either of those things, I think you put yourself and your therapeutic relationship into some kind of jeopardy.

Issues of transference ...

I think it's very interesting because one of the advantages of working with women in this kind of setting, a centre, is that the transference and the connection can occur to the Centre as well as to the therapist. So that it is possible to hold and to help women in a particular kind of way, because of that structure. And I think it is part of what may be containing. Because a very great majority of the work we do is on a once-a-week basis. We have a small group of women who are seen twice a week, and that's sometimes possible in a crisis situation. But the majority of the work is one-to-one and once a week.

I think that the connection into the fact that this is a centre, where there are other women here, not that the client has a connection particularly with anyone else, but the fact that it is a physical setting, can be massively containing, and certainly is a crucial aspect of the transference. I think that that sometimes is a very holding situation, especially if someone comes in quite a distressed state, that the therapist herself doesn't have to feel alone in that holding – the building, the room, and the other therapists can also be an aspect of that holding. Which is quite different to what happens, I think, when someone works in a private setting, where there is one therapist and the person is going in. They're alone in the complete sense. Here I think there is a sense of other people in other situations, being involved in it. So that has an impact on the transference, and also on the countertransference, because I think the therapist is aware of being a part of a centre, rather than alone with a client.

I don't also understand that that is the only transference issue. I do think that there is a connection that happens between women in a particular kind of way. So I think that the possibility of being understood or not understood for that reason, it works in both directions. I mean there certainly are women who come here who find it – even though they've chosen to come here – find it difficult to make an intimate and direct connection with another woman, and that has to be struggled with. And that can set up a countertransference feeling in the therapist as well. Because I think it's difficult if there's a major struggle about that.

How do you weigh up the relative importance of the relationship per se, as opposed to technique alone?

Well I suppose I feel that the most crucial element in a relation *is* the relationship, and is the establishment of a relationship, and that what I understand is that the theoretical elements support that establishment and the continuation of that establishment. Because I think the theory helps you hold the person, but I don't think it should direct you in how you hold the person. I think the theory is there as a resource, and a support rather than a definition. Now clearly that's not necessarily how all therapists work, but I feel if you try to make the client fit into the structure, rather than allow the client to be there and understand the structure as being there to fit around and to be helpful in making something more intelligible, then to me that's being led by a theory rather than being extended and supported and underpinned by it. I think it's interesting to look at the research that's come out in relationship to therapy, and certainly the ones I'm familiar with from the States. There isn't really any kind of strong provable fact that a particular orientation means that the client and the therapeutic relationship will get better. Quicker if you use x theory rather than y theory. So I

suppose to me that proves, or makes me believe, that the whole idea of
the relationship and how that relationship is considered and explored,
and used, and the struggle the therapist goes through about trying to
make it intelligible, and the resources she brings to bear on that, are
the crucial elements. So I think it's possible so long as, say here, there
is an emphasis about women and the way in which they might need to
come into therapy and the effect that the society's had on them. As
long as that is a thread, the way in which the therapist works can differ
to some extent. But I think it has to be underpinned by that position.

How do you conceive of optimum mental health?

Well you see I wouldn't assume to define that. I think that's something
that the woman herself is involved with. Because I don't feel that I want to
see someone to bring them to a certain level, I want to see someone to try
to understand what she is looking for, her well-being if you will. And that
looking at that with her and trying to decide with her how we're going to
move in that direction is, it seems to me, the process in a relationship that
gets developed. That doesn't mean that there aren't certain things that
you'd want to see her being able to do in that process.

What about a woman who doesn't know that?

I think actually to create an environment first, you could begin that
examination. Because I don't think that most people either come into
therapy expecting that, or leave therapy having achieved that. Because I
think therapy is a process, and sometimes the therapeutic experience
may be a contained aspect of that, but it may not be the only therapeutic experience that someone will have in their life. I think that what
you're trying to do is actually to provide some kind of tools and
resources that the woman takes out of the situation, it doesn't end. I
think that if you've had a good therapeutic experience, you take away
from that experience something that you will continue to use, and also
that you will understand therapy as a process that, were you to need it,
you might be able to return to it to use again. That it doesn't have to
be completed all at once. I may believe that now, because I know that
we are not able here always to offer an open-ended situation to a
woman. So that I can believe that in a process, if you have an experience that you feel held and contained by, and also that the resources
there have actually impacted your life, then you might use that again if
something happens. I think that does happen for women, where they
may find another situation, and then they come back and use it in a
different kind of way. I want a woman to be able to choose to do what
she feels is right for her, and to have the space, and the time, and the
clarity to begin to examine that. And to feel entitled to have that. Now
that doesn't mean that women can go out and have whatever they want.
I think that there are always going to be economic realities in that

situation, but I do think that it's actually being able to use what they have in a different kind of way. And feel entitled to do that. I think that often people come into therapy because they feel disconnected from the possibilities that *are* there in their lives, and I suppose what I want from therapy for them, is for them to feel the reconnection with those resources. Perhaps also to come to terms with what is possible, and sometimes what is not.

Do you make some kind of informal contractual agreements with women?

Well I think as far as the contractual arrangement that would happen if it were a brief time-limited situation. There might be a focus in that work. If someone is going to be offered a ten- or twelve-week group of sessions, there might be a focus, or they might have come in for a specific reason. I think in the longer-term contracts, there isn't a specific focus. There may be a cluster of initial issues which may not be touched on again, because the woman may come into therapy thinking she wants to work on something, and discovering once she gets into the relationship that a whole other area opens up. I wouldn't want her to be held by that initial definition, and I think that that's obviously the difference; whether you're doing a very brief piece of focal work, or whether you have in some way the luxury of being able to open it out in a way where she can actually find there are aspects of herself that she really does want to explore, and didn't know that when she came, because it wasn't really safe enough to have that knowledge.

Are there some people you feel unable to work with?

I think there are. Certainly on the telephone if someone presents with their major focus as alcohol or drug abuse, I think we would direct them to agencies where that's their specialty. That doesn't mean we don't see women here who have those as issues in their lives. But if that's absolutely the major focus of it I think we would suggest they go elsewhere. I think that there are women who think they want to work on something, but when they get here find maybe they don't, and we might not offer them space. By and large, we try to create access to as broad a base as possible, because I think lots of psychotherapeutic agencies have very strong identifying factors and boundaries about who is or isn't appropriate. I'm not suggesting that we offer something to everyone that we see, but certainly if it's a space, not a specific space but a space where the woman is just being offered therapy not defined by one of the theme groups or something like that, I think we'd try to see if there was a way in which we felt there could be a working alliance established. And try as much as possible to make that available, because I think we believe in the therapeutic process. There are people who are not available at a particular time, and I think if we felt someone really wasn't available to working in any sense in the inner world situation or with any kind of conscious feelings, then we might suggest they do something else. Might refer them elsewhere, if we felt they couldn't make the best use of what we offer. And I think that's really because of the kind of pressure that we are under all the time, where we are saying 'No' to women on the phone all the time, or referring them to other agencies, because there is a very small group that can get through. That's a responsibility that we take very, very seriously, because we want to make use of the space we have.

How does the Centre monitor its work?

We're actually working on – because of the new language that exists everywhere, and because of our funding requirements – we're working on monitoring/evaluation forms at the moment. I suppose the major way is through the use of supervision, and through clinical discussion. If you were to feel someone were in a situation where they were being overburdened, you would approach that and suggest they might do less, or get more support. Because I think it is something that is an issue where you can't allow yourself to get worn down by it, because then you can't do the work. I think in some way you're in a better position for that to be considered in an ongoing way in a centre than you are in private practice, because I think part of the difficulty therapeutically is that if you are on your own, you're making the assessment about yourself, and no-one else is involved in that process. You can't continually be in a situation where massive demands are being made on you without needing that underpinning. And without knowing that you might need to take breaks. One of the things that we began to do is actually – because we don't have the funding for it – we have encouraged people to take a sabbatical if they feel that it's necessary. We aren't able to pay them but what we can do is hold the job so they can return to it if they decide to. I think it's important that you think in that way, or that you might want to do a course, that you might want to do something that would be refreshing to you, as far as your clinical thinking and your own education for the work is concerned.

Are you interested in the idea of 'emotional literacy' being taught in schools?

I think we are concerned about how to support in some way the whole concept of an emotionally literate society, and that clearly the place to begin is in schools. I think we have at different times sent people into schools, where we've been asked to. That's really the key. The problem is having the resources to be able to do that, and also wondering whether there are young people's agencies who should be doing that in a clearer way, rather than us. But I do think that there are real issues for me about what young women are being shown and taught in relation to their emotional lives. And the literacy that is being developed. I think one of the things that I've found personally very concerning is the number of younger children, younger girls, who are concerned about their weight, and issues around food, in primary school. I think that that is an appalling situation, and in some ways it does need to be addressed. But the problem is *how*, and whether we do have the resources to do it at this point in time.

Robert Bly, 'men's groups' and all that ...

I don't have any difficulty in men looking for ways to connect with softer aspects of themselves or their own intimacy or their relationships in that kind of way. I think I'm very concerned if I feel that connection has to do with being in opposition to women. Because I think in some way that's why I'm very clear that what we offer here is a service for women by women. Not a service that specifically desires to exclude men, but a service that desires to include women. And be for women. I think that for me the problem is if what happens is that in whatever that bonding may be, a continued misogyny exists; I think that's destructive for men as well as women. Because creating access across – between men and women – really to look at the implications of gender in our society, is a crucial issue for both men and women. I think it's in both men's and women's best interests that we understand the difficulties in intimacy that both have, and look at ways of altering that. And anything that will shift that for a man, I'd be very supportive of. But I don't think that the real shift can possibly come through being in opposition, or blaming, or wanting fault to be laid in either direction.

That doesn't mean I don't think that we are in a patriarchal society. It's very clear, all you have to do is look. Look at the issues about women in Parliament, women in different areas, to see that the struggle's still going on. But I don't think it has to be seen as not wanting men to have any availability of emotional literacy. I think it's as important for men to understand those concepts and have access to that way of thinking as it is for women. Because if not, it wouldn't do any good if you had a society where women can do that and men cannot. And I think in some way that's been the situation for far too long. That women have been seen as the carriers of the emotional situation, and I think it doesn't work that women carry it. I think they're taught from early on – that's perhaps something I didn't mention at all – I do think little girls are taught to carry certain things around, feelings and emotional needs, and also meeting other people's needs. I think a lot of therapeutic experience with a woman is to work on her entitlement to have her own needs met. I think it's important that women do feel that, and that men also understand that that's not an attack on them. That for a woman to get her needs met doesn't mean a man cannot. But there has to be a mutuality in that for it to work.

What can help men?

I think therapy offers the same possibility for them actually to examine where they are with regard to a societal connection as well as a personal relationship one. I think it's important for men to feel that possibility – the fact that we don't offer that doesn't mean we don't think it should be offered.

I would like to say that there are lots of things I haven't touched on: our work with black women, and the kind of focus that we have tried to create here for access to therapy for black women, and the struggle with that looking at some of the theory and the practice, as far as analytic therapy and the access to it. The fact that we've actually been able to create a situation here where, from not having very many black or ethnic minority women coming to therapy here, we now have almost half of our client group in that area. That's been a crucial aspect I think of what's underpinned what we've been doing over the last five years, really looking seriously about access to therapy in the broadest way.

Questions of 'identity' ...

Well I think also the whole idea around whatever difference means. The capacity to acknowledge difference. I think therapeutically that that's a crucial part of what we feel we're trying to do as far as creating access goes. Because if someone comes into therapy and there is a difference in the room, I think that in some way that difference has to be acknowledged as a way to be able to deal with it, and I think that certainly has happened as far as working cross-culturally is concerned. We set up a project to try to create access, and I think that one of the things that we tried to do was to have an initial connection into therapy for black women with black therapists. Not that all the work was done, but the first point of contact was there. I think it was very interesting what happened, because massive issues came out about that, because it didn't always make the woman feel more able to come. Sometimes it created other experiences, and I think once you begin to look at that, and look at some of the concepts of what that difference means, it's really powerful and very important. But I think the fact that you're making this struggle, and that you are saying that you are working on this, because certainly I don't think that we have resolved any of these issues. I think we are in process, as I think we probably will be for as long as we exist. We'll be changing, but I think we're trying to address cross-cultural issues, and in a community setting, what therapeutic needs there are.

But you haven't shifted the focus from women to ethnicity?

I think the woman as a woman is still crucial, but I think it's let us know that the issues that one group of women might have may not be exactly the same. Just like in some cultures the idea of coming to therapy and talking in an intimate way with another person may be seen as in opposition to the cultural ideal, and how you struggle with that, and how you actually try to affect that in a way to let the woman see what the needs might be. I think those issues are clearly here for us.

CHAPTER 21

Archetypal Psychology

Noel Cobb

Noel Cobb edits the journal *Sphinx*, an international forum for
new ideas in Archetypal Psychology. He is the author of
Archetypal Imagination and *Prospero's Island – The Secret Alchemy
at the Heart of The Tempest*. He works privately as a psychotherapist in London.

Do you want to just tell me how you became a therapist.

Well I must go back to my childhood to answer that one and I see
three important factors. The first has to do with my mother who was
both – at times – hysterical *and* crazy, and it was a great challenge just
to figure out what was going on with her – so that was a sort of
immediate initiation. She also spoke in a very disturbing way, as Ronnie
Laing would say, and she communicated on many levels at once, so I
learned early on about double-binds and that kind of thing – not how
they are defined, but the experience of them.

The second factor has to do with environment. I was born in the
American Midwest in 1938. It was the time of the great Depression, just
before the War. Both my parents were very uneducated, working class,
extremely uneducated. My father's father committed suicide – he was a
wood-carver from Eastern Europe – when my father, who was the oldest
child, was seven. The kid had to drop out of the first year of school in
order to support the family, selling newspapers. He never got back to
school. He worked his whole life in factories. And when I saw what was
happening to him I vowed that it would never happen to me, I cried my
eyes out for him for years, when I saw the destruction of the man. I had
great anger about the set-up of the factory, the misery of the working-
class person, the devastation of the imagination, and the lack of opportunity for people like my father to experience beauty and to be fully human.

That last thing affected me a lot because the environment that I
grew up in was so poverty-stricken and so ugly, both because people
around me were poor, but also because there was a kind of vulgarity
about all they did. American 'culture' in the Midwest where I grew up –
Grand Rapids, Michigan – was nothing but hamburger joints and funda-
mentalist churches on every other street corner, and that was it. My
parents, of course, belonged to a church, everybody did. Very, very,

redneck, bigoted community, actually. They belonged to a Pentecostal
holy-roller church, which I was taken to from the age of a few months,
until I finally ran away from it in horror, when I was 16.

I wasn't allowed to read any books except the Bible, and Christian
literature. I brought home Aldous Huxley's *Brave New World*, and my
mother found it under my pillow. She said it was filth, and that I would
go mad if I read things like that, and she took it away and burnt it. So
I promptly got another copy [laughs] and read it.

There was this appalling lack of culture, because the Americans, you
must realise, all denied their pasts – if they had any culture, a lot of
them just left it behind, and then tried to become 150 per cent Americans. So whatever folk songs they knew, or whatever customs or traditions, they often just left them behind. And I couldn't find the 'culture'
of my church comforting either [laughs], not with hell-fire sermons two
or three times a week, and prayer meetings that lasted sometimes three
hours, where I'd have to be on my knees until long after midnight,
begging forgiveness for my sins.

Later on – the thing I'd add to that which has made me become a
therapist, actually, was my fascination with beauty. Trying to see what
could evoke it, and why people surrounded themselves with ugliness.
Why they did that, because it made me shrink inside. I remember the
doctor telling my mother that why I misbehaved and was so difficult
was because I was 'hypersensitive'. And I remembered that word as a
kid – 'hypersensitive' – it means that you're not normal, you're more
sensitive than you should be. I used to have terrible fits of temper
about things, and they couldn't understand where it was coming from,
because they said, 'Other kids aren't like this. Why don't you like the
colour we painted the walls in your bedroom?' or 'Why do you hate this
building, or this and that, or what somebody looks like, and what they
say to you? Why do you cry?' I cried all the time, as a kid. Well into my
teens, actually.

I grieved over something, I didn't understand. Today, when I think
back, I think that I was probably grieving over the sister I didn't have. I
finally had a brother, but he was nine or ten years younger, and I
couldn't really talk to him. Anyway by the time I went off to university,
working my way through university, he was only ten, so I couldn't have
great conversations. I was very isolated, partly because of growing up
surrounded by such neurotic religiousness.

So there was that impact of ugliness and beauty. Then, later on,
there was a fascination with things in nature. I found that the only
things that were beautiful were things that were not man-made. As a
young teenager I used to get on my bicycle, and if I could get outside
the city somehow, I'd find plenty of beauty. As soon as I got back into
the city it was ugly. So that struck me very early. The very small
glimpses of beauty that I had when I was little had to do with nature,
really. Trees, animals, things in the Grand Rapids Public Museum I
could go to for free. And there at the Museum, I found that you could

go free on Saturdays to a class in mineralogy, and learn about stones. So I joined a group, and made some friends. We went on expeditions, and were taught by a civil servant – an amenable young lady, just out of university – things about minerals. And I started to make my own collection. I had orange-crates, I would collect them from the supermarkets or wherever, and take the ends off them – the wooden parts, you know these long American orange-crates – and I would make little paper trays on them, so I would get about, maybe 16 or 20 trays of paper, and I would glue them on to these home-made orange-crate shelves which I would then fit into a standing-up orange-crate to make a storage cabinet.

So I had specimens which I had collected, and I began to learn about geology, and about the earth, and of course it came into conflict with Sunday School, where we were taught that the earth was created in 4000 BC, and things like that. But I had a fossilised trilobite that was millions of years old. So I soon had arguments, scientific ones; I read a lot of science. I used to argue with my parents about the Bible. I used to get beaten up and told off because what I said was obviously a very great blasphemy and sin.

But the beauty of the stones was something that in my condition of utter loneliness and feeling that life was almost unbearably brutal around me ... I think the stones were a meditation. I could feel some mysterious force of healing in my soul when I held these stones and looked at them. I would sit around for hours like that.

I had all sorts of stones, and I collected them because of the beauty of them. I loved the radiance and the colours of them, the thin slice of watermelon-pink rhodonite, the tiny peacock-blue crystals sparkling in the indigo velvet of azurite, the miniature Chinese landscape of moss-agate, the dizzy feline magic of tiger's eye ... The rarity of them too. I'd send off, if I could collect a little money from my newspaper round, and buy a few more little rocks for my collection [laughs] ... and that led me to chemistry. Because I had to learn how to do tests. I learned that you needed hydrochloric acid to test stones, and a bunsen burner or an alcohol lamp to see what colour the flame was if you held a stone in it. So gradually I started learning about chemistry. I took chemistry at school and then I decided I really wanted my own lab, so I had two private studies going on during high school outside schooltime. Much to my parents' fright and superstitious anger – they wanted me to stop these things, they didn't know what I was doing. Eventually I had a lab, a storeroom off my bedroom, in the house we had – I cleared it out, I got an old table and some scrapped cooking pots. Finally I got a few test tubes. I had a mortar and pestle. I gradually collected my own chemicals, and all through high school I was doing my own experiments at home, a kind of alternative chemistry. And the transformations of matter were what fascinated me the most. I loved watching matter transform, from one condition to another, and I was also getting interested in science, and I wanted to calculate things too. But more than anything, I was interested in the *qualities* of matter. I'd learned from stones that matter had colour, texture, crystalline forms, and properties – mineral properties – and smell and taste, as well. And that if you put things together, things happened. If you put two chemicals together that were of a certain nature, they created something new. Or if you took a piece of phosphorous out of a bottle where it was sitting in its oil and it came into contact with the air, it would begin spontaneously burning, and things like that. I loved the pungent smell of burning sulphur and the dangerous fragrance of nitric acid as well as the more enchanting smells of esters and alcohols. I would set up incredible experiments. I made gunpowder and rocket fuel, for example. I was interested in the fierceness of things, too, not just in their colours. So there'd be clouds of smoke pouring out of this room all the time, and my parents telling me that I would have to stop, and I would refuse. I would lock the door and carry on [laughs] in this laboratory.

That went on for years really. When I left high school I finally figured out a way to get to university by painting houses 12 hours, 15 hours a day all summer long, and getting enough money together for university for the next academic year. I went into Physics, Chemistry and the Sciences, Maths. But I soon realised that people weren't interested in matter in the same way I was. They all wanted to get jobs with Dow Chemical Company and get on the payroll, making new kinds of aspirin, or with Kodak, testing new emulsions. And I kept thinking: 'There must be more to it than this. I want to understand something here.' It was the mystery, I think, at the root of it. I was really fascinated by the mystery of things. Both in matter and in people. But in the beginning it was more matter, and people were far too terrifying anyway.

So I kept my distance – I had a few friends, and I read. By the time I was 19/20 I was reading Freud's *Collected Papers*, totally immersed in psychoanalysis, reading everything I could find on it, and trying to analyse myself and everyone else. But science didn't satisfy me, and I gravitated gradually into mathematics, and then into pure maths, calculus, topology, vector spaces, and at one point I thought nuclear physics, and then I saw it's the same thing, people are going to work for business or the government. I just wanted to do pure research. I suppose that having left the dogma of the church behind, I had been prey to the dogma of science, which asserts that everything can eventually be explained, you just need the proper scientific tools. I was very, very purist. Finally I realised, 'I'm not really a mathematician. I've got to get out of this', and I took a deep breath and leaped into Philosophy [laughs], and so I did my first degree in Philosophy.

I left America almost a week after my finals. Got a berth on a steamer to Norway, I bought a one-way ticket with the only money I had. I took my precious books, I think two or three cases, and that was it. I said goodbye to America, and I didn't go back until 24 years later, and then it was to see my father who was dying. At that point I had to see him. And, you know, he had finally understood me. It was a good parting.

Why Norway ...

Well, in the middle of the appalling ugliness I was telling you about, there would be these fortuitous meetings with what I can only call 'soul-moving agents' of some kind. Angels, actually. The first was an ex-quarterback in football from Notre Dame University called Lynn Partridge, who ought to have been a very dogmatic Catholic, but became an assistant minister in the Unitarian church and held discussion groups in existentialism in the evenings. I was told about this by a friend of mine in Physics class who brought me along. There we read and discussed Kafka, Kierkegaard, Camus, Sartre; it was fantastic, I really got off on that, and the discussions. Because I couldn't talk about these things at home, there was nowhere in my milieu I could talk about these things, and he was a great guy, really incredible, very generous. That's where I discovered *Brave New World*, for example.

Later on at university – when I was having a very miserable time, with great attacks of anxiety about the whole of existence, feeling alone in the cosmos, having visions that I believed no-one else shared with me, except people long-dead, like William Blake or Rainer Maria Rilke, a guy walked into the university one day who really changed my life. He was a friend of Donald Hall, my professor in poetry at the University of Michigan. One day, Hall said that a friend of his was coming to give a poetry reading – this poet hadn't published much yet, but he was a good poet, and we ought to go and hear him. And I nearly didn't go because we didn't always go to extra-curricular things, but I decided I would give him a try. And it was Robert Bly. This was 1958 – and Robert was great – he conjured up William Blake and read us some of his early translations of Rilke's *Nine Voices*, wonderful: 'The Orphan', 'The Drunkard', 'The Suicide', 'The Dwarf'. And he recited some W.B. Yeats, early Yeats – 'Who will go drive with Fergus now?/And pierce the deep wood's woven shade,/And dance upon the level shore?', and I just loved Robert and the poetry. I thought 'Well this is it, I've met a poet. Now at last I've met a real poet.' Everybody left after the meeting. I went up to the front and very shyly introduced myself, and Robert said 'What are you doing and do you write?' And I said 'Yes, I was writing.'

We started to walk across the campus together, and by the end of the walk we had become friends, and I remember the conversation very well. I told him of my soul's longing for poetry and the great terror that pursued me. He listened. It was such a quiet listening. Then he said, 'It's important to stay close to the edge. That is where great poetry comes from. Rilke's whole life was like that. He was like a man skating – black water on one side, ice on the other – seeing how close to the edge he could skate.' As we parted he said, 'Come and visit me any time in New York', which I did. And two years later when I wanted to leave America, I said to Robert: 'I've got to get out of this country. It's killing me. I've got to go somewhere and I don't really mind where, as long as it's not America. What do you think?' And he said: 'Well I've

been travelling a lot, and I quite like the countries on the edge of
Europe. Don't go to London, Paris, Rome, because you'll just meet
other Americans. Go to somewhere like Lithuania, Finland, Poland,
Norway. And there you will see [this was in the late '50s] the old
culture, and it won't be Americanised. But if you go to London, or
Paris you'll just meet a lot of other Americans; you won't even have to
learn another language. And you won't see the Old World. If you go to
a country like Norway, they won't necessarily know English, and you'll
have to speak another language, but it will be a way to take you *into*
the country.'

I took Robert's advice, and when I got a scholarship to the Oslo
International Summer School in the summer of '59, I sold the few things I
owned to get money for a ticket. My parents had no money. I was 21. It
was a one-way ticket on a huge steamer sailing from New York to Oslo. A
nine-day voyage across the ocean. I was very happy to be going, America
was making me physically ill, though I felt sad to be leaving my few
friends. But Bly said, 'Sometimes I come to Europe; and when I do, I'll
look you up', and he did, actually twice in Norway, in the early days. And
we wrote, kept contact. His journal, *The Fifties*, and, later, *The Sixties*, was
utterly important to me, it was a real lifeline; that and the books of poetry
I brought with me: Blake, Rilke, Lorca and Yeats.

The first year in Norway, when the Summer School had finished and
I was alone, I found a room in a house high in the hills above the Oslo
fjord. I lived alone during the first year up there in the pine forests,
snow sometimes four feet deep in the winter. I got a job washing dishes
in a restaurant in Oslo, and I spent the whole first winter there alone,
because the landlady had gone off to the north of Norway to investigate
some factory of her deceased husband. She left me in charge of her
house, a beautiful log house,and there were skis outside, and she said
'You can use them.' I had learnt to ski in Michigan, so I spent that first
lonely winter skiing at night on paths up and down through the forest,
on an arc-lit ski-path around Oslo, about 20 kilometres long. I'd get
back from work about midnight, put on my skis and climb up the hill to
the ski-path. It was fantastic. Can you imagine? Three o'clock in the
morning, nobody there. I just skied all night.

I began to 'erase all the old tapes', as I called it then. I didn't do a
self-analysis as such, although I had read a lot of Freud, I simply
'played back' my memories of the things that haunted me until the
painful emotions just wore out and I could clear my mind for entering
my new existence. It was a kind of small death. At the end of that first
year, towards the spring, the lady who owned the house said, 'There's a
girl you should meet, her father is a very important Norwegian novelist
and poet, Tarjei Vesaas, and his daughter Guri is about your age and
she also writes.' The landlady knew I was writing by this time and she
introduced us, and through Guri I met the few foreigners living in Oslo.
There were very few, only a handful of foreign residents in those days.

By this time I'd approached the University of Oslo and found that my

American degree was not considered sufficient to enrol. So I had to sit a separate exam to study there. With absolutely no money, I embarked on a six-year degree in Psychology, called an *Embedseksam*, which would make me a *Candidatus Psychologiae*, which means a 'candidate' for a European Professorship. I thought: 'Well, by the end of this, I might know a bit more about people.' At this time I was still very shy and frightened of life. But I was very fascinated by people. I had discovered women. I had had a few relationships, and I was initiated into sex and was very keen to discover what women were like in Norway. I found Norwegian girls open and friendly. They loved warm, physical contact and were not hysterically frigid like the American girls with whom I had grown up. They taught me a lot. Truly. And they healed some very deep wounds in my soul. And taught me Norwegian! It made it bearable to study academic psychology – to have such good, close relationships.

I had started to study, but I still had no income and no chance for a grant – I applied for one which was given to political refugees, but I was told that I did not qualify as a refugee, since there was no such thing as a refugee from America. So I used my barely existent Norwegian to translate sociological research into English – for which they paid good money. I'd stopped working in the vegetable market, getting up at four a.m., which was the second job I had, and I worked as a stevedore for a while on the waterfront. There were no unions, or they didn't have any at that time, so I could clock in at seven in the morning and sit at a big table with a whole lot of guys, and they'd call out shift numbers and you'd get your ticket, and be sent off to the docks, and you'd have to take out whatever was inside the hull of this boat – fucking heavy iron ingots or bags of sugar or whatever. Or get it on to winches. It was very heavy work, but I earned well.

And I *had* to learn how to speak Norwegian, because none of the guys down on the docks were educated, and they all shouted and cursed in Norwegian. And so I started reading Knut Hamsun with a pocket dictionary, and I used to read through my lunchhour, and they would scoff at me, these old sailors and winos who worked on the boats, that I was reading *books*, but nonetheless Hamsun was a good teacher. He writes very beautiful Norwegian.

I was writing poetry too, and, luckily, Guri translated my first poem for *Dagbladet*, one of the big daily newspapers. In those days if you published a poem in the newspaper you could live on that as a student, you could live on what you got for a month, for one little poem in the newspaper. They do print a lot of poetry, and people read it. It's not like here, people like it. My first book of poetry was published by *Gyldendal*. In the end, I published five collections before I left Norway. I was gradually accepted as a Norwegian poet, during my student days, and I was considered as one of the contemporary, up-and-coming poets of that generation, one of a group of guys who are now becoming the 'grand old men' of Norwegian poetry. So my writing also brought in

some money. But a lot of the time at university, I was close to starving.
For a while I ate only brown rice, onions and cabbage.

So I was surviving and I was studying Psychology and it was awful
and I was hating every minute of it. This was the early 1960s, and to
become a 'psychologist' you had to know about statistics and do things
like dissect brains and experiment on frogs. We had to learn a lot of
neurology, which is all right in its place, but the teachers were trying to
connect it up with psychiatry in a very weird way. We were asked to
attend demonstrations, for example, in psychiatry class, where some
poor lady would be wheeled in, and she would be asked what her name
was and how old she was, and what day of the week it was. She might
have been very depressed because her husband of 50 years had died. A
group of us became so incensed about this that we organised a petition.
We said we would not go to this class – the psychiatry class – any more
if they would not stop demonstrating patients. And they accepted our
petition, and stopped the demonstrations.

We formed a little 'revolutionary' unit – in the end there were five of
us – and we were reading all the things that were not on the syllabus:
Laing and Jung, Husserl, phenomenology and existentialism, of course.
So what we did was we went to one of the professors, and we said:
'Look, there are all these empty auditoriums at noon. Nobody is using
them. Can we have one for our little group?' 'Ya, ya, you can have it.'
They didn't know what was going on. They gave us an auditorium. So
we ran and passed out invitations to the other students in the department. 'You'll hear a special free lecture on Existential Psychiatry in the
lunch hour.' And they piled in. We were lecturing our fellow students. It
was great fun. We even brought in Zen. And, of course, Laing. And this
was in Norway, in the early '60s.

Of course, as students we read about things happening in America. A
Harvard professor, Timothy Leary, had written about a newly-discovered
laboratory chemical which mimicked in its effects certain natural, psychotropic compounds used by traditional shamanistic societies. He had written a kind of a guidebook for people using this new and supposedly
'consciousness-expanding' substance, comparing experiences which happened to people using it to experiences described in the ancient Buddhist
manual for navigating the *bardo* or 'intermediate state between death and
re-birth': *The Tibetan Book of the Dead*. He was suggesting that people use
that kind of traditional wisdom to guide themselves through the bewilder-
ing states of mind they might find themselves in were they to ingest such a
substance. So I started reading about that. There was also Evans-Wentz's
translation of the original Tibetan book itself, and I was reading that. In
my spare time, of course.

I was also very keen to understand what was going on in Vietnam.
Having been fortunately protected by my guardian daemon one day in
college when we were given IQ tests – I had scored so high, that the
American military had decided to pass me by for as long as I wished to
be studying – I was never called up for military duty in Vietnam. But, I

was very disturbed by what the Americans were doing to the Vietnamese. I felt ashamed to be American. Although Norway is far away from everything else, there was a lot of interest in the Vietnam war, a lot of intelligent protest about it, in which I also participated. And about this time, I suppose, about halfway through my six-year study programme, I chose Clinical Psychology as my field of specialisation. You had to choose between that and Developmental, Child, Social, or Industrial Psychology. I thought they were all terrible actually. I hadn't known just how awful academic psychology, particularly the Germanic-American kind, could be. I got very angry about what we were being taught. I wrote several essays for the newspapers about how alienating and alienated contemporary psychology had become. I stuck my neck out, and probably shouldn't have, as a student. Some of my professors wrote angry replies in the newspapers condemning me for suggesting that psychologists were traitors toward humanity.

This was about the time Laing's first books were published: *The Divided Self*, and *The Self and Others*. I read them avidly, and I took it all on board, and I thought: 'This is completely right. This is the first person that I've come across who's writing any sense, for fuck's sake!' The other stuff I couldn't bear, the intellectually-constipated dreariness we were forced to read at university. I could almost vomit every time I went to the classes. I had terrible arguments with the professors in Experimental Psychology about the use and value of Behaviourism.

I so much appreciated that story you got out of Ronnie [in *Mad To Be Normal*] about his being in the third year of training at the Institute of Psychoanalysis where Rosenfeld tells the dream of the so-called psychotic, who dreams that there's a vertical cliff. Inside of it a hatch opens and a little mechanical cuckoo comes out and goes 'Cuckoo, cuckoo, cuckoo' and goes back in and the hatch shuts. And in the same dream, in another vertical cliff opposite the first one, a little hatch opens and a cuckoo comes out and says, 'Cuckoo, cuckoo, cuckoo' and goes back in and the hatch shuts – and Rosenfeld's interpretation was that this shows that the psychotic is really split, and that both sides of him are split, and he's psychotic on both sides. And that's it, and that's the name of the game. And Ronnie saying at the table in discussion, maybe as an alternative interpretation, 'Do you think the dream could be a depiction of the state of affairs in analysis between you and him?' And the guy just looking at him and not saying anything, and not even acknowledging Ronnie's comment. The guy obviously had no sense of humour, on top of it. Ronnie says that he thought, 'oh fuck you!' – and never went back again to Rosenfeld's seminars.

I did much the same. I sometimes walked out, but one had to keep something going or one wouldn't get one's degree. It was touch and go at one point, in the end, whether I'd get it or not. In the exams I did very well. I scored, in terms of points, rather high. But I hated it, it was torture, I had to force myself to learn things that, if I wasn't careful, would infect me. Some ideas are like viruses, you know? So, I had to struggle at the same time as I was learning to free myself from what I was learning – to unlearn it.

Along with discovering Laing's books, I also happened to meet someone who actually was in analysis with him at the time. This guy later had the generosity to send me the first volume of Jung's *Collected Works*, to be translated into English. It was Volume Twelve, *Psychology and Alchemy*. He sent it to me as a surprise – out of the blue. It arrived one day, I opened it – I'd never read any Jung before – and I sat down and started leafing through it and I was completely amazed. Because what got me was the alchemy. I understood that this was all about what I had been doing when I was about 14, 15 in my own instinctive way.

I gobbled it up, I stayed up all night reading and I took this precious discovery with me to class next day, and I showed it to professors and my students. Nobody was the slightest bit interested! But I thought it was incredible stuff. And I still do! I think alchemy is a wonderful theme for creative reverie. How it teaches the soul to open its eyes. And it teaches about transformation too.

I don't know if I would agree with contemporary Jungians about alchemy. Alchemy is far more idiosyncratic than most Jungians imagine. But Jung certainly was a great inspiration and I carried that book around with me like a Bible for years. I really loved it. In fact I've only now come to part with it! I've just wrapped it up and put it into a large box of psychology books that I'm sending to Warsaw to the Jung Club, and I've dedicated it to a young woman psychologist there because they have no books, they have no money. When I was teaching there this year, I realised that they just can't get it together to get books, it's far too expensive. They couldn't even buy a single volume of Jung's *Collected Works*. Probably would be a month's wages, or something. It is impossible. So I thought, 'This book meant so much to me, I'll send it to them.'

By the time I finished my degree at the University of Oslo, I'd written to Laing about my next move. He said 'Come and join the dance', and so I did. Packed up everything and came straight to London. I didn't know anyone in England except the guy who had sent me the Jung book and who had been in analysis with Ronnie [Laing]. That was 1966.

Did you get involved with Laing's work at the time?

Within two days of arriving in England, I went to meet Ronnie at his office in Wimpole Street. Aaron Esterson was still working with Laing then. Aaron was, I remember, eating an orange when I walked in. Ronnie and he were standing around, kind of hanging out, I suppose, in the corridors around the consulting rooms. Ronnie said: 'Well, come in, let's have a talk', and we sat down in the wonderful big leather chairs in this very spacious room, very elegant, with hardly anything in it. Plenty of space, and he just sort of laid back in the chair and looked up at the ceiling and just waited, and I thought, 'Great, there's a lot of space here.' [Laughs]

Another time we were talking about all sorts of things, and he said: 'Why don't you come and live at Kingsley Hall, and see what it's like?', which I did within about another week or two, and went straight to the East End. [Laughs] Having arrived in England from beautiful Norway [laughs] you know, the trees and the forest, and the fjords and the mountains, you can walk to them outside your house nearly, or take a train – 15 minutes or half-an-hour and you're in the country – to Bromley-by-Bow in the grim East End. It was quite a shock. I lived there two years. Ronnie was still living at Kingsley Hall and we talked a lot, he participated 100 per cent in the community. A great many wonderful and exciting things happened during that time. All of us there learned from what was happening, each in our own way, and I suppose I started doing therapy then quite naturally, but I didn't call it that. For example, I looked after Mary Barnes on a daily basis for months and months at a time. In any institutional setting, Mary would have been diagnosed as a dangerously regressed schizophrenic, but at Kingsley Hall, she could be herself without that label.

Looking after Mary was quite a job; her supposed therapist, Joe Berke, was not around more than very occasionally – an hour here or there – but the nitty-gritty of listening to her profuse and exhausting ramblings, frequently for three or four hours at an end, was my job. And Paul Zeal's. Paul had arrived more or less the same day I had and we had both come there because of our enthusiasm for Laing's ideas. We had hardly been there one week, though, when the man announced, 'We're going on holiday, we've had enough, we're all exhausted, and you and Paul can look after things here while we're gone!' And Ronnie, and all the rest of the people who had been looking after the place, just left for Greece. Paul and I, being very new to the whole thing, didn't know what had hit us.

It was an extraordinary situation. I'm sure Ronnie knew what he was doing, and I think he trusted us because he knew that we were completely behind his vision. But 'being trusted' is one thing – it doesn't necessarily follow that you know what you should do when Andrew, who has been diagnosed catatonic schizophrenic and hasn't spoken a word in five years, walks out of the building and off into the blue one early morning. We learned that he got picked up by the police virtually every time he went out, so we'd try and prevent that in some way. But we didn't really know what we were doing! [Laughs] We thought we had to protect Andrew from the system, and we tried to talk to Andrew about it. But he wasn't particularly interested in what we had to say. [Laughs] So it was a very funny situation. He would try to 'escape our clutches', as it were, and get out of the door. We gave him a key – but it didn't really matter to him whether he had a key or not, because he would always ring the doorbell when he got back, whether he had a key or not. And David, one of the residents, was so angry about this, that he ripped the wires out of the doorbell [laughs] – so Andrew ended up by climbing over the wall! Next to Kingsley Hall was a children's playground, and the wall dividing it from our building had broken glass stuck in the top of it, but Andrew – never mind – he would climb over this wall, get himself bloody, fall down into the little corridor between the building and the wall where the dustbins were, and then crawl along, get through the back door which was open, through the boiler room, then up the back steps and back to his room. Instead of opening the front door with his key! [Laughs]

On other occasions, the telephone would ring and the police would say: 'One of them blokes from your place is down at the High Street greengrocers, an' there's some kinda fuss, so could you send someone t'collect him?' So I'd arrive, and a typical scene would be: there's Andrew standing in the middle of the road – no traffic because it was a very peaceful little backwater – and around Andrew there would be a whole gaggle of neighbourhood folks, all talking at once, and a bobby [policeman]. I'd walk up and say to the bobby something like, 'Excuse me, but has he done anything?' and the bobby would look somewhat bemused and say, 'Well, actually, no', [laughs] and I'd say 'Well what's all the commotion about?' and he'd say something like, 'We got a call from the people who run the shop, and they said that he's been standing across the street, without moving, for a very long time, looking at the vegetables.' There was the implication that Andrew was planning a lightning raid on the cabbages or something. He might well have been! But on the other hand, he might have just been *standing*, spontaneously arrested, like Socrates in the account in the *Symposium*.

That's what Andrew used to do – perfectly normal behaviour for a philosopher! Ronnie used to say that [laughs] if the Buddha were alive today they'd haul him off and have him labelled 'catatonic' because he was not *moving*, never mind that he took this vow not to move. Anyway, that was Andrew, and he hadn't done anything. He never did harm anyone. Then one of the women who ran the shop would say 'But, he's got something in 'is pockets, he's got a knife in 'is pockets, he's going t'harm somebody', and I'd say to Andrew 'Have you got anything in your pockets?' and Andrew [shrugs], and the policeman would look and there'd be nothing, maybe a comb, maybe his key to Kingsley Hall or something. But it is amazing what the human mind can conjure up given a little encouragement – say, of someone standing completely still and doing nothing ... .

So that kind of situation provoked Paul and I into trying to grapple with how does one behave, or how does one be with someone who is being looked at as crazy by the world at large? In the end we decided that we could only be towards Andrew like we were towards anybody else, like ourselves, although there were times it seems, that we had to try to – for his own good maybe – protect him.

Did you do any therapy in Kingsley Hall?

Well Ronnie suggested that I see a few people in therapy after a while, and I had no supervision actually, I just started off. There was a young guy who was not living at Kingsley Hall, but he could make it there on

the train, which was remarkable, because he had been diagnosed
'schizophrenic' and he was very spaced out. He was in a family that Joe
Berke and I were seeing in family therapy. We were trying to figure out
what was going on in this family, which was very complicated; Joe was
seeing the mother, and I was seeing the son – the young man who had
been diagnosed. Then we'd see all the family together on certain occasions. As the son got 'better', as it were, in the sense of not behaving in
ways that were getting him labelled as 'mad', so did the mother begin to
break down, and we were looking at this family as a system in which
there seemed to be a need for somebody constantly to be carrying some
madness or other. We saw, like Ronnie had suggested, that the madness
'moved about' in the family.

Anyway, to start with I didn't know much, my psychology studies at
the university were of nil value at Kingsley Hall. But I learned. Being
there with Ronnie was an absolute gift, an invaluable source of learning
about sanity and madness. But I also learned from the people who came
to us. I learned from Andrew, and from Mary Barnes – by looking after
her – but also from talking with that young man who used to come to see
me for therapy, and from many other visitors to the building to whom I
used to sit and listen to for hours on end. Being an American and not
having a work permit, I was not supposed to have a job. I didn't have any
money, and I was more or less living on bread and tea. Ronnie finally
worked out that I could be 'Warden' of Kingsley Hall, [laughs] and they
would give me £10 a week, which I could use to live on, which was how I
survived. And [pause] I think that the experiences at Kingsley Hall, which
Ronnie never managed to write about, and I haven't either, except in that
fictionalised account which is very slim really – are very difficult things to
write about actually – what we were doing.

I remember in the last years of his life, I said to Ronnie, 'If you
were going to do something like Kingsley Hall again, how would you do
it? Would you contemplate it?' He said, 'Yes, I'd contemplate it, but it
would be very different next time.' I said 'How?' and he said, 'Well we
were all very green in those days. None of us knew what we were
doing, and we could do it much better. But it would be very different
now. We've learnt a lot.' I think he said in your book, [*Mad to Be
Normal*], how he'd be more authoritarian. I think that's probably right,
because people got away with a lot of fucking nonsense. Ronnie was
always leaning over backwards to let people all do their own thing – we
all were. It was the '60s! [Laughs] Wonderful, but very tiring. We all
got exhausted from it, very exhausted.

What did you do after Kingsley Hall?

In 1967, a Norwegian friend, on leaving the country, asked me to return a
borrowed book to an English teacher who lived in Chelsea. So I rang her
up; she said 'Come over for tea', and I did. One Sunday afternoon we met
for tea, and I was a little nervous, wondering if I smelt too strongly of

Kingsley Hall. We lived like – not like animals exactly – but it was very basic – I had holes in my clothes and a stubble heard, and there was this language teacher, and proper china cups. So, I was sitting there making polite conversation when the doorbell rang, and she said 'Oh, I wasn't expecting anybody.' She got up, opened the door, and there were two guys, she let them in and said, 'I hope you don't mind, I haven't seen these people for a long time.' And she introduced them. One of them was a Tibetan lama called Chogyam Trungpa, the other was the first westerner who'd become a Tibetan monk. And I couldn't take my eyes off this man, I just thought he was the most extraordinary being, it was the first time I'd ever seen anybody from Tibet. But it was not that he was just somebody from the East, he had the most extraordinary quality. His eyes looked almost alien. He looked as if he was from a different planet, and his skin had a sort of golden aura, and he spoke English very well, very fluently, and he had some very nice turns of phrases, and a giggle which was very crazy, and something in his eyes I thought was very interesting. And I thought 'Well, I must meet this guy again', and I did become friends with him. I didn't see much of the woman again, but that's how things happen sometimes. It turned out that he had a centre up in Scotland called Samye Ling and I went up and visited him there a couple of times, and started to meditate, some Tibetan Buddhist meditation, and a bit of study. I even brought him once to see Kingsley Hall, which he loved.

Around this same time I met Fay Russell, a very mysterious Welsh woman, who was at that time a flamenco dancer and a potter – a very spirited, earthy woman. We became very good friends, and then lovers, and when I left Kingsley Hall, I went to live with her. She had a dream of going around the world on a boat with a group of people. I felt that I had to go to India to study meditation. She was curious about the Tibetan lama I had met, so I brought her up to Scotland, and she met him.

The East was exercising a very strong pull on my imagination. In Norway, I had been taken to meet the Indian ambassador by an old friend of his, Vimala Thakar, a Brahmin yogini. This woman was a friend of Krishnamurti and Vinobha Bhave and a fine teacher in her own right. Vimala told me some of her many psychic experiences – like Madame Blavatsky appearing to her in visions and teaching her and the trans-spatial awareness she had of Krishnamurti wherever he happened to be. When she said she wanted to bring me to meet Aba Pant, the then Indian ambassador to Norway, I didn't have any idea why, but I agreed because she was such a canny mystic. She just said one day, 'Come on, I'm going to take you over in a taxi, and you're going to meet the Indian ambassador.' We were ushered in to his office, he was very pleasant and welcoming, and he said, after meeting me, 'You're going to India, aren't you?' and I said 'I don't have any plans to', [laughs] and I didn't have any money either. And he said 'Well, I think India will be a very interesting place for you.' Five years later, when I was living in England and planning to go travelling with Fay, we went into India House in London to get some papers and letters, and there was Aba Pant, now High Commissioner of India in the UK, smiling, and saying that he knew I would eventually get to India.

Ronnie didn't know why I wanted to travel – this was before he decided himself to go to Sri Lanka – and he kept saying things like, 'Thomas Hardy never went more than 40 miles away from the place he lived. What do you want to go travelling for? Besides it's dangerous. If you go to North Africa, take a gun.' It's the only piece of bad advice that Ronnie ever gave me. I didn't follow it, I didn't take a gun. I'm damned glad I didn't take a gun. I would have regretted it.

When Fay and I did embark on our extended journey, it wasn't on a boat, we compromised and fitted-out a Landrover so that we could live in it and that is how we travelled. We also compromised on the aims – she wanted to go through the Sahara desert and then through central Africa to a port like Dar es Salaam, ship the vehicle to Bombay and continue on from there. I basically wanted to get to India, mainly to look for meditation masters. For Fay the travelling itself was the aim, she loved adventure and throwing herself into new and challenging situations. I reluctantly agreed that that could be fun, but I insisted that we must not forget India. Eventually, we agreed on making the expedition into the Algerian Sahara, then a return to Europe and a second leg of the journey overland, through Iran and Afghanistan to India.

This journey, all the parts of it, was an incredible initiation for me. The Sahara, for example, has become a part of my soul, like a sentient being, a vast presence, deeply ingrained in my memory. It's the only place on earth where I have known complete silence and where I began to get a sense for the immensity of the earth's geological time. I realised how tiny we humans are and how short-lived our history has been. I will always carry the Sahara in my soul, it is there even now as we sit here talking in London, the winds blowing centuries of sand across the face of the dunes.

Well, it took us two years to reach India, but we did. And we stayed three years on the subcontinent before returning to the West.

There I met some Tibetan yogis and lamas, very interesting guys really, up in the hills of North India. I took refuge as a Buddhist, then *bodhisattva* vows and *tantric* vows and began receiving teachings from them and started to do solitary retreats, all the time studying Buddhist texts and practising Buddhist tantra, and when I could no longer stay in India – because of the passport/visa problem – I would go to Nepal. There I worked for a year-and-a-half, teaching English at an American school, studying medicine with Ayurvedic doctors, practising my *sadhanas* and learning *tantric* temple dances with a Newari priest. I loved Kathmandu, it was a sacred city and full of magic, the way a city should be.

In terms of being a therapist, these kinds of experiences are invaluable, though you will not find them listed as part of any training programmes. Some of these experiences were of such an intensity and power that I would be hard put to get them into words, but all the same they inform my knowledge of the psyche and of human existence.

Just thinking of life-threatening situations alone, I tried to count them up at the end of my journey, I think there were 22 situations of very-near-death, like a hair's breadth away from death – and that changes your attitude to how you live and what seems important. Again, the experience of meeting alien cultures with totally different values and belief systems and yet needing to communicate is very good experience for being a therapist. It teaches one something of the infinitely varied possibilities of the human soul.

Luckily, Fay was fearless, physically fearless. She was terrified enough on the spiritual level, of various things, mentally. But physically she could walk into any situation and not bat an eye, no matter what was coming at her. It was quite nice to travel with somebody like that. She taught me many things, I'm very grateful to her, really. We both learned a great deal. After an initial scepticism, Fay actually became a very serious practitioner of Tibetan Buddhist meditation.

By the time five years had gone, the West was very far from our consciousness, and so when a telegram arrived saying that Fay's mother had a brain tumour and was in hospital for an operation, we realised that there were forces at work far outside our control and we would have to give up our studies in India and return to Wales to help. I was immersed in a solitary meditation retreat which I'd vowed not to break on pain of death. I had promised my teacher that I wouldn't break the retreat whether there was an earthquake, a war, or if somebody was dying, so I had to stay there until the end.

Fay went on ahead. She was a month earlier in returning to the West. Going overland in a Landrover, slowly, is very different from coming back in a plane, even though it takes 17 hours – which sounds like a long journey. Nothing like going slowly, village by village.... [Laughs] 17 hours, that's something, it blows your mind completely. It completely destroys the traditional idea of the pilgrimage, which is all about the journey itself and the things you encounter on the way; the obstacles, sicknesses, doubt and dangers. I cried at the beauty of the earth from so high, sitting – how high are you – going 300 miles an hour, maybe 17,000 feet up, in a jumbo jet. The dawn, breaking over Pakistan and the long, red rays of the sun stretching for hundreds of miles across the old, wrinkled land of the Indus Valley and casting long shadows over the Khyber Pass into Afghanistan. You could see whole mountain ranges, it was all very clear. Flying over places where the Landrover had crawled along like a beetle, a tiny thread of a road through the Persian desert. Seeing the so-called 'cradle of civilisation' the places where Ur and Uruk had been – completely crumbled into red dust, crumbling walls, old civilisations put to the sword .... [Pause]

Well I didn't get very far with that, are we just going to leave it hanging about how I became a therapist?

No ...

[Later] Shall I pick it up there, and bring it up to the present? Because it's like half the story otherwise. From what I saw at Kingsley Hall I learnt that I knew very little about human beings, really, I became very humble. I saw so-called professionals who were working with Ronnie. I don't know if Ronnie would have defined it that way [laughs], but that is how they saw it. They were setting themselves up as psychotherapists and analysts. And I just felt it was a charade, it couldn't be true. You can't sit in a room with someone who may have gone through ten times more suffering than you and seen depths of the soul that you've not even been conscious existed, or who have travelled long, or lost friends in battles, or have had their hearts broken or watched a friend dying – and expect that what you say can have any relevance for them. You're a novice, you've read the books and been through your training, but does that entitle you to insult the soul with your theories?

I was completely shocked when I saw this. I thought really there's so little I can do until I become wiser in some way, and I just had to throw myself more out into the maelstrom.

As I said Fay was fearless and she was a fantastic travelling companion. In the middle of the Sahara with a hundred miles of sand in any direction, sand, not dunes, but with bits of rock, very hot, cloudless sky. Nothing around. In the distance up ahead we would see a little dot, and we knew that on the piste was another vehicle, and as we got closer we saw it was a lorry, and as we got closer still we saw there were Algerians/Arabs, men, standing around on the sand doing something or other. Nobody around. So you can't just go past, because in the desert there are so few people, obviously. And there's a desert code. If you are on a camel you do the same thing. I'd spent a long time researching this, I knew what I should do. [Laughs] I didn't like the thought of it though, and so we'd stop the car, get out and walk towards each other – they'd walk towards us, we'd walk, it was like the cowboys in the Wild West [laughs] – we'd stop and greet each other and then the next thing was that we would offer them tea, since it wasn't our country and they love having tea. A little brew-up down in the sand, gather a few sticks and make a fire, put your pot on, little glass cups with mint tea. If they were Arabs we might have coffee. We'd make them a present of something and then they might suddenly surprise us by giving us a whole stack of tinned fruit which was lovely, to have something sweet and cool in the middle of the desert when your supplies were very low. Fay was always very good at cutting through the ice and being a woman. She was very beautiful, very dark, a Spanish-looking Welsh lady, a very powerful personality. And she would usually win them over so there were never any advances, nothing ever happened actually. We were in that situation time and time again. And, gradually, I learned to thaw out, to relax and trust myself.

In my own practice, I've seen people from Brazil, Peru, Scandinavia, France, Germany, Armenia, Iraq, many Americans, people with Islamic backgrounds, Jewish, Catholic, Protestants, Buddhists, Hindu. Because I have been with so many different races and religions on my travels and seen them close up, I have a kind of easiness with them. It doesn't mean that I accept everything, I have my own perspective, but I find that it's very helpful in working with someone that I know where they come from, and where their parents and grandparents come from. Often, a whole area of communication opens up when I show them that I know something of their culture or their grandparents' culture.

So all that travel was fantastic. A lot of it was dangerous and very difficult, time and again, but slowly, I suppose, I matured. Something started to change. The greenhorn started to toughen up and, by the time we got to India, it had taken us two years to get there, from the time we left London. Of course, there was the war that stopped us in Pakistan for a while. And I got sick with hepatitis through taking tea with some Austrian hippies up in the Pakistani mountains of Swat. Then the spiritual journey, slow at the beginning: meeting Tibetans, Hindu gurus as well, all sorts of teachers, and gradually gravitating towards one or two teachers, and then deciding to do very, very intense meditation practices.

On my return to England, Ronnie Laing was one of the first people I sought out, then Francis Huxley, a remarkably imaginative and brilliant anthropologist. I had very good conversations with both of them. Very important for re-entry. It was more of a culture shock coming back than going away. I was getting very much used to being in other cultures, and I'd forgotten the violence of my own, the brutality, the ugliness, the poverty of the mind and imagination, it all suddenly hit me again.

What made you turn toward psychotherapy after all your spiritual practice in India?

Soon after I returned to England from India, I had a dream, and this dream said it all. It shocked me – but I saw that it was irrefutable. I dreamt that I saw a Brahmin bull grazing alone on a dusty plain. He was white with a tinge of pinkish cinnamon. He had huge, lyre-shaped horns, a hump-back and dewlaps. He was like an animal-god, beautiful, just quietly grazing. The sun was shining. You could tell that the earth was hot, the grass was dry. Then, suddenly, from the far right side of the plain another animal appeared: it was a powerful, fast, black bull – very black, it had long dangerous horns with dagger-sharp tips – like a Spanish fighting bull. This bull came charging up to the first one, full of battle lust. It pawed the ground and snorted and swung its horns in rage. But the first bull ignored it and kept on grazing. The second bull came closer, pawing the ground and feinting with its horns, trying to engage the first bull in a fight. Only when the second bull actually attacked the first and jabbed it with its horns did the first bull react, and then it was only with a toss of its horns to shoo the other away. But finally, seeing that the black bull would not leave it alone, the Brahmin bull pulled itself up with great dignity, turned and plodded away, down a dry river bed and out of sight, leaving the field to the black bull. When I woke from this dream, I didn't need an analyst to tell me what it was saying! It was clear that the black bull had taken over the field.

It was also clear that the return to my meditation-practice in the East might have to wait a long time, maybe until my next lifetime, or maybe until the end of this life, when I am old and have finished my work here. But with respect to the next chapter, I knew clearly that I had work to do on the 'black bull' of western consciousness. Violence in thought and action is one of the most characteristic attributes of western man. That and the growing lack of any kind of conscience – the godless psychopath in each of us, who lives, cut off, inside a bubble of nihilistic narcissism.

I decided that I would look around for some place to reconnect with psychotherapy. But after looking into some of the existing organisations for analytical and therapeutic training, my previous feelings of distaste returned. I do not think that it was arrogance, I was just unable to feel that any of the people I met in these institutions was worth spending my time and money on.

So I didn't do anything about it for a while, and then, again quite by accident, one weekend, while visiting a Tibetan teaching centre in the north of England, I found myself in conversation with an elderly lady with white hair, blue rinse, very genteel, a highland lady, about 70, sitting at the hearth in this rather gloomy stone hall. Someone I normally would not have struck up a conversation with. Out of all the many people there I was drawn to this elderly lady and we immediately began talking. Like you might do with a good friend, there was an immediate ease in our communication. She told me of a vision she'd had as a little girl, of some wild, colourfully-costumed dancers which she only later understood must have been Tibetan black-hat dancers. After a while, I said, 'What do you do?' I thought she might be a matron of a women's prison – she had moments of great authority – and I thought: 'I wonder what she does?' So I asked her what she did, and she said, 'Well, I'd prefer to remain incognito, if people know what I do, it changes everything, and I'd rather just be here', and I said 'That's fine with me.' I realised she lived in London, so I said: 'Shall we exchange telephone numbers?' – and we did. I later met her, and it turned out that she was a Jungian analyst [laughs], but a very one-off character.

Buntie Wills, for that was her name, had been in analysis with two Jungian analysts. The first was a man called Philip Metman. After that she saw a women called Toni Sussman. Toni had come to England in 1938 – Jung had sent her to be his first training analyst in Britain. Later on, when the Society of Analytical Psychology had set itself up as a Jungian training group, Buntie went along and introduced herself to them and told them of her work with Toni, but they said that they did not recognise Mrs Sussman as a training analyst and that Buntie would have to start all over again, from scratch, with them! Buntie had already completed her own analysis and training analysis, so she wasn't about to start over again, but it did mean that she had to go it alone. And she did. She worked and practised alone for 30 years until she died, as a 'one-woman band', as she called herself.

She was a brave woman. Before becoming an analyst, she had lived a very full life, working as stage designer, then set designer for films, running a saw-mill during the Second World War and generally being very involved with radical art and artists. She had worked with Paul Robeson when he was here in England and had stood up for him when there was a whole scene in a pub about blacks being there. The director of the film they were working on said that she mustn't sit with Robeson in the pub because it would cause trouble, but she disobeyed. It must have been one of the first occasions that a white woman sat in an English pub with a black man. She was not easily intimidated by false authority, no matter what its rank. She was radical, yet very warm, and had an extremely spiritual side of her which recognised why I had gone to India, and what I was doing, and she didn't put it down. That's what I was looking for. I said to her: 'Can we work together', and she said: 'Yes, I think we can work together very well.' And, it was true, we did work well together.

She lived alone. She practised in a small room above some artists' studios in St John's Wood. She said that she always had the impression that she was sitting high up in the branches of a huge tree in her little room and that one day, on examining an old map of the area, she found that there had been a very old and enormous oak growing exactly where this building later was built. So, I always thought of her as 'the Old Woman in the Tree'. I liked her zaniness and her sharp wit, the surprising ways she had of getting a point across. And her compassion.

I wanted to work at making a bridge between all those extraordinary spiritual exercises you'd call them – disciplines of the mind, and the spirit, and the emotions – and the body – that I was going through in India – and Western psychology. And I thought 'Well here's a woman who actually knows the names of a few Indian teachers', she even spoke to me about her personal connection to Ramana Maharishi, which was wonderful. She had never met him, but she absolutely knew that he was her teacher. His imaginable presence was enough for her. Even when he was no longer alive. She didn't have any inclination to go to India to go to meet anybody, but she respected the journey I had made.

We worked many, many hours on my dreams and on the complexes we discovered at work in my life – and in the things which had often caused me considerable pain and discomfort. She took me through the classical path which Jung had mapped out, confronting the Shadow and its devious deceptions, then introducing me to the 'masterwork', as Jung called it: the confrontation with the Anima, those more or less unconscious feminine persons who inhabit a man's psyche. But she also encouraged my love of art and my own writing as a poet and essayist. She had always been connected to artists, she was a great artist in the work of therapy, she had lived on soup and carrots for the first couple of years as an analyst when she had almost no patients coming to see her. She had given up a very well-paid job to begin work as a therapist. She believed in what she was doing. She would have done it if she had had no money at all. She said to me: 'Therapy is an art. It really is an art, and you're born to it. People can go through trainings, but the training in itself doesn't make them therapists.' When she knew she was not going to live long and that I would one day be practising as a therapist, she transmitted as much of her experience and knowledge as she could. But, as with Laing, I knew that her style was unique to her and that I would have to find my own. Of course, she knew that too and said so.

So began a revisioning of my idea of what therapy was about. Until Buntie, my impressions of therapy had been largely negative. In America as a student I had been to see an Adlerian analyst who, as I see it now, must have been very stunted in his imagination. He was incredibly gross in his attempts to manipulate me in our therapy sessions. He was abusive in his language and utterly reductive in his thinking. And filled with an unreflected hatred of artists. Not very much of a human being, nothing unusual, but awful to come across as a vulnerable young person looking for some kind of insight. He was cynical and caustic – he burnt me – I was very young and very wounded – I could not protect myself.

And in Norway I went to see a supposedly Jungian analyst who used a couch, and interpreted every one of the dreams that I brought as having to do with my family, no matter what the content – when I say 'interpreted', she didn't really bother to enter the imagination of them, to wonder about them or to be taught by them or let them come alive, or allow the figures in them to speak, or anything – she killed the images in the dreams with interpretative bullets, and left me with dead concepts.

Buntie Wills was very different – although she was like Laing in that she was completely herself, an individual who had not buckled under the system. One day, in my confusions about how to 'become a therapist', I said to her that I wanted to become 'respectable' like she was – as a therapist. She looked at me with bemused astonishment and laughed, saying, 'My dear, I am not respectable!' And she told me some of the story of her 'non-acceptance' by the Society of Analytical Psychology. Most of her long-term 'sweethearts' as she used to call her patients, knew about her story with the 'establishment', and do you think it made the slightest bit of difference? She was so popular that you had to be on a waiting list for ages to get to see her. I got to know many of her 'sweethearts' [laughs] over the years, and I saw how lightly and magically she had touched their souls and encouraged their uniqueness to blossom. But calling her patients 'sweethearts'! Can you imagine how that would go down in some of the analytical institutions! They just don't have a sense of humour really. But did she! Oh, how we used to laugh! – such wonderful, healing laughter! I have seldom met anyone

who could laugh so freely and with such pleasure. We had some up-
roarious sessions. Really appreciating the divine comedy of existence
and at the same time she had such compassion, on the weekends she
would go out visiting an old friend who might be in the hospital dying,
or she might go to the country to see somebody who was very lonely,
or who didn't have many friends.

She had a great love, a Norwegian man, who was killed in the
Resistance during the War, so she never married. She never felt the
same about anyone else, she said. I understood that it was a great grief
in her life. But she was truly alone, and that's rare in a human being,
and I think the capacity of being alone and being able to sit there and
talk to people who are married or who have children, from her point of
view, was real. She was no longer one of those naive innocents who had
not experienced life, she had seen a great deal. I never felt any lack of
experience in her.

She also used to distinguish in her own way between analysts and
therapists, which I thought was funny, because it wasn't a scientific
distinction. And she meant it jokingly. She said: 'Men make the best
analysts because they're very good at taking things apart.' And if you
think about it, people who want therapy – most people want to see a
woman. I think I began to dare to open that feminine part of myself,
which I hadn't approached before, with her.

She also got me to write my first book on psychology [*Prospero's
Island – the Secret Alchemy at the Heart of The Tempest*]. I was raving
one day to her about having been with a group of people reading *The
Tempest*, and discovering so much through having taken the part of
Caliban. Initially, I was completely identified with Prospero, which was
the part I really wanted to read. Someone had grabbed the part first,
and I was thinking 'Damn it, why did they have to do that? I could read
it much better than they could!' So I rather grumpily took the part, I
began to understand what Shakespeare had done. He had really created
something very unusual and original, a mythical being who was extremely moving, and he'd given a voice to this otherwise mute character
of the soul – words, wonderful words – and I thought 'If only therapists
could teach people how to do this with the persons of the psyche!'

So I got very wrapped up in Caliban. And I spoke about it to Buntie
and she said, 'You must write a book, just write it, write it out. Caliban *is*
the secret of the play, you're right! Nobody has ever written about it like
that.' So I did. And it was a very good idea, because the book became the
bridge I was looking for. A way to join my spiritual experiences in the East
with my psychological experience of the West. *The Tempest* is about a
spiritual man, Prospero, who because of his devotion to the spiritual, loses
touch with the soul and thus his grasp of worldly things. As Duke of Milan
he pays so little attention to the soul of politics that he just loses it, and
one night finds that his enemies are breaking down the door of his ivory
tower and carrying him off with his baby daughter to be put out to sea in a
rotten carcase of a boat ...

And I think in a way that play spoke to me very much, because I saw so many of us – the people who went East – making precisely the same mistake. People went out and got an enormous amount of input from teachers, very high-level beings, and took it in all too fast, in a great rush, and then went off believing that they'd reached some kind of enlightenment and should become gurus themselves and begin teaching the secrets of the great masters. Then terrible things would start happening, because they really hadn't sorted out their western psyches. [Much laughter] They had just put all that to one side, and 'Om Vajra Guru Padme Siddhi Hung Phat!' it boomeranged back with a vengeance – our western psyche is very, very violent and so extroverted compared to the eastern psyche. Jung was very aware of that. So aware that he actually got quite terrified of it all and tried to stop people going East. He wrote terribly damning things about gurus of all kinds. I suppose he thought he should be the only guru. But he used to put people down for having gurus or wanting gurus, going and finding anything like that from the East.

Did you actually do a training?

[Laughs] I *did*, but it was not a training where I got a piece of paper. So, I am not accredited, I do not belong to any register, I'm completely outside and will probably remain so until I die. You know the system needs some outsiders, how else will it keep from becoming blind to its own unconsciousness?

It happened like this: one day I said to Buntie, 'I think I ought to do a training', and she laughed and said, 'Well men need to be recognised, they need much more recognition than women. Women don't mind actually just practising.' [Laughs] She was full of these funny perceptions, and I quite enjoy thinking about them because – although they might strike one as being over-simplified – there's always a grain of truth in them. For her, men were the analysts who could take things apart; women were the healers – the people who could sit with others and help them to come together again after they were broken-hearted, or broken-minded, broken-spirited. Men, she felt, needed recognition. So they were the ones who set up all the training organisations and the accreditation. Now women are also feeling that they have to go through all this accrediting, and so on, but it isn't, according to Buntie, very central to their nature.

Most important, there's something vital being lost in this process. Buntie would probably call it 'spontaneity'. There's a wonderful section in your book [*Mad To Be Normal*] about spontaneity that's absolutely perfect, where he [Ronnie Laing] says that it's so important for therapy, spontaneity. But then, if you use the word, what people think you mean is jumping into bed with someone. Ronnie was incensed that a perfectly good word like that had been condemned by Freud and made suspect. But the difference between someone like Ronnie and his critics is that

they can see only their own filthy propensities. Ronnie said that 'courtesy and respect' were 'written into the bottom and top line' of his
practice and that 'uncultivated undisciplined spontaneity' could possibly
lead to anything. One must use one's intelligence and integrity in questions like this. Not set up rules of ethics. If I have to look up in the
rules of ethics to see whether I can do something or not, then I have
already gone down the path of ethical nihilism. But spontaneity with
'courtesy and respect' is absolutely essential, and I think that's easily
lost in training programmes. Much has been lost, much that really dis-
turbs and troubles my mind, sometimes keeps me awake at night, thinking what's happening to the whole profession.

But I found myself, and this was in the late '70s, saying to Buntie
one day, 'I've heard that there is a group of people lobbying to make
psychotherapy "respectable". I suppose I will have to go somewhere and
get a certificate', and she laughed and said, 'Yes, well, maybe it's time
for you to see a male analyst anyway, and see how that is different from
working with a woman.' I heard about an analyst who had been to
Zurich and who was a training analyst with the Association of Jungian
Analysts. His name was Ean Begg.

So I rang him up, went to see him, I liked him a lot. He had been
something like a wine taster and a food connoisseur for the Automobile
Association, and before that he had been in a monastery and had been
a monk. I think he had parted company with them over his more
Dionysian side [laughs] but he seemed a very cultured man, and he was
a Jungian in the fashion that I could appreciate. I think he's a rare
being, an analyst with a generous heart. And quite free from dogma.
He's very Jupiterian, and I have found that a great asset in an analyst –
to have that much joviality. He wasn't just into a monotheistically masculine mode either, he had a spiritual strength. And he was Scottish as
well. [Laughs] He was a very well-read, very articulate man; spiritual,
but with a toughness. I liked that combination a lot. It was just right. I
felt blessed actually, I felt it couldn't have been better. I began analysis
with him and did another few years. These two people [Buntie Wills and
Ean Begg] were the two best people I could have seen at the time.

I never saw Ronnie as an analyst, and I'm content with that because
our friendship developed without those extra tangles. Whatever closeness we had wasn't anything to do with having been in that sometimes
difficult asymmetrical situation. Although with Ronnie, I'm sure he did
his best to avoid the asymmetry. With him, people put it on to him so
much that no matter what he said, he'd sometimes have to lie on the
floor and rock like a foetus [laughs], for him to cut through some of the
stuff that was flying around him.

So in the middle of my – what Ean called my 'training analysis' – I
applied to the Association of Jungian Analysts of which Gerhard Adler
was Chairman at the time, and while my application was going on there
was a struggle of some kind in that group. Basically Adler was getting on
in years and he was resigning, and so they'd put a vote among the

members of the Association who they would like to replace him, and they chose Ean Begg. Well the story as I heard it was that suddenly Gerhard refused to accept the vote. He held on to his position, and he wouldn't let it go. He said that he wasn't resigning after all. Ean's party which was the majority of the members got together around Ean and as a move of solidarity, said, 'We're leaving, because enough is enough. You cannot act in this way.' They withdrew and formed their own organisation, which is now called the Independent Group of Analytical Psychologists. Ean was the first convenor of that group. They applied to the International Association of Jungian Analysts, and were accepted and they're now a separate Jungian training group. So they're a splinter group of the AJA which is a splinter group of the SAP. It's the second schism among the English Jungians. And this probably will go on and on. It's part of the nature of psychology – its schisms, it's a schismatic subject.

I think it's because the psyche is basically schismatic, and as Jung pointed out, it's full of complexes and splinter psyches and so on. I think Jung, probably in his – wherever he is [laughs] – armchair in the sky, if he looks down on all this may be slightly embarrassed, thinking, 'Well, "individuation", I coined this word, all right, I took it from Nietzsche. Individuation was the thing I pushed, and it meant people becoming more and more truly themselves. So I can't complain when they do, can I now!' So the more yourself you become, the less like others you will be, and the more you have to pull away and make your own psychology, basically. I think in the end all psychologies are one-person affairs, and that's why Jung was so horrified when he found the people calling themselves Jungians. Jaques Lacan couldn't stand the idea of having Lacanians, even publicly announced it and tried to get them to stop, for Christ's sake. But they still go on calling themselves Lacanians.

One of the reasons why I like archetypal psychology is that Hillman, who coined the term in about 1971, avoided from the beginning having a 'Hillmanian' psychology, another personal name. He actually said that archetypal psychology was not only his creation, Jung was one of the fathers, and another father was the French philosopher, Henri Corbin. Then there are these other people he lists going back through the Romantics. A lot of poets and artists, back through the Romantics to the Renaissance, to philosophers like Marsilio Ficino. Back again in time to the Neoplatonic philosophers like Plotinus, and then further back to Plato, even to Heraclitus. There have been lots of influences in archetypal psychology, and Hillman, in his little monograph defining archetypal psychology for the Italian *Encyclopedia del Novecento*, lists a good twenty, thirty contemporary contributors to the field. Friends and acquaintances, people he knows, those he doesn't know that well, who are contributing to archetypal psychology. So I thought that is a generous move on his part. He started to create something and said 'Look, it's out there, if you want to, you may join me, if you like what I'm doing', and he used a phrase to me once when we were talking about this – 'elective affinity'. One of Goethe's phrases ...

... and Max Weber ...

... right. So you know what I mean. And on another occasion Hillman spoke to me about 'sitting in the same tree'. When we look around, who is sitting in the branches of the tree we're in? I have a few different people to Hillman, but a lot of them are the same as the people in his tree. So there's a lot in common there.

So to return to the story of how I became a therapist. One day Ean said, 'Why don't you start seeing people?' Buntie had already said the same, she'd said: 'You might as well start seeing people.' They believed in what I was doing, and I would talk to them, not in a strict supervision sense like: 'I did this, what do you think about that?', but I'd tell them about who I was seeing and if I thought that there was an interesting thing that maybe could use some of their perspicuity I would mention it in the session, and we'd talk about it. And so it went. I knew that I was apprenticing myself to these older, more experienced people, and it felt like the right way to go about it. They also seemed happy with that.

When I put my application in with the Association of Jungian Analysts, it was just at the time when the great split was beginning in the group – which I knew nothing about at the time. Adler had seen me once for a single brief session and had asked me a few questions. Ean said that he had put me forward as his strongest candidate, the one of all those applying who should be taken on. When Adler refused to have me in the training – and this was before they parted company – Ean got angry. He said that I was being used in this situation like a ping-pong ball. He wanted me in and Adler didn't. And Adler had the final say.

Ean said, 'How many years have you been doing this sort of thing?' He said, 'you've been a student long enough.' I was ten years at university, five years travelling, three years in meditation, several years in personal analysis and another three years in training analysis. 'What more do you want?' he said. '*You* should be teaching the students in the programme.' And I said, 'Shouldn't I have some piece of paper?' and he said, 'Oh forget it, in the old days nobody bothered about such things. Why can't you just do it?' I said, 'Well there is talk of setting up some sort of body of accreditation and making the whole thing super-respectable and all that.' He said: 'I don't think it's ever going to get anywhere. I don't think it's going to bother you, you're a clinical psychologist, you've had all this background, why don't you just go ahead?' So I said 'All right, I will.' And I did. So I was saved another five years of boring aggravation. And that's how I became a therapist. [Laughs]

When?

When? Around 1984.

What happens when someone comes to see you? As an 'archetypal therapist' ...

All right, I'll answer that, but first I want to go back and draw some loose ends together. Do you remember at the beginning of our talks, I mentioned three factors that early on played a great part in my becoming a therapist?

Yes ...

The first factor was an early need to understand a disturbed and disturbing mother, that was the first. The second was my American experience of the devastating impact on the soul of the loss of culture and cultural roots. And the third was my longing for beauty. I also mentioned that I was grieving over something in childhood, which I didn't understand. I said that I thought it might have been grief over the sister that I didn't have. But those three factors have occupied me most of my life, more or less in that order.

I spent the first 25 years of my life desperately trying to free myself from the crazy tangle of negative injunctions, double-binds, existential/religious traumas, internalised habits of misperception, and a general terror of life. This was the period in which I read Freud and steeped myself in that kind of analytical thought. As I gradually emerged from this miasma in my late twenties, and was no longer subject to the internal corrosiveness of perpetual fear, I began to realise the extent to which my soul was impoverished.

During my second 25 years I began to accept being embodied, and to enjoy it. I began to have confidence in my natural inclination to explore the world. This was the time of my literal journeys to many countries and cultures, it was also a time of profound inner journeys, explorations of all kinds of psychic and spiritual geographies. This was the period in which Jung became my mentor and guide. But by the end of this period I knew that everything up to this time had been preparation. My longing for beauty was still there, it was beginning to become apparent to me that it was not only missing from my life but from our culture as a whole.

This was the time I discovered the writings of James Hillman, and said: 'Aha, here's a man who's found a way to revision psychology so that it can be given a poetic basis in mind, and can address the appalling repression of beauty in our time.'

In 1987 I was 49 years old. I had been immersed in the work of Hillman since 1979, teaching his ideas since 1983. At last I'd found a psychology which I thought was completely right for me, and there was also plenty of room for my own contribution to it, if I felt that I was up to it. Ean Begg strongly encouraged me to set up an organisation to further the dissemination of archetypal psychology in England. And this suggestion came at precisely the right time. Since 1985 I'd been living with Eva Loewe, who shared all my passion for poetry, painting, music and archetypal psychology. Completely unforeseen, I had at last found the sister I had never had. More than anything else that had so far happened to me, Eva made it possible for me to become the kind of therapist I wanted to be and am becoming. From the moment of our first meeting it was clear that we could create something phenomenal together that we could never do apart. We still, after more than ten years of life together, find this coincidence of destinies astonishing.

It made it possible for us to create the London Convivium for Archetypal Studies, which is a registered charitable Trust. And the annual full-length anthology *Sphinx – A Journal for Archetypal Psychology and The Arts*. Eva has accompanied me during the last ten years in the creation of these two major projects – frequently staying up all night long and working through weekends. But it was all based on our love of the Arts, and the conviction that Art had to be brought to bear on the practice of psychotherapy and psychology. We've had nearly a century of psychotherapy where questions of beauty and ugliness are simply not addressed as central issues. They are what is being repressed. It isn't sexuality any longer, it is beauty that is being repressed.

So you see I have finally begun to address that last factor of crucial importance in my growing up. The combination of Hillman's ideas and the central importance of imagination, and the need for an aesthetic psychology, together with my proximity to Eva and her great sensitivity towards beauty, gave me the confidence to begin working out ways in which the practice of psychotherapy could include the awakening of an aesthetic imagination. This year, 1995, marks the first year in which Eva and I are teaching our ideas on archetypal and cultural psychology in a Foundation Year Course, which we have named 'Thiasos'. It's not a training course [laughs], it's a course about ideas. And *Thiasos* is taken from the Greek name for the company of devotees around Dionysus.

So let's return to your question now. What Hillman has been calling for, and what we, Eva and I, have seen to be imperative, is a complete and radical transformation of psychology, turning it more or less inside out. If psychotherapy means 'attending to the soul', or 'care of soul' – *psyche* meaning 'soul', and therapy meaning 'attending to', I think everybody knows that by now – then we must be clear about what that implies. We must distinguish between the therapy of soul and the therapy of body, for example, or the therapy of spirit. There's a great confusion today, for example, between soul and spirit, as well as between soul and body. And psychotherapy means a primary concern for soul matters. For a start, we as therapists, must be much more aware of the inherent, built-in tendency in psychotherapy of virtually all schools to foster introspection and a narrow preoccupation with the literal persons in our lives, to the exclusion of the non-personal, mythic elements of the soul. And that narrow personal sense with which psychotherapy is confusedly operating today makes it more a *sociology* than a *psychology*, and perhaps should be called that.

So the first thing that I would work on with someone who comes to see me is developing a sense of 'soul'. The meeting with the archetypal dimension to their existence may have to come much later – it usually

isn't on the cards to begin with. It may never be for any of the people I
see. It's a very wonderful mode of perception, though, a way of imagining things and seeing through the obfuscations of the ego. Not everybody who walks into the consulting room is ready for it, however, or is
interested in it, or can grasp it, or sees the point of it. It depends very
much on what people come for.

Some people come in the room and it's obvious that they're going to
fall apart at any moment, or they feel that they're going to fall apart, or
they're suffering so much they can't stop crying, in or out of the session. Other people are so loaded with psychiatric drugs, in up to the
eyeballs with some time-release capsule which is buffering their chakras
and severely cutting them off from the deeper layers of the psyche that
they are completely numbed-out. Or they're working in the city and
they're numbed-out. [Laughs] Many, many different kinds of people
come into therapy. Some people actually do come into therapy who are
passionately interested in the imagination and in the condition of their
souls. There is a growing sensibility which recognises the need to break
out of our self-enclosed subjectivity and to allow soul to again appear in
the things of the world.

A few individuals actually come because they are concerned about
the state of the world we are living in. In my mind this is the best
reason for entering the kind of therapy that I practise – because in the
end it leads to a concern, beyond oneself, a concern for the soul of the
world, what Plato, Plotinus and the Neoplatonists called *Anima Mundi*,
the World Soul. Plotinus maintained that the material world is held in
the soul like a net is held by the sea. They are coterminous – the sea
extends as far as the net extends. There is nowhere any place without
soul, according to this tradition. The interesting thing is that this idea is
shared by virtually all tribal peoples in the world. They know that the
world is ensouled and they regard us as dangerous and crazy because
we reject the idea that trees, mountains, rivers and animals can be
ensouled. In turn, we write all this off as simply superstition and
'animism' – a foolish, primitive belief-system.

Therapy – if it is not to founder in its own narcissism – must begin
to counter its ingrained centripetal force with a centrifugal one. Therapy
must find a way out of its hall of mirrors into the world it has left
behind. On a concrete level, Jung's introduction of the *dialogue* with the
patient and his replacing Freud's couch with two armchairs facing each
other was already a centrifugal move away from the endlessly self-
centred monologues of the patient.

As you see, Eva and I offer the patient a third possibility. They can
sit facing the therapist on the settee or they can choose the other
armchair, which is set oblique to the therapist's chair. In that position,
we are not squarely face-to-face. The patient can look out of the
window! [Laughs] So the world is not shut out. There is an opportunity
to abandon the narcissistic fascination of the analytical mirror and to
look out at the world. This is a metaphor, of course, but the concrete

position of the chairs reflects a governing fantasy – as does the couch and the darkened, heavily curtained room of classical analysis.

Of course, this view of therapy is not only very radical and revolutionary, but it is new and unfamiliar to people. Thus, it is not something that I can expect everyone turning up in the consulting room to understand. But it is this kind of imagination about therapy which informs my practice – it is the larger context, if you like. To begin with: what appears in the consulting room is basically the soul looking for love. The soul looking for love for its symptoms, its terrors and awesome sufferings, its peculiar enigmas, its irrational desires and impossible longings. Gradually, perhaps, with some of the individuals who come into therapy with me, I can introduce the idea of there being another meaning to what has seemed only a literal, single-meaninged event or experience. That move, away from the literal toward the metaphorical, opens the door to a discussion of soul and the realm of mythic images. In other words, of the archetypal patterns and formal modes of the psyche.

In practice I find that it is highly individual how soon a person could be expected to follow an archetypal move. I say archetypal, because we are talking about a move one makes rather than a thing that is. In this sense archetypal psychology is different from Jung's psychology in that we emphasise the adjective, not the noun. We don't talk so much about archetypes. Archetypal psychology – in distinction to Jung, does not consider the numenon, but the phenomenon. For Jung the archetypal patterns of the psyche transcended the empirical world of time and place, and were not in themselves phenomenal. Archetypal psychology, however, considers the archetypal always to be phenomenal.

Archetypal psychology always looks for the archetypal patterns or structures behind what is going on. In therapy, for example, archetypal psychology does not ignore psychopathology, like many new forms of therapy. Psychopathology is seen as central, but I do not consider psychopathologies true pathologies in the medical sense. I work at finding some psychological necessity in the pathologising activity of the soul. Psychopathology is deeply linked to myth. There is a double link: that pathology is always mythologised, and mythology is always pathologised. So a large part of our work in therapy is involved in *seeing through* the symptoms, and syndromes, and pathologies which people bring to the consulting room – to their mythic or archetypal core. This archetypal move is a move of conferring value on the fantasies or symptoms people bring. Archetypal psychology is a psychology of value.

When talking of the figures of mythology, Jung once said that *we ought to stop deriving these figures from our conditions, and rather derive our conditions from these figures.* But in order to be able to do this, one must first know a great deal about the figures Jung is referring to – the gods, the goddesses. That means having an enormous understanding of mythology. That means that you cannot practise an archetypal psychotherapy without a very sound grasp of mythology and the mythological imagination.

Many people don't think in terms of 'soul'; maybe they don't even think it exists. How do you deal with this in a session? Suppose someone comes in and doesn't seem to know what the soul is?

Well, I might give him a poem like this one by Antonio Machado which I love and I occasionally recite to people. It goes like this:

The wind one brilliant day called to my soul with the aroma of jasmine.

'In return for this jasmine odour, I'd like all the odour of your roses ... '

Machado says,

'... I have no roses – all the flowers in my garden are dead ... '

And the wind said,

'Then I'll take the waters of the fountains, and the dried up leaves and the yellow petals.'

The wind left. I wept. And I said to my soul,

'What have you done with the garden entrusted to you?'

I might start there, if somebody doesn't have any sense of what soul is, but, you know, most people do. I find that poetry is incredibly magical in communicating this sense of soul. So I may quote Keats or Blake, Yeats, Lorca, Rilke or Wallace Stevens. But also if you mention 'soul food' or 'soul music', or somebody who 'has soul', there's an immediate understanding in the ordinary mind. It may have been 'cultured out' of psychology [laughs] and maybe philosophy and theology, actually, but it still remains in everyday life.

When you mentioned 'soul' I first thought of Otis Redding.

Exactly, and that is perfectly right. It's right on.

Can you tell me what actually happens when someone comes to see you?

I can't because I don't know what is going to happen and because people are so different there are no two sessions alike. All right, there are certain external parameters to the situation that remain much the same, but that isn't going to tell you the important thing – how the soul appears in the consulting room and how I respond to it, because that is not something that can be standardised. No way!

What are some of the external parameters then ...?

They ring the doorbell. I buzz to open the outer door and let them into
the building. I open the door to my flat and welcome them with a
handshake if it is the first time. I walk with them into the consulting
room and offer them the choice of either the settee or the armchair. I
usually ask them what brought them here. If they want to know something about me and how I practise, I try to give them a sample of my
style of thinking and working – I will probably mention that I value the
dream highly and that if possible I like to have written texts of dreams
to work on – to the extent that they have dreams. If they don't have
dreams, then I suggest that we look at life-situations or work-situations
or plans and goals. I use the first hour to explore the feasibility of
working with this person and whether it looks like we will get on. If we
both feel good about this at the end of the first hour, I discuss my fees
with them, ask them how frequently they would like to come. Normally
I see people once or twice a week, though I am flexible with other
arrangements when people have worked with me for a time. I usually
set a period of time with the person at the end of which we agree to
review the work and to see whether we want to continue – this could be
anything from a month to six months or a year.

What about the more subtle parameters? The internal ones?

What do I do with them? Well, Ronnie Laing said a beautiful thing in
your book [*Mad to be Normal*] which I would hope that I could live up
to. He said that his patients had had his company and his attention,
that he put himself at their service and addressed himself the best he
could to what was troubling them. The form this could take was unpredictable and varied but they would get the best of what he could bring
to bear on the situation – of his intuition, spontaneity and sensibility.
But he couldn't package all that into a model. I'm very grateful to
Ronnie for having found those words, because I think it does say something very true about the difficulties of talking about the kind of soul-
making that goes on in good therapy.

Someone may come into the consulting room with a tremendous
panic, someone on the edge, as it were, a borderline, a real borderline.
It's a very tricky place to be. It's a place that deserves our respect. It's
awesome. You cannot bluff you way around it and analyse it away.
That's why so many doctors and psychiatrists and analysts end up pre-
scribing psychopharmaceuticals in such a case. They don't know how to
address it. They cannot see the god in the dis-ease, as Jung requested
we look for. But I've been there myself, I know what it's like. And I
honour this god. As a therapist you don't do a lot. But you've got to be
there. You've got to give that person 'your company and your attention'.
Well, if someone looks as if they're not breathing, I might suggest that
they breathe. [Laughs] Because you can get so caught by the panic,

that part of your diaphragm isn't actually moving any more. And I will breathe with them. I will consciously tune in to their breathing.

So little things like that one might do. The longer people stay of course, the more we can explore. It's not that they get attached and can't leave, that's a very different thing. I don't encourage people to get attached, really.

Can we talk about transference?

'Transference' as a concept is really an Apollonian defence, and a particularly nasty one, against Eros, and for what perennially in human history has been regarded as friendship. I am not saying that therapists should make friends with their patients, but neither am I saying that they should not. What I am saying is that a lot of psychoanalysis and psychotherapy hides behind a protective shield of concepts like 'the transference' because of a fundamental self-deception. The truth is that a concept like 'transference' is all too frequently used to mask a frightful inability to love. Terrible mockeries of human relationships go on under the name of 'transference' and 'countertransference'. The psychoanalytical use of the word is an appalling abuse of language – because in essence it has the same meaning as the word 'metaphor': 'to carry across'. No poet would be caught dead using the word in the way it has been and is being used in psychological circles. There is no doubt in my mind whatsoever that there are many things which are 'carried across' during the therapeutic encounter, but the kind of theory which interprets all of these marvellous metaphors of the soul as 'parental projections' and so on is absolutely absurd. It is an act of hubris of such proportions that the gods must either fall sick from laughter when they observe it or go berserk with rage.

You know, I led a kind of 'practise-revisioning' group for professionals in analysis, psychiatry and psychotherapy, and one of the members was someone who had trained with one of the so-called 'Jungian' analytical training groups in London. When he first came to see me, he had been a practising analyst for over ten years, and he wanted to revision his way of practising through archetypal psychology. He said to me, 'You know, you're the first person that I've been able to talk to about imagination and dreams in therapy. In my training we were taught that every remark of the patient had to be interpreted in terms of "the transference".' This is the sort of thing which kills the imagination. It doesn't have any dignity. And it isn't even decent.

Of course, there are occasions when people come into the consulting room, sit down and begin behaving as if I were their father or mother, and you don't have to train for five years to see that. But that is not something that happens consistently with every single individual who enters therapy. And one does not have to behave in such a way as to encourage it. It is easy to discourage it! Usually, it is easy to side-step. Therefore, I find it morally reprehensible when the therapeutic hour is

used to force the patient into a 'transference' and then to browbeat him
endlessly about it and to refer everything that takes place back to it. It
is so tedious and so degradingly trivial to the soul. There is so much
else which is being 'carried across', archetypally, which calls out to be
recognised. By interpreting all that happens during the hour exclusively
in the name of the 'family romance', therapy is in danger of losing
touch with soul altogether. There's something about it that's very disturbing. It's vampiric. I don't like it and I wouldn't encourage it. I know
that there are many groups who teach it, and of course, this is just my
own individual assessment.

Unfortunately, some of the most established and respectable psychotherapeutic organisations around have built their entire conception of
therapy around ideas like 'the analysis of "the transference"'. It is so
embedded in them that you would have to take the whole theoretical
system apart, piece by piece, down to the ground, in order to get rid of
its insidious influence.

*Do you try to deal with patients' everyday concerns or do you try to take
them further?*

Are they mutually exclusive, those two things? [Laughs] No. One can
do both. Somehow bringing in an archetypal move, say in connection
with a marital row or with a feeling a person has – an emotion, or an
emotional attack, or a mood – bringing an archetypal mood to bear on
that somehow values it in a very special way.

*Could you give an example of what you might draw upon, how it might
illuminate someone's problems?*

In archetypal psychology there is always the idea that every 'problem'
conceals a fantasy at its core, and so it is necessary to dissolve the
problem into the fantasy within it. A woman might come into the consulting room with an enormous fear that she might be a lesbian. She
calls this a 'problem'. She is terrified that something is going to push
her into that, and is also terrified maybe that I'm going to try to
encourage her to act that out or be that. But it's a fantasy that keeps
her awake at night, and it feels like an obsession and it haunts her. So
gradually in working with that person, I may come to discover that
there's been very little of the feminine in their lives – maybe they lost
their mother very young, there were no sisters around, they've had to
get out into a man's world and work – and have somehow neglected,
not by their own choice but because of life itself, they have neglected a
particular aspect of the garden that Machado talks about, which in
archetypal terms would be a fantasy of beauty. The fantasy that may
haunt this young women is of getting close, intimately close with
women, and finding them attractive. But within the attraction-power of
the feminine is a goddess, there is a mythic person within the eroticism

and seductiveness of the feminine. She was called Aphrodite by the Greeks, Venus by the Romans.

So I might introduce that person to the myths and stories and images of Aphrodite, rather than to stay within a discussion of whether she should become a lesbian or not. Whether she does or not, anyway is her decision, but what's very clear in how she's presenting her 'problem' is that something is missing from her life. Now, moral philosophy is an abuse here. I cannot join her in condemning her fantasies, because they are the soul's own voice speaking. If I were to get caught by the ideology of middle-class humanism of mental health and mental illness, attempting to judge what is 'healthy' in this case, I would miss the archetypal person in this patient's fantasies. Ideas of mental health and illness are ideas about the psyche. When we are told what is mentally ill we are being told what ideas, fantasies and behaviour are wrong. Too much of therapy and analysis is trapped in this kind of moral philosophy.

With the pagan Greeks, if something was bothering them, or they were disturbed about something in their life – something was wrong – a friend might say to them, 'Have you remembered to make offerings to such and such a god or goddess? Perhaps you have not paid enough attention to Aphrodite? Maybe some of your misery is because she's feeling that you haven't noticed her.' Well if you look at the Greek tragedies that's often clearly stated so that the audience will know what deity is presiding over the action of the play. Euripides is very precise with that link. Like in his play, *Hippolytus*, where Aphrodite comes on stage before the play begins and has a little prologue, where she says 'Hippolytus is always out hunting with Artemis. He is always going to Artemis's altar. He says that I am the most pernicious of all the gods. He's not interested in girls, or in making love. I'm going to get him because of his contempt for me. I'm going to have my revenge.' And the rest of the play is Aphrodite's vengeance – it's how she gets Hippolytus's stepmother Phaedra to fall in love with him, and a great tragedy then ensues where he's finally dragged to death by his horses.

The Greeks took the gods very seriously. Now archetypal psychology doesn't worship the gods, rather it imagines them – that is a big difference. It sees them phenomenologically, as *places* in which to put things, so that we can order our existence in some way. These are ordering principles. The gods and goddesses. So, for example, certain forms of depression, and there are many kinds, certain kinds are obviously very linked to what the Renaissance mythographers called Saturn. And so I might make an archetypal move with respect to someone's depression and introduce them to the image of Saturn, and to talk about melancholy as it was seen by Renaissance physicians and philosophers and artists as a particular gift of Saturn. Introducing them maybe to some of the art that's involved with Saturnian images, and see whether or not they might be able to allow that depression into their lives as something that would deepen their sense of soul. I might mention Marsilio Ficino, who was a kind of archetypal psychologist of the Renaissance, and who

devised numerous imaginative ways of working with his depression, having accepted melancholy as an aspect of his character or destiny. He
lived with it his whole life, and regarded Saturn as a prominent part of
his nature. It was the dominant in his astrological chart, and significant,
and therefore he knew he had to give Saturn his due. And he would do
that by making very melancholy music, or dressing in black on certain
days, or any number of things.

So in a way archetypal psychology isn't about treatment and cure. It
doesn't operate out of the 'treatment fantasy'. Therefore again it's very
different.

Are you saying that 'coming to terms' with things actually changes them?

There is that possibility. But I don't set out to 'treat' symptoms, which
usually means getting rid of things without really understanding them.
Jung used to see the symptom as a really creative energy the psyche
produced, and that if it was understood correctly, it could lead to a marvellous blossoming in a person's life. Incorrectly understood, on the other
hand, it could lead to a narrowing and closing down – the feeling of being
psychologically crippled – but that's because of a lack of understanding of
the symptom. Therefore, when we surgically remove symptoms, as with
behaviour therapy, or with various forms of psychopharmaceuticals, like
Prozac, or all the different ways we have of getting rid of symptoms, we're
actually cutting off our nose to spite our face, we're losing something that
in most cases would be able to benefit us, to enrich our lives rather than
to impoverish us.

It won't seem obvious to the patient at the time ...

No, no. And that's what this kind of therapy's about. Which is a lot to
do with education, I suppose, and counter-education with respect to
what one already thinks about what one is into.

Do people ever come to see you with the idea of a 'quick fix'?

Seldom, and if they only want that, they don't usually stay. They can see
that I'm not offering that, and I'm usually quite clear about it. I don't
encourage people to stay if that is the case: why would I, if they are not
interested in how I see the world at all. No, it's not a big problem. People
come to me usually because they've either read my writing, my books, or
they've met me somewhere giving a talk, or somebody whom I've seen has
liked what's happening in their therapy and recommends me. So I don't
advertise. I don't work much with GPs – who might also have the idea of
'quick fix' from their medical model.

Very rarely somebody does come from that sort of referral, and sometimes by complete chance, fortune, it works. And other times it doesn't. If
what they're looking for is a kind of medical/treatment approach.

If someone comes who is expecting that kind of therapy, do you tell them what you offer and how it is different?

Yes, of course. I will usually do that with a person who is coming from that rather unknown area like I just described – from a GP, for example – and who doesn't know my work. But if it's someone who actually knows what I'm on about, it's not necessary. They've come because they've read my book called *Archetypal Imagination – Glimpses Of The Gods In Life And Art*. So that's what they're here for, they want to understand how that works in their own lives.

I'm still unclear, is it about patterns ...

Well. You could rephrase all that and say it's to give the person coming here a sense of soul. Because sometimes they don't have it. And if they do have it, maybe it's not in any way supported in their lives. So coming here is a kind of confirmation, or an affirmation of something that they dimly feel. Our work gives them more confidence to follow something which they know to be true for themselves. So first of all it is giving them a sense of soul. Another way to rephrase it might be the activation or catalysation of the imagination – the creative imagination. Because in our society this is in a sorry state, mainly through the school system and the media, through almost everything. The imagination is not recognised as what William Blake would have called a 'Divine power' – the divine imagination in man. And the link to the realm of the divine, the gods. Our religion, which has only one God, and one that is an imageless abstraction at that, our religion has fought the many gods of pagan polytheism and thus also the imagination, which naturally imagines them.

So that's another way to rephrase what happens here, it's an activation of the creative imagination. And that can happen in so many different ways. If you don't have imagination, you can't practise archetypal psychotherapy. [Laughs] Obviously, that's what it's all about. But to the extent that I can tap into certain resources of imagination, so can I perhaps encourage that in another. It may be, for example, that we embark on a revisioning of their biography, their 'story' – perhaps they're trapped in a view of it that is largely to do with pop psychology, or television or some books they've read, or even some therapies they've been into where they've come to a complete dead end, and it just feels like they're going nowhere. So maybe the therapy in the beginning takes the form of a revisioning of their biography, and we're like two writers. We sit down and we see how we could write this story in a different way, do you see? Every good novelist knows that you can tell the same story in about ten different ways, but if you're stuck with only one, that can be quite an unhappy situation. Only one way to see what's happened to yourself in your life.

Do you draw on a number of theories, insights – Laing, Jung, Freud ...?

Yes, but in the end it is the person who 'tells' me what kind of language
I need to speak in order to communicate most appropriately with them.
It's up to me to hear that. I know women who did not have a father in
their childhood, but who grow up with an incredible assurance with
men, and who also develop an impressive masculine intelligence and an
impressive assertiveness – and you wouldn't imagine, looking at them, if
you were say, a Freudian or a psychoanalytically-trained therapist, that
that person could possibly be a person who grew up without a father.
But that happens all the time. There are anomalies and exceptions to
the rule. It would be useless to talk to that kind of person in Freud's
language. Have you ever heard of Pataphysics? It is a new science,
invented by the French surrealist, Alfred Jarry, which sets out to study
the laws of 'exceptions to the rule' [laughs] and I think something like
that should be considered by psychotherapists. It happens a lot. You
can't generalise.

Do you keep to a regular hour or 50 minutes ...

I have very few rules like that.

This is what I am trying to find out.

[Laughs] Very few rules. Though I aim at a full hour for everyone I see.
You know, the soul has a pace all of its own, and it's not honoured in
our manic society. I have found that some individuals need an hour and
a half in order for the soul to speak. You can't force it. By cutting down
the hour to 50 minutes, you are depriving the soul of its own slow
rhythm and constantly frustrating the patient. With many patients I
need to work at slowing everything down before anything can happen.
Everything in the soul moves slowly. And I have no rules about talking
or silence. It's happened that I've spent a whole hour in silence with
somebody when I felt it was necessary. It's also happened that I've
talked a great deal, and told stories and jokes, and recited poetry, or
got up and looked for books that I wanted to show someone. Again, I
usually do not interfere or interrupt someone's fantasy. One of my rules
is to follow the fantasy they bring, not judge it or moralise over it.
Sometimes if I have the feeling that someone is just 'reporting' the past
week's events in a very literal way in session after session, I might try
to stop them and encourage them to see what they're doing and to see
that there are other things that they could be doing in this precious
time that we have together, this hour.
    Another area where I do not put myself into a strait-jacket of fixed
rules is to do with the actual place of the session. Because archetypal
psychology has had, from its beginning in 1970 when Hillman first
named it as such, the intention of moving beyond clinical inquiry within
the consulting room and situating itself within the culture of western
imagination, the actual place at which the session takes place is not

eternally fixed in one literal spot – in my consulting room. Because soul is not only an individual matter but is present everywhere in the world, according to my masters like Plato and Plotinus, sometimes something can be gained by meeting the patient in a particular place in which the *anima loci*, the soul of the place, can be met as a part of the therapy. This is not a very common occurrence, the sheer mechanics of organising it is far too complicated, but both Eva and I have had sessions 'out in the world' with our patients. Early morning in the great flower market in New Covent Garden, for example. Or in the Greek section of the British Museum, or at the Spider House in Regents Park Zoo. Once one stops confining the soul inside the body, one sees that the care of the soul can take one into the world – must take one into the world in many different ways. Or, by bringing the world into the consulting room which we do as much as possible, by discussing the plan of the office in which one works, or the details of the architecture of the place in which one lives, or the ethical implications of the job one is in. Following Jung's dictum of *Esse in anima*, or *being in soul*, we work with the understanding that we are in soul, not that soul is in us, merely.

Is there a goal?

Well I mentioned a few, like giving the person a sense of soul, like activating the imagination, like making connections between their personal life and the life of the gods – the archetypal structures of existence.

How would you know when enough has been achieved?

I largely leave it up to them, but if I feel somebody is hanging on too long, and things have come to some kind of conclusion, and they should have left, I will probably tell them that, most certainly I would say: 'You know, it's about time we think of finishing.' But I don't encourage people to come all that often, or to stay for that long. I don't feel that it's feasible for most people to come more than once – or at the most twice – a week, in London. First of all, because it's an expense. Second of all it's difficult – you may live in South London, and getting up to Hampstead twice a week is quite an ordeal, especially if you're in a full-time job. But most important of all, I don't think that therapy should substitute for their lives, and I don't think that I want to encourage people to think that. There's a lot of work that I encourage people to do between sessions. I send them out to the library, or I get them to write things for me or to paint pictures, or to rethink things. But people are so amazingly individual and different. I find it really difficult to answer your question, because people are so individual.

Presumably 'training' in your approach is possible or is it overwhelmingly intuitive?

That is a difficult question, because it's taken me a very long time in my life to arrive where I am, and I don't know how to cut through some of the mistakes that I made in order to bring people more quickly to the same place. I think the mistakes were perhaps part of it, and living is part of it. I think apprenticeship is about the closest I can get to this idea of training. An apprenticeship is something quite particular. I have arrived where I am because all through my life I have looked for truly gifted and experienced people who had something to teach. When I found them, I stuck with them and tried to learn what they had to offer. I didn't stick around the ones who I felt were doing it wrong, the ones who were possessed of a fear of imagination and a phobia of the soul, a psychophobia. And, unfortunately, there are also people like that in training programmes. They can cause a lot of harm, because they are in positions of power and their 'victims', the trainees, have no recourse or way to criticise them – if they do, they're out. I know of many sad cases of this happening. There is no evidence that the licensing and accreditation schemes will actually stop people in training programmes from this continual abuse of the imagination.

If you were a young man in the Renaissance and you wanted to be an artist or a painter, you would approach Verocchio, Bellini, Leonardo, or somebody and you'd say 'Can I work with you?', and he'd say: 'Well, I'm painting this mural up in the dome of the cathedral. I need someone to carry the buckets of paint up and down the ladder for me.' And after a while he'd say: 'Well, you could start grinding colours or filling in that part of the sky, behind that cloud. And when you can do that, I'll show you how to paint clouds. And, after a while, when you know how to mix the paints properly, I can show you how to draw. And once you've learned how to draw and to mix the paints, maybe you can start painting parts of the landscape and clothes.' Finally, one day you would be taught about the human body and the expressions of the human face. But none of that would work if there wasn't a really good rapport between the apprentice and the artist. If one of them didn't like the other one – no way.

So it was based on Eros. The 'training programme' which we are used to is that you've got an institute or a centre or something like that, and you go along and you get interviewed to see whether you are the 'right sort of material', and if you've got the right qualifications – which might be having a Doctorate, or having 500 hours of therapy, or whatever – you pay their fees, and then you're accepted. Eros is left out. Talent is left out. And aesthetics is left out. Nobody's looking at the creative relationship an applicant might have with the people he or she might be studying with, as I see it. Somehow, for me, it's got off on the wrong foot, the whole idea of the training programme. There is no Eros. I don't know what the solution is, but I know that there's something inherently wrong with the standard training programme as it's set up today.

Do you remember that passage, I think it's in the last quarter of your book [*Mad To Be Normal*], maybe in the section on therapy, where

Ronnie says – you asked him about his practice, and he says, 'I realised that I was doing very unorthodox things.' That to me is the clue to Ronnie, and why Ronnie was so great – a great man, a great healer, a great therapist, a great thinker – his genius is involved with this one fact: that is, that he didn't go the conventional way. Genius doesn't follow conventional ways, it's inimical to them, it doesn't do it. Either you can get strung out alone, and people think you're daft or something, or they accept you, if you keep at it long enough, and then you become institutionalised!

I was very amused at Ronnie saying [in *Mad To Be Normal*] that he didn't want to set up a training thing because people would run away with bits of it and call themselves Laingian, and it would be subject to unbearable corruption and misunderstanding and he would find it 'absolutely detestable' [laughs]. I think that that is true of anyone who has arrived at something worth while, I completely understand him. It isn't that there is no value at all in training programmes, but that they don't transmit the essential thing – *that* is missing – and where do you find it? That's the mystery. You either have it or you don't. You can take your cue from someone you admire, whom you think has got it, but you have to then go out and find it for yourself and create your *own* method. It's virtually impossible to teach that essential thing, because it has to do with what Jung called 'individuation', that which is truly unique in ourselves. It's different for everyone who ever found it. The things that I learnt from Ronnie were subtle things. They were not: 'this is how you practice psychotherapy, this is what you do when someone comes in and says "I'm afraid I'm going mad"'. They were wonderful little things, spontaneous exchanges between free spirits. I learned them standing around the piano, singing while he played. Or talking about scales, or syncopation ... so many little things like that ... things which have to do with the real art of living. [Pause]

What has happened to people, your clients, when you know they have achieved enough?

Well again it's very different for each person. It may be that one particular person, say, has come as far as they can go along a particular road with me, though they might return to that road later in their lives – but at the moment they've come to a 'turning point' and it feels like a good time to end. And, I mean it does happen, and I think every therapist should know this, that an individual can only go so far and should be encouraged to quit therapy at that point. I think that one must be very honest, and if it's the case that I really cannot help you any more as a therapist, I should say so. But it is usually quite clear to me when someone has had enough. It may be that they're beginning to let their dreams teach them and their dreams indicate that the dream-ego has now accepted, and been accepted by, the figures of the dream-world – that is always a good sign, or I see that the imagination has really come awake and through it, they are opening the questions of life to mythic and culturally imaginative reflection. They begin to have such really good ideas about the things which used to block and baffle them, that I think: 'Well, what do they need to keep coming to see me for? It's time for them to take their independence and what they've learnt, and go off with it, and fly.' [Laughs]

I want to be sure there's a connection between these great imaginings and the presenting problems ...

You want to be sure that there's a connection ...? Well so do I. [Laughs] I wouldn't be doing my job at all if I didn't help to make that connection.

It seems you don't concentrate on immediate presenting, mundane problems ...

Oh yes, I can do. For as long as they feel they want to. It's no good interrupting someone in a flow when they're really feeling it's very important for them to talk about some urgent matter, what you call the mundane things. But I can nevertheless be still sitting here listening to what they're saying, hearing it with my third ear as it were. And later on I may make some comment or something. But there's also this question of how to dislodge people from the viewpoint that it is really the done thing to come to a therapist and talk endlessly about yourself, and be listened to and encouraged to do more of it, and to think more about yourself in that particular 'psychological way', that we've developed in our century. We may literally, like Nero, be playing the fiddle while Rome burns.

I think it's important that we really put our minds to this, because the world isn't really in such a wonderful shape. I don't think that the people coming out of consulting rooms, on the whole, are that much more able to address the sufferings of, say, the World Soul – let's put it that way. I think that the world – in some ways – is in a very dire situation. And there are many problems – there are problems of say, city life, national life, political life that are not being addressed by psychotherapy. On the contrary, they are being forced to a place of secondary importance. First is 'me': 'my' development, 'my' self-realisation, 'my' progress in therapy, 'my' analysis, 'my' individuation.

People come to a therapy session, and they've spent many hours on the motorway from Cambridge, say, coming down to see me in Hampstead, and they feel completely shattered from driving on the motorway. Now, I can interpret their bad mood as having to do with 'the transference' or I can ignore it and jump right into getting them to talk about their 'inner' problems, or I can also bring the question of the motorway experience itself into the session, or they could. Because we need to pay attention to soul in the world. And very little is being done about the fact that we are being submerged in one environmental misery after another, many directly linked to the number of cars on the road, which is an excruciating problem in our time. And we all suffer from it. The whole ecological space of the countryside, let alone the neighbourhood and the street and 'village life' has changed. These once soulful places have become places of alienation and strangeness and brutality; rather than places of neighbourliness, friendliness, human exchange, and play or creativity. What happens in the streets now, that's fun? [Laughs] Well, it did when I was a boy.

So there are all kinds of things related to our life in the city that could be addressed in the session. And all those things also have archetypal aspects to them, those things that affect us so deeply.

Can we talk about the archetypal aspects of these things?

Well, one that – it's not easy off the top of one's head – but one of the, I think, archetypal structures that perhaps we should consider is the belief in technological progress as being the solution to all ills. The mythic person who embodies this view is Prometheus. And not only Prometheus, but in fact really the Titans themselves, of which Prometheus was one. The Titans of myth were very interesting figures. They were super-huge figures, and there's something very titanic, in fact, about our emphasis now on enormity – whether it's the supermarket, or the mega-multinational company, or whether it's larger vegetables and fruits at the cost of their nutritional component and taste. Super highways, superstars, giant skyscrapers, jumbo jets, overstuffed American paunches and Big Macs. Western society is suffering from a kind of gigantism. James Hillman has made a very insightful study of this megalomania of the western world. But, coming back to Prometheus, in particular, he is the mythic person in the fantasy of endless progress and technological solutions to life's 'problems' – the 'quick fix'.

And how exactly is this going to help the patient?

This kind of psychologising, or 'seeing through' a situation to its archetypal background, is a way of realising just how much our existence is permeated through and through with mythic realities, archetypal structures and patterns. It helps to know where something is 'coming from'. And we need to know how much responsibility we can assume for what is going on. As Jung said, we have to stop deriving the gods from our conditions, and rather derive our conditions from the gods. So having understood that, one cannot just say, 'Well, we're going to reverse all this.' We have to learn a little humility. There are things going on which are largely out of our control, certain aspects of our national and political life and so on. But recognising what the mythic structures are which inhabit these events is maybe a help. And perhaps one could try in one's way to invoke something to balance that, or to contact something that would meet that titanic energy. It might be – as Hillman once suggested – it might be the imagination of Zeus, who was well known for his prolific generative powers. Taken metaphorically, Zeus' abundant fertility means a very wide-ranging and prolific imagination, and perhaps that's what we need to bring to bear on the situation of the Titans. We need to deal with the monstrousness of things. The monstrous shopping malls, the very large – what are they called in America? – 'Edge Cities' that are being built. With these very, very tall office buildings, where there's no human scale any longer, what the Renaissance felt was so important, the scale of the human body in architecture.

Personally, I would invoke Aphrodite, in terms of her pleasure in elegance and beauty, bringing beauty into the details of the bland monstrosities – small things, the textures and the fragrances, the soul qualities of Aphrodite – as a balance to the titanic, and the outsizedness of things. The return to close attention to details. Buildings in most places in the world that draw our attention, and which we love to visit and return to are buildings and places where there is an enormous wealth of detail. Things that the eye stays with and can look at again and again. And our wonder about it – 'How did they do it? How could they make such exquisite windows? – the craftsmanship!' What can you do when you're faced with a 30-storey building faced entirely of glass? [Laughs] What is there to feast your eyes upon?

So the work of finding soul in the world and re-ensouling the world – or re-enchanting the world as somebody once said – is also a very important part of psychotherapy, and maybe it can happen here in the consulting room. So that in a small way a person feels more connected to the city in which he lives and gradually he begins to reclaim his citizenship. Patient becomes Citizen, truly. Because although he or she may be a citizen in name, he or she may not be a citizen in soul. Here's somebody who's a citizen, but is not actually involved with his city. He's a dysfunctional citizen, relegated to the side. He's marginalised, psychologically de-politicised, he's got nothing to say about what's going on, it's a nightmare – he cannot even feel that he has any say about what happens on his street, let alone the city in which he lives – the whole thing is out of control. That to me is just as important as his talking about his childhood traumas. The trauma of his everyday life is also important and how to address that. What can we do to bring beauty and community back into our world, to make it more pleasurable and desirable, more liveable? Should therapy not ultimately be a therapy of soul in the world we all share?